THE PSYCHOLOGY OF DESIGN

D1430324

Design plays an increasingly larger role today in creating consumer desire for products and attraction to commercial messages. However, the psychological processes involved are only partially understood. In addition, design is inherently interdisciplinary, involving (among others) important elements of aesthetics, anthropology, brand strategy, creativity, design science, engineering, graphic design, industrial design, marketing, material science, product design, and several areas within psychology.

While researchers and practitioners in all of these fields seek to learn more about how and why "good" design works its magic, they may benefit from each other's work. The chapters in this edited book bring together organizing frameworks and reviews of the relevant literatures from many of these contributing disciplines, along with recent empirical work. They cover relevant areas such as embodied cognition, processing fluency, experiential marketing, sensory marketing, visual aesthetics, and other research streams related to the impact of design on consumers. Importantly, the primary focus of these chapters is not on product design that creates functional value for the targeted consumer, but rather on how design can create the kind of emotional, experiential, hedonic, and sensory appeal that results in attracting consumers. Each chapter concludes with implications for a theory of design as well as for designers.

Rajeev Batra is the S.S. Kresge Professor of Marketing at the Ross School of Business at the University of Michigan, USA.

Colleen Seifert is Professor of Psychology at the Department of Psychology at the University of Michigan, USA.

Diann Brei is Professor of Mechanical Engineering and Associate Chair for Undergraduate Education at the University of Michigan, USA.

THE PSYCHOLOGY OF DESIGN

Creating Consumer Appeal

*Edited by Rajeev Batra,
Colleen Seifert,
and Diann Brei*

Routledge
Taylor & Francis Group

NEW YORK AND LONDON

First published 2016
by Routledge
711 Third Avenue, New York, NY 10017

and by Routledge
2 Park Square, Milton Park, Abingdon, Oxon OX14 4RN

*Routledge is an imprint of the Taylor & Francis Group,
an informa business*

Library of Congress Cataloging-in-Publication Data
The psychology of design : creating consumer appeal / edited by
  Rajeev Batra, Colleen M. Seifert, and Diann E. Brei.
    pages cm
  Includes bibliographical references and index.
 1. Product design.   2. Marketing—Psychological aspects.
 I. Batra, Rajeev.   II. Seifert, Colleen M.   III. Brei, Diann.
  TS171.P79 2015
  658.5′752—dc23
  2015004477

ISBN: 978-0-7656-4759-7 (hbk)
ISBN: 978-0-7656-4760-3 (pbk)
ISBN: 978-1-315-71480-6 (ebk)

Typeset in Bembo
by Apex CoVantage, LLC

CONTENTS

FIGURES

TABLES

CONTRIBUTORS

Joshua Ackerman, University of Michigan
Pankaj Aggarwal, University of Toronto
Aditi Bajaj, Georgia Institute of Technology
Rajeev Batra, University of Michigan
Peter Boatwright, Carnegie Mellon University
Samuel D. Bond, Georgia Institute of Technology
Simona Botti, London Business School
Diann Brei, University of Michigan
Ravindra Chitturi, Lehigh University
Luca Cian, University of Virginia Darden School of Business
Shanna R. Daly, University of Michigan
Ping Du, Iowa State University
Ryan S. Elder, Brigham Young University
Samuel Franssens, London Business School
Tanuka Ghoshal, Indian School of Business
Richard Gonzalez, University of Michigan
Jeffrey Hartley, General Motors
Kelly B. Herd, Indiana University
He (Michael) Jia, University of Southern California
James J. Kellaris, University of Cincinnati
Aradhna Krishna, University of Michigan
Minu Kumar, San Francisco State University
Jan R. Landwehr, Goethe University Frankfurt
Tina M. Lowrey, HEC Paris
Jonathan Luffarelli, IE University

Malika M., Indian School of Business
Erin MacDonald, Stanford University
Ahreum Maeng, University of Kansas
C. Page Moreau, University of Wisconsin
James A. Mourey, DePaul University
Anirban Mukhopadhyay, Hong Kong University of Science and Technology
Don Norman, University of California San Diego
C. Whan Park, University of Southern California
Gratiana Pol, United Talent Agency, Beverly Hills
Keiko I. Powers, MarketShare Japan
Sarah Roche, Texas Wesleyan University
Bernd Schmitt, Columbia University and ACI Singapore
Colleen Seifert, University of Michigan
L. J. Shrum, HEC Paris
Sanjay Sood, University of California: Los Angeles
Antonios Stamatogiannakis, IE University
Aparna Sundar, University of Oregon
Claudia Townsend, University of Miami
Matteo Visentin, London Business School
Tingting Wang, Hong Kong University of Science and Technology
Lawrence E. Williams, University of Colorado Boulder
Haiyang Yang, Johns Hopkins University
Seda Yilmaz, Iowa State University

FOREWORD

The "Science" in the Psychology of Design

Designers create practical goods and services. This is what makes design so special, so very different than most academic disciplines that do in-depth studies of the topic of interest. Design is a wonderful field because it actually creates things that change people's lives. This is all very nice, but the question before us is whether there is a science to this behavior or whether it depends upon the whims, insights, and creativity of talented designers.

Today, much of design is done through the intuition, instincts, and insights of the designers, honed by years of practice, training, and mentoring. Some parts of design, especially interaction and visual appearance, have considerable basis in the cognitive sciences of interaction and perception. Other parts lack a solid base of evidence. Can design be a science? Many in the design community think the answer is no. I find this misguided.

In a recent posting to a mailing list that discusses such problems I classified the different types of rigor possible in a field like design. Here is what I said (edited slightly):

> Can design be a science, driven by theory? Or can we at least enhance the quality of our methods through evidence-based design, where practices are studied, evaluated, and then codified with statements about their efficacy and the conditions where they are appropriate. Or should design remain as it is today, based upon the skills and talents of designers? My answer? All three.
>
> 1. I strongly prefer design theory as a way to proceed: theory supported by evidence.
> 2. Most areas of design today do not have appropriate theories—indeed, it may be impossible to develop appropriate theories—and in these cases I strongly argue for evidence-based design as the way to proceed.

3. Many areas of design today do not have a base in evidence—indeed, it may be impossible to develop appropriate evidence—and in these cases we rely on the skills and insights of skilled designers as the way to proceed.

In the history of science, this is a common path. First come observations. Then comes classification. Then simple measurements of some components. With time, a theoretical basis develops. The scientific method is a procedure for probing, testing, disputing, and eventually converging upon useful, tested theory. Not all science or engineering practice today is theory based. Some is still evidence-based. Medicine is a good example of a field with a mixture of deep theory, a non-theoretical component based upon evidence, and numerous components not well supported by either evidence nor theory.

Design is following these paths, but in its own way, for each field has different goals, methods, and techniques. In many disciplines the problems to be tackled are well defined. In design, the activities and issues that we address are so vast that I believe that most of design will fall into my categories 2 and 3: no appropriate theory, but a combination of evidence-based best practices, and the skills and insights of designers.

Design is a complex field. Some components of design already are based upon good science, usually from the behavioral and cognitive sciences. Some are at the pre-scientific level of understanding. I believe that with a proper attitude toward evidence-based studies, these areas can also become either scientific, or at least rigorously proven to be effective when used under well-understood circumstances. Some aspects of design seem primarily based upon human creativity, sense of style, and other socially mediated conventions. These may never be scientific, but they do play a critically important role in the quality and acceptance of design. So, can design be a science? Sometimes yes, sometimes no. Can it be empirically based, evidence driven? Yes. Will it have to reply on intuition and the creativity of individual designers? Sometimes, yes.

The power of design lies with its methods. In modern design, the process starts with observation of the people for whom the design is intended, spending time observing, studying, and developing a deep appreciation for the underlying issues. I have a rule when I'm asked to consult: "Do not solve the problem I am asked to solve." Strange rule: why do I have it? Because the problem given to us is seldom the fundamental, root problem—it is usually the surface problem or the symptom. Design is powerful because we do not just solve problems: we define them. We spend a lot of time trying to understand the fundamental issues that should be worked on, not the superficial issues that are easily observed.

Many of the important problems in the world cannot be solved, either because not enough is known or because they are fundamentally unsolvable: there are too many factors, too many competing constraints, too many issues that are fundamentally incompatible. "Wicked" is the term applied to these problems by both economists and designers: wicked problems. Design differs from most disciplines in that it is not searching for truth. It is searching for "good enough," or sometimes, simply for "better." In the words of Herbert Simon, we satisfice. Design has to create real value, it has to make a difference. It has to look for large effects, not small ones, things that make a significant difference, whether or not they are optimal or perfect. Design is the field of practical accomplishment, where the results are continuously studied, modified, and improved. Big effects, not small ones. Significance in people's lives, not the tiny difference of statistical significance.

Designers think by drawing and by making. Not with words, not with equations, but by drawing, sketching, and building. It's a different kind of thinking. Drawing and sketching are powerful because they readily allow two, three, or even four dimensions to be represented. Space and time, both.

Part of design is a form of applied art. Yes, we want things that work well, but we also want them to be attractive, to give pleasure: nice to look at and that feel good in their operation. That's an art form, and we still don't quite know how it happens. Many parts of the design process remain art rather than science.

Let me give you an example. On today's smartphones and modern operating systems, when scrolling through a list by gesture, when the finger is lifted off the screen or track pad, the list keeps scrolling, slowing gently. It has a virtual "momentum" and "viscous friction" so that it slows non-linearly. At the end of the list, what does it do? It bounces! What is the function of the bounce? None whatsoever, except that it makes us happy. That's what great designers put into products: pleasure, feeling good, making us happy.

What is the science behind the addition of the tiny little pleasures these products provide? We don't know. Maybe we'll never know. I don't have an answer for what kind of theory might ever develop in the artistic, pleasurable, fun, and emotional component of design, even though these are crucial aspects of successful design.

This essay has been about the traditional area of design. Many of the chapters of this book come from the field called "consumer psychology," which include lots of insights and evidence about people's preferences, the importance of sensory look and feel, the impact of color, and how price affects adoption. These issues overlap the concerns of the traditional product designer, but should be a fundamental part of the design process, considered during the early phases of design.

Design is a multi-faceted, complex enterprise. It involves the initial choice of what to make, a deep understanding of people, of materials, and of technology. It requires understanding how people decide upon purchase, and then use products. It covers an extremely wide range of activities and different disciplines of study and training. It is this depth and richness that makes design such a wonderful, fascinating field.

Don Norman
University of California San Diego

INTRODUCTION

Rajeev Batra, Colleen Seifert, and Diann Brei

UNIVERSITY OF MICHIGAN

This book is the product of an interdisciplinary conference held in May 2014 in Ann Arbor on the subject of "the Psychology of Design." Design plays an increasingly larger role today in creating consumer desire for products and liking for commercial messages. However, the psychological processes involved are only partially understood. In addition, design is inherently interdisciplinary, involving (among others) important elements of aesthetics, anthropology, brand strategy, creativity, design science, engineering, graphic design, industrial design, marketing, material science, product design, and several areas within psychology. While researchers and practitioners in all of these fields seek to learn more about how and why "good" design works its magic, they may benefit from each other's work. The goal of our conference—the 33d Annual Advertising and Consumer Psychology (ACP) Conference of the Society for Consumer Psychology—was to bring together top researchers and scholars, as well as thoughtful practitioners, from these different contributing domains in order to build our understanding of the "psychology of design." Importantly, the primary focus of this conference and book was not on product design that creates functional value for the targeted consumer, but rather on how design can create the kind of emotional, experiential, hedonic, and sensory appeal that results in attracting consumers.

In this book, we have attempted to create a volume that not only presents very useful literature reviews and integrative frameworks, but also contains syntheses and suggestions by the authors that will help us move our knowledge of design forward. The chapters therefore end with the authors' implications for practicing designers, as well as for new theories of design.

The themes of the conference included Embodied Design, Designing Product Features, Aesthetics and Emotions in Design, and Methods for Design. Each of the contributions to this volume provides a diverse perspective on the themes.

Embodied Design

Given the increasing recent interest in "grounded" and "embodied" cognition, we begin the book with four chapters that show how our study of such phenomena can help us better understand consumer response to design elements. Joshua Ackerman draws implications from theories and studies about people's haptic (touch-related) experience (e.g. of heaviness, or roughness, or hardness) for product and environmental design (such as perceptions and feelings about importance, or difficulty, or stability). Lawrence E. Williams then shows how knowledge developed in infancy—called conceptual scaffolding—serves as the foundation for conceptual knowledge developed later in life, so that later physical experiences (such as physical brightness, or temperature) activate related psychological concepts (such as purity, or emotional warmth), and then influence higher-order thoughts and feelings (including feelings of product efficiency, or trust). He argues that while embodiment effects can operate via scaffolding, this need not always be the case; and that scaffolding can occur in ways that go beyond conceptual metaphors.

Luca Cian explores how the concrete experience of verticality can convey specific and unconscious abstract connotations of power, divinity, morality and valence—via the cognitive mechanisms of conceptual metaphors—leading to effects on consumer recognition, memory, accuracy and preferences. Aradhna Krishna, a keynote speaker at our conference, links design phenomena to recent research on sensory marketing, an area that she has championed.

Designing Product Features

From these general and overall conceptual and cognitive principles, the book segues to specific characteristics of products, to see how they might shape consumer perceptions and responses.

Two chapters address the role of color. Aparna Sundar and James J. Kellaris discuss how colors—not just green, but also blue (but not red)—affect ethical judgments. In their studies, they show colors impacting ethically ambiguous retailer practices, and they argue that this occurs via halo effects of eco-friendliness. Then, Keiko I. Powers looks at how vehicle color affects emotions, and those emotions then affect the prices that consumers are willing to pay for their (used) automobile purchases. She presents a regression-method study that shows how vehicle color affects the price depreciation rates of used cars.

Tanuka Ghoshal, Peter Boatwright, and Malika M. detail how the angular versus curved shape of products can work better to communicate functional versus hedonic benefits respectively. They show that while there seems to be a general predisposition for curves over angles, preferences seem to vary across product categories, depending on the nature of benefits sought. Two other chapters examine the effects of visual symmetry on brand personality inferences. Aditi Bajaj and Samuel Bond show that a product's visual symmetry can create perceptions of greater sophistication, while asymmetry suggests excitement.

Experimental evidence shows the mediating role of arousal, the effects of which are then (mis)attributed to properties of the brand. Antonios Stamatogiannakis, Jonathan Luffarelli, and Haiyang Yang also show such brand personality effects (including effects on sincerity, competence and ruggedness) for brand logos, but then also show how these brand perceptions need to be congruent with the nature of the product.

In their chapter, Ahreum Maeng and Pankaj Aggarwal propose and test the interesting proposition that products which are anthropomorphized to become associated with a humanlike face (e.g., a car), will also show an association between the width-to-height ratio of the product face and the product's perceived dominance. Specifically, they suggest that consumers prefer such dominant products since they allow consumers to achieve a higher status/power. As such, these products enjoy an advantage over products that show a lower width to height ratio of the product face.

Looking at a different configuration of a product's "facial features," Tingting Wang and Anirban Mukhopadhyay present a review of the research on consumer response to "cute" products—such as Hello Kitty. They examine the stimulus-based characteristics that create perceptions of cuteness; cognitive (inferential) and affective responses to it; and individual differences in approach motivation to these antecedent features. He (Michael) Jia, Gratiana Pol, and C. Whan Park address similar issues, examining in addition how cuteness differs from other types of attractiveness, and the multiple types of behavioral tendencies that follow from it.

Sarah Roche, L. J. Shrum, and Tina M. Lowrey examine auditory stimuli— how the sound of a product or brand name can drive consumer perceptions of its physical, tangible and functional aspects, which then affect attitudes towards it. After reviewing prior research on phonetic effects, they present research on how the sound of stock market ticker symbols can actually affect the initial performance of stock IPOs (initial public offerings).

Bernd Schmitt, a keynote speaker at our conference and leader in the field of "experience design," presents his perspective on how experiences are shaped by design, not just for brands but also in other domains such as architecture. He argues that there are general principles—applicable across domains—that underlie the way in which specific dimensions of design relate to specific types of experiences and object perceptions. He urges that these be used in our efforts to create a broad theory of design.

Underlying Processes

Naturally, we also have several frameworks and investigations about the underlying mechanisms through which various design elements impact the level and type of consumer desire.

Claudia Townsend and Sanjay Sood show why and how the influence of product aesthetics on evaluation and choice may not be a straightforward deliberative process. While functional attributes usually require serial and effortful information processing, a product's aesthetic qualities (when perceived visually) can be processed all at once, therefore more quickly, and without awareness. They show experimentally, via a cognitive load manipulation, that product aesthetics play more of an evaluation-driving role when cognitive resources are depleted.

In his chapter, Jan R. Landwehr asks: "What concrete design features exert a systematic effect on consumers' aesthetic experience, and for what reason?" His chapter begins by presenting the key tenets of the processing fluency account of aesthetic pleasure. This theory posits that the experience of cognitive ease when processing a visual stimulus triggers aesthetic pleasure. Landwehr summarizes empirical studies examining this theory, and introduces the idea that the valence of fluency may change based on processing mode (affective/automatic vs. cognitive/controlled processing). This new perspective allows the integration of some contradictory empirical findings, which indicate positive effects of disfluent visual characteristics.

Minu Kumar discusses the neural and biological mechanisms that might underlie the relationships between aesthetic aspects of product form (e.g., balance, harmony) and the emotions they evoke. Objective components of these aesthetic aspects might match the appraisal dimensions that underlie specific emotions.

Naturally, emotional pathways are explored, too. Ravindra Chitturi shows how product aesthetics can evoke the positive promotion emotions of excitement and pride, as well as the positive prevention feelings of confidence. These emotions then increase willingness-to-pay by improving three types of perceived benefits—functional, experiential, and self-expressive. Experimental evidence shows that visual aesthetics significantly change the feelings of confidence with functional benefits, the feelings of excitement with experiential benefits, and the feelings of pride with self-expressive benefits.

James A. Mourey and Ryan S. Elder examine arousal. They argue that while consumers may not notice the specific changes made to product design over the years ("change and inattentional blindness"), their subtle experience and feeling of change ("visual sensing") may impact their evaluations through a process they call Dynamic Transference. Operating through arousal mechanisms, changes in one domain (such as size or color), although not consciously attended to, can be misattributed and impact subjective evaluations in an unrelated domain.

Matteo Visentin, Samuel Franssens, and Simona Botti look at the frustration of too much choice. How does perceived usability of a product affect post-purchase satisfaction when consumers have to choose from large versus small assortments? They find that consumers are less satisfied and less confident when choosing from large assortments, but only when they are characterized by a high-usability design. That is, in large assortments, high-usability designs appear to exacerbate feelings of choice overload, and can be detrimental to post-choice evaluations of the outcome, relative to low-usability designs.

Finally, Kelly B. Herd and C. Page Moreau review self-signaling, or how consumers examine their own behavior to make inferences about their personal characteristics. In empirical studies, they show that using attractive products can cause consumers to gain confidence and evaluate themselves more favorably. But, the presence of an audience may lessen the aesthetic self-signaling effect.

Design Methods

A set of chapters then examine ways in which practitioners and researchers can better study and create designs.

Ping Du and Erin McDonald show how eye-tracking data can facilitate our understanding of consumer product evaluations. They review measurement approaches and types of equipment, then show application issues specific to the design domain.

Jeffrey Hartley shows how the many different silos and mindsets in a large organization that are involved with creating, manufacturing, and marketing designed objects (such as cars) can be made to converge on a deeper understanding of the customer, via what he calls "inspirational research." Such research can build both a deep, intuitive understanding of how the organization's customers think, and help build a shared intuition on what is required to delight them. He presents ways to plan and implement design research.

Colleen Seifert, Richard Gonzalez, Seda Yilmaz, and Shanna R. Daly present a method for generating new designs. They report on the development of Design Heuristics, a set of cognitive strategies useful in finding innovative product designs. Their design method is based on empirical studies of designers across fields.

In sum, the chapters provide wide-ranging insight into the varied ways that consumers' desires can be influenced by design.

Acknowledgements

We conclude here with some heartfelt acknowledgements. Intellectual support and inspiration came from Don Norman, "Dean" of the Design community and a keynote speaker at our conference, who also contributes a thoughtful foreword to this book. The Society for Consumer Psychology, under whose aegis the conference was held, provided invaluable support and guidance. Financial support for the conference came from the Yaffe Center, the Dean's Office and the Marketing Department at the Ross School of Business, University of Michigan, as well as the Design Science program and Psychology Department at the University of Michigan. The Marketing Science Institute provided major financial support. The Association for Consumer Research helped support attendance by Doctoral students. And Yaffe Center administrator Clea Davis made sure the conference ran without a hitch. Thanks, too, to our commissioning editor at Routledge, David Varley, and the helpful editorial staff there.

PART I
Embodied Design

1

IMPLICATIONS OF HAPTIC EXPERIENCE FOR PRODUCT AND ENVIRONMENTAL DESIGN

Joshua Ackerman

UNIVERSITY OF MICHIGAN

It seems relatively uncontroversial to declare that what a decorative vase looks like or how a speaker system sounds are important elements of product design. Yet, do we consider the physical feel of these items to be equally as critical to their design? Does the heaviness of the vase matter for how we perceive its functionality? Could the firmness of the box that the speakers are packaged in affect our judgment of this system? The aim of this chapter is to make the case for the experience of touch as a central factor in our impressions and decisions regarding people, situations, and products, and thus its general importance for design. The study of haptics—referring to the sensation and movement associated with tactile experience—is flourishing, nowhere more so than in the social and decision sciences (Peck, 2010). This is because research has increasingly shown that how things feel, and whether we have the chance to feel them in the first place, has wide ranging psychological implications well beyond the straightforward idea that something can feel good or bad.

Touch is one of the five classic senses we learn about in primary school (humans actually experience other sensations, such as balance and pain, as well). Touch is also the first of these senses to develop, emerging relatively early in embryonic development, and it utilizes the widest bodily distribution of receptors of any sense—our entire skin can detect elements of tactile experience (Gallace & Spence, 2010; Gottlieb, 1971; Montagu, 1971). Whereas many senses function primarily for information acquisition, haptic abilities are uniquely involved in two functions: (1) gathering of information and (2) direct manipulation of stimuli and environments. Recent research indicates that tactile sensation further affects two mental analogues of these physical functions, impression formation (analogue of information acquisition) and decision making (analogue of environmental manipulation), making it quite important in an array of individual and interpersonal domains of judgment. One such domain of particular relevance for the topic of design is consumption, or consumer, behavior.

People use haptics to interact with a wide array of items and products on a daily basis, both in the physical world and increasingly in digital formats. Data on consumer evaluation of products indicates that people not only prefer the opportunity to touch products, but they also will put effort into seeking out such opportunities (Accenture, 2014). Two interesting examples of this effort that have emerged widely in the internet age are showrooming and webrooming. In showrooming, people visit brick-and-mortar stores to physically interact with and evaluate products but then go online to actually purchase these products. In webrooming, people evaluate products online (presumably where more information exists) but then visit retail locations to actually purchase these products. Both of these behaviors are common (showrooming: 73% of consumers; webrooming: 88% of consumers; Accenture, 2013) and both involve the choice to shop in-person at stores where the ability to touch products exists.

Data like these indicate that touch matters to people. But exactly how does it matter? What kinds of influences does haptic experience have on consumption outcomes? What are the implications for design of consumer products and environments? This chapter is organized into three key sections that address these questions. First, I will outline the basic elements of haptic experience, including differences in the ability, motivation, and type of touch. Next, I will review literature on the various influences of haptic experience, considering both direct and indirect influences and focusing on a hot topic in psychological and consumer research—embodied cognition. This section will cover the diverse routes by which tactile sensation and motion shape impressions and decisions and also identify areas of emerging research. Finally, I will suggest several domains where designers could beneficially attend to the implications of haptic experience. This chapter cannot hope to review every piece of research in the broad fields of haptics and sensation, but it should provide a starting point for understanding the many and often indirect ways that touch matters, both for design and for our everyday lives.

Elements of Haptic Experience

There are many ways to conceptually carve up experiences of tactile sensation and bodily movement. The framework I will present highlights three aspects of haptic experience that vary between people and situations: the ability to touch, the desire to touch, and the type of touch.

Ability to Touch

Tactile interaction with items requires both the situational opportunity for contact and the physical capability to engage in that contact. Though it might seem rather obvious that people must be able to mentally and physically process tactile sensations and movements in order for these to play a strong role in impressions and decisions, little consumer research has confronted the fact that not everyone can feel to the same degree. A number of disorders, some quite prevalent, can impair aspects of sensation, balance, and movement (e.g., diabetes, Parkinson's), and these impairments can manifest cognitively through deficits in processing action-related concepts and words (Boulenger et al., 2008). Such problems could certainly affect consumer behaviors as well.

Many situational elements also can prevent people from touching items. In consumer settings, products may be shown but not available for interaction due to factors such as company norms and rules, restrictive packaging, or storage of products in locations not readily accessible (e.g., display cases). Certain products, including experiential products and services, are not even touchable. Clearly, the situational possibility for physical product interaction is an important factor for leveraging the different influences of haptic experience. It is, however, not 100% necessary for these influences to emerge. Research suggests that mentally simulating the enactment or reenactment of touching a product can produce some effects very similar to actually touching that product (Kamleitner, 2011; Peck, Barger, & Webb, 2013). This work suggests that, although the experience of touch involves a physical sensation, much of this sensation's action on our behavioral responses is fundamentally psychological. I'll review this research more in a later section of the chapter.

Desire to Touch

The desire to touch refers to people's motivation to engage in haptic experience and their awareness of the extent to which this experience is occurring. Within the consumer literature, internal motivation has largely been captured by one individual difference measure—need for touch. The need for touch (NFT) is conceptualized as a "preference for the extraction and utilization of information obtained through the haptic system" (Peck & Childers 2003a, p. 431). This construct is fundamentally motivational in nature and is multidimensional in structure. NFT has two dimensions, instrumental and autotelic, which differ in multiple ways. From a motivational standpoint "self-attributed motives corresponding to the instrumental dimension of NFT are characterized by organized analytic thought that is initiated by an explicit goal that drives behavior. In contrast, more implicit motives represented by autotelic touch reflect compulsive and affective themes intrinsic to an activity that are not elicited by reference to unmet goals" (p. 431). Thus, the instrumental dimension is concerned with how people solve problems using touch, from gathering information to manipulating products. The autotelic dimension is instead concerned with how people have fun and seek sensory stimulation for its own sake through touch. Highly instrumental people prefer haptic elements that provide key information about items whereas highly autotelic people prefer products with pleasurable "touchability" (Klatzky & Peck, 2012; Peck &

Childers, 2003a). Peck and Childers (2003a) also make a comparison between the NFT distinctions and explicit vs. implicit goals (McClelland, Koestner, & Weinberger, 1989), with the instrumental dimension presumably being more explicit and conscious than the autotelic dimension.

Research on need for touch has variously considered NFT as a single or a multidimensional construct, but empirical findings from its use appear consistent. People high in NFT interpret their product judgments to be more confident when they are able to haptically interact with products, and less confident when some barrier prevents them from doing so (Peck & Childers, 2003a, 2003b). Messages that encourage consumers to touch products elevate positive affect and are more persuasive to high autotelic people and can persuade high instrumental people as well when the touch experience is logically related to the message (Peck & Wiggins 2006). Low autotelics are particularly persuaded by touch when they are not strongly involved with the persuasive message (Peck & Johnson, 2011). Further, people high in autotelic NFT also appear to better correct for the influence of haptic cues compared to people low in autotelic NFT (Krishna & Morrin, 2008).

Individual differences in motivation clearly matter to the likelihood that consumers will physically engage with products as well as the implications of that engagement, yet the degree to which these implications will affect aspects of cognition also relies on people's motivation to attend to their internal bodily states. People vary in factors such as body awareness and self-focus (Miller, Murphy, & Buss, 1981), which relate to the degree to which people prefer to pay attention to and incorporate knowledge about sensations and changes in their bodily condition. High self and body consciousness can make people more susceptible to haptic cues and interactions (e.g., Häfner, 2013; Kronrod & Ackerman, 2014). Thus, the desire to touch items, and to understand the impact of tactile feedback on one's body, represent important motivators of haptic experience.

Types of Touch

Despite the general significance of haptic input, all touch is not created equal. Types of tactile sensation can be divided into two broad categories. The presence vs. absence of touch has a number of psychological effects, making simple contact the first (and most basic) category of haptic experience. Apart from contact, touch can be broken down into individual forms of sensation and motion. For instance, one of the most influential papers in the field of haptics delineates multiple types of object-based haptic qualities (Lederman & Klatzky, 1987). These include three distinct sets: substance-related, structure-related, and functional properties. Within the substance-related set, objects can provide tactile sensations of texture, hardness, weight, and temperature. Within the structure-related set, objects can provide volume, global shape, and exact shape. Finally, within the set of functional properties, objects can provide part motion and specific motion. Each of these kinds of sensations (each representing a specific piece of information to be acquired) is paired with an "exploratory procedure" that refers to the motor movement necessary to perceive the sensory element (Lederman & Klatzky, 1987, Table 1). For example, evaluations of texture require lateral motions in order to determine how rough or smooth an object is. Judgments of weight require unsupported holding to freely evaluate heaviness or lightness. Thus, both sensory and motor subsystems are integral components of haptic experience. Further, although we can think of basic contact as having one variety of influence on cognition, each type of sensorimotor element has a (somewhat) unique influence as well. In the following section, I review the current literature highlighting what we know about these influences.

Influence of Haptic Experience

Haptic experiences have an influence on thoughts and actions at a number of levels. Direct and indirect influences refer to those effects that occur due to intended touch and incidental touch, respectively. Additionally, a large and growing body of literature points to embodied influences of touch, particularly those tactile sensations and body movements that mentally activate associated concepts and metaphors. I detail each of these types of influences in this section, focusing most strongly on the embodied cognition literature.

Direct Influences

Real and imagined contact creates a sense of connection between person and item. With respect to consumer behavior, touching products can lead consumers to feel a heightened sense of ownership over those products (even products they do not actually own), which then translates into elevated valuation judgments (Peck et al., 2013; Peck & Shu, 2009). For example, study participants who were asked to touch either a Slinky or a mug increased their estimates of the monetary value of these items by over 20% compared to participants who simply observed but did not touch the items (Peck & Shu, 2009). For consumers high in autotelic need for touch, messages encouraging direct contact result in more impulsive purchasing (Peck & Childers, 2006). Highly vivid haptic imagery can produce similar effects when people merely imagine physical contact with products, and this imagery can also elevate perceptions of control, which then increase feelings of ownership (Peck et al., 2013).

As mentioned earlier, direct contact also affects direct perceptions about products by increasing quality judgments for those products, and it also affects perceptions of one's own judgments by increasing confidence in those judgments (Peck & Childers, 2003a, 2003b). Thus, not only do people see the products they touch as better, they believe that their own product-related judgments are better as well. These effects seem to suggest that all touch is good (particularly from the view of businesses and marketers). From a cognitive viewpoint, this does appear to be true. Even touching relatively unpleasant products can elevate the sense of ownership over these products (Peck & Shu, 2009). However, from an affective standpoint, people tend to better like those products they touch, but only when those products are pleasing to the touch (Peck & Shu, 2009). In sum, the role of direct contact on perceptions and judgments is relatively straightforward. Contact brings people mentally closer to items, improving feelings of control, positivity (for positive items), and ownership, which can result in the belief that items are better and more desirable. The role of indirect contact is more complex.

Indirect Influences

Research has documented a number of indirect effects of haptic experience. These influences emerge in two broad settings: (1) when people see others touching items, and (2) when people engage in touch-related actions for a purpose unrelated to the immediate judgment or decision context. Effects that occur when observing other people in contact with items emerge from several types of mental processes, including associative links, contagion beliefs, and emotions. Either positive or negative consequences can result. On the negative side, people treat products that other consumers have touched as though those products have been contaminated, evaluating them as worse and expressing less interest in purchasing them (Argo, Dahl, & Morales, 2006). These effects occur because people experience disgust as a result of consumer contamination. However, negative reactions in such contexts are not inevitable. Seeing celebrities and attractive, opposite sex people touch products increases positive evaluations and willingness to buy those products because people perceive the positive qualities from such others to transfer contagiously to the products (Argo, Dahl, & Morales, 2008; Newman, Diesendruck, & Bloom, 2011).

The second setting in which indirect influences of haptic experience emerge involves people touching products themselves. However, unlike contexts of direct haptic influence, in these situations, influential tactile feedback occurs because people are either incidentally in contact with items or engaging with items for reasons that are irrelevant to how they feel. A great deal of research has identified a range of ways in which this influence plays out, much of it focusing on specific types of object-based sensory cues. For instance, in the substance-related domain of weight, a series of papers has shown that holding heavy objects can lead people to perceive effortful activities as more strenuous, even though the objects are presumably unrelated to these activities. People wearing heavy backpacks see hills and slants as steeper (Proffitt, 2006; Proffitt & Linkenauger, 2013), and people throwing heavy balls at a target judge the distance to the target to be greater (Witt, Proffitt, & Epstein, 2004). Such effects likely emerge due to the anticipated effort that perceivers judge necessary in order to walk up the incline. Consistent with this interpretation, people who are less fit (in worse physical shape, elderly, etc.) show stronger weight-slant effects (Bhalla & Proffitt, 1999).

In a somewhat similar line of work, the weight of food service items has been found to alter consumers' perceptions of the food they consume. Holding a heavier plate, which is presumably not rationally connected to the amount of food one eats, can distract people from the food they end up adding to their plates. Because of this distraction, people tend to default to pleasure-based choices and thus select more indulgent food options, increasing the likelihood that they will over-consume these relatively unhealthy foods (Tal, Grinstein, Kleijnen, Ackerman, & Wansink, 2014).

Many indirect influences of haptic experience can be described as carryover effects. With such effects, tactile sensations activate certain concepts within mental networks, making those concepts more mentally accessible. This increased accessibility increases the chances these concepts will be applied to unrelated outcomes and situations. Consider the following examples. Consumers using flimsy cups to drink water rate that water as lower quality, and are willing to pay less for it, than consumers drinking the same water out of firm cups (Krishna & Morrin, 2008). Shoppers who stand on soft flooring, like carpets, evaluate other products (e.g., lamps) more positively than shoppers standing on hard flooring because soft floors trigger feelings of comfort which are then applied to the irrelevant product judgments (Meyers-Levy, Zhu, & Jiang, 2010). Finally, spatial confinement (e.g., from narrow aisles) can create restrictions on bodily freedom of movement, resulting in consumers seeking product variety as a means of exerting freedom of choice (Levav & Zhu, 2009). A number of situational and individual differences moderate effects such as these, but the consistent finding in this literature is that haptic experiences can exert an indirect influence on the judgments and decisions we make across a range of contexts.

Embodied Influences: Overview

The last decade has seen an enormous increase in empirical attention given to embodied models of cognition (Joy & Sherry, 2003; Krishna & Schwarz, 2014; Meier, Schnall, Schwarz, & Bargh, 2012). These models posit that perceptual-motor simulations are an integral part of mental representations and the processing of concepts. Activating one aspect of a representation makes other components of that representation, including bodily states, action tendencies, and meanings, more accessible in working memory (Barsalou, 2008; Meier et al., 2012; Niedenthal, Barsalou, Winkielman, Krauth-Gruber, & Ric, 2005; Reimann et al., 2012). Thus, the sensations and movements of the body are necessary players in how we understand, interact with, and remember both the physical world as well as the more abstract and social world. Clearly, our brains work in fundamentally embodied ways.

One particularly fruitful area of representational research within the embodied cognition literature focuses on the role of metaphorical constructs as a means of linking physical experiences and abstract concepts. Metaphors have been considered from a variety of angles in this work, including as drivers of embodiment effects (Lakoff & Johnson, 1999), reflections of them (Landau, Meier, & Keefer, 2010), or as manifestations of their development (Williams, Huang, & Bargh, 2009). A full examination of the role of metaphor in embodiment research is beyond the scope of this chapter (see Landau et al., 2010; Williams, this volume), but several examples that researchers have uncovered include links between scent and trust (e.g., "something smells fishy"; Lee & Schwarz, 2010), between vertical space and constructs such as power, emotion, and religion (e.g., "high status," "feeling down"; Meier, Hauser, Robinson, Friesen, & Schjeldahl, 2007; Meier & Robinson, 2004; Schubert, 2005), and between unethical behavior and the desire to physically clean oneself ("washing away sins"; Lee & Schwarz, 2010; Zhong & Liljenquist, 2006), among others. With respect to haptic experience specifically, metaphorical associations between physical and social warmth lead people who are in contact with warm objects (e.g., a cup of coffee) to perceive others as "warmer" people (Williams & Bargh, 2008) and people in contact with cold objects to prefer "warm" romantic movies (Hong & Sun, 2012). These effects occur nonconsciously, such that people are not explicitly aware of the increased mental accessibility of the metaphorical concepts. In sum, touching some stimulus can convey sensory information (e.g., temperature changes in the finger), perceptual information (e.g., this feels warm), and higher-order cognitive information (e.g., increased accessibility of concepts related to social warmth).

In the following paragraphs, I review in detail a set of studies we conducted that demonstrates the implications of active, embodied concepts for outcomes that are ostensibly irrelevant to the touch-related embodiment context (Ackerman, Nocera, & Bargh, 2010). Much of this work focuses on the meaning conveyed by sensory information rather the physical manipulation of objects, but many of the principles remain the same. To preview, the physical experience of haptic sensations and movements nonconsciously activates mental representations that contain specific associations, which are then applied to unrelated targets. These studies draw the two physical functions of haptic experience—information acquisition and environmental manipulation—by examining two conceptual analogues—impression formation and decision making.

Embodied Influences: Empirical Focus

Apart from temperature, three types of substance-related haptic dimensions exist—weight, texture, and hardness (Lederman & Klatzky, 1987). Each dimension is commonly associated with a particular concept through metaphors. These metaphors are apparent in the language we use to describe abstract ideas and events. Weight is linked with concepts of seriousness and importance (e.g., "weighty matters," "gravity of the situation"). Texture is linked with concepts of difficulty and harshness ("having a rough day," "coarse language"). Hardness is linked with concepts of stability and rigidity (e.g., "hard-hearted," "she is my rock"). The studies described below should help to demonstrate these linkages in more detail, but for now, try this simple thought experiment. Imagine two houses. One is a suburban, single-family bungalow made of brick. The other is also a single-family home, but is located on the savannah, and is a hut made entirely of straw. Visualize what these houses look like in your mind. Now, consider these questions. Which of these houses is more set in its ways? Which is stricter? Although these questions seem to be nonsensical with regards to housing options, I bet you are able to answer them. In fact, if you answered "the brick house," you are like the vast majority of people to whom I have given this thought experiment. Why is this the case? A strong possibility is that your mental representations of strictness and set-ness are associated with being unmalleable. Being set in one's ways refers to a firm, unchanging opinion. Bricks are also more resistant to (physical) change than is straw. If your mental representations about strictness and building materials involve such overlapping concepts, these concepts are likely to be applied (or misapplied) when you answer the previous questions.

So what did we find in our studies? We conducted a series of six experiments to understand how physical experiences with each haptic dimension affected impressions and decisions (see Ackerman et al., 2010). Recall that the first dimension, weight, is associated with concepts of seriousness and importance (see Jostmann, Lakens, & Schubert, 2009). In the first experiment, we approached people on the street, much like someone seeking charitable donations, and asked whether people would agree to take part in a study on impressions of job candidates. People viewed the resume of an academic candidate and evaluated it on scales related to judgments of the candidate's seriousness of interest in the job and his/her sociability with other employees. Participants were told that their evaluations would be compared to experts in order to determine whether novice raters can perform equally as well as expert raters (because the embodiment effects described here involve activating concepts outside of conscious awareness, cover stories are used so that study participants do not intentionally or unintentionally change their natural behavior). In order to trigger the haptic sensation of weight, participants evaluated the resume on one of two clipboards—a regular light one or a secretly-weighted heavy one. On the scales mentioned above, the study results indicated that people holding a heavy clipboard rated the job candidate as significantly more serious about the position than participants holding a light clipboard. This finding is interesting because it shows that tactile sensations can influence judgments that apparently have nothing to do with the weight of the clipboard, and they do so without people being aware of this influence. Moreover, this effect is specific to the content of the embodied concept—the weight of the clipboard affected only judgments of candidate seriousness, and not sociability. This specificity helps to reveal the underlying associative structure linking the haptic experience and the relevant concepts within a shared mental representation.

A second weight experiment demonstrated that a more "manipulative" form of cognition—decision making—is also influenced by physical weight. In this study, passersby on a university campus made decisions about whether to increase or decrease government funding for a variety of issues by marking a sheet again presented on either a heavy or light clipboard. These issues included a set of important social topics (e.g., air pollution standards) and a set of topics more idiosyncratic in importance (e.g., regulating the number of sinks in public bathrooms). If people indeed view the first set of topics as important in nature, their decisions should be swayed by metaphors linking weight and importance. Indeed, participants holding the heavier clipboard decided to increase funding for important social issues more than participants holding the lighter clipboard. There was no effect of the clipboard on decisions for the idiosyncratic issues. Thus, even though we typically presume that the impressions and decisions we make about abstract, intellectual issues are disconnected from irrelevant influences such as current bodily sensations, the first two studies indicate that this presumption is not correct.

The next two studies investigated the role of a different haptic dimension, that of texture. Common metaphors for texture (rough vs. smooth) associate rougher sensations with concepts such as difficulty and harshness. To better understand these sensations, we used a somewhat different experimental context. In the first texture experiment, passersby completed an easy puzzle which was presented as a measure of cognitive abilities that might inform social judgments. In one version, the pieces were made of smooth poster-board, whereas in the other version, the pieces were covered in rough sandpaper. They then read and formed an impression about a written passage describing both positive components (e.g., kidding around) and negative components (e.g., exchange of sharp words) of a social interaction and thus was ambiguous as to the overall tenor of the interaction (Kay, Wheeler, Bargh, & Ross, 2004). After reading, participants rated the interaction on measures relevant to difficulty and harshness (e.g., was the interaction adversarial/friendly, competitive/cooperative?) and on irrelevant measures (e.g., was the interaction business/casual in tone?). How did touching the pieces of this puzzle affect people's impressions about the social interaction? The results indicated that participants completing the rough puzzle rated the interaction as significantly more adversarial, competitive, and so on—that is, more difficult and harsh—than participants completing the smooth puzzle. Importantly, this did not occur for the irrelevant measures suggesting that perceptions of the interaction were changed only for those dimensions consistent with the metaphor of roughness.

In the second texture experiment, we measured actual choices that people made after touching the same either rough or smooth puzzle. Participants completed one of the puzzles and then engaged in an Ultimatum game, a measure of fairness and selfish/altruistic decision making (Güth, Schmittberger, & Schwarze, 1982). In this economic game, each participant received 10 tickets for a $50 lottery. Participants could give 0–10 of the tickets to an anonymous participant (who didn't actually exist) with the rule that the split became official if the other participant accepted the offer, but neither participant would receive any tickets if the other participant rejected the offer. Because choices in the Ultimatum game are often strongly influenced by chronic individual differences, participants also completed a Social Value Orientation (SVO) scale identifying chronic interaction styles such as "prosocial/cooperator" and "individualist" (Messick & McClintock, 1968; Van Lange, 1999).

Analyses of the lottery ticket decisions showed that participants who completed the rough puzzle offered significantly more lottery tickets than participants who completed the smooth puzzle. This was a somewhat surprising result, as a surface-level prediction might be that people who touch rough things experience greater accessibility of difficult/harsh concepts, and this would lead to more selfish choice behavior. In fact, SVO classifications suggest that the generosity of rough-puzzle participants was not necessarily due to being more cooperative. Of participants classified prosocial/cooperative, 70.6% actually completed the smooth puzzle, whereas of those classified individualistic, 75.0% completed the rough puzzle. This means that the rough puzzle participants were in a sense more likely to look out for themselves. So why did they offer more tickets to an anonymous person? If we take into account the results of the previous study, in which roughness made a social interaction appear more difficult, here roughness similarly may have led people to interpret the decision context of the Ultimatum game as more difficult. Participants therefore may have engaged in compensatory bargaining behavior (i.e., giving more tickets so that the offer was not rejected) in a rough situation. Although this conclusion is tentative, we do know that the rough puzzle did not merely show more negative behavior overall.

The last two studies I will review focused on yet another substance-related haptic dimension—hardness. Metaphors for hardness (vs. softness) tend to involve both positive concepts like stability as well as negative concepts like strictness. In the first hardness experiment, passersby were told that the initial task involved watching a magic act and attempting to guess the "trick." Participants then examined one of two objects, a soft piece of blanket or a hard block of balsa wood. The magic act was then postponed (forever) while participants completed the second half of the study—forming an impression of a social interaction in a passage much like that from the first texture study, but here between a boss and an employee. Participants evaluated the employee's personality on trait terms relating to general positivity (e.g., kind) and rigidity/strictness (e.g., unyielding). Would simply touching a hard or soft object change people's impressions of someone's personality? On composites of the two trait dimensions, participants who handled the hard block rated the employee as significantly more rigid/strict than participants who handled the soft blanket. Again, this embodiment effect was specific to the relevant metaphorical quality associated with hardness: Examination of the magic act object had no influence on ratings of the employee's overall positivity. Thus, this finding was not simply an outcome of feeling better or worse.

The last experiment featured two important changes to the prior designs. Participants completed two outcome measures, both a social interaction impression task and a decision task that involved negotiating a price on a new car. If metaphorical concepts related to stability become active as a result of hardness sensations, then people may show less flexibility in their negotiation strategies (specifically, the concepts of stability and rigidity should reduce people's willingness to change their offer prices). Perhaps more uniquely, we also decided to push the haptic envelope to investigate whether these embodiment effects emerged following contact on other parts of the body. Instead of having people actively touch objects with their hands, we placed people in different types of chairs, meaning that haptic experiences occurred passively by the seat of one's pants. Participants sat in either a hard, wooden chair or a soft, cushioned chair. They then read and evaluated the same social interaction passage as in the previous study using a modified trait list (e.g., emotional, stable). Next, participants completed the negotiation and decision making procedure. Participants imagined shopping for a new car (sticker price $16,500) and subsequently placed two offers on the car (the second assuming that the dealer rejected the first offer).

On the social impression task, participants sitting in hard chairs judged the employee to be significantly more stable and less emotional (i.e., "like a rock") but not any more or less positive than participants sitting in soft chairs. Analysis of people's changes from first to second car negotiation bid showed that, among participants who made a second offer, hard chairs produced less change in offer price than soft chairs (a decrease of approximately 39% for participants in hard chairs). Thus, hardness elevates perceptions of strictness and stability, and also reduces change from one's initial decisions, even when the touch experience is passive in nature. These findings again reinforce the metaphorical specificity of haptic embodiment effects. Hard objects can make others seem both more negative (strict and rigid) and more positive (stable), and they can make ourselves act in similar ways.

In sum, these experiments help to emphasize how physical interactions with three key dimensions of haptic experience influence our impressions and decisions, even those which are entirely unrelated to what is being touched. Each dimension—weight, texture, and hardness—is mentally represented not simply as a physical sensation but in concert with the abstract and metaphorical content we attach to those sensations. These embodied cognitions are critical components of our mental development and social lives, and they can be leveraged to change the ways that consumers and everyday people think.

Embodied Influences: Emerging Research

The studies just reviewed demonstrate the importance of embodied influences, but they represent just a small set of the work being conducted in this fruitful and often controversial research area. To give a sense of some of this emerging research, we can consider both process-level embodiment work and work that extends the boundaries of effects typically found in the embodiment literature.

Process

The underlying processes and mechanisms on which embodiment effects rest is currently one of the most hotly debated topics in the field. Some investigations focus on elements of the individual that inform the underlying mental representations relevant to specific embodied contexts. For example, in the domain of weight sensations, Chandler, Reinhard, and Schwarz (2012) have found that heavy sensations can influence the impressions that people form about books. Books that feel heavier (through inclusion of artificial weights) are rated as more important pieces of literature, but this is only the case when people have prior knowledge about the particular book. This finding advances our understanding of the processes that drive embodiment effects by suggesting that metaphor activation either influences the accessibility of existing knowledge (i.e., if people know nothing about the book, then "importance" cannot be made more accessible) or that the weight cue helps to confirm an existing hypothesis (i.e., knowing something about the book makes it seem more important). Which of these possibilities actually carries the most weight remains to be determined.

A second line of work has considered how focusing on the self (including its bodily states) can either heighten or weaken embodiment effects. Many sensations originate through contact with stimuli outside the body, but the changes those interactions produce within the body (e.g., in the skin, nerves, viscera) may themselves act as stimuli that people can sometimes detect. This process of *interoception* has been found to moderate the effect of haptic experiences on cognition. For instance, people who are more attuned to their bodily sensations are strongly influenced by weight and hardness cues relative to people less attuned to such internal states (Häfner, 2013). A further extension investigated whether people who are more sensitive to internal states (assessed by self-monitoring differences) are similarly more sensitive to haptic movements compatible with the use of certain products. For example, people who move their hands in a gentle fashion are more interested in products that require gentle handling (e.g., grapes) than people moving their hands in a more rowdy manner, but this is true only for people low in self-monitoring (i.e., people who pay increased attention to internal states) (Li, Briley, & Gorn, 2013).

Lastly, one of the big, unresolved issues in the field of embodied cognition has involved the question of directionality. Different models of embodiment predict different routes to the development of mental representations. These fall primarily into one of two camps. The first proposes that people develop conceptual and linguistic metaphors through application of primary knowledge about the physical world (which develops relatively early in life). Thus, in a sense, physical knowledge is more fundamental than abstract knowledge. In any given context, perceiving physical sensations or movements should be more likely to influence later-developed concepts than activation of those concepts is to influence physical perceptions (Ackerman et al., 2010; Lakoff & Johnson, 1999; Landau et al., 2010; Williams et al., 2009). The second possibility follows more standard associative models of cognition by proposing that links between physical sensations and conceptual knowledge occur through experience and are fundamentally bidirectional in nature (Niedenthal, 2007; Niedenthal et al., 2005; see also Lee & Schwarz, 2010). Many papers have focused on testing only one direction of effects, but recent evidence has begun to accumulate that at least some level of bidirectionality is present in embodied processes. For instance, reversing the operational direction of the Chandler et al. (2012) studies mentioned above, manipulations of a book's perceived importance lead to higher estimations of its physical weight (Schneider, Rutjens, Jostmann, & Lakens, 2011; but see Zhang & Li, 2012). Work on this issue is ongoing, and perhaps the next step is to move beyond testing the basic presence of bidirectionality toward tests of the relative strength of physical-to-conceptual effects as compared to conceptual-to-physical effects.

Extensions

In addition to the many process-based streams of research that have begun to emerge, research has expanded our understanding of where and when haptic embodiment effects exist. For instance, one line of work has linked experiences with physical weight to the cognitive processing of secrets. It appears that people associate secrets with heaviness, and people who hold or suppress important secrets (e.g., infidelity, sexual orientation) estimate hills to be steeper, perceive distances to be farther, and judge physical tasks to require more effort (Slepian, Masicampo, Toosi, & Ambady, 2012). In fact, the bigger the secret, the greater the burden it has on physical perceptions. Whether cueing weight would similarly increase the felt size of the secret (i.e., reversing the direction of causality) remains to be seen.

From a consumer behavior perspective, perhaps one of the most timely and relevant questions concerning haptic experience involves the influence of tactile sensation that occurs during use of touch screens. Touch screens are fast becoming a ubiquitous aspect of technological life, from cell phones to automobile dashboards to online shopping. Recent work has investigated how use of touch screens alters consumer shopping outcomes and has found that the more interactive the tactile experience, the greater the effect it has on perceived product ownership and product endowment effects (Brasel & Gips, 2014). This work highlights how touch screens engage the feeling of connection with products (see also Peck & Shu, 2009), and future research might consider the dual role of such interfaces to facilitate usability and establish felt connection, particularly with respect to whether these dual roles complement or interfere with each other.

Finally, although the majority of research on haptic experiences focuses on the influence of tactile sensation, some work has expanded into questions of bodily movement and posture (e.g., Van den Bergh, Schmitt, & Warlop, 2011). In a project on interpersonal communication, we investigated how restrictions on these states alter people's ability to effectively communicate. If people naturally simulate action when talking about that action (e.g., moving one's hands while giving directions), then limiting the physical ability to properly simulate might impair effective communication about that action. In fact, we have found that having people stand while describing sitting tasks (and vice-versa), or confining their hand motions while describing hand-related household activities, leads to deficits in both language comprehension and language production (Kronrod & Ackerman, 2014). Thus, not only are people worse at understanding when embodiment is restricted, they are actually worse at speaking too.

Implications of Haptic Experience for Design

The previous sections of this chapter have laid out a framework for understanding the basic elements of haptic experience and the broad influences these experiences have. Given this framework, we can now ask about the implications of touch for design. Perhaps the most conspicuous design category in which touch plays an important role involves product design, but we can also include two other categories as well—environmental and packaging design. I consider each of these in brief below.

Environmental Design Implications

For the purposes of this chapter, environmental design refers to design of spaces, retail store locations, and even online settings. Each of these kinds of environments can potentially benefit from attention to the relevance of haptic experience for people and consumers. Clearly, in consumer settings, one overarching rule applies: contact matters. Spaces that facilitate contact between shoppers and products will engage a variety of psychological processes, the most beneficial of which for sellers is perceived ownership. We see examples of such stores in those that encourage direct interaction with cell phones (e.g., Apple), consumer goods more generally (e.g., Best Buy), and even contact with spaces themselves (e.g., climbing walls at REI). Environmental contact can also offer useful indirect influences on consumer behavior (Levav & Zhu, 2009; Meyers-Levy & Zhu, 2007). For consumers, the ability to have direct contact with spaces and items affords the ability to try before you buy, and it also makes the shopping experience more entertaining.

Many retail locations have enacted changes to amplify the sensory experiences of shoppers, but touch often lags behind other types of sensations like scent and sound. Stores that limit tactile interaction, such as those that place items behind display cases or encourage staff members to enact rigid policies toward consumer touch will suffer from being unable to leverage these automatic processes. For those stores where contact is difficult for whatever reason (e.g., those selling experiential products), proxies for touch can help. The previously mentioned research on use of touch screens (Brasel & Gips, 2014) suggests that contact with symbolic markers of products and situations, such as thumbnail images, can still elicit an important level of engagement and ownership on the part of consumers. With the advent of tablets and other touch screen shopping, this is especially beneficial for online stores.

Designing environments to facilitate touch is clearly important for how people engage with items and products, but it is also important for another, often overlooked reason—how people engage with other people in those environments. As earlier research indicated (e.g., Kronrod & Ackerman, 2014), limitations on haptic experiences such as movement and posture can inhibit effective communication. In customer-seller and customer-support interactions, clear communication is essential. Impaired communication is also likely to lead to impaired social connection between people in non-consumer environments. Research on interpersonal contact, a domain of touch outside the scope of this chapter, has demonstrated that touch can facilitate increased trust, security and credibility, even between strangers (e.g., Burgoon, Walther, & Baesler, 1992; Crusco & Wetzel, 1984; Levav & Argo, 2010; but see Martin, 2012). Thus, designing environments that promote some level of contact (under appropriate circumstances of course) could benefit communication and affiliative interactions within a number of settings.

Packaging Design Implications

Packaging is often designed for functional or visual purposes, but the haptic dimension can prove useful for engaging and shaping consumer opinions. Many forms of packaging prevent shoppers from interacting with the product itself and thus limit perception of touch-related information. This may be a missed opportunity, particularly for products that involve physical use such as furniture, computer interfaces, sports equipment, and so on. One underutilized method of allowing consumers to interact with such products is cutout packaging. Other, more commonly used techniques include trial and floor display items. Those types of packaging that allow for easy customer access are likely to best leverage psychological ownership and endowment effects.

Beyond ease of access, other forms of package design can directly and indirectly shape shopper impressions and decisions. Often the touch-related aspects of packaging are intended to promote consumer interest and engagement (e.g., Hinestroza & James, 2014; Underwood & Klein, 2002), but little attention is given to the manner in which that packaging is processed at a sensory and conceptual level. Some work has focused on the role of visual content to engage relevant processes, as when brand logos that appear in high locations on packages convey power-related information compared to when those same logos appear low on packaging (Sundar & Noseworthy, 2014). As reviewed here, the tactile dimensions of packaging (e.g., texture, weight, hardness) also have the ability to trigger carry-over influences onto product perceptions and decisions more generally. For instance, research indicates that taste perceptions of drinks are affected by the packaging of those drinks. Mineral water tastes worse when drunk from a flimsy cup than when the same water is drunk from a more firm (hard) cup (Krishna & Morrin, 2008). We may expect similar effects to emerge for products that vary in the type of packaging they use (e.g., baby food is sold in both hard glass jars and relatively malleable foil pouches). Increased attention to the sensory qualities of product packaging may represent an opportunity for designers, producers, and retailers to craft more precise brand images and encourage specific kinds of shopper perceptions.

Implications for Design

Finally, it should be quite clear at this point that touch matters for how people engage with and interpret products themselves. Contact, whether with actual products or by proxy, can heighten felt connections between people and products. But of course, how we touch (the degree of contact, the specific sensations, the type of motion), and what that touch means both explicitly and implicitly, can be equally important (see Williams & Ackerman, 2011). Much of this has been reviewed earlier in this chapter, but it is worthwhile to emphasize that a focus on haptic experience is in some ways still in its infancy within the realm of product design. Many basic questions remain to be answered. Should we design primarily for function or for the autotelic and pleasurable aspects of touch? How do we best harness the representational aspects of tactile sensations (the concepts likely to be triggered when touching products)? What product elements are necessary to maximize a designer's ability to deliver and communicate key sensations and experiences?

This last question is particularly important within many technological product spaces. As of the present time, digital devices have been woefully underequipped for facilitating variable haptic interaction. Buzzing cell phones and minimal force feedback gaming gadgets have been perhaps the most ubiquitous sources of such tactile sensation. Touch screen items have been a step in the right direction, but these provide only a basic degree of contact with products and product depictions. Additionally, consumers often report more negative attitudes toward use of digital-only vs. "real" interfaces (e.g., digital keyboards vs. keyboards with physical keys; Das, 2013). Work is increasingly pushing the boundaries of this interaction in order to change haptic qualities on the fly, but thus far it has been limited to fixed interfaces such as bubble overlays on keyboards (e.g., Barde & Purkar, 2013; http://tactustechnology.com/), feedback knobs (Whitfield, 2002), actuators (Poupyrev, Maruyama, & Rekimoto, 2002), and the use of electrostatic vibration to create the sensation of friction on smooth screens (Bau, Poupyrev, Israr, & Harrison, 2010). In the latter case, a periodic signal is applied to an electrode pattern (e.g., on a screen), creating a weak electrostatic attraction between the finger and the electrode, which is perceived as vibration when the finger is moved. This vibration slows movement and is interpreted by the brain as friction. Firms have begun implementing such technology in a range of touch screen devices, including cell phones and car dashboards (Banter, 2010). However, more functional means of delivering real-time sensation through changes in weight, texture, temperature, and hardness remain to be developed and implemented.

Similar ideas can be brought to the fore on more stable aspects of product design. For instance, how much does material flexibility matter to consumers, and in what ways? What do design styles emphasizing more modern styling (e.g., smooth lines, synthetic materials) versus traditional styling (e.g., natural shapes and materials) communicate to people, even in nonconscious ways? What is the best weight for handheld electronic devices? Consider the cell phone market. Phone makers who have moved from traditional plastic housings to harder and heavier metal housings have enjoyed perceptions from the public that their phones are of better quality (Petrovan, 2013), consistent with the conceptual and embodied implications of weight and hardness. Sales of the metal-body iPhone 5s (which does offer other additional features) far outpaced sales of the plastic-body iPhone 5c (Curtis, 2013). In situations where products can reflect on one's social- and self-images, attention to the higher-order cognitive implications of haptic experience may be quite important, but this focus may be misguided for products more purely associated with function (or perhaps not!). Such issues are significant in their own right, but also because the information derived from haptic input can bias impressions and judgments in unforeseen ways (e.g., Krishna, 2006). Research and implementation in this direction is clearly of value given consumers' strong desire to physically interact with products (Accenture, 2014) and because the haptics market is predicted to grow by 1600% in the next decade (Koetsier, 2013).

Implications for a Theory of Design

Given the implications of this work for various types of environmental, packaging, and product design, it is worthwhile to consider the contributions this perspective might make for a generalized theory of design. First and foremost, research in the domains of sensory perception and marketing strongly suggest that theories of design should incorporate both a conceptual attunement to and empirical focus on the role of haptic experience. Haptic sensations and their consequences can act across consumer information search, integration, decision making, use, and disposition processes, highlighting their importance for design. Design that is intended to facilitate psychological connection and feelings of ownership is particularly relevant to haptic factors. Further, haptic experiences can change users' views of products and spaces by cuing semantic and metaphorical information, and by encouraging physical interaction from users. This interaction moves design from an abstract and conceptual enterprise to a tangible and dynamic one.

This shift is true for designers as well as for consumers. The cognitive and emotional implications of haptic experience suggest that touch should not remain a static construct in our approach to design, but should be integrated in both the generation of new ideas and the refinement and reinterpretation of existing ones. How exactly this will work in practice depends on the type of contact or sensation being implemented as much as on the problem or concept domain in which designers are working. Nevertheless, the new insights reviewed here into how haptic experience can shape the mind offer an increasingly expansive set of opportunities for which designers, and a theory of design, can engage.

Conclusion

The goal of this chapter was to make the case for touch as a central factor in our impressions and decisions regarding people, situations, and products, and thus its general importance for design. Clearly, haptic experience affords a wide range of influences on how consumers think and act. Whether these influences are direct, indirect or embodied, a sizeable set of possibilities remains to be tapped. This is particularly true in the world of design, where tactile sensations and motor movements can inform not only for product development, but packaging and environmental design as well. Despite the technological and operational hurdles to overcome, touch really does matter, and we should grab opportunities to use it effectively.

References

Accenture. (2013, April 15). Accenture study shows U.S. consumers want a seamless shopping experience across store, online and mobile that many retailers are struggling to deliver. Retrieved from http://newsroom.accenture.com/news/accenture-study-shows-us-consumers-want-a-seamless-shopping-experience-across-store-online-and-mobile-that-many-retailers-are-struggling-to-deliver.htm

Accenture. (2014, February 3). More U.S. shoppers plan to buy from stores but want the in-store shopping experience to match convenience of online, Accenture study finds. Retrieved from http://newsroom.accenture.com/news/more-us-shoppers-plan-to-buy-from-stores-but-want-the-in-store-shopping-experience-to-match-convenience-of-online-accenture-study-finds.htm

Ackerman, J. M., Nocera, C. C., & Bargh, J. A. (2010). Incidental haptic sensations influence social judgments and decisions. *Science, 328*(5986), 1712–1715.

Argo, J. J., Dahl, D. W., & Morales, A. C. (2006). Consumer contamination: How consumers react to products touched by others. *Journal of Marketing, 70*(2), 81–94.

Argo, J. J., Dahl, D. W., & Morales, A. C. (2008). Positive consumer contagion: Responses to attractive others in a retail context. *Journal of Marketing Research, 45*(6), 690–701.

Banter, B. (2010). Touch screens and touch surfaces are enriched by haptic force-feedback. *Information Display, 26*(3), 26–30.

Barde, M. C., & Purkar, M. K. (2013). A dynamic touch screen interface like Tactus for mobile and automotive devices. *International Journal of Emerging Technology and Advanced Engineering, 3*(4), 351–356.

Barsalou, L. W. (2008). Grounded cognition. *Annual Review of Psychology, 59*, 617–645.

Bau, O., Poupyrev, I., Israr, A., & Harrison, C. (2010). TeslaTouch: Electrovibration for touch surfaces. In *Proceedings of the 23nd Annual ACM Symposium on User Interface Software and Technology* (pp. 283–292). New York, NY: ACM.

Bhalla, M., & Proffitt, D. R. (1999). Visual–motor recalibration in geographical slant perception. *Journal of Experimental Psychology: Human Perception and Performance, 25*(4), 1076.

Boulenger, V., Mechtouff, L., Thobois, S., Broussolle, E., Jeannerod, M., & Nazir, T. A. (2008). Word processing in Parkinson's disease is impaired for action verbs but not for concrete nouns. *Neuropsychologia, 46*(2), 743–756.

Brasel, S. A., & Gips, J. (2014). Tablets, touchscreens, and touchpads: How varying touch interfaces trigger psychological ownership and endowment. *Journal of Consumer Psychology, 24*(2), 226–233.

Burgoon, J. K., Walther, J. B., & Baesler, E. J. (1992). Interpretations, evaluations, and consequences of interpersonal touch. *Human Communication Research, 19*(2), 237–263.

Chandler, J. J., Reinhard, D., & Schwarz, N. (2012). To judge a book by its weight you need to know its content: Knowledge moderates the use of embodied cues. *Journal of Experimental Social Psychology, 48*(4), 948–952.

Crusco, A. H., & Wetzel, C. G. (1984). The Midas touch: The effects of interpersonal touch on restaurant tipping. *Personality and Social Psychology Bulletin, 10*(4), 512–517.

Curtis, S. (2013, December 2). Apple iPhone 5s outsells 5c three to one in Britain. Retrieved from http://www.telegraph.co.uk/technology/apple/10484648/Apple-iPhone-5s-outsells-5c-three-to-one-in-Britain.html

Das, S. (2013, February 13). A keyboard that rises up from flat touch screens. Retrieved from http://www.cnet.com/news/a-keyboard-that-rises-up-from-flat-touch-screens/

Gallace, A., & Spence, C. (2010). The science of interpersonal touch: an overview. *Neuroscience & Biobehavioral Reviews, 34*(2), 246–259.

Gottlieb, G. (1971). Ontogenesis of sensory function in birds and mammals. *Biopsychology of Development,* 67–128.

Güth, W., Schmittberger, R., & Schwarze, B. (1982). An experimental analysis of ultimatum bargaining. *Journal of Economic Behavior & Organization, 3*(4), 367–388.

Häfner, M. (2013). When body and mind are talking: Interoception moderates embodied cognition. *Experimental Psychology, 60*(4), 255–259.

Hinestroza, N. B., & James, P. T. (2014). The effects of sensory marketing on the implementation of fast-food marketing campaigns. *Journal of Management & Marketing Research, 14*, 1–11. Retrieved from http://www.aabri.com/jmmr.html

Hong, J., & Sun, Y. (2012). Warm it up with love: The effect of physical coldness on liking of romance movies. *Journal of Consumer Research, 39*(2), 293–306.

Jostmann, N. B., Lakens, D., & Schubert, T. W. (2009). Weight as an embodiment of importance. *Psychological Science, 20*(9), 1169–1174.

Joy, A., & Sherry, J. F., Jr. (2003). Speaking of art as embodied imagination: A multisensory approach to understanding aesthetic experience. *Journal of Consumer Research, 30*(2), 259–282.

Kamleitner, B. (2011). When imagery influences spending decisions: The role of ownership simulations. *Zeitschrift für Psychologie/Journal of Psychology, 219*(4), 231.

Kay, A. C., Wheeler, S. C., Bargh, J. A., & Ross, L. (2004). Material priming: The influence of mundane physical objects on situational construal and competitive behavioral choice. *Organizational Behavior and Human Decision Processes, 95*(1), 83–96.

Klatzky, R. L., & Peck, J. (2012). Please touch: Object properties that invite touch. *IEEE Transactions on Haptics, 5*(2), 139–147.

Koetsier, J. (2013, August 6). Touchy-feely haptics market to balloon 1600% by 2025 (report). Retrieved from http://venturebeat.com/2013/08/06/touchy-feely-haptics-market-to-balloon-1600-by-2025-report/

Krishna, A. (2006). Interaction of senses: The effect of vision versus touch on the elongation bias. *Journal of Consumer Research, 32*(4), 557–566.

Krishna, A., & Morrin, M. (2008). Does touch affect taste? The perceptual transfer of product container haptic cues. *Journal of Consumer Research, 34*(6), 807–818.

Krishna, A., & Schwarz, N. (2014). Sensory marketing, embodiment, and grounded cognition: A review and introduction. *Journal of Consumer Psychology, 24*(2), 159–168.

Kronrod, A., & Ackerman, J. M. (2014). *Inference-making in language comprehension is contingent on embodied states.* Working paper.

Lakoff, G., & Johnson, M. (1999). *Philosophy in the flesh: The embodied mind and its challenge to western thought.* New York, NY: Basic Books.

Landau, M. J., Meier, B. P., & Keefer, L. A. (2010). A metaphor-enriched social cognition. *Psychological Bulletin, 136*(6), 1045.

Lederman, S. J., & Klatzky, R. L. (1987). Hand movements: A window into haptic object recognition. *Cognitive Psychology, 19*(3), 342–368.

Lee, S. W., & Schwarz, N. (2010). Dirty hands and dirty mouths: Embodiment of the moral-purity metaphor is specific to the motor modality involved in moral transgression. *Psychological Science, 21*(10), 1423–1425.

Levav, J., & Argo, J. J. (2010). Physical contact and financial risk taking. *Psychological Science, 21*(6), 804–810.

Levav, J., & Zhu, R. J. (2009). Seeking freedom through variety. *Journal of Consumer Research, 36*(4), 600–610.

Li, E., Briley, D., & Gorn, G. (2013, June). *Moving hands move mind: Embodied gentleness effect.* Proceedings of the 7th Global Business and Social Science Research Conference, Beijing, China.

Martin, B. A. (2012). A stranger's touch: effects of accidental interpersonal touch on consumer evaluations and shopping time. *Journal of Consumer Research, 39*(1), 174–184.

McClelland, D. C., Koestner, R., & Weinberger, J. (1989). How do self-attributed and implicit motives differ? *Psychological Review, 96*(4), 690.

Meier, B. P., Hauser, D. J., Robinson, M. D., Friesen, C. K., & Schjeldahl, K. (2007). What's "up" with God? Vertical space as a representation of the divine. *Journal of Personality and Social Psychology, 93*(5), 699–710.

Meier, B. P., & Robinson, M. D. (2004). Why the sunny side is up: Associations between affect and vertical position. *Psychological Science, 15*(4), 243–247.

Meier, B. P., Schnall, S., Schwarz, N., & Bargh, J. A. (2012). Embodiment in social psychology. *Topics in Cognitive Science, 4*(4), 705–716.

Messick, D. M., & McClintock, C. G. (1968). Motivational bases of choice in experimental games. *Journal of Experimental Social Psychology, 4*(1), 1–25.

Meyers-Levy, J., & Zhu, R. J. (2007). The influence of ceiling height: The effect of priming on the type of processing that people use. *Journal of Consumer Research, 34*(2), 174–186.

Meyers-Levy, J., Zhu, R. J., & Jiang, L. (2010). Context effects from bodily sensations: Examining bodily sensations induced by flooring and the moderating role of product viewing distance. *Journal of Consumer Research, 37*(1), 1–14.

Miller, L. C., Murphy, R., & Buss, A. H. (1981). Consciousness of body: Private and public. *Journal of Personality and Social Psychology, 41*(2), 397.

Montagu, A. (1971). *Touching: The human significance of the skin.* New York, NY: Columbia University Press.

Newman, G. E., Diesendruck, G., & Bloom, P. (2011). Celebrity contagion and the value of objects. *Journal of Consumer Research, 38*(2), 215–228.

Niedenthal, P. M. (2007). Embodying emotion. *Science, 316*(5827), 1002–1005.

Niedenthal, P. M., Barsalou, L. W., Winkielman, P., Krauth-Gruber, S., & Ric, F. (2005). Embodiment in attitudes, social perception, and emotion. *Personality and Social Psychology Review, 9*(3), 184–211.

Peck, J. (2010). Does touch matter? Insights from haptic research in marketing. In A. Krishna (Ed.), *Sensory marketing: Research on the sensuality of products* (pp. 17–31). New York, NY: Routledge.

Peck, J., Barger, V. A., & Webb, A. (2013). In search of a surrogate for touch: The effect of haptic imagery on perceived ownership. *Journal of Consumer Psychology, 23*(2), 189–196.

Peck, J., & Childers, T. L. (2003a). Individual differences in haptic information processing: The "need for touch" scale. *Journal of Consumer Research, 30*(3), 430–442.

Peck, J., & Childers, T. L. (2003b). To have and to hold: The influence of haptic information on product judgments. *Journal of Marketing, 67*(2), 35–48.

Peck, J., & Childers, T. L. (2006). If I touch it I have to have it: Individual and environmental influences on impulse purchasing. *Journal of Business Research, 59*(6), 765–769.

Peck, J., & Johnson, J. W. (2011). Autotelic need for touch, haptics, and persuasion: The role of involvement. *Psychology & Marketing, 28*(3), 222–239.

Peck, J., & Shu, S. B. (2009). The effect of mere touch on perceived ownership. *Journal of Consumer Research, 36*(3), 434–447.

Peck, J., & Wiggins, J. (2006). It just feels good: customers' affective response to touch and its influence on persuasion. *Journal of Marketing, 70*(4), 56–69.

Petrovan, B. (2013, March 18). The great plastic debate of 2013: Is plastic that bad? Retrieved from http://www.androidauthority.com/is-plastic-bad-galaxy-s4–173494/

Poupyrev, I., Maruyama, S., & Rekimoto, J. (2002, October). Ambient touch: designing tactile interfaces for handheld devices. In *Proceedings of the 15th Annual ACM Symposium on User Interface Software and Technology* (pp. 51–60), Paris, France.

Proffitt, D. R. (2006). Embodied perception and the economy of action. *Perspectives on Psychological Science, 1*(2), 110–122.

Proffitt, D. R., & Linkenauger, S. A. (2013). Perception viewed as a phenotypic expression. In W. Prinz, M. Beisert, & A. Herwig (Eds.), *Action science: Foundations of an emerging discipline* (pp. 171–197). Cambridge, MA: MIT Press.

Reimann, M., Feye, W., Malter, A. J., Ackerman, J. M., Castaño, R., Garg, N., . . . & Zhong, C. B. (2012). Embodiment in judgment and choice. *Journal of Neuroscience, Psychology, and Economics, 5*(2), 104–123.

Schneider, I. K., Rutjens, B. T., Jostmann, N. B., & Lakens, D. (2011). Weighty matters importance literally feels heavy. *Social Psychological and Personality Science, 2*(5), 474–478.

Schubert, T. W. (2005). Your highness: Vertical positions as perceptual symbols of power. *Journal of Personality and Social Psychology, 89*(1), 1–21.

Slepian, M. L., Masicampo, E. J., Toosi, N. R., & Ambady, N. (2012). The physical burdens of secrecy. *Journal of Experimental Psychology: General, 141*(4), 619–624.

Sundar, A., & Noseworthy, T. J. (2014). Place the logo high or low? Using conceptual metaphors of power in packaging design. *Journal of Marketing, 78*(5), 138–151.

Tal, A., Grinstein, A., Kleijnen, M., Ackerman J. M., & Wansink, B. (2014). *Pound per pound: Do heavy burdens make heavy people?* Working paper.

Underwood, R. L., & Klein, N. M. (2002). Packaging as brand communication: Effects of product pictures on consumer responses to the package and brand. *Journal of Marketing Theory and Practice, 10*(4), 58–68.

Van den Bergh, B., Schmitt, J., & Warlop, L. (2011). Embodied myopia. *Journal of Marketing Research, 48*(6), 1033–1044.

Van Lange, P. A. (1999). The pursuit of joint outcomes and equality in outcomes: An integrative model of social value orientation. *Journal of Personality and Social Psychology,* 77(2), 337–349.

Whitfield, K. (2002). Touch and go. *Automotive Design & Production, 114*(6), 36–38.

Williams, L., & Ackerman, J. (2011, December 15). Please touch the merchandise. Retrieved from http://blogs.hbr.org/cs/2011/12/please_touch_the_merchandise.html

Williams, L. E., & Bargh, J. A. (2008). Experiencing physical warmth promotes interpersonal warmth. *Science, 322*(5901), 606–607.

Williams, L. E., Huang, J. Y., & Bargh, J. A. (2009). The scaffolded mind: Higher mental processes are grounded in early experience of the physical world. *European Journal of Social Psychology, 39*(7), 1257–1267.

Witt, J. K., Proffitt, D. R., & Epstein, W. (2004). Perceiving distance: A role of effort and intent. *PERCEPTION-LONDON, 33,* 577–590.

Zhang, M., & Li, X. (2012). From physical weight to psychological significance: The contribution of semantic activations. *Journal of Consumer Research, 38*(6), 1063–1075.

Zhong, C. B., & Liljenquist, K. (2006). Washing away your sins: Threatened morality and physical cleansing. *Science, 313*(5792), 1451–1452.

2

THE BUILDING BLOCKS OF DESIGN

Conceptual Scaffolding as an Organizing Framework for Design

Lawrence E. Williams

UNIVERSITY OF COLORADO BOULDER

Modern-day approaches to industrial design emphasize that an understanding of humans must be central to the designers' efforts (Kreuzbauer & Malter, 2005; Norman, 2013). Given that successful design is largely determined by commercial success, designs must resonate with consumers (Venkatesh, Digerfeldt-Månsson, Brunel, & Chen, 2012). In addition to understanding consumers' preferences for forms (Bloch, 1996) and functions (Bailetti & Litva, 1995), an understanding of how people interact with the physical environment can help designers connect with consumers. For example, knowing that consumers direct the bulk of their attention to stimuli at eye-level informs the design of retail spaces (Dreze, Hoch, & Purk, 1995), and understanding consumers' preferences for touch informs the design of product packaging (Peck & Childers, 2003).

It is clear that designers must be acutely aware of the fact that human behavior occurs within a physical context. However, such awareness is only part of the story. Recent advances in psychology have begun to specify myriad ways in which people's bodily experiences with the physical world shape their mental lives (see review in Reimann et al., 2012). For example, people's experiences with physical distance, physical brightness, and physical temperature have all been shown to alter their emotional states (McGraw & Warren, 2010; Chiou & Cheng, 2013; Williams & Bargh, 2008a, 2008b). Therefore, it also behooves designers to understand the psychological ramifications of consumers' experiences with the physical world, in order to effectively establish emotional connections with consumers and satisfy their needs.

Why would experiences with the physical world meaningfully alter psychological states? The answer lies in a consideration of how humans develop conceptual knowledge. *Conceptual scaffolding* refers to the set of processes by which knowledge developed in infancy (based on interactions with the physical environment) serves as the foundation for conceptual knowledge developed later in life (Williams, Huang, & Bargh, 2009). In this view, the abstract notion of emotional attachment is scaffolded (built) upon the concrete concept of physical distance, just as moral darkness is scaffolded upon physical darkness, and social warmth is scaffolded upon physical warmth. An important consequence of scaffolding is that the associative links between physical concepts and their psychological analogues remain intact. As a result, physical experiences can activate corresponding psychological concepts, bringing these to the 'top of mind' where they then influence people's higher-order thoughts, feelings, and behaviors.

In this chapter, I aim to shed light on the relationship between scaffolding processes (for developing and refining psychological concepts), and the psychological processes underlying consumers' response to design. Similar to how design researchers and practitioners historically have drawn upon Gestalt theory and Gibson's affordances view (Bloch, 1996; Still & Dark, 2013), I propose that a scaffolding perspective can provide a useful framework for guiding consumer-oriented, human-centered design, by taking into account the sensory, motor, and perceptual foundations for higher-order thought.

In what follows, I provide an overview of scaffolding as a basic mechanism of human thought and detail the correspondence between existing theoretical perspectives on design and the scaffolding view. I then review evidence in support of the scaffolding view within the psychology and consumer behavior literatures. I conclude by considering the potential implications of adopting a scaffolding view for three critical discussions within the design literature: user experience, form/function, and establishing emotional connection with consumers. For the designer, the key takeaways from the following review are (1) oft-overlooked, seemingly innocuous and inert features of the physical environment are capable of exerting measurable influences on people's judgments, feelings, thoughts, and behaviors, and (2) the scaffolding perspective provides insight into the underlying reasons for such influences, allowing us to make informed predictions in advance.

Scaffolding: The Physical Begets the Psychological

Drawing upon the social cognition, developmental psychology, and evolutionary psychology literatures, my colleagues and I introduced the term *conceptual scaffolding* to refer to the process by which an early understanding of lower-order physical (foundational) concepts passively and nonconsciously supports the development of higher-order (scaffolded) concepts (Williams et al., 2009). Others have defined scaffolding differently, thus for the sake of clarity it is important to distinguish our intended meaning from others found in the literature.

Distinguishing scaffolding from related perspectives. Developmental psychologists interested in children's ability to learn via observing their primary caregiver's actions first introduced the term scaffolding to describe how a mother's behavior (or explicit instruction) serves as the foundation upon which the child's mental abilities develop (cf. Vygotsky, 1934/1962). Indeed, this treatment of the term scaffolding is not wholly at odds with my own; I am simply focusing on different elements of early childhood experience (implicit knowledge of physical concepts versus explicit parental instruction).

More recently, neuroscientists have used the term scaffolding to describe the process by which neural circuitry for a specific psychological process is supported by other neural circuits, suggesting a wide, diffuse pattern of neural activity when concepts (skills) are being formed, and a more narrow, efficient pattern of neural activity once concepts are well-understood (Petersen, van Mier, Fiez, & Raichle, 1998; Park & Reuter-Lorenz, 2009). Again, this use of the term scaffolding does not fundamentally conflict with mine; in fact such neuroplasticity may represent the physiological mechanism by which conceptual scaffolding occurs.

It is also instructive to distinguish the scaffolding perspective from the related notions of embodiment and conceptual metaphor. Over the past 20 years, researchers have conducted numerous investigations of embodiment effects on higher-order judgment and choice, demonstrating the tight link between physical and psychological states (Reimann et al., 2012). Embodiment refers to the role of the body's sensory and perceptual apparata on psychological outcomes. Such effects could be built into a person's mental representation of concepts, via scaffolding, but this need not be the case. For example, Strack, Martin, and Stepper (1988) found that facial configurations influenced participants' judgments of the humor in cartoons, such that engaging the zygomatic muscles implicated in smiling led participants to judge the cartoons as more humorous. This classic effect demonstrates a bodily influence on cognition, but does not implicate scaffolding at all.

Similarly, the notion that abstract knowledge arises from concrete knowledge is also related to conceptual metaphor theory, introduced by Lakoff and Johnson (1980) and recently expanded by Landau, Meier, and Keefer (2010). Conceptual metaphor may represent a specific mechanism by which scaffolding occurs, but is not scaffolding itself. Indeed, not all conceptual metaphors involve scaffolding. Landau, Sullivan, and Greenberg (2009) find that it is possible to shape participants' preference for social policy by invoking a metaphorical association between immigration and communicable disease. In other work, Morris, Sheldon, Ames, and Young (2007) find that the type of metaphor used to describe price trajectories affects people's valuation of stocks. When the stocks were described using agent (object) metaphors, investors expected trends to continue (reverse). In both of these cases, the metaphors are shaped by idiom and language usage learned later in life and do not appear to be linked to early experiences with the physical environment. Hence, although it is clear that the notions of conceptual metaphor and conceptual scaffolding are intimately linked, they are distinguishable constructs (cf. Landau et al., 2010).

Ecological basis for scaffolding. A useful feature of the scaffolding perspective is that it specifies why some early emerging concepts are more likely candidates to serve as foundational concepts compared to others. Such specification is informed by work in developmental psychology. Children appear to have a natural, possibly innate readiness for processing information related to the physical world (Premack, 2010). It has been shown that infants as young as three months demonstrate an early understanding of physical concepts such as gravity and physical support (Baillargeon, Needham, & Davos, 1992; Kim & Spelke, 1992; Needham & Baillargeon, 1993). Young humans are amazingly adept at quickly gaining a rudimentary understanding of the realities of the physical world (Premack, 2010). For example, lifting an object up from a surface suggests an implicit understanding of gravity, force, spatial relationships, and object solidity (Mandler, 1992). Indeed, it appears to be the case that an understanding of physical principles developmentally precedes the application of those principles, such that 3-month-old infants are capable of demonstrating their understanding of object permanence via their perceptual activity (looking times), but only at 8 months do infants appear to be able to use that knowledge to reach for occluded objects (Munakata, McClelland, Johnson, & Siegler, 1997).

Based on this analysis, the scaffolding view maintains that foundational concepts are those physical concepts that are critically linked to humans' ability to do things, concepts that support the development of action tendencies. Foundational concepts underlie adaptive motor action and perception. That is to say, an understanding of core physical concepts permits people to successfully navigate and interact with their physical environments. Hence, I argue that the features of the physical environment that are relevant for goal-directed action shape the architecture of the mind. To the extent that industrial design is similarly focused on understanding how people efficiently and effectively accomplish their goals, designers can be aided by an appreciation of the relationship between physical (foundational) concepts, on one hand, and psychological (scaffolded) concepts on the other.

Relationship to theoretical perspectives on design. Indeed, previous theoretical treatments of the study of industrial design have emphasized the relationship between consumers' perceptual abilities and the constraints afforded by the natural environment (Bloch, 1996; Gibson, 1979; Still & Dark, 2013). For example, researchers have noted that product designs succeed when they adhere to the principles of Gestalt psychology, such that consumers' find designs more aesthetically appealing when they feature unity (Veryzer & Hutchinson, 1998). These findings account for basic, low-level features of the human perceptual apparatus, which is more attuned to perceptual unity than perceptual discord (Köhler, 1959; Wertheimer, 1923/1938). Likewise, in his influential work Gibson (1979) emphasized the constraints placed on people's representational system by features of the physical environment. People's perceived ability to interact with physical objects are partially determined by the actions those objects *afford* (e.g., a solid, non-porous, opaque object affords being held). Taking such low-level considerations into account, designers can help consumers form the appropriate mental representations needed to successfully interact with a product by building in indicators of the actions afforded by the product (Norman, 2013). Still and Dark's (2013) recent extension of the affordances perspective corresponds neatly with the scaffolding view; both accounts suggest that people's mental representations (of affordances on one hand and scaffolded relationships on the other) are shaped by a lifetime of consistent interactions with the physical environment.

Like Gestalt psychology and Gibson's affordances theory before it, the scaffolding view holds the potential to serve as a guiding framework for design. Product designers can use scaffolding to develop a fuller understanding of the psychological consequences of consumers' exposure to the physical features of designs. Consider for example the potential implications of the white versus black version of Apple's iPhone. Via scaffolding, the brightness of a white iPhone may activate the concept of moral purity (Zhong, Bohns, & Gino, 2010); however such concept activation would be absent for a black iPhone engineered to be identical in every other way. Knowledge of how the physical begets the psychological can help designers effectively anticipate and modulate consumer responses to the physical properties of products.

These properties include (but are not limited to) the spatial configurations of things, the luminosity of things, and the temperature of things. Even though these three elements are all critically important features of the physical environment, they are not the only physical concepts shown to shape consumer behavior (indeed see Ackerman, this volume, for a review of the role physical tactile sensations play in judgments and decisions). Space, luminance, and temperature are highlighted because (1) they are ecological invariants that play a critical role in guiding human action (cf. Clark, 1973), (2) they have been shown to serve as important foundations for scaffolded thought, and (3) they represent core properties of product experiences under the designer's control. Accordingly, the influences of these three aspects of the physical environment on higher-order thought are considered in turn.

Scaffolding at Work: Space, Luminance, and Temperature

Recent investigations examining the embodied nature of human thought provide evidence for the scaffolding view. This work largely demonstrates how exposure to low-level, bodily- and/or physical concepts (e.g., via priming manipulations) activates high-level, psychological, abstract concepts. Much of this work has been conducted within the field of social cognition, but there have been a number of investigations examining the effects of scaffolding on consumer behaviors. Again, for the designer the key takeaway from the following review is that features of the physical environment are capable of shaping people's judgments, feelings, thoughts, and behaviors in predictable and systematic ways.

Space. Spatial perception is irresistible. At every turn, humans perceive the varying spatial relationships between objects in the world (how close is that car to that bicyclist?), and we maintain an egocentric sense of the distances between our bodies and other entities in our environments (Hall, 1966). The spatial configuration of the physical environment provides people with information regarding goal pursuit, social connections, and causal relationships. From a design standpoint, the spatial configuration of elements of a product can be used to provide users with information regarding their purpose and relationship. For example, buttons placed far away from each other on an electronic device conveys different sets of functions, whereas light switches placed close to each other on a wall (usually) indicates some shared relationship (e.g., controlling all of the lights in one room, but not in other rooms). Critically for our analysis, recent evidence supports the view that the perception of varying spatial distances provides the foundation for the concept of psychological distance.

Psychological distance is the subjective sense of how near versus far people feel to mental representations (of other people, places, ideas, or points in time; Trope & Liberman, 2010). Psychological distance has been shown to have a pervasive influence on consumers, including their consideration of product usage situations (Alexander, Lynch, & Wang, 2008), the weights placed on product attributes during choice (Malkoc, Zauberman, & Ulu, 2005), and the intensity of their reactions to emotional events (Williams, Stein, & Galguera, 2014). Although there is currently a lack of consensus on the precise nature of psychological distance (e.g., we do not know precisely how the subjective sense of distance is instantiated at a neural level), the scaffolding view proposes that the construct of psychological distance originates from people's early childhood experiences with physical distance and the spatial organization of their environments.

If the abstract concept of psychological distance is scaffolded upon the lower-order, bodily understanding of physical distance, then, given spreading activation and the schematic organization of memory contents, the mere perception of physical distance should be capable of activating a sense of psychological distance. Accordingly, Williams and Bargh (2008a) found that the spatial distance between elements in a visual array influences judgments of emotional attachment, as well as the degree to which people were emotionally affected by violent or otherwise aversive media experiences. In that research, the experimenters asked participants to plot two points on a Cartesian plane. Compared to those who plotted points close to each other, those who plotted distant points reported being less bothered by violent media, and less connected to significant people and places in their lives.

At first glance, this effect may seem surprising. However, this type of priming effect is consistent with previous evidence and theory suggesting that starting from an early age, people inject themselves and their world-view into what they perceive. For example, infants as young as five months old attribute agency and goals to self-propelled objects (Luo & Baillargeon, 2005; Premack & Premack, 1997). In this research, abstract arrays featuring inert and moving shapes have been used to demonstrate infants' understanding of both causality ("that ball caused the block to move") and causal intent ("that ball pushed the block because it wanted the block to move"; Premack, 1990). In the same vein, the work of Williams and Bargh (2008a) suggests that people spontaneously apply their understanding of physical distance to objects in an array. The result of this application is the activation of the concept of psychological distance.

Accordingly, physical distance perception has been shown to alter other emotional reactions as well. McGraw and Warren (2010) show that when people plot points on a Cartesian plane that are distant from each other, they perceive more humor in a severe moral violation. The authors view this effect as a demonstration of how spatial distance produces a sense of psychological distance in consumers. Psychological distance is capable of producing a protective frame through which consumers can safely engage with frightening or otherwise disturbing content (Andrade & Cohen, 2007). Distancing permits people to be less negatively affected by the moral violation, allowing them to safely find the humor in the situation (cf. McGraw, Williams, & Warren, 2014). Again here, we see evidence of how exposure to physical distance produces meaningful psychological outcomes.

In the marketing literature, Chae, Li, and Zhu (2013) show that the spatial layout of advertisements shapes people's judgments of the effectiveness of advertised products. In this work, the experience of perceiving physical separation feeds into higher-order causal attributions, such that perceived closeness between a product such as beauty cream and the usage situation leads consumers to expect the product to work better. Here again we see the relationship between a foundational physical concept and higher order psychological processes. Taken together, all of these investigations provide evidence that low-level experiences with physical distance serve as the foundation for our concept of psychological distance. This relationship has downstream consequences for people's emotional experiences and evaluations.

Luminance. Shifting away from spatial perception, a number of researchers have shown that luminance (the brightness of objects and experiences) shape people's psychological responses. Similar to distance, nearly every visual experience involves an appreciation of the varying levels of luminance objects afford. Indeed, people's largely invariant experience with the circadian cycle has taught humans that the light of day brings with it clarity and safety and hence affords action, whereas the darkness of night is tied to a decreased ability to detect threats and hence affords rest. Designers have long known that physical brightness denotes purity whereas darkness denotes imperfection; this understanding is believed to underlie Apple's decision to delay the release of the white model of the iPhone 4, as they sought to perfect the process to generate a pure white chassis that would not darken over time or with usage (Lai, 2010). People's experiences with physical brightness and darkness serve as the experiential foundation for the development of abstract concepts related to emotional valence and morality.

In support of this view, Meier, Robinson, and Clore (2004) found that people are quicker to associate positive words—like puppies—with light colors, and negative words—like cancer—with dark colors. Related, Chiou and Cheng (2013) have also found that physical brightness automatically brings to mind concepts related to morality, highlighting the experiential basis for the reason why people associate the divine with the light and the damned with the shadows. Similarly, Zhong and colleagues (2010) found that dimly lit rooms facilitate dishonest behavior, whereas brightness brings the truth to light. Such findings show that people's cognitive, emotional and behavioral responses are tied to the physical realities of our experiences with light and darkness. Early sensory and perceptual experiences with brightness versus darkness structure the way in which people mentally represent abstract concepts such as goodness and purity. Being attuned to the psychological ramifications of consumers' experiences with physical brightness can help designers ensure that they do not inadvertently limit consumers' desire to forge a connection with their products.

Temperature. The final stream of research reviewed here in support of the scaffolding view demonstrates the relationship between physical and psychological temperatures. As with space and luminance, temperature is an ever-present feature of the physical environment. Indeed, temperature information can be extracted from all cutaneous tactile perception experiences (Craig et al., 2000). Furthermore, as mammals, humans crave warmth. Typically, our initial experiences with abstract notions of love, concern, and care simultaneously feature close physical contact with a warm object, namely our caretakers (cf. Harlow, 1958; Lakoff & Johnson, 1980). Through this repeated association early in life we build the concept of psychological warmth onto the foundational concept of physical warmth.

Supporting this view, Williams and Bargh (2008b) showed that exposure to physical warmth led people to perceive more emotional warmth in an ambiguous other and to make emotionally warmer choices—choosing to give a gift to a friend instead of taking a reward for oneself. Building upon these initial findings, Kang and colleagues (2011) show that exposure to physically warm objects enhances trust, leading people to invest more with a stranger in an economic trust game. In both of these investigations, the authors hypothesized that physical experience with warm (versus cold) temperatures would activate the notion of psychological warmth; this activation then has downstream consequences for people's social judgments, decisions, and emotional states.

Others have corroborated these findings. Importantly, Inagaki and Eisenberger (2013) showed that there are shared neural mechanisms underlying feelings of physical and social warmth. In their study, participants holding a warm heating pad felt more connected to their loved ones, and both physical warmth and social warmth were associated with increased activity in the insula and ventral striatum. In marketing, it has been found that exposure to physical cold motivates a desire for emotional warmth (Hong & Sun, 2012). Here the researchers find that consumers show a stronger preference for romantic (emotionally warm) movies during the winter. Such effects mirror the work of Zhong and Leonardelli

(2008), who showed that feeling socially cold and excluded led people to prefer physically warm products such as hot tea. Last, recent work shows that physically warm temperatures increase people's valuation of products, such that they report stronger purchase intentions and are willing to pay more for products after being exposed to warm (versus cold) temperatures (Zwebner, Lee, & Goldenberg, 2014).

The scaffolding view maintains that it is our early childhood experience with the physical environment that gives rise to these relationships between foundational and abstract concepts. IJzerman and his colleagues (2013) demonstrate the importance of such experience by examining the effect of temperature priming on children's sharing behavior. Children exposed to warmth were more likely to share stickers with others, but only if they were securely attached. For insecurely attached children, the temperature manipulation had no effect on their generosity. This pattern supports the scaffolding view. The relationship between physical warmth and psychological warmth results from close, caring, physical contact with warm caretakers early in life, contact that is likely absent for insecurely attached children.

Implications for Design

Designers succeed when they incorporate a deep understanding of humans into their work (Norman, 2013). Like Gestalt psychology and affordances theory before it, the scaffolding perspective represents one lens through which designers can gain a deep understanding of how people's experiences with the physical environment translate into psychological experiences. The following section speculates about ways in which an understanding of the scaffolded nature of mind can help designers connect with consumers.

User experience. Some of the most important challenges of the modern technological age revolve around the design of effective user interfaces. As consumer products become increasing complex, multifunctional, and digital, the relationship between consumers' concrete product experiences and the outcomes of those experiences becomes increasing abstract. Mechanical button presses no longer produce immediate mechanical changes; instead a single virtual button press can accidentally delete large bundles of digitally stored information. Modern designers are tasked with building user experiences and interfaces that are sensitive to the fact that the users are human, with human tendencies (Norman, 2013).

Taking the scaffolding perspective into account can potentially help designers build user experiences that are consistent with the way in which users understand the world. People's expectations for how things work will be guided by their existing knowledge, and baked into that knowledge are schema-based relationships between foundational and abstract concepts. If designers know that consumers' experiences with the physical environment reflect not only physical outcomes but also psychological outcomes, then they can build user interfaces that capitalize on the relationship between the physical and the psychological.

Consider, for example, virtual keyboards on mobile and tablet touchscreen devices. One design challenge is how to provide users with clear and consistent information that a virtual key is active versus inactive (e.g., the keyboard's shift key can be inactive, actively shifting, or actively engaged in a "caps lock"; all three states require a distinct visual appearance). The designer can solve this problem in various ways (for example, by changing the hue, transparency, or size of the key), and indeed a cursory review of all of the iterations of the iOS, Android, and Windows Phone virtual keyboards suggest that no single standard approach has emerged. However, guided by knowledge on the correspondence between physical and psychological brightness, designers may wish to use luminance as a way to distinguish between states, as brightness is associated with action whereas darkness is associated with rest. In this way, dark, dull colored keys would be inactive, whereas brightly lit keys would be actively engaged in their specified functions. These considerations also may be fruitfully applied to the design of pop up messages that do versus do not require immediate action on the part of the user (warning messages can be brightly lit, whereas notification messages can be more dim).

Form and function. Another area in which adopting the scaffolding perspective may assist designers involves helping consumers appreciate the relationship between a product's form and its function. To borrow language from Norman (2013), I suggest that when the relationships between physical experiences and the abstract concepts associated with the product are consistent with people's natural schemas, it makes it easier for them to form a "conceptual map" for the relationship between the more observable "form" of a product and the less-observable "function" of a product.

Imagine, for example, a brand new, discontinuous, innovative product designed to promote social networking and connectivity. To the extent that the function of this product (which could potentially take the form of a physical object, a web site, or some other yet-to-be-commercialized interface) is to bring people together, then building in physical elements that connote closeness will be beneficial. Physical closeness will activate the concept of psychological closeness, which will facilitate user's ability to understand the function of such an extremely new product. We can understand this process via the mechanisms of associative priming (Tulving & Schacter, 1990) and processing fluency (Schwarz et al., 1991). In this view, when designs "prime" people's long-standing, well-understood associations between foundational (physical) concepts and their corresponding scaffolded (abstract) concepts, this can increase the ease with which people infer an association between (physical) forms and (abstract) functions. Such predictions can be borne out by future research.

Now it can be argued that perhaps designers should be playful with the relationship between the physical elements of a product and its intended function. For example, deliberately creating a mismatch between the physical appearance of a product and its function might prompt consumers to think more deeply about the product experience (cf. Pocheptsova, Labroo, & Dhar, 2010). Take, for example, Terje Ekstrom's chair, which does not give off the immediate impression of supporting an adult's weight. In this case, the physical form does not offer many clues to the product's function and may activate undesired higher-order thoughts and feelings (such as mistrust). However, such an argument is insensitive to the fact that consumers engage in deep thought as an exception, not a rule (Bargh & Morsella, 2008; Hoyer, 1984). Given that the goal of industrial product design is to successfully satisfy consumer needs, designers cannot afford to rely on the slim chance that consumers will tolerate inconsistent and disfluent relationships between the physical and psychological elements of a design. Such a luxury is reserved largely for fine artists.

Emotional connection. Last, by capitalizing on the relationship between foundational and scaffolded concepts, designers can more strongly foster emotional connections between consumers and products. To do this, designers can ensure that the emotional features associated with the basic physical aspects of the design—via scaffolding—are consistent with the intended emotional features of the product. For example, Starbucks' Oprah Chai Tea offerings aim to promote self-growth, positivity, and generosity in consumers. Further, these products are tied to the firm's corporate social responsibility agenda. Given these goals, the scaffolding perspective suggests that integrating physical closeness, physical brightness, and physical warmth into the design (of both the product and marketing communications) should stimulate a desired emotional response in consumers, compared to the use of physically distant, dark, and cold cues. Indeed, guided by the scaffolding perspective, it is reasonable to hypothesize that consumers would be less interested in charitable donations after ordering the iced versus hot version of Oprah's Chai Tea.

Implications for Theories of Design

Incorporating the scaffolding perspective can augment current theories of design. For example, the present review suggests that an understanding of the relationship between foundational and abstract concepts may be used as a backdrop for thinking through the four stages of Norman's (2013) double diamond model of human centered design. In this view, it may be the case that divergent thinking processes are enhanced when designers appreciate how the physical world shapes psychological experiences in unexpected, nonobvious ways. Such thinking may prompt a deeper exploration of all of the downstream psychological ramifications of design choices. At the same time, convergent thinking may be aided by an appreciation that consumers' thoughts and feelings are intimately tethered to their experiences with the physical world; foundational concepts provide meaningful constraints on the ways in which consumers process information embedded in product designs. Future research can bear out the extent to which design theory and practice benefit from a consideration of the scaffolded nature of human thought.

Conclusion

Here I sought to introduce the notion of conceptual scaffolding to the study of product design. In reviewing the theoretical rationale and empirical evidence for scaffolding, it becomes clear that physical experiences are capable of shaping the way people think, feel, and subsequently act. Remembering that consumers' experiences with the physical environment can have systematic (but not immediately obvious) psychological ramifications can guide designers' attempts to recognize and solve the problems consumers face.

References

Alexander, D., Lynch, J. G., Jr., & Wang, Q. (2008). As time goes by: Do cold feet follow warm intentions for really-new vs. incrementally-new products? *Journal of Marketing Research, 45*, 307–319.

Andrade, E. B., & Cohen, J. B. (2007). On the consumption of negative feelings. *Journal of Consumer Research, 34*, 283–300.

Bailetti, A. J., & Litva, P. F. (1995). Integrating customer requirements into product designs. *Journal of Product Innovation Management, 12*, 3–15.

Baillargeon, R., Needham, A., & Devos, J. (1992). The development of young infant's intuitions about support. *Early Development and Parenting, 1*, 69–78.

Bargh, J. A., & Morsella, E. (2008). The unconscious mind. *Perspectives on Psychological Science, 3*, 73–79.

Bloch, P. H. (1996). Seeking the ideal form: Product design and consumer response. *Journal of Marketing, 59*, 16–29.

Chae, B. G., Li, X., & Zhu, R. J. (2013). Judging product effectiveness from perceived spatial proximity. *Journal of Consumer Research, 40*, 317–335.

Chiou, W.-B., & Cheng, Y.-Y. (2013). In broad daylight, we trust in God! Brightness, the salience of morality, and ethical behavior. *Journal of Environmental Psychology, 36*, 37–42.

Clark, H. H. (1973). Space, time, semantics, and the child. In T. E. Moore (Ed.), *Cognitive development and the acquisition of language* (pp. 27–63). New York, NY: Academic Press.

Craig, A. D., Chen, K., Bandy, D., & Reiman, E. M. (2000). Thermosensory activation of insular cortex. *Natural Neuroscience, 3*, 184–190.

Dreze, X., Hoch S. J., & Purk, M. E. (1995). Shelf management and space elasticity. *Journal of Retailing, 70*, 301–326.

Gibson, J. J. (1979). *The ecological approach to visual perception.* Boston, MA: Houghton Mifflin.

Hall, E. T. (1966). *The hidden dimension.* Garden City, NY: Doubleday.

Harlow, H. (1958). The nature of love. *American Psychologist, 13*, 673–685.

Hong J., & Sun Y. (2012). Warm it up with love: The effect of physical coldness on liking of romance movies. *Journal of Consumer Research, 39*, 293–306.

Hoyer, W. D. (1984). An examination of consumer decision making for a common repeat purchase product. *Journal of Consumer Research, 11*, 822–831.

IJzerman, H., Karremans, J. C., Thomsen, L., & Schubert, T. W. (2013). Caring for sharing: How attachment styles modulate communal cues of physical warmth. *Social Psychology, 44*, 160–166.

Inagaki, T. K., & Eisenberger, N. I. (2013). Shared neural mechanisms underlying social warmth and physical warmth. *Psychological Science, 24*, 2272–2280.

Kang, Y., Williams, L. E., Clark, M., Gray, J. R., & Bargh, J. A. (2011). Physical temperature effects on trust behavior: The role of the insula. *Social Cognitive and Affective Neuroscience, 6*, 507–515.

Kim, I. K., & Spelke, E. S. (1992). Infants' sensitivity to effects of gravity on visible object motion. *Journal of Experimental Psychology: Human Perception and Performance, 18*, 385–393.

Köhler, W. (1959). Gestalt psychology today. *American Psychologist, 14*, 727–734.

Kreuzbauer, R., & Malter, A. J. (2005). Embodied cognition and new product design: Changing product form to influence brand categorization. *Journal of Product Innovation Management, 22*, 165–176.

Lai, R. (2010). White iPhone 4 delay: The challenges faced by Apple's glass supplier. Engadget. Retrieved from http://www.engadget.com/2010/07/18/white-iphone-4-delay-the-challenges-faced-by-apples-glass-supp/

Lakoff, G., & Johnson, M. (1980). *Metaphors we live by*. Chicago, IL: University of Chicago Press.

Landau, M. J., Meier, B. P., & Keefer, L. A. (2010). A metaphor-enriched social cognition. *Psychological Bulletin, 136*, 1045–1067.

Landau, M. J., Sullivan, D., & Greenberg, J. (2009). Evidence that self-relevant motives and metaphoric framing interact to influence political and social attitudes. *Psychological Science, 20*, 1421–1427.

Luo, Y., & Baillargeon, R. (2005). Can a self-propelled box have a goal? Psychological reasoning in 5-month-old infants. *Psychological Science, 16*, 601–608.

Malkoc, S. A., Zauberman, G., & Ulu, C. (2005). Consuming now or later? The interactive effect of timing and attribute alignability. *Psychological Science, 16*, 411–417.

Mandler, J. M. (1992). How to build a baby: II. Conceptual primitives. *Psychological Review, 99*, 587–604.

McGraw, A. P., & Warren, C. (2010). Benign violations: Making immoral behavior funny. *Psychological Science, 21*, 1141–1149.

McGraw, A. P., Williams, L. E., & Warren, C. (2014). The rise and fall of humor: Psychological distance modulates humorous responses to tragedy. *Social Psychological and Personality Science, 5*, 566–572.

Meier, B. P., Robinson, M. D., & Clore, G. L. (2004). Why good guys wear white: Automatic inferences about stimulus valence based on brightness. *Psychological Science, 15*, 82–87.

Morris, M. W., Sheldon, O. J., Ames, D. R., & Young, M. J. (2007). Metaphors and the market: Consequences and preconditions of agent and object metaphors in stock market commentary. *Organizational Behavior and Human Decision Processes, 102*, 174–192.

Munakata, Y., McClelland, J. L., Johnson, M. H., & Siegler, R. S. (1997). Rethinking infant knowledge: Toward an adaptive process account of successes and failures in object permanence tasks. *Psychological Review, 104*, 686–713.

Needham, A., & Baillargeon, R. (1993). Intuitions about support in 4.5-month-old infants. *Cognition, 47*, 121–148.

Norman, D. A. (2013). *The design of everyday things*. New York, NY: Basic Books.

Park, D. C., & Reuter-Lorenz, P. (2009). The adaptive brain: Aging and neurocognitive scaffolding. *Annual Review of Psychology, 60*, 173–196.

Peck, J., & Childers, T. L. (2003). To have and to hold: The influence of haptic information on product judgments. *Journal of Marketing, 67*, 35–48.

Petersen, S. E., van Mier, H., Fiez, J. A., & Raichle, M. E. (1998). The effects of practice on the functional anatomy of task performance. *Proceedings of the National Academy of Science, 95*, 853–860.

Pocheptsova, A., Labroo, A., & Dhar, R. (2010). Making products feel special: When meta-cognitive difficulty enhances evaluation. *Journal of Marketing Research, 47,* 1059–1069.

Premack, D. (1990). The infant's theory of self-propelled objects. *Cognition, 36,* 1–16.

Premack, D. (2010). Why humans are unique: Three theories. *Perspectives on Psychological Science, 5,* 22–32.

Premack, D., & Premack, A. (1997). Infants attribute value +/– to the goal-directed actions of self-propelled objects. *Journal of Cognitive Neuroscience, 9,* 848–856.

Reimann, M., Feye, W., Malter, A. J., Ackerman, J. M., Castaño, R., Garg, N., Kreuzbauer, R., et al. (2012). Embodiment in judgment and choice. *Journal of Neuroscience, Psychology, and Economics, 5,* 104–123.

Schwarz, N., Bless, H., Strack, F., Klumpp, G., Rittenauer–Schatka, H., & Simons, A. (1991). Ease of retrieval as information: Another look at the availability heuristic. *Journal of Personality and Social Psychology, 61,* 195–202.

Still, J. D., & Dark, V. J. (2013). Cognitively describing and designing affordances. *Design Studies, 34,* 285–301.

Strack, F., Martin, L. L., & Stepper, S. (1988). Inhibiting and facilitating conditions of the human smile: A nonobstrusive test of the facial feedback hypothesis. *Journal of Personality and Social Psychology, 54,* 768–777.

Trope, Y., & Liberman, N. (2010). Construal-level theory of psychological distance. *Psychological Review, 117,* 440–463.

Tulving, E., & Schacter, D. L. (1990). Priming and human memory systems. *Science, 247,* 301–306.

Venkatesh, A., Digerfeldt-Månsson, T., Brunel, F. F., & Chen, S. (2012). Design orientation a grounded theory analysis of design thinking and action. *Marketing Theory, 12,* 289–309.

Veryzer, R. W., & Hutchinson, J. W. (1998). The influence of unity and prototypicality on aesthetic responses to new product designs. *Journal of Consumer Research, 24,* 374–394.

Vygotsky, F. (1962). *Thought and language* (E. Hanfmann & G. Vakar, Trans.). Cambridge, MA: MIT Press. (Original work published 1934)

Wertheimer, M. (1938). Laws of organization in perceptual forms. In W. Ellis (Ed.,) *A source book of Gestalt psychology* (pp. 71–88). London: Routledge and Kegan Paul. (Original work published 1923)

Williams, L. E., & Bargh, J. A. (2008a). Keeping one's distance: The influence of spatial distance cues on affect and evaluation. *Psychological Science, 19,* 302–308.

Williams, L. E., & Bargh, J. A. (2008b). Experiencing physical warmth promotes interpersonal warmth. *Science, 322,* 606–607.

Williams, L. E., Huang, J. Y., & Bargh, J. A. (2009). The scaffolded mind: Higher mental processes are grounded in early experience of the physical world. *European Journal of Social Psychology, 39,* 1257–1267.

Williams, L. E., Stein, R., & Galguera, L. (2014). The distinct affective consequences of psychological distance and construal level. *Journal of Consumer Research, 40,* 1123–1138.

Zhong, C.-B., Bohns, V. K., & Gino, F. (2010). Good lamps are the best police: Darkness increases dishonesty and self-interested behavior. *Psychological Science, 21,* 311–314.

Zhong, C.-B., & Leonardelli, G. J. (2008). Cold and lonely: Does social exclusion literally feel cold? *Psychological Science, 19,* 838–842.

Zwebner, Y., Lee, L., & Goldenberg, J. (2014). The temperature premium: Warm temperatures increase product valuation. *Journal of Consumer Psychology, 24,* 251–259.

3

THE CONCEPTUAL EFFECTS OF VERTICALITY IN DESIGN

Luca Cian

UNIVERSITY OF VIRGINIA DARDEN SCHOOL OF BUSINESS

Vertical dimension is omnipresent in any design product. Any building, car, object, or picture has a higher and a lower part. The vertical axis is one of the basic elements of the visual grammar (Cian, 2012). However, designers, when deciding where to place elements along the vertical dimensions, usually follow their aesthetic taste and some functional principles. Does such placement involve more than taste and principles, however? Does verticality convey specific and unconscious connotations?

In daily language, we associate verticality with numerous concepts. For example, "We had a *high*-level intellectual discussion" (something that is "up" is associated with rationality), "the discussion *fell to* the emotional level" (emotions are connected with something that is "down" or "below"), and leaders have a *high* status and *super*vise their employees, whereas employees are *sub*ordinates and are at the *lower* levels of a hierarchy (power is connected with something "higher" along the vertical dimension). Are these terms just figures of speech, or are they implicit modalities through which we understand reality?

In this chapter, we tackle this question by providing a general review of some recent empirical findings. We begin by briefly outlining the literature for which metaphors are the cognitive mechanism people use to understand and manipulate abstract concepts. We review experimental findings that document the conceptual links between verticality and several conceptual domains (power, divinity, morality, and valence). We conclude by addressing specific contributions and implications of this research for designers.

Are Metaphors Just Figures of Speech?

Western philosophy, linguistics, and related cognitive sciences have traditionally viewed metaphorical language as both an imaginative and practical way to convey meaning. Writers, for example, employ it in their poems, plays, and novels to express themselves in a manner that might bear little resemblance to common thinking.

On the other hand, cognitive linguists such as Lakoff and Johnson (1980, 1999) argue that more than being figures of speech, metaphors allow people to communicate about what they cannot see, hear, taste, touch, or smell. Thus, a metaphor is a mapping (a tight set of correspondences) from a source domain to a target domain (Lakoff, 1993), with the former domain representing the shared and concrete knowledge from which we draw metaphorical expressions (e.g., "up" or "down"). By contrast, the latter domain represents conceptual and abstract thinking (e.g., power, morality). These mental associations allow people to use knowledge from the source domain to understand information regarding the target domain. Thus, Lakoff and Johnson (1980, 1999) argue that conceiving abstract concepts is possible because we can connect them with concrete sensory experiences. Without such connection, concepts would lack reference to the physical world and would be difficult to elaborate on and communicate. Such connection is primarily unconscious, as an automatic cognitive mechanism able to facilitate representation. In conclusion, Lakoff and Johnson (1980, 1999) argue that metaphors represent the basic structure through which we understand and manipulate abstract concepts. Simply speaking, metaphors reflect how we think rather than how we speak.

The conceptual metaphor framework is consistent with a grounded view of cognition (see Landau, Meier, & Keefer, 2010, for a comparison of these two frameworks). Grounded cognition is based on the theoretical assumption that cognition is generally grounded in a multitude of possible ways (e.g., simulations, situated actions, bodily states, etc.; see Barsalou, 2008). Historically, researchers have long debated whether the knowledge representations in cognition are "amodal" or "modal." In psychology and philosophy, a long tradition—beginning with Descartes's division between *res extensa* ("corporeal substance") and *res cogitans* ("mental substance") and culminating in artificial intelligence—has assumed that mental representations are symbolic, abstract, and separated from perception. They are "amodal" knowledge structures with no correspondence to the perceptual states that produced them. On the contrary, Barsalou (1999) proposed that cognition is intrinsically perceptual. When we perceive entities or events, sensory-motor neurons capture information inside and outside the body. Barsalou calls a record of such neural activation a "perceptual symbol." Perceptual symbols are unconscious, schematic, and multimodal, arising across different sensory modalities, proprioception, and introspection. Perceptual symbols are organized and grouped into "simulators" that allow the cognitive system to assemble specific simulations of an entity or event in its absence ("offline"). In this theoretical framework, a *simulator* is equivalent to a *concept* because it represents the knowledge and the associated processes that allow us to represent and think about entities and events. For example, when pressing the accelerator on a car, the "online" process of perception captures sensory information (visual details, the sound of the engine, the vibration of the car, etc.), the proprioception experience of pressing the pedal, and the introspective sensation of excitement. Later, when we think about the same event "offline" (when we are not accelerating in a car), we use a simulator of the event, which, being based on perceptual symbols, reenacts (unconsciously and schematically) the sensorimotor state we perceived. Barsalou (1999, 2008) provides some evidence showing that perceptual symbols can be the underlying base of more abstract concepts (e.g., "truth") that are grounded in several temporally distributed simulations of internal and external events.

Bargh (2006) and Williams, Huang, and Bargh (2009), within this same framework, proposed the concept of scaffolding. The authors describe scaffolding as a natural process by which new concepts become integrated with extant knowledge structures. Specifically, during their earliest years, individuals gain an understanding of physical concepts based on their direct experiences. Over time, they develop more abstract and complex knowledge structures that build on these first experiences. Thus, they link the meanings of the older, more basic concepts with the newer, higher-level concepts. Then, an activation of the more basic physical concept (which may even occur outside direct experience) will automatically activate the higher-level concept because of their shared metaphorical link.

Conceptual metaphor theories and grounded cognition share the fundamental assumption that the meaning and the interpretation of abstract constructs are intrinsically connected with bodily experience and physical perceptions, because of the intrinsically sensory-based nature of humans. Many studies provide evidence for this framework in several fields, such as marketing (for a review, see Krishna, 2012; Krishna & Schwarz, 2014), social psychology (for a review, see Meier et al., 2012), cognitive psychology (for a review, see Barsalou, 2010), decision-making (for a review, see Lee & Schwarz, 2014), and organizational behavior (e.g., Giessner & Schubert, 2007).

Next, we will focus specifically on the studies that have examined the relationship between physical verticality and abstract concepts.

What Conceptual Metaphors Does Verticality Hold?

Vertical-space positioning (i.e., something being physically higher or lower than something else) is a common and basic human experience. Thus, people have come to use it for multiple metaphorical associations (Lakoff & Johnson, 1999; Meier et al., 2007). Several studies have investigated the relation between verticality and abstract constructs, such as power, valence, morality, divinity, and rationality/emotions. They all found these metaphorical associations to be not simple communication elements, but rather, representations of a deeper mode of knowledge representation. We will discuss them in detail.

Most of the studies presented in this chapter, which test if a specific metaphor is a figure of speech or a deeper mode of knowledge representation, have used the so-called metaphoric transfer strategy (Landau, Meier, & Keefer, 2010). This empirical strategy involves assessing whether manipulating one domain (source or target domain) changes how people process the other domain (the target or the source domain, respectively) following the metaphorical relation.

Verticality and Power

Our daily language frequently uses metaphors to link power to verticality (dominance is up, submission is down; "high" status vs. "low" status; "upper" vs. "lower" classes). In a scene from the movie *The Great Dictator* (1940), Charlie Chaplin depicts this association in a clever and humorous way. Before the meeting between Hynkel (the caricature of Hitler) and Napaloni (the caricature of Mussolini), Garbitsch (Hynkel's Minister of Propaganda) indicates to Hynkel how to appear more powerful than Napaloni using psychology. Garbitsch continues, saying, "This can be done in many subtle ways. For instance, at this interview I have so arranged that he will always be *looking up* at you. You looking *down* at him. At all times his position will be *inferior*" (1:30.08–1:30.52).

Schubert (2005) wanted to empirically test if vertical positions are indeed perceptual symbols of power. If they are, the perception of vertical spatial differences should affect one's thinking regarding power (and/or vice versa). In a first study, the author found that people more quickly recognized stimuli representing power when the stimuli appeared at the top of the page than when they appeared at the bottom. In a second study, Schubert tested the ease with which participants judged a group as powerful or powerless when they were asked to perform a movement that fit the metaphor (in this case, participants were asked to make their judgments using the up or the down cursor key on their keyboards). He found that participants more quickly and accurately judged a group as powerful when they were asked to answer using the up (vs. down) cursor key. On the contrary, participants more quickly and accurately judged a group as powerless when they were asked to answer using the down (vs. up) cursor key. In a final study, Schubert (2005) showed how the amount of power attributed to an agent (in particular, to animals) is influenced by their position on the vertical dimension; that is, animals appearing in the upper part of a computer screen were more respected than those appearing at the bottom.

Similarly, Giessner and Schubert (2007) showed that the physical representation of vertical position influences judgments of a leader's power. In a series of studies, the authors changed the length of a line in an organization chart, asking participants to evaluate the leader's power. The longer the vertical line separating the leader from the rest of the employees in the charter, the more powerful the leader was evaluated. In a second set of studies, the authors reversed the metaphorical direction. In other words, participants received information about the power of a leader and were then asked to place the picture of the leader on a screen to a position that would best represent that leader's relation to his followers. Results showed that the more powerful the leader was described to be, the higher he was placed in the chart. Similarly, studies investigating the way authority status influences individuals' perceptions of size have found that prestigious titles result in height distortions. Wilson (1968) conducted an experiment on five classes at a college in Australia. The instructor introduced a man as a visitor from Cambridge University, and in each of the five classes, described the man's status differently: a student, a demonstrator, a lecturer, a senior lecturer, and a professor. After the man left the room, the class was asked to estimate his height. Wilson found that with each increase in status, the man gained an average half-inch in height, such that the "professor" was perceived as being 2 1/2 inches taller than the "student." Another study found that following an election, the citizenry perceives the winning politicians as being taller than they were before the election (Higham & Carment, 1992).

Moller, Robinson, and Zabelina (2008) hypothesized that because dominant individuals think in terms of power hierarchies, they should favor the vertical dimension (following power vertical metaphors such as "upper class," "lower class," etc.). In two studies, the authors showed that more dominant individuals were faster than less dominant individuals in responding to probes arranged along the vertical dimension of space. In a similar fashion, Robinson et al. (2008) found that attention is biased upwards in the case of dominant people and downwards in the case of submissive subjects.

Finally, Meier and Dionne (2009) built upon evolutionary psychology's theories suggesting that males are generally attracted to young and faithful females (i.e., powerless) and females are generally attracted to males with status and resources (i.e., powerful). Using vertical position as a proxy for power, the authors showed that men found women more attractive when their images appeared in a lower position on a computer screen, whereas women rated males as more attractive when their images appeared in a higher position.

Verticality and Valence

Our daily language has many associations between something that is positive and something that is up (e.g., "thumbs *up*," "feel *up*"), and between something that is negative and something that is down (e.g., "thumbs *down*," "feel *down*"). Meier and Robinson (2004), in a first study, found that people more quickly recognize positive words appearing at the top of the screen than those same names appearing at the bottom. In addition, participants were faster to recognize negative words when presented at the bottom (vs. top) of the screen. In a second study, participants had to evaluate a positive or a negative word (positioned at the center of the screen); immediately following this verbal evaluation, participants were asked to recognize a stimulus appearing either at the top or at the bottom of the computer screen. Participants were able to more quickly recognize a stimulus appearing in the higher part of the screen (vs. the lower) after they evaluated a positive word. The reverse happened for negative words.

Crawford et al. (2006) deepened the analysis about the association, showing that this conceptual metaphor influences memory. Specifically, they found that participants remembered positive stimuli as having appeared higher in space than negative stimuli. Finally, Meier and Robinson (2006) found that participants who scored higher (lower) in neuroticism or depressive symptoms were faster to respond to or detect lower (higher) regions of visual space.

Verticality and Morality

In the case of morality, in daily language, we can find many common metaphors that associate the abstract concepts of moral and immoral with something that is physically higher or lower (e.g., "*high* minded" and "*under*handed"). Meier, Sellbom, and Wygant (2007) found that people recognize words with a moral meaning (e.g., caring, charity, nurture, truthful, and trustworthy) more quickly when they appear in the higher part of the screen. Conversely, people recognize words with an immoral meaning (e.g., adultery, corrupt, dishonest, evil, and molest) more quickly when they are shown in the lower part of the screen.

Verticality and Divinity

In a similar fashion, many metaphors associate God with something that is up or higher (e.g., "Glory to God in the *Highest*") and Devil with something that is down or lower (residing in the "*under*world"). Meier et al. (2007) found that people were faster to recognize God-related words when they were associated with up rather than down, whereas the reverse occurred for Devil-related words. In a second study, participants were asked to categorize whether a word was more related to God or Devil. Meier et al. (2007) used several words that appeared one by one at the top or at the bottom of a computer screen. People were faster to categorize a God-related word when it was presented on the higher part (vs. the lower part) of the screen, whereas the reverse occurred for Devil-related words. In a third study, the authors found this association biased participants' memories of the stimuli. In other words, people remembered images of God (Devil) as being higher (lower) than they actually were. Finally, the authors showed that participants rated strangers as more religious when their pictures appeared in the higher part of the computer screen than when they occurred in the lower part. Chasteen, Burdzy, and Pratt (2010) reported similar findings. The authors, using a target detection task, determined that God-related words triggered attentional shifts to upward and rightward areas of the visual field. Analogously, Devil-related words caused attentional shifts to downward and leftward areas of the visual field. The authors also found that these results did not depend on participants' level of religiosity.

Verticality and Construal Level

Aggarwal and Zhao (2015) related physical verticality with construal level theory. Construal level theory divides mental construals into two levels: high and low. High-level construals encourage individuals to think about the "big picture."

They are superordinate thought processes that focus on the overall idea of a situation in order to extract the main point. On the other hand, low-level construals are detail-oriented or subordinate thought processes (Trope & Liberman, 2003, 2010). Aggarwal and Zhao (2015) hypothesized that as children, we learned that being physically higher offered a wider view and being physically lower provided a more restricted view. Therefore, we have gradually and subconsciously created a link between physical height and perceptual perspective such that the activation of the more basic concept of height now activates the corresponding perceptual processing.

Five studies supported Aggarwal and Zhao's hypotheses. For example, in one study, the authors asked participants to imagine purchasing a new computer desk and considering two options, one with higher-feasibility characteristics and one with higher-desirability characteristics. Participants who were primed with pictures from a *lower* angle (something physically low) preferred the more feasible desk, because they had a local focus (lower construal level). On the contrary, participants who were primed with pictures from a *higher* angle (something physically high) preferred the more desirable desk, because they had a higher perceptual construal level with a global focus.

Verticality and Rationality/Emotions

When connoting whether a person acted rationally or emotionally in a situation, we often invoke the concept of verticality. Thus, we say things such as, "he couldn't rise above his emotions," "the discussion fell to an emotional level," and "we had a high-level intellectual discussion." Cian, Schwarz, and Krishna (2014) explored this conceptual metaphor and its effects on consumer behavior. In a series of studies, they showed a systematic link between rationality and emotionality and physical verticality. The manipulation of this subconscious association has an impact on consumers' perceptions of information, and thus on attitudes and preferences. The authors found the association is strongest when consumers are unaware of it, and that brand familiarity moderates the metaphorical effect.

Implications for Design

The possible implications and applications of these notions in the design practice are countless because every design work entails the vertical dimension. A building's height may affect the sensation of power the people who work or live in it experience (indeed, architects designed the exaggerated verticality of the gothic churches to convey a sense of powerlessness for the people entering them, while magnifying the power of divinity). The height of chairs may impact the sense of power and, consequently, the ability to be persuaded (the more powerful and in control one feels, the less one is prone to being persuaded by others' opinions). If a chair's height affects one's perceived power, does designing "high" chairs for offices make more sense than designing them for homes? Similarly, imagine a meeting in an organization's conference room. Should the chairs be the same height? To corroborate differences in power, hierarchical organizations (e.g., military organization) should prefer differences in the height of chairs (i.e., higher chairs for people higher in status). All other interior design choices should be organized accordingly as well. Organizations that favor a non-hierarchical communication would benefit from an internal and external building design that presents no differences in height. Sergio Marchionne applied this approach when he became CEO of Fiat Chrysler Automobiles (FCA). Before him, at Chrysler, the chairman and three vice chairmen offices were located on the top floor of the building. Marchionne decided to locate those offices on the fourth floor, which is where the engineering department is located, while the top-floor penthouse now sits empty.

Besides power, issues related to affect, divinity, and rational thinking are also extremely relevant to product design. Images, logos, and slogans in advertising, the position of goods on grocery shelves, and the position of catalog descriptions of goods and services can benefit from the good (bad), moral (immoral), or higher (lower) construal-level associations with a higher (lower) vertical position. For example, companies can position their most expensive or highest-quality products at the top of their webpage and the cheapest or lowest-quality products at the bottom. Similarly, consider a consumer choosing between a multi-function desk requiring self-assembly and a desk with basic features that comes pre-assembled. Following Aggarwal and Zhao's research (2015), the level at which the store is located will affect consumers' preferences. If the store is located on a mall's upper level, consumers will focus more on the desk's functions and thus prefer the self-assembly desk. If the store is on the lower level, however, they will focus more on convenience and prefer the pre-assembled desk. Menus on phones or on vehicles can be designed to correspond to the metaphorical link between rationality/emotionality and physical verticality. Cian et al. (2014) show that the position of a political slogan (higher/lower) on a poster can influence voters' preferences. Individuals are more likely to vote for the candidate whose slogan position matches the slogan's rational/emotional content. In other words, a rational slogan in the higher part of a poster generates higher intention to vote for the candidate than the same slogan in the lower part of the poster. On the other hand, an emotional slogan generates more intention to vote for the candidate when it is in the lower part of a poster.

Interestingly, Cian et al. (2014) show how these conceptual metaphors can have downstream effects on consumer behavior, influencing peoples' preferences. Building on their work, we can assume that when a stimulus (a picture, a product, an environment, etc.) matches a specific conceptual metaphor (e.g., something that is good is up, something that is powerful is up, etc.), people will evaluate the stimulus itself more positively than when the stimulus and metaphor do not match.

A final question could be the following: How might manufacturers incorporate height in their products? Considering all the studies we have discussed, we can think of at least four different methods for generating differences in height: manipulating the display's height, the viewer's height, the imagined height, and the abstract domain. Manipulating the display's height consists of varying the product verticality while keeping the viewer's height constant. Examples are the variation of the product (or message) position on grocery shelves, on digital screens, or in advertisements. Changing the viewer's height is also possible via positioning him/her on taller/smaller chairs or on higher/lower floors, for example. Display height and viewer height are highly correlated. Indeed, pictures taken from different camera angles can suggest different viewer heights. Because viewing pictures taken from a high angle gives one the sensation of seeing the objects from above, individuals will feel they are at a physically higher level. Viewing the pictures taken from a low angle, on the other hand, provides the sensation of seeing the objects from below. Individuals will therefore feel they are at a physically lower level. If changing the display's or the viewer's physical verticality is not feasible, manipulating the imagined height might be an option. Indeed, encouraging people to imagine a physical experience can change their attitudes or behaviors without requiring them to change their bodily states (Barsalou, 2008; Elder & Krishna, 2012). Aggarwal and Zhao (2015) successfully manipulated verticality by having people imagine being on a building's upper or lower level. Finally, manipulating the abstract domain could result in a variation of the physical verticality. As such, variations of power status, morality, or valence could influence people's perception of height.

Implications for a Theory of Design

So far, we have described some of the most relevant works exploring the conceptual metaphors associated with verticality. Other conceptual metaphors involving verticality may be studied in the future. Some verticality metaphors may be conceptual, whereas others may be merely linguistic. However, not all associations are necessarily present simultaneously in consumers' minds, nor are they necessarily correlated. For example, a designer may want to use verticality to convey something with a positive valence (using the association up → good) but may not want to suggest power (given the association up → powerful). The contextual triggers that activate one conceptual metaphor (e.g., up → good) instead of another (up → powerful) have received little attention in the literature.

Contextual effects and stimuli properties can likely determine which conceptual metaphor is more salient in the consumer mind. In other words, the way in which the work of design is presented and the context in which it is immersed can trigger a specific metaphorical association. Perceivers adopt the most accessible interpretation, as rendered by the task and its context. Moreover, once people have adopted a given interpretation, competing interpretations become less accessible, and they reach judgments that contradict the conclusions to which the same input in a slightly different context (Schwarz, 2010) or with a reversed question order (Cho & Schwarz, 2008) would have otherwise led them.

However, more research is needed on this point, and designers should carefully consider the manner in which they present their work if they want to elicit a specific association.

Association Directionality

Some metaphors seem to be unidirectional. In Meier and Robinson's (2004) studies about verticality and valence, positive and negative words activated spatial attentions (i.e., "good" activated "up"). In other words, people were quicker to recognize a stimulus in the higher (lower) portion of the screen after having seen a positive (negative) word. However, spatial attention did not prime evaluation; that is, stimuli placed in the higher or lower part of the screen did not enable participants to more quickly identify if a word has a positive or negative meaning (i.e., "up" did not activate "good").

In other studies, such as in Giessner and Schubert (2007), the conceptual metaphor is bidirectional. In a series of studies, they showed that the more powerful the leader was described to be, the higher participants placed him in the chart (i.e., "power" activated "up"). In another series of studies, the longer the vertical line separating the leader from the rest of the employees in the charter, the more powerful the leader was evaluated to be (i.e., "up" activated "power").

The directionality of conceptual metaphors (unidirectionality vs. bidirectionality) is a topic that, despite considerable debate (cf. Landau, Meier, & Keefer, 2010; Lee & Schwarz, 2014; Zhang & Li, 2012; Zhang & Wang, 2009; Zhong & Leonardelli, 2008), remains poorly understood. In conclusion, designers should not assume that a change in the source domain (verticality) will affect the target domain (valence, power, etc.) and vice versa for all the conceptual metaphors we have discussed.

Culture

Culture represents another variable worth discussing. Most of the experiments described in this chapter were indeed conducted in Western countries. Investigating if these conceptual metaphors manifest in different cultures would be of much interest.

On the one hand, linguistic analyses show that some metaphors persist across cultures (Asch, 1958; Kövecses, 2005; Sweetser, 1990). Similarly, anthropological evidence shows that collective systems of cross-cultural verbal and imagistic meaning reflect metaphors that link social power/status with vertical position (Fiske, 2004; Schwartz, Tesser, & Powell, 1982). Bodily constraints, relational models, and early sensorimotor experiences as foundations of more abstract concepts may explain why some conceptual metaphors have emerged universally across cultures (Landau, Meier, & Keefer, 2010; Williams, Huang, & Bargh, 2009).

On the other hand, as IJzerman and Koole (2011) noted, conceptual metaphors can also be culturally specific. In any case, as Landau, Meier, and Keefer (2010) point out, researchers can use the metaphoric transfer strategy to determine whether members of different cultures construe or merely talk about aspects of the social world in different ways.

In conclusion, this brief review shows how visual positioning along the vertical dimension can affect consumer recognition, interpretation, memory, accuracy, and preferences toward information or stimuli.

References

Aggarwal, P., & Zhao, M. (2015). Seeing the big picture: The effect of height on the level of construal. *Journal of Marketing Research, 5*(1), 120–133.

Asch, S. E. (1958). The metaphor: A psychological inquiry. In R. Tagiuri & L. Petrullo (Eds.), *Person perception and interpersonal behavior* (pp. 86–94). Stanford, CA: Stanford University Press.

Bargh, J. A. (2006). What have we been priming all these years? On the development, mechanisms, and ecology of nonconscious social behavior. *European Journal of Social Psychology, 36*(2), 147–168.

Barsalou, L. W. (1999). Perceptions of perceptual symbols. *Behavioral and Brain Sciences, 22*(4), 637–660.

Barsalou, L. W. (2008). Grounded cognition. *Annual Review of Psychology, 59*, 617–645.

Barsalou, L. W. (2010). Grounded cognition: Past, present, and future. *Topics in Cognitive Science, 2*(4), 716–724.

Chasteen, A. L., Burdzy, D. C., & Pratt, J. (2010). Thinking of God moves attention. *Neuropsychologia, 48*(2), 627–630.

Cho, H., & Schwarz, N. (2008). Of great art and untalented artists: Effort information and the flexible construction of judgmental heuristics. *Journal of Consumer Psychology, 18*(3), 205–211.

Cian, L. (2012). A comparative analysis of print advertising applying the two main plastic semiotics schools: Barthes' and Greimas'. *Semiotica, 190*, 57–79.

Cian, L., Schwarz, N., & Krishna, A. (2014). *Top or bottom of the screen? Vertical position as a representation of rationality and emotionality*. Manuscript submitted for publication.

Crawford, E. L., Margolies, S. M., Drake, J. T., & Murphy, M. E. (2006). Affect biases memory of location: Evidence for the spatial representation of affect. *Cognition and Emotion, 20*(8), 1153–1169.

Elder, R. S., & Krishna, A. (2012). The "visual depiction effect" in advertising: Facilitating embodied mental simulation through product orientation. *Journal of Consumer Research, 38*(6), 988–1003.

Fiske, A. P. (2004). Four modes of constituting relationships: Consubstantial assimilation; space, magnitude, time, and force; concrete procedures; abstract symbolism. In N. Haslam (Ed.), *Relational models theory: A contemporary overview* (pp. 61–146). Mahwah, NJ: Erlbaum.

Giessner, S. R., & Schubert, T. W. (2007). High in the hierarchy: How vertical location and judgments of leaders' power are interrelated. *Organizational Behavior and Human Decision Processes, 104*(1), 30–44.

Higham, P. A., & Carment, D. W. (1992). The rise and fall of politicians: The judged heights of Broadbent, Mulroney and Turner before and after the 1988 Canadian federal election. *Canadian Journal of Behavioural Science/Revue canadienne des sciences du comportement, 24*(3), 404.

IJzerman, H., & Koole, S. L. (2011). From perceptual rags to metaphoric riches—Bodily, social, and cultural constraints on sociocognitive metaphors: Comment on Landau, Meier, and Keefer (2010). *Psychological Bulletin, 137*(2), 355–361.

Kövecses, Z. (2005). *Metaphor in culture: Universality and variation.* Cambridge: Cambridge University Press.

Krishna, A. (2012). An integrative review of sensory marketing: Engaging the senses to affect perception, judgment and behavior. *Journal of Consumer Psychology, 22*(3), 332–351.

Krishna, A., & Schwarz, N. (2014). Sensory marketing, embodiment, and grounded cognition: A review and introduction. *Journal of Consumer Psychology, 24*(2), 159–168.

Lakoff, G. (1993). The contemporary theory of metaphor. *Metaphor and Thought, 2,* 202–251.

Lakoff, G., & Johnson, M. (1980). *Metaphors we live by.* Chicago, IL: University of Chicago Press.

Lakoff, G., & Johnson, M. (1999). *Philosophy in the flesh: The embodied mind and its challenge to western thought.* New York, NY: Basic Books.

Landau, M. J., Meier, B. P., & Keefer, L. A. (2010). A metaphor-enriched social cognition. *Psychological Bulletin, 136*(6), 1045–1067.

Lee, S. W., & Schwarz, N. (2014). Metaphors in judgment and decision making. In M. J. Landau, M. D. Robinson, & B. P. Meier (Eds.), *The power of metaphor: Examining its influence on social life*, (pp. 85–108). Washington, DC: APA.

Meier, B. P., & Dionne, S. G. (2009). Downright sexy: Verticality, implicit power, and perceived physical attractiveness. *Social Cognition, 27*(6), 883–892.

Meier, B. P., Hauser, D. J., Robinson, M. D., Friesen, C. K., & Schjeldahl, K. (2007). What's "up" with God? Vertical space as a representation of the divine. *Journal of Personality and Social Psychology, 93*(5), 699–710.

Meier, B. P., & Robinson, M. D. (2004). Why the sunny side is up: Associations between affect and vertical position. *Psychological Science, 15*(4), 243–247.

Meier, B. P., & Robinson, M. D. (2006). Does "feeling down" mean seeing down? Depressive symptoms and vertical selective attention. *Journal of Research in Personality, 40*(4), 451–461.

Meier, B. P., Schnall, S., Schwarz, N., & Bargh, J. A. (2012). Embodiment in social psychology. *Topics in Cognitive Science, 4*(4), 705–716.

Meier, B. P., Sellbom, M., & Wygant, D. B. (2007). Failing to take the moral high ground: Psychopathy and the vertical representation of morality. *Personality and Individual Differences, 43*(4), 757–767.

Moeller, S. K., Robinson, M. D., & Zabelina, D. L. (2008). Personality dominance and preferential use of the vertical dimension of space evidence from spatial attention paradigms. *Psychological Science, 19*(4), 355–361.

Robinson, M. D., Zabelina, D. L., Ode, S., & Moeller, S. K. (2008). The vertical nature of dominance-submission: Individual differences in vertical attention. *Journal of Research in Personality, 42*(4), 933–948.

Schubert, T. W. (2005). Your highness: Vertical positions as perceptual symbols of power. *Journal of Personality and Social Psychology, 89*(1), 1–21.

Schwartz, B., Tesser, A., & Powell, E. (1982). Dominance cues in nonverbal behavior. *Social Psychology Quarterly, 45,* 114–120.

Schwarz, N. (2010). Meaning in context: Metacognitive experiences. In B. Mesquita, L. F. Barrett, & E. R. Smith (Eds.), *The mind in context* (pp. 105–125). New York, NY: Guilford.

Sweetser, E. (1990). *From etymology to pragmatics: The mind–body metaphor in semantic structure and semantic change.* Cambridge: Cambridge University Press.

Trope, Y., & Liberman, N. (2003). Temporal construal. *Psychological Review, 110*(3), 403.

Trope, Y., & Liberman, N. (2010). Construal-level theory of psychological distance. *Psychological Review, 117*(2), 440.

Williams, L. E., Huang, J. Y., & Bargh, J. A. (2009). The scaffolded mind: Higher mental processes are grounded in early experience of the physical world. *European Journal of Social Psychology, 39*(7), 1257–1267.

Wilson, P. R. (1968). Perceptual distortion of height as a function of ascribed academic status. *Journal of Social Psychology, 74*(1), 97–102.

Zhang, M., & Li, X. (2012). From physical weight to psychological significance: The contribution of semantic activations. *Journal of Consumer Research, 38*(6), 1063–1075.

Zhang, M., & Wang, J. (2009). Psychological distance asymmetry: The spatial dimension versus other dimensions. *Journal of Consumer Psychology, 19*(3), 497–507.

Zhong, C. B., & Leonardelli, G. J. (2008). Cold and lonely: Does social exclusion literally feel cold? *Psychological Science, 19*(9), 838–842.

4

SENSORY IMAGERY FOR DESIGN

Aradhna Krishna

UNIVERSITY OF MICHIGAN

In the last decade, there has been a lot of momentum in the area of sensory marketing, both in the corporate world and within academia—consultancies and market research firms devoted to sensory engagement have grown in number, as has the sheer volume of research focused on the area. In many efforts, I have attempted to provide a common ground for conversation and information dissemination in the area, with a hope to foster informed interest in the area and help it grow. In 2008, I brought together researchers in marketing, psychology, and neuroscience who worked on disparate senses, and also scent marketing practitioners, and held the first academic conference under the umbrella of "Sensory Marketing." The conference helped me put together an edited volume on Sensory Marketing with key research organized by each sense (Krishna, 2009). In *Sensory Marketing: Research on the Sensuality of Products*, I provided a definition for Sensory Marketing as "sub-conscious triggers that affect how people make purchase and consumption decisions." In a later review article (Krishna, 2012), I updated the research covered in the edited book, placed sensory marketing within a broader framework, showing its relationship to embodied cognition—another emerging popular field which highlights that thinking is guided by feeling (or that cognition is impacted by sensory perception)—and pointed out areas that needed further investigation. A trade press book showed examples for how sensory marketing can be used by managers (Krishna, 2013). Finally, I edited a special issue of the *Journal of Consumer Psychology* on embodied cognition and sensory marketing (Krishna & Schwarz, 2014b), and wrote another review article (Krishna & Schwarz, 2014a) where I elaborated on the role of sensory experiences in judgment and decision-making. Readers are referred to all these sources for reviews of sensory marketing. In this short chapter, however, I will focus on how sensory imagery can impact product design by: (i) encouraging mental simulation through visual design of advertisements (ads), (ii) inducing dynamic imagery through design of logos and icons, and (iii) encouraging smell imagery through ad design. I will discuss each in turn.

Encouraging Mental Simulation Through Visual Design of Ads

For years, marketers have encouraged consumers to use their imagination, by slogans such as "Imagine the Possibilities" (Intel and Apple), or simply "Imagine" (Samsung). These slogans have been quite successful (e.g., Bone & Ellen, 1992; MacInnis & Price, 1987; McGill & Anand, 1989). However, can the advertiser induce the consumer to imagine product-use without explicitly asking them to do so? Elder and Krishna (2012) build upon recent models of cognition and perception and demonstrate that simply altering the way in which a product is visually depicted can induce consumers to imagine interacting with the product, and increase purchase intention. More specifically, they show that when there is a match between handed-ness and product orientation (e.g., a right-handed person sees a picture of a bowl of soup with a soup spoon on the right), versus a mismatch (e.g., a right-handed person sees a picture of a bowl of soup with a soup spoon on the left), then mental simulation of product-interaction is higher. This, in turn, leads to higher purchase intention. Their results are robust in that they hold over varied stimuli (bowls of ice cream, cake, soup, and coffee mugs). They also show that mental simulation requires similar resources as actual perception—if right-handed subjects are holding a clamp in their right hand, then the elevation in purchase intention does not occur.

Thus, even very subtle manipulation of object-orientation in an ad design can impact purchase behavior. Advertisers can increase purchase intentions by facilitating mental simulation through their visual depictions of the product. They can do this simply by orienting a product (e.g., a cake with a fork) toward the right side. While this may not suit the smaller percentage of left-handers, the larger percentage of right-handers will have better mental product-interaction. These results also hold for shelf display design in retail environments. For example, a very slight change in display design of mugs in the window of a coffee shop could affect purchases with consumers imagining picking up that coffee mug and drinking from it. Including an instrument (e.g., a spoon for eating an advertised soup) that facilitates mental simulation should also increase purchase intentions. These consequences of visual depiction impact not just advertising design, but product packaging design and display design as well.

Besides mental simulation of hands, ad design can also impact mental simulation of other bodily parts. For example, in an ad, placing a pair of cozy bedroom slippers vertically with the openings towards the bottom versus the top should enhance mental simulation of putting on the slippers. Similarly, showing a soda with the cap off versus on should enhance imagination of drinking from it; showing a car door open versus closed should enhance imagination of entering the car and sitting on the seat; and showing a bed with the sheets turned down versus not should increase imagining slipping between the sheets. These are all very subtle ways of facilitating consumer mental simulation through ad design.

Inducing Dynamic Imagery Through Design of Logos and Icons

Marketers use many tools to engage consumers with their brand, including using celebrity spokespeople (e.g., smartwater with Jennifer Aniston) and beautiful models (e.g., Buick with Marisa Miller) in ads, or by trying to evoke strong emotions through the use of humor, drama, and even fear. Another way to increase consumer engagement with visuals pertaining to the brand (e.g., logo or ad) can be through evocation of dynamic imagery. Cian, Krishna, and Elder (2014) propose and demonstrate that (static) visuals that generate greater dynamic imagery tend to result in higher consumer engagement than those that evoke less dynamic imagery. By dynamic imagery, they mean "an image evoked by the viewer that has a sense of movement."

They focus their attention on brand logos and see how a small change in logo design to increase dynamic imagery can enhance consumer attitudes toward brands. Logo design has become increasingly important, because it not only captures awareness, but is also often the first exposure a consumer has to a brand or company. Logos appear in several marketing communications that have little or no copy, making them even more important. For instance, the brand logo can be placed on the product itself (e.g., Nike, Puma, and Starbucks), in banner ads in electronic media, in small one-column inch ads in print media, on product packaging, and in other ways.

Cian, Krishna, and Elder (2014) show that static (i.e., non-animated) brand logos can be designed in ways so that consumers perceive movement, increasing their level of engagement with the brand logo, and impacting consumer attitudes toward the brand. For instance, in one of their studies, they created two versions of a logo for a fictitious brand, "Cilian." The lower dynamism logo contained a simplistic drawing of a seesaw in a horizontal position, whereas the higher dynamism logo contained an identical drawing, but with the seesaw at a diagonal angle—suggesting a seesaw frozen in motion. In other studies, they similarly used a running horse and a child playing with a ball on a string. They showed that engagement (measured through self-reports and also eye-tracking measures of amount of attention) is higher with the high dynamism logo which then results in higher attitude towards the logo.

While Cian, Krishna, and Elder (2014) focus on dynamic imagery from logo design and its impact on attitude towards the brand, Cian, Krishna, and Elder (forthcoming) focus on dynamic imagery from icon design and its effect on responsible locomotive behavior (e.g., driving, walking). While there are many arenas for responsible consumption (e.g., not polluting, recycling, keeping children away from electrical sockets), none is more important than road safety. Every year, in the United States, 37,000 people die in road crashes, and another 2.35 million are either injured or disabled (ASIRT, 2014). The victims of these accidents are not just drivers and passengers in the cars, but also pedestrians—nearly 20% of children between the ages of 5 and 9 who are killed in traffic crashes were pedestrians outside the car (AAC, 2010).

To decrease accidents, the whole world uses traffic signs, and people are taught to follow these traffic signs; else they will be penalized. While all countries have traffic laws and traffic signs, visual icon design for the same signs (i.e., children crossing sign) varies a lot between countries. Cian, Krishna, and Elder (forthcoming) focus on the connection between traffic icons and resultant behavior. They show that static (non-animated) traffic signs with higher dynamism (vs. lower dynamism) icon design result in earlier attention to and identification of signs, earlier indication of safe behavior (quicker reaction time), and stopping at a safer distance.

Hopefully, their research findings will help change traffic signs and reduce accident-related injuries. Indirect but important effects can be a decrease in automobile repair expenses, as well as car insurance health care costs. One other point to note is that such dynamic imagery is especially useful in a consumer setting where most icons (e.g., brand logos, traffic signs) are not animated because that can be prohibitively expensive.

Encouraging Smell Imagery Through Ad Design

The prior examples dealt with visual imagery, which is what one thinks of when the word "imagery" is mentioned. However, imagery can be of any sense—olfactory, auditory, haptic, gustatory, or visual. Recent work has focused on olfactory imagery from an ad, how it interacts with visual imagery from the ad, and its effect on ad effectiveness (Krishna, Morrin, & Sayin, 2014).

It is interesting to note that while the existence of visual imagery is well accepted and documented (Adaval, Isbell, & Wyer, 2007; Adaval & Wyer, 1998; Dahl, Chattopadhyay, & Gorn, 1999; Escalas, 2004; Hung & Wyer, 2011; Peck & Shu, 2009; Rajagopal & Montgomery, 2011; Shiv & Huber, 2000; Unnava, Agarwal, & Haugtvedt, 1996; Wyer, Hung, & Jiang, 2008), there has been debate on whether olfactory imagery even exists (Crowder & Schab, 1995; Engen, 1991; Herz, 2000). Now, however, there is increasing evidence that it does and that humans respond to imagined smell in similar ways as they do to actual smells (Stevenson & Case, 2005).

Krishna, Morrin, and Sayin (2014) focus on food ads and demonstrate olfactory imagery of foods encouraged through food ads can enhance consumer response to the advertised food—as measured by consumers' physiological (i.e., salivation), evaluative (i.e., desire to eat), and consumptive (i.e., amount eaten) responses. That is, when consumers are exposed to a picture of chocolate chip cookies and asked to imagine the smell, they salivate much more than they do when they are exposed to the picture but not asked to imagine the smell. Krishna, Morrin, and Sayin (2014) also find that this olfactory-imagery response happens when consumers can see the food vividly (either in a picture or through really good visual imagery), and is much weaker otherwise. They also replicate the more expected effect that ad effectiveness is also higher when ads have a real smell (i.e., actual and not imagined smell) versus not.

So far, smells have typically been used in ads for personal products (e.g., deodorant, perfume, roll-on, after-shave), but not for foods. Krishna, Morrin and Sayin's (2014) results suggest that food ads could also benefit from real smells and imagined smells. Thus, like deodorants, food ads can benefit from a scratch-n-sniff strip (as long as the strip can meticulously reproduce the food smell). Importantly, simply asking consumers to imagine what the advertised food smells like, or "smellizing" it (Krishna, Morrin, & Sayin, 2014), can make consumers desire the food more (if the ad also has a picture of the food).

Implications for Design

This chapter tries to highlight new types of sensory imagery in the context of design. Thus, the chapter discussed the notions of mental simulation, whereby the easier it is for people to simulate interaction with an object, the higher is their purchase intentions. The chapter also expounds on dynamic imagery, which allows for images within the mind to continue in motion, resulting in perception of motion from a static image. This automatic completion of movement has several effects on attention, attitudes, and consumer behavior. Finally, the chapter introduces the concept of olfactory imagery (or "smellizing"), for which the simple suggestion to imagine a smell leads to physiological, evaluative, and consumptive effect.

Implications for Theories of Design

There is much innovative work that can be done both in terms of further research in the field of sensory imagery, and also by managers in applying such sensory imagery to ad, logo, icon, and product design. This chapter attempts to nudge researchers in that direction.

References

AAC—Advocate Auto Consultants. (2010). Parking lots account for 1.26 million car accidents in the U.S. annually, with a 20% jump. Retrieved from http://www.reuters.com/article/2010/12/20/idUS183731+20-Dec-2010+MW20101220

Adaval, R., Isbell, L. M., & Wyer, R. S., Jr. (2007). The impact of pictures on narrative- and list-based impression formation: A process interference model. *Journal of Experimental Social Psychology, 43*(3), 352–364.

Adaval, R., & Wyer, R. S., Jr. (1998). The role of narratives in consumer information processing. *Journal of Consumer Psychology, 7*(3), 207–245.

ASIRT—Association for Safe International Road Travel. (2014). 2013 road crash statistics. Retrieved from http://www.asirt.org/KnowBeforeYouGo/RoadSafetyFacts/RoadCrashStatistics/tabid/213/Default.aspx

Bone, P. F., & Ellen, P. S. (1992). The generation and consequences of communication-evoked imagery. *Journal of Consumer Research, 19*(1), 93–104.

Cian, L., Krishna, A., & Elder, R. S. (2014). This logo moves me: Dynamic imagery from static images. *Journal of Marketing Research, 51*(2), 184–197.

Cian, L., Krishna, A., & Elder, R. S. (forthcoming). A sign of things to come: Behavioral change through dynamic iconography. *Journal of Consumer Research.*

Crowder, R. G., & Schab, F. R. (1995). Imagery for odors. In F. R. Schab & R. G. Crowder (Eds.), *Memory for odors* (pp. 93–107). Mahwah, NJ: Erlbaum.

Dahl, D. W., Chattopadhyay, A., & Gorn, G. J. (1999). The use of visual mental imagery in new product design. *Journal of Marketing Research, 36*(1), 18–28.

Elder, R. S., & Krishna, A. (2012). The "visual depiction effect" in advertising: Facilitating embodied mental simulation through product orientation. *Journal of Consumer Research, 38*(6), 988–1003.

Engen, T. (1991). *Odor sensation and memory.* New York, NY: Praeger.

Escalas, J. E. (2004). Imagine yourself in the product: Mental simulation, narrative transportation, and persuasion. *Journal of Advertising, 33*(2), 37–48.

Herz, R. S. (2000). Verbal coding in olfactory versus nonolfactory cognition. *Memory & Cognition, 28*(6), 957–964.

Hung, I. W., & Wyer, R. S., Jr. (2011). Shaping consumer imaginations: The role of self-focused attention in product evaluations. *Journal of Marketing Research, 48*(2), 381–392.

Krishna, A. (Ed.). (2009). *Sensory marketing: research on the sensuality of products.* New York, NY: Routledge.

Krishna, A. (2012). An integrative review of sensory marketing: Engaging the senses to affect perception, judgment and behavior. *Journal of Consumer Psychology, 22*(3), 332–351.

Krishna, A. (2013). *Customer sense: How the 5 senses influence buying behavior.* New York, NY: Palgrave Macmillan.

Krishna, A., Morrin, M., & Sayin, E. (2014). Smellizing cookies and salivating: A focus on olfactory imagery. *Journal of Consumer Research, 41*(1), 18–34.

Krishna, A., & Schwarz, N. (2014a). Sensory marketing, embodiment, and grounded cognition: A review and introduction. *Journal of Consumer Psychology, 24*(2), 159–168.

Krishna, A., & Schwarz, N. (Eds.). (2014b). Sensory perception, embodiment, and grounded cognition: Implications for consumer behavior [Special issue]. *Journal of Consumer Psychology, 24*(2), 159–168.

MacInnis, D. J., & Price, L. L. (1987). The role of imagery in information processing: Review and extensions. *Journal of Consumer Research, 13*(4), 473–491.

McGill, A. L., & Anand, P. (1989). The effect of vivid attributes on the evaluation of alternatives: The role of differential attention and cognitive elaboration. *Journal of Consumer Research, 16*(2), 188–196.

Peck, J., & Shu, S. B. (2009). The effect of mere touch on perceived ownership. *Journal of Consumer Research, 36*(3), 434–447.

Rajagopal, P., & Montgomery, N. V. (2011). I imagine, I experience, I like: The false experience effect. *Journal of Consumer Research, 38*(3), 578–594.

Shiv, B., & Huber, J. (2000). The impact of anticipating satisfaction on consumer choice. *Journal of Consumer Research, 27*(2), 202–216.

Stevenson, R. J., & Case, T. I. (2005). Olfactory imagery: A review. *Psychonomic Bulletin & Review, 12*(2), 244–264.

Unnava, H. R., Agarwal, S., & Haugtvedt, C. P. (1996). Interactive effects of presentation modality and message-generated imagery on recall of advertising information. *Journal of Consumer Research, 23*(1), 81–88.

Wyer, R. S., Jr., Hung, I. W., & Jiang, Y. (2008). Visual and verbal processing strategies in comprehension and judgment. *Journal of Consumer Psychology, 18*(4), 244–257.

PART II
Designing Product Features

5

BLUE-WASHING THE GREEN HALO

How Colors Color Ethical Judgments

Aparna Sundar

UNIVERSITY OF OREGON

James J. Kellaris

UNIVERSITY OF CINCINNATI

> *Color is one of the most powerful tools a designer has to communicate a client's message. It can symbolize an idea, can invoke meaning, and has cultural relevancy.*
>
> —Sherin (2011)

The use of color is ubiquitous in visual communication. When harnessed in the service of marketing, color can wield profound and far-reaching influences on consumers through its ability to please the senses and at the same time communicate with power (Bleicher, 2011). Humans respond to not just the perception of color, but to emotions and thoughts evoked in the presence of color (Elliot & Maier, 2012). It is no wonder then that researchers from diverse backgrounds are interested in the study of color. For example, whereas artists study the interaction and contrast of color, physicists study properties of color, such as light, waves, frequencies, and their measurement (Portillo, 2010). Psychologists study the sensation, perception, and responses to color (Portillo, 2010). Ultimately it is the marketer who is intrigued and motivated to study the influence of color on consumers' perceptions of brands (Bellizzi & Hite, 1992; Gorn, Chattopadhyay, Yi, & Dahl, 1997; Meyers-Levy & Peracchio, 1995).

Consider the example of the color green. Some research has indicated that green is associated with positive affect (De Bock, Pandelaere, & Van Kenhove, 2013). Specifically, De Bock and colleagues demonstrated that when good behavior by customer service personnel is described against a green background, consumers rate the behavior more positively. The authors attributed this effect to a result of the emotional valence associated to the color green. However, research in psychology has indicated that there are many different effects and influences of color on decision making. Colors can communicate meanings visually. As background to the different effects of color, we provide a brief review of color research in psychology.

Chapter Overview

In this chapter we contend that colors can evoke halo effects with far-reaching consequences for human judgment and decision making. When colors are used in logos, for example, they can prime inferences about the eco-friendliness of the organization represented by the logo. Whereas ethically ambiguous actions are deemed more acceptable when performed by an eco-friendly organization, color cues influence ethical judgment by casting a multi-stage halo effect: evoking perceptions of eco-friendliness, establishing an implied association between eco-friendliness and a firm, and thereby coloring ethical judgments about the firm's actions. Moreover, any color that primes eco-friendliness—not just green—should produce a "green halo" effect. Under some circumstances, blue may be greener than green.

Psychophysics Perspective

Psychophysics refers to the study of how and why physical stimuli influence sensations and perceptions. There is a long history of psychophysical research, dating back to the pioneering work of Fechner and Wundt in the 1890s (Hawkins 2011). Interest in the psychophysics of color continues today, in part because of the implications for the use of color in marketing. The reason we study the use of color in marketing is because color is used as a fashion statement (Grossman & Wisenblit, 1999). Certain colors are used as heuristic indicators of flavors (Kostyla, Clydesdale, & McDaniel, 1978), taste perceptions (Spence, Levitan, Shankar, & Zampini, 2010) and quality inferences (Francis, 1995).

Evolutionary Perspective

Human and nonhuman species are attracted to certain common colors. The color red specifically has been linked to love and passion across different cultures (Aslam, 2006; Jacobs, Keown, Worthley, & Gyhmn, 1991; Neto, 2002). In fact, the female attraction to the color red is not unique to our species (Elliot et al., 2010). Attraction to male red has been documented for species such as crustaceans, fish, birds, and nonhuman primates such as rhesus macaques (see Elliot et al., 2010, for a detailed review). Palmer and Schloss (2010) proposed that according to the ecological valance theory, people on average like colors that they strongly associate with objects they like (e.g., blue skies and water).

Social Psychology

From a social psychological perspective, many researchers have studied the meaning, character, association, and connotation of color. However, Elliot and Maier (2012) note that just as the meaning of words in a language is context dependent, so is the meaning of color (Kinsch & Mangalath, 2011). Certain colors have meaning that is consistent across time and is not affected by variations of language and culture (Berlin & Kay, 1969; Kay & Maffi, 1999; Kuehni, 2007). Relevant examples are the colors white, black, and red (Elliot & Maier, 2012). Default meanings that are represented by color are activated under most conditions. Women have been shown to show preferences for colors that symbolize status (e.g., red; Li, Bailey, Kenrick, & Linsenmeir, 2002).

Research of Color in Psychology

Over the past century, psychologists have researched the effect of the physics, physiology, and psychology of color on human perception and behavior (Elliot et al., 2007). The study of the physics of color mainly entails the study of light and vision (Maloney, 1999). Colorimetry investigates individual perceptions of color contrast and harmony (Nemcsics, 2007). This field of study assumes that individuals evaluate combinations of colors in an objective fashion. Hence, combinations of colors that are considered complementary, harmonious, balanced, and so on are computed by providing objective values to each color on the color wheel. The three dimensions of hue, saturation, and brightness are also quantified. Variations to these dimensions allow for formulaic prescriptions of combinations of colors that are complementary or harmonious (Szabo, Bodrogi, & Schanda, 2010). However the influence of color on emotion and thought is based on individual perceptions and experiences, and research on the psychological reactions to color provides some insights.

Effects of Color Have Been Noted on Behavior, Affect, and Cognition

Exploration into the psychological reactions to color indicates that colors with longer wavelengths (such as red and orange) are arousing; and, in contrast, shorter wavelengths (such as green and blue) are calming (Stone & English, 1998). Downstream effects on behavior are influenced by the affective valence of color. Affective valence refers to the tendency to associate colors with positive or negative feelings. Behavioral effects include the influence of color on outcomes such as performance in a task (Elliot et al., 2007), motivation to complete a task (Bargh Gollwitzer, Lee-Chai, Barndollar, & Trotschel, 2001), and even judgments of ethical behavior (De Bock et al., 2013). For instance, exposure to the color red has been shown to impair performances at subsequent tasks because red activates a need for avoidance (Elliot et al., 2007). Color does not just have an impact on affect; it communicates or symbolizes specific meaning. Evidence suggests that the meanings we infer or the associations we make with a presented color are rather important. Consider the color black for example. In general, black is associated with evil and death (Frank & Gilovich, 1988). Similarly, the color blue is known to be associated with sadness (Elliot & Maier, 2007). Elliot and colleagues (2007) therefore argued that research on the psychology of color should consider specific meanings intrinsic in a color. In this context, it is important to note that although many associations of color are ingrained in the evolutionary response to color (Mollon, 1989), the meaning associated with a specific color can be learned. It is in this respect that the study of halo effects evoked by color can be useful. The halo effect is defined as the transfer of positivity based on a single dimension to other unrelated dimensions (Asch, 1946; Dion, Berscheid, & Walster, 1972; Nisbett & Wilson, 1977). Colors convey meaning, which influences behavior, affect, and cognition.

Research of Color in Marketing

Marketers have indeed leveraged the use of color in many contexts. The following section details the study of color in different consumption contexts.

Color and Brand Personalities

Color is usually used as a strategic tool in marketing. Marketers use color as an effective communication tool (Meyers-Levy & Peracchio, 1995). Tavassoli (2001) notes that colors play an important role in the trademark practice of a brand. Brands such as Pepsi, Apple, M&M, and IBM are known to have made strategic decisions to associate themselves with one color to create a clear identity. Color has been shown to influence brand evaluations (Gorn et al., 1997) and at the same time aid recognition and retrieval in consumers of different ages (Macklin, 1996). Research in this domain also indicates that bright colors like reds and yellow are associated with exciting brands and colors such as browns and earthly tones are associated with sincere brands (Aaker, Fournier, & Brasel 2004).

Color and Advertising

Color in advertising is used to increase attention to an ad and hence the impact of an ad (Schindler, 1986). Studies have demonstrated that color ads actually capture higher readership in comparison to black and white ads (Finn, 1988). Use of complementary colors and contrast in colors have specifically been known to increase consumer attention (Sloane, 1968). Gorn et al., 1997 noted that a combination of the hue, chroma, and brightness are effectively used as executional cues in advertising.

Use of Color in Logos

Despite the large body of research in the area of color in consumer behavior and marketing, few studies have looked at the effect of color in a logo on consumption attitudes and behavior. In attempting to fill this gap in the literature, we begin by first presenting research in consumer psychology that evaluate the role of color in shaping consumer perceptions.

Valence Associated With Color in a Logo

De Bock et al. (2013) showed that the valence of a color cues moral acceptability of undesirable behavior. This research evaluated the effect of affective valence associated with the color used in a background to describe the behavior of customer service personnel (Studies 1 and 2). It is our contention that in contrast to the use of color in describing the action of a firm, when color is used to represent the firm itself, color communicates meaning inherent in the color rather than emotion in response to the color. Hence, color used in the logo of a brand or a retailer informs moral evaluations in the form of the positive halo of eco-friendliness of color rather than the valence associated with color.

This proposition is not farfetched. Think of the word *green* used in a logo to symbolize environmentally responsible behavior. When we know that a firm is environmentally responsible, it generates a positive halo. Hence, communicating to a consumer that a firm engages in positive practices regarding the environment should transfer to judgments about unrelated, ambiguous practices. When this perception is unfounded (i.e., the firm engages in unethical practices but brands itself as green), we call it greenwashing (Parr, 2009). It seems intuitive then that the use of the word *green* in a logo can bias a consumer into thinking that the firm it represents is environmentally friendly. This makes one wonder about the sight of color. Would the actual color operate similarly to the word used to describe the color?

Meaning vs. Valance Associated in the Color of a Logo. Seeing a color communicates meaning that is embodied in the color (i.e., attributes embodied in the aesthetic stimulus). This is different from the meaning associated with the word used to label the color or the referential meaning of color (i.e., meaning that emerges from semantic association of concepts evoked by the aesthetic stimuli; Labrecque, Patrick, & Milne, 2013). In recent years, linguists have begun to uncover the value of meaning embodied in color, and the color green is one such example. The word *green* when used to define eco-friendliness is not used to indicate a single meaning, but rather a complex network of events and practices. We predict that not just the use of the word green, but the use of the color in branding too should produce far-reaching effects. This includes consumer inferences regarding the morality of a firm, brand, or retailer.

Our research journey began simply with a desire to understand how different colors can evoke a positive halo of eco-friendliness. The research summarized in this chapter evaluates the effects of using color to symbolize the brand in a logo. Indeed the color used to symbolize the brand when used in packaging for a product or branded interior is important. Essentially, we propose that the image of the retailer in the mind of the consumer causes a halo effect regarding the retailer such that perceptions of the retailer inform moral judgments of acts performed by the retailer. Further, we also propose that the concept of eco-friendliness of the retailer is the underlying mechanism informing ethical judgments. Our prediction is that the role of color in informing the eco-friendly colors is due to embodied rather than referential transfer of meaning. To test the prediction that a logo color should influence perceptions of ethicality of an ambiguous retail practice, we conducted a series of empirical studies.

Pretests

We conducted a pretest to determine consumer reactions to different colors featured in a logo. In the pretest, participants were exposed to a logo featuring 1 of 16 different colors adopted from various retailer logos, selected to represent the full range of the color spectrum. The two colors that represented high and low eco-friendliness were carried over to the study. The main finding of this pretest was that green is symbolic of eco-friendliness and red is not. Surprisingly, blue was rated as more eco-friendly than the color green.

We conducted another pretest to identify ethically ambiguous retailer practices. Ten statements were pretested. Two statements that were rated as ethically ambiguous were carried forward as the test statements in the studies. In all studies, each participant was asked to rate the ethicality of the retailer based on one of the two test statements that were randomly presented.

Empirical Work

In all studies, responses of participants who failed a color test (Birch, 1997) were not considered in the analysis. The first study evaluated whether ethical ratings (Dabholkar & Kellaris, 1992) would be influenced by the logo color accompanying the description of the retailer. We conducted this study using an online panel. The findings indicated that blue positively influenced the ethical judgments about the practices tested such that the same ethically ambiguous statement was rated as more ethical when the retailer was represented with a blue logo (vs. a red logo).

We conducted a second study to determine whether the observed effect held for the transfer of the embodied versus referential meaning of the two colors under consideration. We conducted this study using student participants in a behavioral lab. Ethical ratings were captured as in the first study. In addition, ratings of eco-friendliness of the retailer and individual processing styles were also captured using Childers, Houston, and Heckler's (1985) scale. This scale measures individual differences in visual versus verbal information processing.

The results indicated that although the influence of color affected ethical judgments of visual processors, the differences in ethical judgments of individuals who were predominantly verbal processors were not significant. Further, the perceived eco-friendliness of the retailer mediated the effect of color on ethical ratings.

We conducted a third study to replicate the findings of Study 2 and, more importantly, to see whether the results held when the mode of presentation was manipulated. Participants took part in an online study. The results were consistent with Study 1. In addition, the analysis supported the prediction that perceived eco-friendliness of the retailer caused participants to rate the practices as more ethical but only when they saw the color in a logo, not when they read the name of the logo color.

In a fourth study, we wanted to evaluate the effect of the embodied versus referential meaning of green on ethical ratings. To do so, we tested the effect of visual versus verbal transfer of meaning of the color green compared with another eco-friendly color, blue. Participants took part in an online study. The results of this study showed that unlike other eco-friendly colors, the color green is an exception in that it evokes eco-friendliness through not just embodied transfer of color but also referential transfer of meaning. Further, the results suggested that eco-friendliness embodied in green does not inform ethicality judgments differently than does the color blue.

Summary of Findings

The review of literature and research presented in this chapter captures the importance of color symbolism. Specifically, a series of four studies demonstrated that colors such as green and blue (but not red) embody the concept of eco-friendliness. Further, the findings illustrated that the color blue is perceived to be more eco-friendly than is green. Color informs the perception of eco-friendliness, and this mediates the effect of color on ethical judgments of a retailer practice, which is otherwise rated ambiguously. The effect of color on judgments of ethicality is moderated by both an individual's style of processing and the mode of presentation. That is, only when color is seen does the embodied meaning of color influence ethical judgments. Despite the fact that blue and green share the same embodied meaning of eco-friendliness, the referential meaning of eco-friendliness of the color green is distinct from that of blue. Consequently, color can shape ethical perceptions of a retailer's behavior.

Implications for Designers

Popular wisdom holds that color is the first thing consumers notice about a logo (Miller, 2012). Color is a fundamental design tool that affects consumers viscerally, emotionally, or cognitively. Importantly, the influence of color on consumers depends on cultural context. As opposed to past research that demonstrates the effect of the valence of color (Bargh et al., 2001; De Bock et al., 2013; Elliot et al., 2007), the current research shows that the color in a logo embodies meaning communicated to consumers, and thereby creates a halo effect with downstream consequences.

When it comes to the use of the actual color, this research is the first of its kind that debunks the clichéd use of the color green to represent or communicate an eco-friendly concept. The empirical findings in this research suggest that although it is counterintuitive, the concept of *greenness* (eco-friendliness) can be conveyed by blue. Consequently, an implication for designers is to consider multiple possibilities of color consideration in design. Future research could evaluate the effect that other colors have on perceptions of eco-friendliness. Other halo effects can be evaluated too.

Notably, the research in this chapter calls attention to the distant, downstream effects of color in a logo. Color in a brand's logo may influence other identity-branding elements, such as colors of store interiors, packaging, service personnel attire, and so on. Colors in branding a firm thus need to be thought out, deliberate, and purposeful. After all, once the color of a logo has been established, a firm will probably retain the color to maintain sustainable brand identity within its consumer base.

Color is an important part of branded identity. We did not find evidence that the colors we tested were associated with a particular brand or retailer. However, it is well known that certain brands are associated with specific colors: for example, the UPS brand is associated with brown. Hence further research into the effects of color on identity branding is needed. Whereas this research suggests that strategically using color can benefit firms that are perceived negatively in general, we wish to add a cautionary note and call to policy makers responsible for regulating the use of color in trademarks.

Implications for Designers

The United States Patent and Trade Office (USPTO) currently restricts the use of the word *green* in branding. In 2013, it revised its guidelines to prevent companies that are not environmentally friendly from using the word *green* in their trademarks (Collen, 2012). This regulation attempted to control greenwashing, a practice used by companies that are not environmentally friendly (Collen, 2012). However, as this research indicates, elements of trademarks can be embodied in color rather than just in the use of the word *green*. A trademark search revealed that more companies actually use the color blue (136,024 times) more often than they use the color green (106,418 times; USPTO). Although these numbers indicate the favorable use of the color blue in branding, certainly more attention in this area of research is needed to inform policy.

Practitioners are aware of the power of a logo. The logo is not just symbolic of the brand; it determines most identity branding endeavors of the firm. The

USPTO does not typically allow the trademark of color, shape, or typeface of a logo (Bailey, 2010). However, consumers do make color and brand associations (e.g., brown and UPS). Hence future research in the area of such associations and how these interact with the meaning of color is certainly warranted.

Furthermore, once the logo of a brand is established, reconfiguring the logo (e.g., Walmart, Pepsi, Starbucks, and Apple) can be an expensive and onerous process. This research suggests that firms can do well by testing and evaluating the reactions to the logo. Indeed, the evolution of color in logos, such as that of Starbucks (from brown to green), Walmart (from black, to brown, to blue), and Apple (multicolored, to blue, to white), in some way indicates that firms are attuned to consumer reaction and symbolism in a logo. The empirical research in this chapter was focused on downstream effects (of ethical evaluations of practices by the retailer) rather than perceptions of the retailer or brand. Future research on color, identity branding, and consumer reactions to the brand is needed in this area.

Implications for a Theory of Design

Design is subjective and multidisciplinary. Existing theories of design encompass an understanding of aesthetic principles and the way design influences consumer behavior. However, a theory of design must account for the multiplicities of consumer responses to design (Hansen et al., 2014). The inherent challenge in formulating such a theory goes beyond understanding or framing aesthetic principles. The challenge for marketers is to frame a theory of design differently from a theory of consumer psychology. Our work shows that design features such as color can have far-reaching consequences due to multi-stage halo effects. The main implication for a theory of design stemming from this work is that the use of color symbolizes meaning, which can be strategically used in managing branded identity.

Design is reflective of different ways in which humans respond to the world. It follows, therefore, that the reaction consumers have to the world can be studied at different levels (i.e., visceral, emotional, cognitive, and cultural). Our work highlights the symbolic representation of a concept using color. Whereas the current research focuses on a single concept represented by the color green, this chapter provides a useful framework in which a theory of design can be formulated, with the ultimate goal of more fully describing, explaining, and predicting the multiple and far-reaching consequences of design features.

References

Aaker, J., Fournier, S., & Brasel, S. A. (2004). When good brands do bad. *Journal of Consumer Research, 31*(1), 1–16.

Asch, S. E. (1946). Forming impressions of personality. *Journal of Abnormal and Social Psychology, 41*(3), 258–290.

Aslam, M. M. (2006). Are you selling the right colour? A cross-cultural review of colour as a marketing cue. *Journal of Marketing Communications, 12*, 15–30.

Bailey, J. (2010, August 12). Trademark, copyright and logos. *Plagiarism Today*. Retrieved from http://www.plagiarismtoday.com/2010/08/12/trademark-copyright-and-logos/

Bargh, J. A., Gollwitzer, P. M., Lee-Chai, A. Y., Barndollar, K., & Trotschel, R. (2001). The automated will: Nonconscious activation and pursuit of behavioral goals. *Journal of Personality and Social Psychology, 81*(6), 1014–1027.

Bellizzi, J. A., & Hite, R. E. (1992). Environmental color, consumer feelings, and purchase likelihood. *Psychology and Marketing, 9*(5), 347–363.

Berlin, B., & Kay, P. (1969). *Basic color terms: Their universality and evolution*. Berkeley: University of California Press.

Birch, J. (1997). Efficiency of the Ishihara test for identifying red-green colour deficiency. *Ophthalmic and Physiological Optics, 17*(5), 403–408.

Bleicher, S. (2011). *Contemporary color: Theory and use*. Boston, MA: Cengage Learning.

Childers, T. L., Houston, M. J., & Heckler, S. E. (1985). Measurement of individual differences in visual versus verbal information processing. *Journal of Consumer Research, 12*(2), 125–134.

Collen, J. (2012). Gang green: Rules are tightening. Don't say green if you don't mean green. Retrieved from http://www.forbes.com/sites/jesscollen/2012/10/04/theres-no-debate-about-this-you-cant-call-your-pesticide-green-and-ask-the-trademark-office-to-help-you/

Dabholkar, P. A., & Kellaris, J. J. (1992). Toward understanding marketing students' ethical judgment of controversial personal selling practices. *Journal of Business Research, 24*(4), 313–329.

De Bock, T., Pandelaere, M., & Van Kenhove, P. (2013). When colors backfire: The impact of color cues on moral judgment. *Journal of Consumer Psychology, 23*(3), 341–348.

Dion, K., Berscheid, E., & Walster, E. (1972). What is beautiful is good. *Journal of Personality and Social Psychology, 24*(3), 285.

Elliot, A. J., & Maier, M. A. (2007). Color and psychological functioning. *Current Directions in Psychological Science, 16*(5), 250–254.

Elliot, A., & Maier, M. A. (2012). Color-in-context theory. *Advances in experimental social psychology, 45*, 61–125.

Elliot, A. J., Maier, M. A., Moller, A. C., Friedman, R., & Meinhardt, J. (2007). Color and psychological functioning: The effect of red on performance attainment. *Journal of Experimental Psychology: General, 139*(3), 399–417.

Elliot, A. J., Niesta Kayser, D., Greitemeyer, T., Lichtenfeld, S., Gramzow, R. H., Maier, M. A., & Liu, H. (2010). Red, rank, and romance in women viewing men. *Journal of Experimental Psychology: General, 139*(3), 399.

Finn, A. (1988). Print ad recognition readership scores: An information processing perspective. *Journal of Marketing Research, 25*(2), 168–177.

Francis, F. J. (1995). Quality as influenced by color. *Food quality and preference, 6*(3), 149–155.

Frank, M. G., & Gilovich, T. (1988). The dark side of self and social perception: Black uniforms and aggression in professional sports. *Journal of Personality and Social Psychology, 54*(1), 74–85.

Gorn, G. J., Chattopadhyay, A., Yi, T., & Dahl, D. W. (1997). Effects of color as an executional cue in advertising: They're in the shade. *Management Science, 43*(10), 1387–1400.

Grossman, R. P., & Wisenblit, J. Z. (1999). What we know about consumers' color choices. *Journal of Marketing Practice: Applied Marketing Science, 5*(3), 78–88.

Hansen, O. E., Simonsen, J., Svabo, C., Malou Strandvad, S., Samson, K., & Hertzum, M. (2014). *Design thinking, design theory*. Boston, MA: MIT Press.

Hawkins, S. L. (2011). William James, Gustav Fechner, and early psychophysics. *Frontiers in Physiology, 2*, 1–129.

Jacobs, L., Keown, C., Worthley, R., & Gyhmn, K. (1991). Cross-cultural color comparisons: Global marketers beware! *International Marketing Review, 8*, 21–30.

Kay, P., & Maffi, L. (1999). Color appearance and the emergence and evolution of basic color lexicons. *American Anthropologist, 101*, 743–760.

Kinsch, W., & Mangalath, P. (2011). The construction of meaning. *Topics in Cognitive Science, 3*, 346–370.

Kostyla, A. S., Clydesdale, F. M., & McDaniel, M. R. (1978). The psychophysical relationships between color and flavor. *Critical Reviews in Food Science & Nutrition, 10*(3), 303–321.

Kuehni, R. G. (2007). Nature and culture: An analysis of individuals focal color choices in world color survey languages. *Journal of Cognition and Culture, 7*, 151–172.

Labrecque, L. I., Patrick, V. M., & Milne, G. R. (2013). The marketers' prismatic palette: A review of color research and future directions. *Psychology & Marketing, 30*(2), 187–202.

Li, N. P., Bailey, J., Kenrick, D. T., & Linsenmeir, J. A. W. (2002). The necessities and luxuries of mate preferences: Testing the tradeoffs. *Journal of Personality and Social Psychology, 82*, 947–955.

Macklin, M. C. (1996). Preschoolers' learning of brand names from visual cues. *Journal of Consumer Research, 23*(December), 251–261.

Maloney, L. T. (1999). Physics-based approaches to modeling surface color perception. In K. R. Gegenfurtner & L. T. Sharpe (Eds.), *Color vision: From genes to perception* (pp. 387–416). Cambridge: Cambridge University Press.

Meyers-Levy, J., & Peracchio, L. A. (1995). Understanding the effects of color: How the correspondence between available and required resources affects attitudes. *Journal of Consumer Research, 22*(September), 121–138.

Miller, J. (2012). True colors: What your brand colors say about your business. Retrieved from http://blog.marketo.com/2012/06/true-colors-what-your-brand-colors-say-about-your-business.html

Mollon, J. D. (1989). Tho' she kneel'd in that place where they grow . . . *Journal of Experimental Biology, 146*(1), 21–38.

Nemcsics, A. (2007). Experimental determination of laws of color harmony. Part 1: Harmony content of different scales with similar hue. *Color Research & Application, 32*(6), 477–488.

Neto, F. (2002). Colors associated with styles of love. *Perceptual and Motor Skills, 94*, 1303–1310.

Nisbett, R. E., & Wilson, T. D. (1977). The halo effect: Evidence for unconscious alteration of judgments. *Journal of Personality and Social Psychology, 35*(4), 250–256.

Palmer, S. E., & Schloss, K. B. (2010). An ecological valence theory of human color preference. *Proceedings of the National Academy of Sciences, 107*(19), 8877–8882.

Parr, A. (2009). *Hijacking sustainability*. Cambridge, MA: MIT Press.

Portillo, M. (2010). *Color planning for interiors: An integrated approach to color in designed spaces*. Hoboken, NJ: John Wiley & Sons.

Schindler, P. S. (1986). Color and contrast in magazine advertising. *Psychology & Marketing, 3*(2), 69–78.

Sherin, A. (2011). *Design elements, color fundamentals: A graphic style manual for understanding how color impacts design*. Minneapolis, MN: Rockport.

Sloane, P. (1968). *Color: Basic principles and new directions.* New York, NY: Reinhold.

Spence, C., Levitan, C. A., Shankar, M. U., & Zampini, M. (2010). Does food color influence taste and flavor perception in humans? *Chemosensory Perception, 3*(1), 68–84.

Stone, N. J., & English, A. J. (1998). Task type, posters, and workspace color on mood, satisfaction, and performance. *Journal of Environmental Psychology, 18*(2), 175–185.

Szabo, F., Bodrogi, P., & Schanda, J. (2010). Experimental modeling of colour harmony. *Color Research & Application, 35*(1), 34–49.

Tavassoli, N. T. (2001). Color memory and evaluations for alphabetical and logographic brand names. *Journal of Experimental Psychology: Applied, 7*(2), 104–110.

6

COLOR DESIGN AND PURCHASE PRICE

How Vehicle Colors Affect What Consumers Pay for New and Used Cars

Keiko I. Powers

MARKETSHARE PARTNERS

Do consumers pay more just for the vehicle color when buying a car? For example, does it makes sense if the price a consumer paid for a red car is higher than for a white car with the same vehicle attributes? Some auto-related industry websites that deal with the topic of vehicle color (e.g., "Which colour?: Does colour choice really matter?" 2012; "Black, white top most popular vehicle color list," 2013) endorse the importance of color as a key vehicle attribute in purchase decision. This practical question about vehicle color has some important implications from the consumer psychology perspective. A key aspect of this question is related to the fact that the vehicle color does not provide any functional values for many consumers as a driver. This idea is related to the aesthetic vs. utilitarian distinction of design (Veryzer, 1995), and unlike functional attributes such as the engine size, the number of seats, the body type (e.g., sedan versus SUV), the color attribute does not offer any practical benefits as the means for transportation. For this reason, it would be reasonable to see a higher purchase price for a car with, for example, a bigger engine or more seats, but how could it be rationalized if consumers pay more for a car simply because of its color?

In the United States, when consumers are at a dealer site to purchase a car, they typically do not pay the manufacturer's suggested retail price (MSRP). Instead, they go through price negotiation with a salesperson at the dealer before completing the purchase process (see, e.g., Loomis, 2012; Reed, 2013; Kelley Blue Book, 2014, on pricing vs. MSRP for vehicle purchase). This situation creates the condition where the final negotiated price reflects the consumer's subjective price perception of a given car in addition to the utility-based "value" of the car. In other words, the consumer judgment could be affected not only by objective factors (e.g., negotiation dynamics between the consumer and the dealer, knowledge about the vehicle model, etc.), but also by the subjective perception, such as the "feel" for the car.

Powers (2006) has demonstrated that the vehicle color affects how much consumers pay for new cars, in particular with sporty cars where the image or design of the car is an important factor.

The same negotiation process takes place for new cars as well as for used cars. Among industry experts on used cars, it is often said that the price depreciation of cars is affected by the vehicle color—i.e., everything else being equal, cars with certain colors are worth more than others in the used car market (see the website by Kirsten, 2012). The present paper investigates the relationship between color and decision making for the price, focusing on the case of used car purchase. With this type of purchase occasions, the interaction between the two should be comprehended as an emotional experience. As car purchase is what is considered as a high-involvement process, the price negotiation could be an emotional experience as well.

After literature review on the color studies in the related fields, the present paper includes an empirical study that illustrates and further demonstrates the impact of product color on price decision for used cars, and the attempt will be made to look into this dynamics from the perspective of psychology of design. First, the literature review section summarizes past research studies that focused on color impacts in the market place as an emotional attribute. In addition, the emotional aspect of price decision will be covered. Next, an empirical study that investigated the relationship between vehicle color and price depreciation of used cars will be presented. The analysis was based on a large database that captured prices paid for luxury cars at the transaction level. Finally, the findings will be discussed in the light of color and price decision making from the emotion perspective.

Literature Review

Past research on color has linked it to emotion in various marketing contexts (e.g., Bagchi & Cheema, 2013; Bellizzi & Hite, 1992). In many of the related studies, color is often considered as an image attribute where its impact on consumers is based on emotion/affect rather than cognition (e.g., Kaya, & Epps, 2004; Nezhad & Kavehnezhad, 2013; Plass, Heidig, Hayward, Homer, & Um, 2014; Reimann, Zaichkowsky, Neuhaus, Bender, & Weber, 2010; Singh, 2006; Valdez & Mehrabian, 1994). In addition, there have been various research studies addressing the interaction between price and emotion (e.g, O'Neill & Lambert, 2001; Powers, 2006). Given these relationships, it would be difficult to address psychological dynamics associated with color or price decision making without considering the notion of emotion. There has been extensive deliberation in the past literature on the precise definitions for emotion and affect or the distinction between emotional versus cognitive mental processing (see for example, Kemp, Bui, & Chapa, 2012; Pham, 2007; Ruth, 2001; Schwarz, 2004, for related discussions), and it is beyond the scope of this chapter to address all the viewpoints regarding this complex psychological concept. For the purpose of the present study, this chapter will follow a more general definition by Pham (2007), who stated that "the term 'emotion' will be used somewhat broadly to refer to the presence of affect in general. . . . If one is to have a full appreciation of the rationality or irrationality of emotional phenomena, it is important not to restrict one's analysis to the most intense emotional experiences" (p. 156).

The following sections review past studies focusing on the two relationships—color and emotion, and then price and emotion. As can be seen, many studies on these topics explicitly or implicitly encompass the notion of emotional dynamics.

Color and Emotion from the Consumer Psychology Perspective

Recently, there have been more research studies focusing on the impact of color on consumer behavior in various settings (see Labrecque, Patrick, & Milne, 2013, for a literature review on the topic). There are various empirical studies that have examined impacts of environmental color on consumer behavior, such as purchase decision, search time, or perception of time (e.g., Babin, Hardesty, & Suter, 2003; Bellizzi, Crowley, & Hasty, 1983; Bellizzi & Hite, 1992; Gimba, 1998; Gorn, Chattopadhyay, Sengupta, & Tripathi, 2004; Jansson, Marlow, & Bristow, 2004; Middlestadt, 1990). Separate from the research on color as an external environmental factor, there are also studies looking into the impact of product color on its preferences (e.g., Akcay, Dalgin, & Bhatnagar, 2011; Akcay, Sable, & Dalgin, 2012; Deng, Hui, & Hutchinson, 2010), as described in the following section.

Product Color and Emotion

Akcay and his colleagues (2011, 2012) conducted surveys to ask college students how important the product color attribute is when choosing a particular product, such as mobile phones, etc., and found gender-related differences in product color preferences. Hekkert and Leder (2008) demonstrated with their experiments that attractive product packaging would increase initial positive response to a product and explained that the attractiveness generated affective expectations that were associated with a consumption experience. Similarly, Galli and Gorn (2011) showed in their experiments that participants' evaluations of the brand names depended on consistency between the external colors being used for the products packaging and the product themselves. The study by Bottomley and Doyle (2006) indicated that choosing product colors that are connotatively congruent is important. They demonstrated with their empirical studies that colors and products have connotative meanings that are shared by consumers. Kareklas, Brunel, and Coulter (2014) introduced the notion of automatic color preference where consumers have implicit tendency to prefer a certain color when choosing a product.

Some studies on the role of color in marketing focused on cross-cultural differences. The studies on color and product preferences by Akcay and his colleagues (2011, 2012) found that there exist cross-cultural differences in the influence of product colors on their preferences among various ethnic groups in the U.S. as well as across countries, i.e., U.S., India, China, and Turkey. Mantua (2007) also described color-related differences with cross-cultural communication between China and Finland. For general discussions on color and cross-cultural marketing, Sable and Akcay (2010) provided an overview paper on topics, such as color and branding or cross-cultural meanings and associations of individual colors.

Color and Psychological Functioning

There are studies that looked into the color-emotion link more explicitly, where the semantic meanings of colors and psychological states such as motivation, anxiety, or aggression were explored. Guéguen, Jacob, Lourel, and Pascual (2012) investigated whether the color of cars is related to an aggressive behavior with their field experiment and found the red car elicited early aggressive response. Jacobs and Suess (1975) examined the relationship between four primary colors and the anxiety state and found those who were exposed to red and yellow experienced a higher anxiety level than those exposed to blue and green. Some studies introduced the notion of multiple dimensions with human responses to color (Crowley, 1993; Sakuta & Gyoba, 2006). Crowley (1993) introduced two-dimensional conceptualization of responses to color—activation dimension and evaluation dimension. Sakuta and Gyoba (2006) identified three factors, i.e., Activity, Potency, and Evaluation, in their studies on impression formation that involves color. Labrecque and Milne (2012) conducted four empirical studies that provided support for the relationship between color and brand personality being influenced by semantic meaning of the color. Meyers-Levy and Peracchio (1995) addressed the impacts of ads' colors on consumers' product attitudes from the motivation perspective and concluded that the use of color in ads could be effective or ineffective, depending on how motivated consumers are in processing information in the ads.

Elliot and his colleagues conducted a series of studies to propose and address their general model on color and psychological functioning (Elliot et al., 2010; Elliot & Maier, 2007, 2014; Elliot, Maier, Binser, Friedman, & Pekrun, 2009; Elliot, Maier, Moller, Friedman, & Meinhardt, 2007; Elliot & Niesta, 2008). A premise by their general model states that color carries psychologically relevant meaning (Elliot & Maier, 2007). Applying their model, their empirical studies attempted to explain avoidance behavior where the color red affects achievement tasks (Elliot et al., 2007, 2009) or heterosexual attractiveness associated with men's red clothing (Elliot et al., 2008, 2010).

Price, Decision Making, and Emotion

The importance of emotion for decision making cannot be understated, and in fact decision making itself is often considered as an emotional process (Zeelenberg, Nelissen, Breugelmans, & Pieters, 2008). When a consumer is in the process of price negotiation for a high-involvement purchase occasion such as an automobile, it likely creates a difficult tradeoff situation, which could often trigger a negative emotion status (Luce, Bettman, & Payne, 1997, 1999). Similarly, Zeitham (1988) discussed the concept of perceived price and mentioned that accurate knowledge of prices in the case of durable goods is often deterred by such factors as complexity or lack of price information. Orth, Campana, and Malkewitz (2010) demonstrated with their empirical analyses that package design has the ability to influence consumer price expectation via consumer judgments of quality and attractiveness.

Pfister and Böhm (2008) claimed decision making is all under the influence of emotion with differential weights applied to the four emotional functions—information, speed, relevance, and commitment. Babin et al. (2003), in their atmospherics research where lighting, color, and product price were controlled, showed how physical store characteristics frame purchase decisions and affect perceptions of price fairness. O'Neill and Lambert (2001) focused on the notion of price affect, or consumers' emotional reactions to prices, and identified various relationships between price and emotion. For example, their analyses indicated that as product involvement increases, enjoyment with the price increases.

Powers (2006) investigated if there are differential effects of the product "image" attributes—i.e., color, engine size, and body type—on the purchase price, focusing on new cars with more image appeal, such as sporty cars. The results indicated consistently higher price for red and black among the design-conscious vehicle models. Similarly, though not specifically with respect to color, Landwehr, Labroo and Herrmann (2009) found impacts of visual design attributes of cars on their retail prices and brand preferences in their field study.

An Empirical Investigation of Vehicle Color and Price Decision Making

To explore the relationship between color and price decision further, similar analyses to Powers (2006) was carried out, this time focusing on the price depreciation of used cars and how they vary among different colors. The purpose of this investigation was to examine if the colors of automobiles alone are associated with different price depreciation rates of used vehicles, while controlling for various other attributes, such as the engine size, the body type, etc. *It was hypothesized that the purchase price depreciation rate of automobiles, measured by the regression coefficient of vehicle age (in years) on price, varies depending on the vehicle color.* The investigation further illustrates and provides additional empirical evidence on if/how color influences consumer behavior.

Data

The analysis data consisted of auto dealers' transaction records of new and used vehicles purchased by end consumers between 2001 and 2005 in the California market. The database included over 200,000 transactions, which would help ensure that the analysis findings are statistically robust. In order to ensure that the investigation of price depreciation was not affected by the variance associated with the broad range of automobiles in U.S., the current study focused on the luxury vehicle segment, including such brands as BMW, Cadillac, and Lexus. In addition, each of the "vehicle models" was defined as the unique combination of all the vehicle functional attributes, including engine size, body type, wheel type, etc. Those vehicle models with the sample size being at least 10 were kept for further analyses, and therefore the selected vehicle models each had a sample size sufficient for various analyses.

New car purchase data were also included in the analyses for the baseline price assessment. In addition, the odometer reading was included in the analysis to test for the possible impact of car usage history variation on the relationship between vehicle age and price. For the vehicle colors, the following colors were included— black, blue, gray, green, red, silver, and white. The remaining colors were combined as the 'baseline' color for the purpose of statistical comparisons.

Analysis

An analysis of covariance (ANCOVA) was performed to investigate how the purchase prices of cars depreciate as they age and if/how the depreciation rate varies by vehicle color. In addition to the vehicle model and vehicle age, the analysis included consumer age and gender as control variables. Odometer reading (i.e., mileage of the car) was also considered and first examined for its appropriateness as an explanatory variable.

Preliminary analyses indicated that the relationship between purchase price and vehicle age is nonlinear. The relationship was best represented as exponential as shown in Figure 6.1. It is clear from the chart that the vehicle price declines the fastest when the car is newer and then the depreciation rate becomes slower as the vehicle gets older. To reflect the non-linear relationship, the variables for vehicle age (in years) and vehicle price (in dollars) were log-transformed for the ANCOVA model.

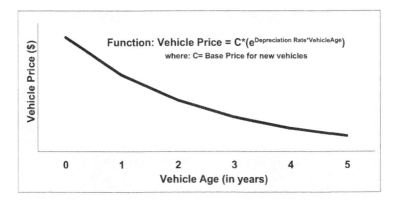

FIGURE 6.1 The relationship between purchase price and vehicle age is nonlinear, and best represented as exponential.

Source: Keiko Powers.

During the preliminary analyses, the odometer reading was examined with respect to (1) the correlation with vehicle age (in years) and (2) the relationship with the vehicle price. The correlation between vehicle age and odometer reading was very high with the coefficient over 0.90. The correlations with price were equally high between odometer reading and vehicle age, with –0.41 and –0.45, respectively. These results indicated that vehicle age alone without the odometer reading was sufficient to assess the price-vehicle oldness relationship, and it was in fact better for the ANCOVA model to avoid the multicollinearity problem with highly correlated independent variables.

Results

Overall, the analysis results based on ANCOVA confirmed the differential effect of color on the vehicle price depreciation (see Table 6.1). For various luxury automobiles investigated here, there was a significant interaction effect between vehicle age and color, indicating the vehicle price depreciation rate varies depending on the color. As shown in Table 6.1, the interaction term between vehicle age and color in the model—Log (Vehicle Age) × Vehicle Color—was statistically significant.

Next, the parameter estimates for Vehicle Age for each Vehicle Color in the ANCOVA model were compared and contrasted for assessing the differential effects on vehicle price in more depth. Figure 6.2 summarizes the parameter estimates of Vehicle Age that represent the price depreciation rates. With over 80 vehicle models (e.g., Audi A4, Cadillac Deville) being tested, the vehicle color = white resulted in the least price depreciation rate, followed closely by red and black, compared to the other colors, including gray, blue, and silver.

The results indicate that *the price deprecation rates for the vehicle colors, white and black, were much slower than the remaining colors, with white being the slowest.* The color red also displayed a slower depreciation rate compared to the "base" color, but its relatively smaller sample size should be considered for its interpretation.

To highlight the color impacts on price deprecation rates, the charts in Figure 6.3 show the price depreciation patterns for white (the slowest depreciation rate) and

TABLE 6.1 ANCOVA Model Results (Based on Type III SS)

Source	DF	SS	MS	F Value	ProbF
Consumer Age	1	0.28	0.28	41.19	< .0001
Gender	1	0.01	0.01	0.94	0.3328
Vehicle Color	7	0.91	0.13	19.02	< .0001
Vehicle Model	37	1368.74	36.99	5419.08	< .0001
Log (Vehicle Age)	1	399.15	399.15	58470.70	< .0001
Log (Vehicle Age) × Vehicle Model	37	60.33	1.63	238.87	< .0001
Log (Vehicle Age) × Vehicle Color	7	0.24	0.03	4.97	< .0001

Note: Dependent variable = Vehicle price (Logged); Sample size = 44553.

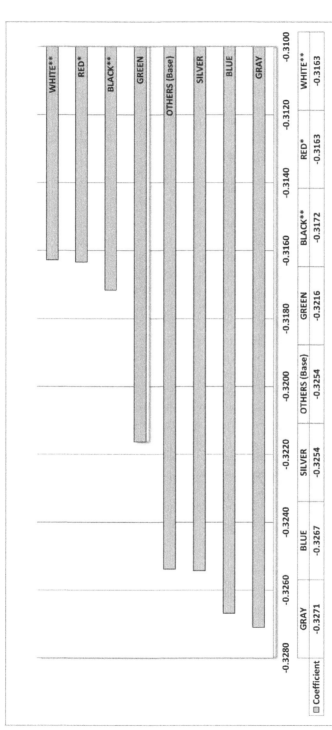

Note: * The coefficient for RED was based on a smaller sample size compared to other color groups ($p < 0.05$).

** The coefficients for WHITE and BLACK were significant ($p < 0.001$).

The coefficients for the remaining colors were not statistically significant compared to OTHERS (Base).

	GRAY	BLUE	SILVER	OTHERS (Base)	GREEN	BLACK**	RED*	WHITE**
Coefficient	-0.3271	-0.3267	-0.3254	-0.3254	-0.3216	-0.3172	-0.3163	-0.3163

FIGURE 6.2 Parameter estimates of Vehicle Age that represent the price depreciation rates for automobiles.

Source: Keiko Powers.

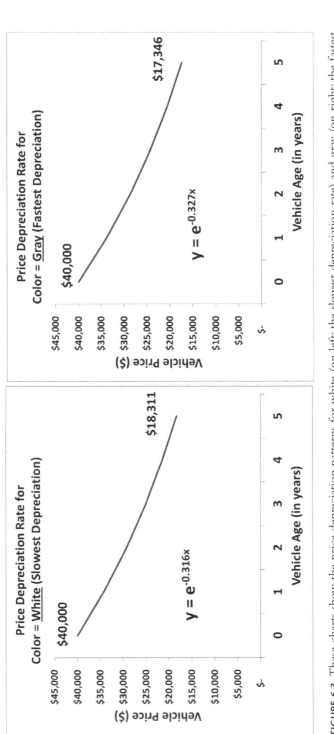

FIGURE 6.3 These charts show the price depreciation patterns for white (on left: the slowest depreciation rate) and gray (on right: the fastest depreciation rate) colors.

Source: Keiko Powers.

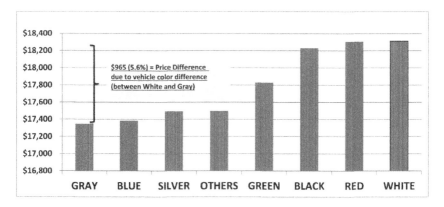

FIGURE 6.4 Predicted vehicle prices by color for new vehicle price: $40,000 & Vehicle Age = 5 years.

Source: Keiko Powers.

gray (the fastest depreciation rate) colors. They depict how the price goes down as the vehicle gets older, choosing $40,000 as the new car price for illustrating purposes. These two slopes appear very similar, but the estimated price difference between the two is not negligible ($18,311 vs. $17,346) when the vehicle is 5 years old.

Finally, using the same $40,000 as the new car price scenario, the vehicle price was estimated for the condition where the vehicle age is 5 years old for each of the colors separately. Figure 6.4 compares and contrasts the predicted vehicle prices for each color. As can be seen, the price difference between white and gray is $965 with the $40,000 new car example. It should be reminded that this price difference is after controlling for various moderating factors, such as vehicle functional attributes, odometer reading, etc.

Discussion and Conclusion

The present chapter examined the relationship between color and price decision, focusing on the case of car purchase. As has been seen in the literature review, many studies in the related fields have demonstrated the impacts of color on consumer behavior in various settings. These studies support the idea that consumers' perception and their "emotional" evaluation of color plays such an important role in the purchase decision that it has a significant influence on consumer's evaluation about the price. The results of the current empirical investigation on color and price depreciation confirmed such impacts of color on prices of used cars. This implies that emotionally appealing attributes such as color can be a very influential factor for automobile design as well as for pricing strategies.

Whereas past studies focusing on the related topics were mostly conducted in an experimental setting, the point-of-sales data used for the current study allowed an assessment of the prevalence and the nature of price differences associated with vehicle color in the real-life situation. There have been a few firms in the industry that looked into the price depreciation rate of used cars and how it varies due to different colors. An article titled "Vehicle colour choice impacts on depreciation and visibility" on an auto industry website mentioned that cars with inoffensive colors, such as white, black, gray, or silver tend to retain higher prices as they age (Kirsten, 2012)—i.e., the price depreciation is slower for cars with these colors. The current empirical investigation supported this claim and confirmed that the price depreciation difference among different vehicle colors is present and statistically significant. The results of the present analyses also showed a pattern with white and black having the slowest depreciation rate.

The empirical study introduced in this paper is limited to the overall analysis across all the vehicle models. Further analysis could focus on how the relationship differs by vehicle type (e.g., more utility-based versus image-based), how the interaction differs by consumer age (the current results show a significant impact), etc. It would also be interesting to further explore how these differences due to color are influenced by consumer characteristics (e.g., gender or age), regions (e.g., urban versus rural), and how they interact with vehicle types (e.g., luxury versus non-luxury).

It should be noted that the empirical findings in this paper are observational in nature and do not allow us to determine what underlying dynamics causes the consumers to pay more just for the color of the car. Besides the psychological drive in the consumer's mind, there are other possibilities such as the supply and demand mechanism in the market that could influence manufacturer's production and distribution or dealer's pricing. These possibilities would be worth further investigation. Regardless of these other possible influences, however, the price difference due to color—an image attribute with no utility value—has been confirmed to be present in the market environment, and this fact itself allows us to infer that there exists underlying dynamics rooted to emotion that drives color to influence consumer purchase in a complex manner. It would be beneficial to supplement the current findings with a controlled experiment (such as conjoint analysis) or consumer survey (Koizumi, Kanke, & Amasaka, 2013) for a more in-depth understanding of the dynamics.

Implications for a Theory of Design

In studying the relationship between color—an "image" or design attribute—and price decision in the auto industry, one of the main purposes was to address if/how emotion can affect consumer behavior in various contexts, including price decision or product feature evaluation where cognitive information processing would seem to dictate the mental processing. This chapter highlighted the importance of a better understanding of emotion for discussing design attributes in various contexts. For example, a recent paper by Townsend and Shu (2010) highlighted how some complex psychological processing could affect the perception of design in the least likely context. They investigated and identified when and how aesthetic design influences decision-making in a domain where aesthetics are considered to be of low importance—i.e., financial decisions. Per Townsend and Shu (2010), we would expect that "financial decision-making is an area where use of cognition over emotion is particularly encouraged and aesthetics may be expected to have little effect" (p. 452). Based on their study results, they emphasized the importance of accurately assessing the return on extra investment with aesthetic design.

Clearly, consumer research on visual design such as color could influence designers in hypothesizing and testing consumer responses to the design (Chrilly & Clarkson, 2006). In fact, Yamamoto and Lambert (1994) noted that product aesthetics could be more influential than product performance attributes on sales for some industry products. Crilly, Moultrie and Clarkson (2004) provided a review paper on consumer response to visual design for products, where they discussed all the factors affecting the communication that is being offered to the consumer by designers. In doing so, they noted it is important to distinguish emotional and cognitive responses to product design. Desmet, Hekkert, and Jacobs (2000) developed and introduced an instrument to measure 18 product emotions for assessing emotional responses to product design, which can be applied to various contexts on emotional impacts of color.

O'Neill and Lambert (2001) stated that "as students of consumer behavior, researchers need to pay more attention to the role of emotion in all aspects of marketing, including those surrounding price" (p. 232). As Srinivasan, Lovejoy, and Beach (1997) stated, it is clear that "customer choices are not solely a function of quantifiable product attributes" (p. 158).

Implications for Designers

Image attributes can be a very influential factor for decision making with respect to how much consumers are willing to pay. This can be interpreted as the reflection of the consumer's perception of the product value, which could be affected by the color of the product, even when the color does not provide any functional value. Hekkert and Leder (2008) stated that designers are becoming more and more aware of the power of emotion with designed objects. Powers (2006) identified price differences among new cars with different colors, especially among highly 'image' sensitive cars, such as sporty cars. The present empirical study also demonstrated the existence of differential color impacts on prices among used cars in the luxury segment where price depreciation rates vary depending on the vehicle colors. The findings suggest that certain vehicle colors are associated with higher market prices when all the other attributes are controlled for. These empirical findings, though indirectly, support the notion that there exist an emotion-driven value assessment and decision making process where the non-functional attribute, color, can influence how much the consumer agrees to pay for the car.

This implies that the role of color in the market is very likely much higher than what our common sense would indicate. From the product design perspective, knowing the exact nature and extent of how color can influence at various stages of the consumer-product interaction is essential and valuable for succeeding in today's competitive market. A study conducted by Yazaki, Tanitsu, Hayashi, and Amasaka (2012) focused on instrumentation design in the automobile industry, and they described how the survey on consumers' subjective preferences and their various research investigations led to an introduction of auto instruments that met preferences identified in the survey results. Such collaborative work between designers and consumer researchers would be beneficial for a better understanding of the relationship between color and design in the context of consumer marketing.

References

Akcay, O., Dalgin, M. H., & Bhatnagar, S. (2011). Perception of color in product choice among college students: A cross-national analysis of USA, India, China and Turkey. *International Journal of Business and Social Science, 2*, 42–48.

Akcay, O., Sable, P., & Dalgin, M. H. (2012). The importance of color in product choice among young Hispanic, Caucasian, and African-American groups in the USA. *International Journal of Business and Social Science, 3*, 1–6.

Babin, B. J., Hardesty, D. M., & Suter, T. A. (2003). Color and shopping intentions: The intervening effect of price fairness and perceived affect. *Journal of Business Research, 56*, 541–551.

Bagchi, R., & Cheema, A. (2013). The effect of red background color on willingness-to-pay: The moderating role of selling mechanism. *Journal of Consumer Research, 39*, 947–960.

Bellizzi, J. A., Crowley, A. E., & Hasty, R. W. (1983). The effects of color in store design. *Journal of Retailing, 59*, 21–45.

Bellizzi, J. A., & Hite, R. E. (1992). Environmental color, consumer feelings, and purchase likelihood, *Psychology and Marketing, 9*, 347–363.

Black, white top most popular vehicle color list. (2013). Retrieved from http://autos.jdpower.com/content/blog-post/0C45k4e/black-white-top-most-popular-vehicle-color-list.htm

Bottomley, P. A., & Doyle, J. R. (2006). The interactive effects of colors and products on perceptions of brand logo appropriateness. *Marketing Theory, 6*, 63–83.

Crilly, N., & Clarkson, P. J. (2006). *The influence of consumer research on product aesthetics.* DS 36: Proceedings DESIGN 2006, the 9th International Design Conference, Dubrovnik, Croatia.

Crilly, N., Moultrie, J., & Clarkson, P. J. (2004). Seeing things: Consumer response to the visual domain in product design. *Design Studies, 25*, 547–577.

Crowley, A. E. (1993). The two-dimensional impact of color on shopping. *Marketing Letters, 4*, 59–69.

Deng, X., Hui, S. K., & Hutchinson, J. (2010). Consumer preferences for color combinations: An empirical analysis of similarity-based color relationships. *Journal of Consumer Psychology, 20*, 476–484.

Desmet, P. M., Hekkert, P., & Jacobs, J. J. (2000). When a car makes you smile: Development and application of an instrument to measure product emotions. *Advances in Consumer Research, 27*, 111–117.

Elliot, A. J., Kayser, N. D., Greitemeyer, T., Lichtenfeld, S., Gramzow, R. H., Maier, M. A., & Liu, H. (2010). Red, rank, and romance in women viewing men. *Journal of Experimental Psychology: General, 139*, 399–417.

Elliot, A. J., & Maier, M. A. (2007). Color and psychological functioning. *Current Directions in Psychological Science, 16*, 250–254.

Elliot, A. J., & Maier, M. A. (2014). Color psychology: Effects of perceiving color on psychological functioning in humans. *Annual Review of Psychology, 65*, 95–120.

Elliot, A. J., Maier, M. A., Binser, M. J., Friedman, R., & Pekrun, R. (2009). The effect of red on avoidance behavior in achievement contexts. *Personality and Social Psychology Bulletin, 35*, 365–375.

Elliot, A. J., Maier, M. A., Moller, A. C., Friedman, R., & Meinhardt, J. (2007). Color and psychological functioning: The effect of red on performance attainment. *Journal of Experimental Psychology: General, 136*, 154–168.

Elliot, A. J., & Niesta, D. (2008). Romantic red: Red enhances men's attraction to women. *Journal of Personality and Social Psychology, 95*, 1150–1164.

Galli, M., & Gorn, G. (2011). Unconscious transfer of meaning to brands. *Journal of Consumer Psychology, 21*, 215–225.

Gimba, J. G. (1998). Color in Marketing: Shades of Meaning, *Marketing News, 32*, 6.

Gorn, G. J., Chattopadhyay, A., Sengupta, J., & Tripathi, S. (2004). Waiting for the web: How screen color affects time perception. *Journal of Marketing Research, 41*, 215–225.

Guéguen, N., Jacob, C., Lourel, M., & Pascual, A. (2012). When drivers see red: Car color frustrators and drivers' aggressiveness. *Aggressive Behavior, 38*, 166–169.

Hekkert, P., & Leder, H. (2008). Product aesthetics. In H.N.J. Schifferstein & P. Hekkert (Eds.), *Product experience* (pp. 259–285). Amsterdam: Elsevier.

Jacobs, K. W., & Suess, J. F. (1975). Effects of four psychological primary colors on anxiety state. *Perceptual and Motor Skills, 41*, 207–210.

Jansson, C., Marlow, N., & Bristow, M. (2004). The influence of colour on visual search times in cluttered environments. *Journal of Marketing Communications, 10*, 183–193.

Kareklas, I., Brunel, F. F., & Coulter, R. (2014). Judgment is not color blind: The impact of automatic color preference on product and advertising preferences. *Journal of Consumer Psychology, 24*, 87–95.

Kaya, N., & Epps, H. (2004). Relationship between color and emotion: A study of college students. *College Student Journal, 38*, 396–405.

Kelley Blue Book. (2014). Know when the price is right: 10 steps to buying a new car. Retrieved from http://www.kbb.com/car-advice/car-buying/step-5-know-when-the-price-is-right/

Kemp, E., Bui, M., & Chapa, S. (2012). The role of advertising in consumer emotion management. *International Journal of Advertising, 31*, 339–353.

Kirsten, B. (2012). Vehicle colour choice impacts on depreciation and visibility. Retrieved http://www.fleetcare.com.au/news-info/fleet-beat-blog/november-2012/vehicle-colour-choice-impacts-on-depreciation-an.aspx

Koizumi, K., Kanke, R., & Amasaka, K. (2013). Research on automobile exterior color and interior color matching. *International Conference on Management and Information Systems, 22*, 201–211.

Labrecque, L. I., & Milne, G. R. (2012). Exciting red and competent blue: The importance of color in marketing. *Journal of the Academy of Marketing Science, 40*, 711–727.

Labrecque, L. I., Patrick, V. M., & Milne, G. R. (2013). The marketers' prismatic palette: A review of color research and future directions. *Psychology and Marketing, 30*, 187–202.

Landwehr, J. R., Labroo, A., & Herrmann, A. (2009). The pervasive effect of aesthetics on choice: Evidence from a field study. *Advances in Consumer Research, 36*, 751–752.

Loomis, T. (2012). New car MSRP vs. invoice: Which price should you pay? Retrieved from http://www.newcars.com/news/msrp-vs.-invoice

Luce, M. F., Bettman, J. R., & Payne, J. W. (1997). Choice processing in emotionally difficult decisions. *Journal of Experimental Psychology: Learning, Memory, and Cognition, 23*, 384–405.

Luce, M. F., Payne, J. W., & Bettman, J. R. (1999). Emotional trade-off difficulty and choice. *Journal of Marketing Research, 36*, 143–159.

Mantua, K. (2007, March). *Is green the colour of cash or conviction? Colour culture in China as seen by managers of Finnish MNCs: Report on a pilot study.* Proceedings of the Association for Business Communication 7th Asia-Pacific Conference, Hong Kong.

Meyers-Levy, J., & Peracchio, L. A. (1995). Understanding the effects of color: How the correspondence between available and required resources affects attitudes. *Journal of Consumer Research, 22*, 121–138.

Middlestadt, S. E. (1990). The effect of background and ambient color on product attitudes and beliefs. *Advances in Consumer Research, 17*, 244–249.

Nezhad, Z. H., & Kavehnezhad, K. (2013). Choosing the right color: A way to increase sales. *International Journal of Asian Social Science, 3*, 1442–1457.

O'Neill, R. M., & Lambert, D. R. (2001). The emotional side of price, *Psychology and Marketing, 18*, 217–237.

Orth, U. R., Campana, D., & Malkewitz, K. (2010). Formation of consumer price expectation based on package design: Attractive and quality routes. *Journal of Marketing Theory and Practice, 18*, 23–40.

Pfister, H. R., & Böhm, G. (2008). The multiplicity of emotions: A framework of emotional functions in decision making. *Judgment and Decision Making, 3*, 5–17.

Pham, M. T. (2007). Emotion and rationality: A critical review and interpretation of empirical evidence. *Review of General Psychology, 11*, 155–178.

Plass, J. L., Heidig, S., Hayward, E. O., Homer, B. D., & Um, E. (2014). Emotional design in multimedia learning: Effects of shape and color on affect and learning. *Learning and Instruction, 29*, 128–140.

Powers, K. I. (2006). Image attributes of automobiles and their influence on purchase price decision. In L. Kahle and C.-H. Kim (Eds.), *Creating images and the psychology of marketing communications* (pp. 291–307). Mahwah, NJ: Lawrence Erlbaum Associates.

Reed, P. (2013). Pricing basics for new-car buying: Understanding the terms will help you get a great deal. Retrieved from http://www.edmunds.com/car-buying/pricing-basics-for-new-car-buying.html

Reimann, M., Zaichkowsky, J., Neuhaus, C., Bender, T., & Weber, B. (2010). Aesthetic package design: A behavioral, neural, and psychological investigation. *Journal of Consumer Psychology, 20*, 431–441.

Ruth, J. A. (2001). Promoting a brand's emotion benefits: The influence of emotion categorization processes on consumer evaluations. *Journal of Consumer Psychology, 11*, 99–113.

Sable, P., & Akcay, O. (2010, February). *Color: Cross cultural marketing perspectives as to what governs our response to it.* Proceedings of ASBBS Annual Conference, Las Vegas, NV, pp. 950–954.

Sakuta, Y., & Gyoba, J. (2006). Affective impressions and memorability of color-form combinations. *Journal of General Psychology, 133*, 191–207.

Schwarz, N. (2004). Metacognitive experiences in consumer judgment and decision making. *Journal of Consumer Psychology, 14*, 332–348.

Singh, S. (2006). Impact of color on marketing. *Management Decision, 44*, 783–789.

Srinivasan, V., Lovejoy, W. S., & Beach, D. (1997). Integrated product design for marketability and manufacturing. *Journal of Marketing Research, 34,* 154–163.

Townsend, C., & Shu, S. B. (2010). When and how aesthetics influences financial decisions. *Journal of Consumer Psychology, 20,* 452–458.

Valdez, P., & Mehrabian, A. (1994). Effects of color on emotions. *Journal of Experimental Psychology: General, 123,* 394–409.

Veryzer, R. W. (1995). The place of product design and aesthetics in consumer research. *Advances in Consumer Research, 22,* 641–645.

Which colour?: Does colour choice really matter? (2012). Retrieved from http://www.theaa.com/motoring_advice/car-buyers-guide/cbg_colour.html

Yamamoto, M., & Lambert, D. R. (1994). The impact of product aesthetics on the evaluation of industrial products. *Journal of Product Innovation Management, 11,* 309–324.

Yazaki, K., Tanitsu, H., Hayashi, H., & Amasaka, K. (2012). A model for design auto instrumentation to appeal to young male customers. *Journal of Business Case Studies, 8,* 417–426.

Zeelenberg, M., Nelissen, R. M., Breugelmans, S. M., & Pieters, R. (2008). On emotion specificity in decision making: Why feeling is for doing. *Judgment and Decision Making, 3,* 18–27.

Zeithaml, V. A. (1988). Consumer perceptions of price, quality, and value: A means-end model and synthesis of evidence. *Journal of Marketing, 52,* 2–22.

7

CURVATURE FROM ALL ANGLES

An Integrative Review and Implications for Product Design

Tanuka Ghoshal

INDIAN SCHOOL OF BUSINESS

Peter Boatwright

CARNEGIE MELLON UNIVERSITY

Malika M.

INDIAN SCHOOL OF BUSINESS

Academic researchers and marketers alike understand the importance of product design as an opportunity for differential advantage in the marketplace (Bloch, 1995; Creusen & Schoormans, 2005; Hertenstein, Platt, & Veryzer, 2005; Landwehr, Labroo, & Hermann, 2011), but does the angularity or curvature (henceforth used interchangeably) of the product play a role in influencing product perceptions? Also, given that a vast majority of products in the marketplace are rectangular (Raghubir & Greenleaf, 2006), a question that naturally arises is whether consumers have inherent preferences for either products with angular shapes or contours, or curved contours. There is a significant body of work spanning different domains, such as empirical aesthetics, social psychology, marketing, and neurobiology, that has looked at how angular and rounded contours are processed by human beings, in a wide variety of contexts. In this chapter, we attempt to integrate the findings from all these different streams and provide comprehensive implications for product design in terms of shape, from the perspective of angularity or curvature. Additionally, using primary research conducted in India, we propose that angular or rounded contours could be used strategically depending on the intended functionality and hedonic perceptions of the product. Extant literature suggests that contours of products communicate information to consumers that may stem from hardwired or primitive human goals. We therefore recommend that marketers thoroughly evaluate the objectives and personalities of their brands or products, as consumers may well draw inferences about a product from its contours that may not be aligned with the brand objectives.

In the following sections we review the literature on curvature from different domains including empirical aesthetics, social psychology, neurobiology, and marketing. Our review is laid out as follows. We first present empirical evidence that suggest a general predisposition of human beings towards curves over angles, then discuss research that provides evidence for the underlying process, followed by a review of various moderators identified in the literature. We additionally present research findings on cross-sensory perceptions related to shape as studied by Gestalt psychologists, this being particularly relevant for product designers, and close the review in this segment with more specific research findings on curvature and product perceptions. We additionally present findings from an original study investigating product perceptions in terms of functionality and hedonics as influenced by angularity. We finally discuss implications for product designers and issues which remain unanswered in the theoretical domain, and we suggest future research questions for academicians and marketers alike.

Empirical Evidence for a Generally Favorable Predisposition Toward Curves

As early as 1909, it was observed that curves are generally felt to be more beautiful than straight lines (as note in *Esthetics,* popularly regarded as the first textbook for psychological aesthetics; Gordon, 1909). In Lundholm (1921)'s experiment, participants were asked to draw lines to express feelings, in which more angles were used to express adjectives like "hard," "harsh," "cruel," while more curves were drawn to denote adjectives like "weak," "gentle," "mild," etc. Other researchers have similar findings with jagged lines denoting feelings like "agitating," "furious," "hard," and "serious" versus curved lines depicting "sad," "quiet," "lazy," "merry," and "gentle" (Poffenberger & Barrows, 1924). A positive attitude towards circular, organic shapes has been found even when complexity (Parise & Spence, 2012) and other aesthetic properties, such as symmetry and balance, are controlled for (Silvia & Barona, 2009). Thus the literature in this domain suggests that curved contours would generally be perceived more favorably than angular contours, although no theory is proposed.

Process Explanations for a Generally Favorable Predisposition Toward Curves

Explanations for the underlying process behind shape preferences are offered in the evolutionary and neurobiological literature. There are two lines of reasoning from an evolutionary perspective that suggest why organic, curved shapes are generally favored above sharp or angular shapes, both emphasizing how geometry of the stimuli can convey emotional meaning. Darwin (1872/1998) proposed, and Ekman (1972) and Izard (1977) confirmed, that emotions provide a common biological communication system that expresses and comprehends meaning in similar ways across all cultures.

The first perspective suggests that simple geometrical shapes underlie facial expressions of emotions, and convey semantic meaning without the need for thorough processing of the stimuli. In a study by Bassili (1979), faces were covered with black makeup and numerous white spots, and were video recorded for different emotions. The results showed that in a happy face, a burst of points expanded outward to form a rounded shape, whereas in an angry face points imploded downward and inward to form a V-shaped angle. Happy faces are seen to have visual properties of roundedness (e.g., curves found in the cheeks, eyes, and mouth while smiling) whereas angry facial displays have visual properties of diagonality and angularity (e.g., angles in the eyebrows, cheeks, chin, and jaw; Aronoff, Woike, & Hyman, 1992).

The second perspective from an evolutionary viewpoint is based on the notion that humans prefer objects that promote safety rather than impede it. This literature, which explains the undesirability of sharp or angular shapes, suggests that angular forms are inherently associated with potentially life-threatening or injuring stimuli such as the sharp edges of the teeth of a tiger, or the thorns of a cactus (Bar & Neta, 2006). On the other hand, an infant's rounded head and facial features have been found to evoke feeling of warmth, care, and protectiveness in humans (Papanek, 1995), which provides an explanation for other research findings such as a preference for baby-faced (faces that are more rounded) CEOs among adults (Gorn, Jiang, & Johar, 2008). The association of aggressive traits with jagged human figures in which shoulders, elbows, and knees are angular (Guthrie & Wiener, 1966) also support this notion of threat being associated with angularity. This preference of objects with curved contours over objects with sharp contours is not only based on semantic meaning of the stimuli, such as a knife, but also comes across among emotionally neutral everyday objects such as cars, watches, furniture, etc. (Bar & Neta, 2006; Leder & Carbon, 2005). The above evolutionary explanation has been alluded to by these researchers in the presentation of their results.

Larson, Aronoff, and Steuer (2012) used the Implicit Association Test (IAT; Greenwald, McGhee, & Schwartz, 1998) to study associations between three shapes (downward, and upward-pointing triangles and circle) and pleasant, unpleasant, and neutral scenes. The results showed that subjects categorized downward pointing triangles more quickly as unpleasant than as pleasant or neutral. These results support the argument that this preference bias for rounded stimuli may be automatic and implicit rather than involving extended cognitive processing.

A speedy identification of threat is considered to be as important as a detection of threat in the first place (Darwin, 1872/1998), and researchers have found that searching for an angry face in a photograph of a happy crowd is quicker than searching for a happy face in an angry crowd (Hansen & Hansen, 1988). Similarly, Larson et al. (2007) find that simple geometric configurations of angry faces (downward pointing "V's") was searched more efficiently than upward pointing V's and circles, suggesting a sustained capture of attention by this shape of threat. Moreover, the superior detection of downward-pointing V's is present in children as young as three years as well as in adults (LoBue & Larson, 2010), providing further evidence that the association of is an implicit biological process. It is to be noted, however that the inclination towards rounded objects is adaptive, and is absent in semantically negative stimuli such as a bomb (Leder, Tinio, Fuchs, & Bohrn, 2010).

In a similar vein, eye-tracking studies have shown that there is preferential looking at curved contours compared to straight ones, both in 5-month-old infants and adults (Amir, Biederman, & Hayworth, 2011). Neurological imaging techniques have also been extensively used to study associations between curvature and brain activity. The amygdala is the part of the brain concerned with the processing of emotions, especially fear, and it is activated by arousal level (Paton, Belova, Morrison, & Salzman, 2006). When testing mundane, emotionally neutral objects differing by shape as either angular or rounded, functional magnetic resonance imaging (fMRI) activity in the amygdala was found to be significantly higher for the sharp-angled objects, compared to their curved counterparts (Bar & Neta, 2007). Similarly, Larson, Aronoff, Sarinopoulos, and Zhu (2009) found that presentations of downward-pointing V-shapes evoke greater activation of the amygdala compared to upward-pointing V-shapes. This pattern of brain activation validates previous behavioral findings from evolutionary research, which purported that the simple geometrical figure of a downward V-shape (devoid of other contextual or affective cues) can function as an indicator of threat.

Moderating Factors for Curvature Preferences

While evolutionary psychology suggests that shape predilections are universal and not affected by cultural or individual disparities, or context, several researchers in social psychology have found otherwise. While studying logos in particular, researchers have found that individualistic cultures prefer angular, and collectivistic cultures prefer rounded shapes (Henderson, Cote, Leong, & Schmitt, 2003; Zhang, Feick, & Price, 2006). Tzeng, Trung, and Rieber (1990) found that students of Mexico, Colombia, and Japan rated the same icons and graphics differently: for instance, Japanese participants rated graphics with round shapes to be powerful and beautiful, whereas Colombian counterparts rated them to be ugly and powerless. In their book *Marketing Aesthetics*, Schmitt and Simonson (1997) discuss the architecture of the Bank of China building in Hong Kong, which is quintessentially angular with triangular shapes throughout. They suggest that in a culture that values harmony, while this structure signals a display of authority and power, it also signals conflict, strife, and bad luck. Similarly, Henderson et al. (2003) found that university students of Singapore and China rated rounded elements of logos more preferably than angular features, and angularity in logos was associated with bad luck.

In a field study, Zhang, Feick, and Price (2006) asked coders from a design school to rate actual logos from seven countries: Japan, Hong Kong, South Korea,

United States, United Kingdom, Canada, and Germany. The results showed that logos from collectivistic countries (the first three) were more rounded than those from individualistic countries (the latter four). These researchers further found that participants' self-construal acted on their conflict resolution style to affect shape preferences. They manipulated self-construal accessibility, and found that those with an independent self-construal tended to confront conflict and preferred angular contours. In contrast, those with interdependent self-construal tended to avoid conflict and preferred rounded elements.

Social identity theory (Tajfel & Turner, 1986) postulates a distinction between two portions of one's self-concept: personal identity (i.e., private self) and social identity (i.e., the self dependent on group(s) membership). Two basic human needs underlie these segments of self: the former being associated with the need to be unique, and the latter being associated with the need to belong. Recently, Zhu and Argo (2013) demonstrated how rounded and angular shapes might elicit these needs and consequently affect persuasion. They manipulated seating arrangements in a room to be angular vs. round, consequently priming either a need to be unique or a need to belong. Circular seating arrangements primed the need to belong, as a result of which participants appreciated persuasive material more when it expressed family-oriented information or majority endorsement. On the contrary, angular seating arrangements primed the need to be unique, and as a result participants appreciated persuasive material more when it expressed self-oriented information or minority endorsement.

Context has also been shown to have an influence on consumer preference for specific shapes. Presentation of visual assortments of simple geometric shapes in a certain format—for instance, the presence of a unique shape in an array—leads to the activation of a "uniqueness" concept, and subsequently favors choices of products that are unique in shape (Maimaran & Wheeler, 2008).

While in general, products in the market that are targeted to men appear to be more angular whereas products targeted to women appear more rounded, research findings regarding gender and shape preference are mixed. In an early research involving a drawing completion task, men showed a tendency to draw sharper (angular) or protruding lines, whereas women appeared inclined to draw round or blunt lines (Franck & Rosen, 1949). In a later field experiment by Munroe, Munroe, and Lansky (1976), male and female children were given the choice of either spherical or cubic shaped candies. Whereas boys preferred angular (cube) shaped candies and girls preferred rounded (spherical) candies, this preference was significant for girls only. A more recent study among infants aged 12, 18, and 24 months found that both genders looked longer at circles, rounded triangles and rounded stars than at squares, triangles, and stars (Jadva, Hines, & Golombok, 2010).

In terms of consistency of preferences, researchers have found that responses of people experiencing synesthesia, a condition in which physical stimulation of a sensory modality gives rise to automatic and involuntary perception of a different stimulus modality, are more consistent over time (Fernay, Reby, & Ward, 2012; Ramachandran & Hubbard, 2001) compared to the general population. All in all, despite some underlying evolutionary motivations, there certainly appears to be a fair amount of evidence that preferences for curvature may be context-dependent.

Curvature and Cross-Sensory Perceptions

Gestalt psychologist Wolfgang Kohler (1929) was perhaps the first to associate angular and curved shapes with other sensory attributes, starting with the auditory. He found that given two unusual shapes and meaningless words, adults matched the more rounded sound of "Bouba" (later also "Maluma") to the rounded shape of overlapping eclipses, and the more harsh sound of "Kiki" (later also "Takete") to angular, star-like shapes. The vowels "u," as in "Sue," and "o," as in "bode," are labeled as rounded vowels and are associated with curvy and organic shapes, whereas the vowel "e" as in "bead" and "u" as in "sun" are labeled unrounded or non-rounded vowels, and are with associated sharp, angular shapes. Similar patterns of results were found for different cultures (Davis, 1961) and different age groups ranging from 2.5 years to adults (Maurer, Pathman, & Mondloch, 2006; Ramachandran & Hubbard, 2001).

While Cheskin (1957) discussed this idea of "sensation transference" as the association of product with other sensory information like image or color, the concept was defined more formally by Spence (2012) as *cross-modal correspondence*: "a tendency for a feature, or attribute in one sensory modality to be matched (or associated) with a sensory feature or attribute in another sensory modality" (Parise & Spence, 2012). Spence (2012) also uses the term "shape symbolism" to specifically denote the crossmodal mapping between abstract shapes and other sensory attributes, and reviews research studying the association between shape and different sensory modalities of food and beverage products. For instance, angular (or sharp or pointy) shapes have been associated with bitter tastes (dark chocolates), sour tastes (cranberry jam, salt and vinegar crisps), sharp tastes (cheddar cheese), and carbonated drinks (sparkling water), whereas rounded shapes have been linked to sweet tastes (blueberry jam), creamy, smooth, and rich textures (milk chocolate, brie cheese), and still water (Gallace, Boschin, & Spence, 2011; Ngo, Misra, & Spence, 2011; Spence & Ngo, 2012).

Other auditory features, like pitch and timbre, have also been related to specific shapes: for instance, lower auditory pitches are found to be related to rounded, curvy forms while higher pitches are related to sharper, angular forms (Melara & O'Brien, 1987). In a recent study, Adeli, Rouat and Molotchnikoff (2014) found that harsh timbres, for example, from crash cymbals, are associated with angular contours, whereas soft timbres, such as from a piano, are linked to rounded contours.

Researchers have also studied the association of proprioceptive (related to position and movement) sensations with angularity. Aronoff, Woike and Hyman (1992) while studying movements of ballet dancers found that performances conveying threat involved jagged movements, whereas performances conveying warmth involved circular movements. Other researchers also find that smooth rhythms lead to more positive (relaxed and peaceful) affect than sharp rhythms (Koch, 2014), providing further evidence for associations of positive (negative) affect with rounded (angular) contours.

Researchers have sought to understand cross-sensory associations, for instance, the association of shapes with auditory sensations, from a biological perspective as well (Kohler, 1929). Ramachandran and Hubbard (2001) speculated that the "Maluma/Takete" phenomenon results from (a) connections among adjoining areas of the cerebrum that unite the visual perception of shape (round or angular) with the auditory, (b) the appearance of the speaker's lips (open and round versus wide and narrow), and (c) the feeling of the phonemic inflection and movement of the tongue when one says the words (rounded lips, large mouth opening, or lips stretched to produce a small mouth opening). In a study of the associations of phonological attributes of labels with round and angular shapes, Kovic, Plunkett, and Westermann (2010) found that there was a faster performance on a task when subjects were asked to categorize names of labels in congruent shape categories (e.g., "dom" with rounded shape and "shick" with angular shape) compared to incongruent counterparts. This stream of research therefore provides biological evidence for the faster processing of shape-congruent stimuli, and inherent associations in the brain of threat with angular stimuli.

Curvature and Product Perceptions

Several studies have looked at how angularity of a product influences aesthetic evaluation and purchase likelihood. Becker, van Rompay, Schifferstein, and Galetzka (2011) found that yogurt in angular containers was perceived to be more intense in terms of taste, but only by those people sensitive to design, as determined by higher scores on the centrality of visual product aesthetics scale (CVPA; Bloch, Brunel, & Arnold, 2003). Rounded shapes have been related to pleasant emotions for various products like furniture (Dazkir & Read, 2011), cars (Carbon, 2010), car interiors (Leder & Carbon, 2005), and other everyday objects (Bar & Neta, 2006). A preference for rounded designs was also found when studying shape of packaging for products as diverse as a box of chocolates, a water bottle, and a bleach bottle (Westerman et al., 2012), and this was over and above preference for design typicality and perceived ease of use. In our study, described in the following section, we study functional and hedonic perceptions as evoked by curvature in many common product categories, and find that hedonic (functional) perceptions are higher for products with rounded (angular) contours.

Our Study: Functionality and Hedonic Perceptions of Angular Versus Rounded Products

Elder and Krishna (2012) suggest that when consumers are exposed to a product or even an image of it, they mentally simulate the experience of interacting with the product. Therefore, simply looking at the contours of the packaging or product are very likely to impact perceived functionality and/or hedonic perceptions of a product, which is what we investigate in our study. The goal of our study was to assess whether curvature influences consumer perceptions of hedonic or utilitarian attributes for product categories where the shape is unrelated to the functionality of the product, and whether this is moderated by factors identified in prior literature.

A total of 438 subjects (254 female; average age 27 years) from the general population participated in our study. We selected 30 common product categories for testing, which varied on their perceived hedonic and utilitarian dimensions (Batra & Ahtola, 1991; Dhar & Wertenbroch, 2000) and their degree of public versus private consumption (Ratner & Kahn, 2002), as confirmed by pretests. For each category we selected a pair of products that looked almost identical in terms of design except for the contours of the product, which were either curved or angular (see Figure 7.1 for sample stimuli).

Each participant evaluated a selection of six products, either angular or curved, representing six categories on attitude (3 items; like/dislike, good/bad, would buy/not buy), hedonic attributes (4 items; fun/not, exciting/not, delightful/not, enjoyable/not), utilitarian or functional attributes (4 items; effective/not, helpful/not, functional/not, practical/not), and involvement with the product category (3 items; adapted from Zaichkowsky, 1994).

Apart from demographics like age and gender, we included specific individual factors that could impact curvature preferences, as have been identified in prior literature. These items, shown in Table 7.1, include individual design acumen as measured on the Centrality of Visual Product Aesthetics scale (CVPA; Bloch, Brunel, & Arnold, 2003), consumer need for uniqueness (CNFU; Tian, Bearden, & Hunter, 2001), and individual penchant for thinking, or need for cognition (NFC; Cacioppo, Petty, & Kao, 1984). While it is intuitive to expect that consumers with a higher CVPA or higher CNFU would be more sensitive to aspects of product design, it is possible that those with a higher NFC could tend towards making more cognitive inferences about a product from its shape, and therefore NFC may emerge to be a significant covariate.

Our estimation revealed that overall there was no preference for either angular or curved versions for specific categories, although there were some specific differences by categories. We did not find any gender differences regarding preferences for either curved or angular products. While level of involvement with a category, CVPA, CNFU, and NFC were significant factors that affected people's attitude toward products in general, we did not find that these specifically moderated preference for curvature or angularity. More interestingly, functional perceptions ($\alpha = 0.92$) were higher for several angular products, and

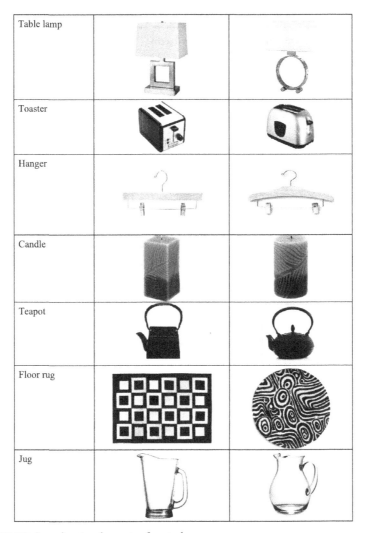

FIGURE 7.1 Sample stimulus pairs for study.

Source: Tanuka Ghoshal.

hedonic perceptions ($\alpha = 0.93$) were higher for curved products across almost all product categories with only a few exceptions (see Table 7.2).

Our results suggest that for products where perceived functionality is more critical than perceived hedonics, it may be advantageous for product contours to be designed angular rather than curved. Conversely, for products where hedonic perceptions are more critical, contours of the product should be curved or rounded, rather than angular. A limitation of our study is that while evaluation of products is typically at a holistic Gestalt level, we isolated only one aspect of

TABLE 7.1 Individual Factor Scales Used for the Study Responses ranged from "Disagree strongly" to "Agree strongly" on a 5-point scale

Centrality of Visual Product Aesthetics Items

A product's design is a source of pleasure for me.

Owning products that have superior designs makes me feel good about myself.

I have a pretty good idea about what makes a product look better than others.

I have the ability to imagine how a product will fit in with designs of things I already own.

When I see a product that has a really great design, I feel a strong urge to buy it.

Consumer Need for Uniqueness Items

I collect unusual products as a way of telling people I'm different.

The products and brands I like best are the ones that express my individuality.

I often look out for new products or brands that will add to my personal uniqueness.

Products don't seem to hold much value for me when they are purchased regularly by everyone.

Need for Cognition items

Thinking is not my idea of fun.

I like tasks that don't require much thinking once I have learned them.

I only think as hard as I have to.

TABLE 7.2 Study Results Comparing Functional and Hedonic Perceptions of Angular Versus Curved Products Across Categories

Functional

Curved rated higher than angular	*Angular rated higher than curved*	*No significant difference*
Floor lamp, table lamp, baking tray, wall clock, ashtray	Teapot, sports bottle, storage jar, wall mirror, toaster, weighing machine, external hard drive, mp3 player, flower vase, storage tray, handbag	Other categories: jug, hanger, candle, floor rug, perfume bottle, camera, wristwatch, compact mirror, guitar, garden pot, dumbbells, chopping board

Hedonic

Curved rated higher than angular	*Angular rated higher than curved*	*No significant difference*
Floor lamp, storage jar, sports bottle, wall mirror, table lamp, candle, external hard drive, cordless phone, baking tray, wall clock, chopping board, wristwatch, handbag, compact mirror, ashtray, garden pot, guitar	Teapot, toaster, dumbbells	Other categories: jug, hanger, floor rug, weighing machine, perfume bottle, mp3 player, camera, flower vase, storage tray

the design—the external shape or contours of the product—deliberately holding other factors constant. Further, we did not control for product category characteristics, other than including a range of products that differ on dimensions like hedonic-utilitarian and public-private consumption. We are therefore unable to comment theoretically on why curvature influences hedonic and functional perceptions for specific product categories, and leave this question for future research.

Conclusions and Limitations

This chapter is meant to provide insights specifically in the context of angularity by providing an integrative review of the rich research on this topic in different areas, along with new insights from our own research. A limitation of our review is that we focused only on primitive associations and general efficacy and hedonic perceptions as impacted by the contours of objects. Notably, we did not review or discuss the literature on size, volume, quantity, or area perceptions as may be affected by the shape of contours, and could potentially impact product evaluations in other important ways. There is a fair amount of research evidencing that shape of a container can impact perceived quantity perceptions and consumption (Raghubir & Greenleaf, 2006; Wansink & van Ittersum, 2005; Yang & Raghubir, 2005); for a brief review of this research please refer to Krider, Raghubir, and Krishna (2001). In our research we had pretested to ensure that pairs of products differing only on angularity of contours were perceived equivalent in volume or area perceptions.

Our research and our review adopt a more general approach to studying angularity and its impact on product evaluations. Because we focus only on one aspect of product design, angularity, it is to be noted that when other aspects like color, etc., are considered in conjunction, an important aspect to take into consideration is congruency between the various aspects, as discussed in the review segment on cross-sensory perceptions. Accounts of processing fluency (Reber, Schwarz, & Winkielman, 2004) suggest that when stimuli are congruent (example, angular shape with more intense color saturation; Becker et al., 2011), processing is more fluent, indicating no threat in the environment, and thereby leading to more favorable evaluations. Thus, all aspects of the design of a product (curvature, color, size, etc.) and other factors like brand name, etc., need to be evaluated for congruency.

Implications for Designers

In general, across research spanning decades, there does seem to emerge a preference for curved products, which appears to be more prevalent among women, despite some mixed results. While ease of transportation and storage could be what drives marketers to produce more angular products and packages, perhaps it is time for more product designers to think "outside the box." However, this is by no means a universal recommendation for all kinds of products, as we do see differences by category, even in our research, for which angular versions connote higher functionality. For products for which hedonic perceptions may be more important than functionality, a curved shape would perhaps be more recommended than angular.

As discussed earlier, all aspects of the design of a product (curvature, color, size, etc.) and other factors like brand name need to be evaluated for congruency, as there is substantial evidence from the literature that cross-sensory semantic transference is common. For a more powerful brand communication, all sensory aspects of the design including curvature need to be in sync with one another. Table 7.3

TABLE 7.3 Summary of Research Findings on Associations With Curvature or Angularity Across Domains; Implications for Product Designers

Domain	Curvature	Key Associations
Empirical aesthetics	Angular	Danger, agitating, hard, and furious
	Curved	Happy, gentle, sad, quiet, and lazy
Evolutionary theory	Angular	Downward-pointing V's associated with angry faces, elicit threat, faster unpleasantness associations Angular shapes associated with sharp harmful objects (e.g., knife)
	Curved	Circles and semi circles associated with happy faces, faster pleasantness associations Baby faces (round) evoke care and protection
Neurobiology	Angular	Greater activation of the amygdala, therefore associated with fear or threat
	Curved	Less activation of the amygdala
Social psychology	Angular	Preferred in individualistic cultures (western countries), by independent self-construal Elicits need to be unique
	Curved	Preferred in collectivistic cultures (eastern countries), by interdependent self-construal Elicits need to be belong
Design, psychology, and marketing	Angular	Preferred by men* Associated with negative affect* Higher functionality perceptions
	Curved	Preferred by women* Associated with positive affect* Higher hedonic perceptions
Cross-sensory perceptions	Angular	Gustatory: Bitter, crunchy/crispy, sourness, citrus Auditory: Non-rounded vowels, lower pitch Proprioceptive: Jagged movements, sharp rhythms, convey movements related to threat
	Curved	Gustatory: Sweet, creamy, smooth Auditory: Rounded vowels, higher pitch Proprioceptive: Circular movements, smooth rhythms, convey relaxed or peaceful movements

*Research shows mixed results

contains a summary of research findings from different domains on curvature or angularity, and associations therein, which we hope will be useful as a quick reference for product designers.

Implications for a Theory of Design

Since we do find differences in terms of preferences and perceptions for curvature or angularity for certain products, an interesting question remains regarding the moderating influence of product categories. One idea would be to measure category characteristics or category personalities (Batra, Lenk, & Wedel, 2010) and see whether congruency between category personality traits and personality traits as suggested by angular or curved contours determine whether angular or curved contours are preferred for different products, or lead to differential perceptions. As of now, we are unable to provide a theoretical basis for whether certain kinds of products should be designed with angular or curved contours, and future research could thus lead to a rich conceptual model for angularity or curvature, as part of the product design schema.

References

Adeli, M., Rouat, J., & Molotchnikoff, S. (2014). Audiovisual correspondence between musical timbre and visual shapes. *Frontiers in Human Neuroscience, 8.*

Amir, O., Biederman, I., & Hayworth, K. J. (2011). The neural basis for shape preferences. *Vision Research, 51*(20), 2198–2206.

Aronoff, J., Woike, B. A., & Hyman, L. M. (1992). Which are the stimuli in facial displays of anger and happiness? Configurational bases of emotion recognition. *Journal of Personality and Social Psychology, 62*(6), 1050.

Bar, M., & Neta, M. (2006). Humans prefer curved visual objects. *Psychological Science, 17*(8), 645–648.

Bar, M., & Neta, M. (2007). Visual elements of subjective preference modulate amygdala activation. *Neuropsychologia, 45*(10), 2191–2200.

Bassili, J. N. (1979). Emotion recognition: The role of facial movement and the relative importance of upper and lower areas of the face. *Journal of Personality and Social Psychology, 37*(11), 2049.

Batra, R., & Ahtola, O. T. (1991). Measuring the hedonic and utilitarian sources of consumer attitudes. *Marketing Letters, 2*(2), 159–170.

Batra, R., Lenk, P., & Wedel, M. (2010). Brand extension strategy planning: Empirical estimation of brand-category personality fit and atypicality. *Journal of Marketing Research, 47*(2), 335–347.

Becker, L., van Rompay, T. J., Schifferstein, H. N., & Galetzka, M. (2011). Tough package, strong taste: The influence of packaging design on taste impressions and product evaluations. *Food Quality and Preference, 22*(1), 17–23.

Bloch, P. H. (1995). Seeking the ideal form: Product design and consumer response. *Journal of Marketing, 59*(3), 16–29.

Bloch, P. H., Brunel, F. F., & Arnold, T. J. (2003). Individual differences in the centrality of visual product aesthetics: concept and measurement. *Journal of Consumer Research, 29*(4), 551–565.

Cacioppo, J. T., Petty, R. E., & Feng Kao, C. (1984). The efficient assessment of need for cognition. *Journal of Personality Assessment, 48*(3), 306–307.

Carbon, C. C. (2010). The cycle of preference: Long-term dynamics of aesthetic appreciation. *Acta Psychologica, 134*(2), 233–244.

Cheskin, L. (1957). *How to predict what people will buy.* New York, NY: Liveright.

Creusen, M. E., & Schoormans, J. P. (2005). The different roles of product appearance in consumer choice. *Journal of Product Innovation Management, 22*(1), 63–81.

Darwin, C. (1998). *The expression of the emotions in man and animals* (3rd ed.). New York, NY: Oxford University Press. (Original work published 1872)

Davis, R. (1961). The fitness of names to drawings. A cross-cultural study in Tanganyika. *British Journal of Psychology, 52*(3), 259–268.

Dazkir, S. S., & Read, M. A. (2011). Furniture forms and their influence on our emotional responses toward interior environments. *Environment and Behavior, 44*(5), 722–732. doi:10.1177/0013916511402063

Dhar, R., & Wertenbroch, K. (2000). Consumer choice between hedonic and utilitarian goods. *Journal of Marketing Research, 37*(1), 60–71.

Ekman, P. (1972). Universals and cultural differences in facial expressions of emotion. In J. Cole (Ed.), *Nebraska symposium on motivation* (Vol. 19, pp. 207–282). Lincoln: University of Nebraska Press.

Elder, R. S., & Krishna, A. (2012). The "visual depiction effect" in advertising: Facilitating embodied mental simulation through product orientation. *Journal of Consumer Research, 38*(6), 988–1003.

Fernay, L., Reby, D., & Ward, J. (2012). Visualized voices: A case study of audio-visual synesthesia. *Neurocase, 18*(1), 50–56.

Franck, K., & Rosen, E. (1949). A projective test of masculinity-femininity. *Journal of Consulting Psychology, 13*(4), 247.

Gallace, A., Boschin, E., & Spence, C. (2011). On the taste of "Bouba" and "Kiki": An exploration of word–food associations in neurologically normal participants. *Cognitive Neuroscience, 2*(1), 34–46.

Gordon, K. (1909). *Esthetics.* New York, NY: Henry Holt.

Gorn, G. J., Jiang, Y., & Johar, G. V. (2008). Babyfaces, trait inferences, and company evaluations in a public relations crisis. *Journal of Consumer Research, 35*(1), 36–49.

Greenwald, A. G., McGhee, D. E., & Schwartz, J. L. (1998). Measuring individual differences in implicit cognition: The implicit association test. *Journal of Personality and Social Psychology, 74*(6), 1464.

Guthrie, G., & Wiener, M. (1966). Subliminal perception or perception of partial cue with pictorial stimuli. *Journal of Personality and Social Psychology, 3*(6), 619.

Hansen, C. H., & Hansen, R. D. (1988). Finding the face in the crowd: An anger superiority effect. *Journal of Personality and Social Psychology, 54*(6), 917.

Henderson, P. W., Cote, J. A., Leong, S. M., & Schmitt, B. (2003). Building strong brands in Asia: Selecting the visual components of image to maximize brand strength. *International Journal of Research in Marketing, 20*(4), 297–313.

Hertenstein, J. H., Platt, M. B., & Veryzer, R. W. (2005). The impact of industrial design effectiveness on corporate financial performance. *Journal of Product Innovation Management, 22*(1), 3–21.

Izard, C. E. (1977). *Human emotions.* New York, NY: Plenum Press.

Jadva, V., Hines, M., & Golombok, S. (2010). Infants' preferences for toys, colors, and shapes: Sex differences and similarities. *Archives of Sexual Behavior, 39*(6), 1261–1273.

Koch, S. C. (2014). Rhythm is it: Effects of dynamic body feedback on affect, attitudes and cognition. *Psychology for Clinical Settings, 5*, 537.

Kohler, W. (1929). *Gestalt psychology.* New York, NY: Liveright.

Kovic, V., Plunkett, K., & Westermann, G. (2010). The shape of words in the brain. *Cognition, 114*(1), 19–28.

Krider, R. E., Raghubir, P., & Krishna, A. (2001). Pizzas: π or square? Psychophysical biases in area comparisons. *Marketing Science, 20*(4), 405–425.

Landwehr, J. R., Labroo, A. A., & Herrmann, A. (2011). Gut liking for the ordinary: Incorporating design fluency improves automobile sales forecasts. *Marketing Science, 30*(3), 416–429.

Larson, C. L., Aronoff, J., Sarinopoulos, I. C., & Zhu, D. C. (2009). Recognizing threat: A simple geometric shape activates neural circuitry for threat detection. *Journal of Cognitive Neuroscience, 21*(8), 1523–1535.

Larson, C. L., Aronoff, J., & Stearns, J. J. (2007). The shape of threat: Simple geometric forms evoke rapid and sustained capture of attention. *Emotion, 7*(3), 526.

Larson, C. L., Aronoff, J., & Steuer, E. L. (2012). Simple geometric shapes are implicitly associated with affective value. *Motivation and Emotion, 36*(3), 404–413.

Leder, H., & Carbon, C. C. (2005). Dimensions in appreciation of car interior design. *Applied Cognitive Psychology, 19*(5), 603–618.

Leder, H., Tinio, P. P., Fuchs, I. M., & Bohrn, I. (2010). When attractiveness demands longer looks: The effects of situation and gender. *Quarterly Journal of Experimental Psychology, 63*(9), 1858–1871.

LoBue, V., & Larson, C. L. (2010). What makes an angry face look so . . . angry? Examining visual attention to the shape of threat in children and adults. *Visual Cognition, 18*(8), 1165–1178.

Lundholm, H. (1921). The affective tone of lines: Experimental researches. *Psychological Review, 28*(1), 43.

Maimaran, M., & Wheeler, S. C. (2008). Circles, squares, and choice: The effect of shape arrays on uniqueness and variety seeking. *Journal of Marketing Research, 45*(6), 731–740.

Maurer, D., Pathman, T., & Mondloch, C. J. (2006). The shape of boubas: Sound–shape correspondences in toddlers and adults. *Developmental Science, 9*(3), 316–322.

Melara, R. D., & O'Brien, T. P. (1987). Interaction between synesthetically corresponding dimensions. *Journal of Experimental Psychology: General, 116*(4), 323.

Munroe, R. H., Munroe, R. L., & Lansky, L. M. (1976). A sex difference in shape preference. *Journal of Social Psychology, 98*(1), 139–140.

Ngo, M. K., Misra, R., & Spence, C. (2011). Assessing the shapes and speech sounds that people associate with chocolate samples varying in cocoa content. *Food Quality and Preference, 22*(6), 567–572.

Papanek, V. J. (1995). *The green imperative: Natural design for the real world.* New York, NY: Thames and Hudson.

Parise, C. V., & Spence, C. (2012). Audiovisual crossmodal correspondences and sound symbolism: A study using the implicit association test. *Experimental Brain Research, 220*(3–4), 319–333.

Paton, J. J., Belova, M. A., Morrison, S. E., & Salzman, C. D. (2006). The primate amygdala represents the positive and negative value of visual stimuli during learning. *Nature, 439*(7078), 865–870.

Poffenberger, A. T., & Barrows, B. E. (1924). The feeling value of lines. *Journal of Applied Psychology, 8*(2), 187.

Raghubir, P., & Greenleaf, E. A. (2006). Ratios in proportion: What should the shape of the package be? *Journal of Marketing, 70*(2), 95–107.

Ramachandran, V. S., & Hubbard, E. M. (2001). Synaesthesia—a window into perception, thought and language. *Journal of Consciousness Studies, 8*(12), 3–34.

Ratner, R. K., & Kahn, B. E. (2002). The impact of private versus public consumption on variety-seeking behavior. *Journal of Consumer Research, 29*(2), 246–257.

Reber, R., Schwarz, N., & Winkielman, P. (2004). Processing fluency and aesthetic pleasure: Is beauty in the perceiver's processing experience? *Personality and Social Psychology Review, 8*(4), 364–382.

Schmitt, B., & Simonson, A. (1997). *Marketing aesthetics: The strategic management of brands, identity, and image.* New York, NY: Free Press.

Silvia, P. J., & Barona, C. M. (2009). Do people prefer curved objects? Angularity, expertise, and aesthetic preference. *Empirical Studies of the Arts, 27*(1), 25–42.

Spence, C. (2012). Managing sensory expectations concerning products and brands: Capitalizing on the potential of sound and shape symbolism. *Journal of Consumer Psychology, 22*(1), 37–54.

Spence, C., & Ngo, M. (2012). Capitalizing on shape symbolism in the food and beverage sector. *Flavour, 1*, 12.

Tajfel, H., & Turner, J. C. (1986). The social identity theory of intergroup behavior. *Psychology of intergroup relations* (pp. 7–24). Chicago, IL: Nelson Hall.

Tian, K. T., Bearden, W. O., & Hunter, G. L. (2001). Consumers' need for uniqueness: Scale development and validation. *Journal of Consumer Research, 28*(1), 50–66.

Tzeng, O.C.S., Trung, N. T., & Rieber, R. W. (1990). Crosscultural comparisons on psychosemantics of icons and graphics. *International Journal of Psychology, 25*, 77–97.

Wansink, B., & van Ittersum, K. (2005). Shape of glass and amount of alcohol poured: Comparative study of effect of practice and concentration. *BMJ, 331*(7531), 1512–1514.

Westerman, S. J., Gardner, P. H., Sutherland, E. J., White, T., Jordan, K., Watts, D., & Wells, S. (2012). Product design: Preference for rounded versus angular design elements. *Psychology & Marketing, 29*(8), 595–605.

Yang, S., & Raghubir, P. (2005). Can bottles speak volumes? The effect of package shape on how much to buy. *Journal of Retailing, 81*(4), 269–281.

Zaichkowsky, J. L. (1994). The personal involvement inventory: Reduction, revision, and application to advertising. *Journal of Advertising, 23*(4), 59–70.

Zhang, Y., Feick, L., & Price, L. J. (2006). The impact of self-construal on aesthetic preference for angular versus rounded shapes. *Personality and Social Psychology Bulletin, 32*(6), 794–805.

Zhu, R. J., & Argo, J. J. (2013). Exploring the impact of various shaped seating arrangements on persuasion. *Journal of Consumer Research, 40*(2), 336–349.

8

BEYOND BEAUTY

Design Symmetry and Brand Personality

Aditi Bajaj and Samuel D. Bond

GEORGIA INSTITUTE OF TECHNOLOGY

Symmetry is a fundamental component of design, and its role in aesthetic experience has long fascinated a range of interdisciplinary researchers. As typically defined, visual symmetry indicates the extent to which an image can be reflected about its central axis (without assuming any specific orientation); as such, symmetry in its extreme form is represented by a "mirror image." A broad and well-replicated finding is the tendency for observers to prefer symmetric stimuli over asymmetric stimuli (Arnheim, 1974; Birkhoff, 1933; Gombrich, 1984; Humphrey, 1997), and several explanations have been advanced for this finding.

Although research on visual design in marketing is a growing area, the majority of existing work has focused on the antecedents and consequences of valenced aesthetic response. Among other findings, positive aesthetic response has been associated with an immediate desire to own a product (Norman, 2004), and higher willingness to pay for it (Bloch, Brunel, & Arnold, 2003). While acknowledging the importance of such research, we believe that visual design elements such as symmetry are worthy of attention for reasons that go beyond aesthetics. For marketers, the goal of design and visual branding is not only to engender favorable response, but also to enhance specific brand associations. Therefore, our research moves beyond aesthetic response to examine the effects of visual design on consumer judgments and behaviors towards the brand.

Building on recent scholarship into the use of visual elements to communicate brand associations (Henderson & Cote, 1998; Henderson, Giese, & Cote, 2004; Orth & Malkewitz, 2008), and also on the phenomenon of "spillover effects" (e.g., Hagtvedt & Patrick, 2008), we assert that salient characteristics of visual brand elements are often assimilated into impressions regarding the brand itself. Specifically, we argue that the presence or absence of symmetry in visual brand elements, such as logos and promotional materials, is often assimilated into impressions regarding brand personality. Our approach is consistent with Keller and Lehmann (2006), who note that logos and symbols (Nike's swoosh and McDonald's golden arches), packaging (Coke's contoured bottle), and slogans (BMW's "Ultimate Driving Machine") play an important role in communicating brand personality.

To establish a framework for our predictions, we draw on Aaker's (1997) five-factor model of brand personality (*sincerity, competence, excitement, ruggedness,* and *sophistication*). We propose two complementary hypotheses relating visual symmetry to distinct personality perceptions. Our first prediction is that brands positioned as sophisticated (i.e., luxurious, prestigious, or tasteful) will benefit from identification with symmetric visual elements. Our second prediction is that brands positioned as exciting (i.e., daring, trendy, or up-to-date) will benefit from identification with asymmetric (as opposed to symmetric) visual elements.

Literature Review

Visual Design Symmetry

The perception of symmetry is a fundamental and ever-present component of human visual processing. Prior research has established that perceivers are able to detect symmetry with little or no effort, across a vast range of stimuli and viewing conditions (Barlow & Reeves, 1979; Julesz, 1971). As a topic of inquiry, the notion of symmetry has fascinated artists and philosophers since the ancient Greeks. Within academic research, symmetry has been studied not only by scholars in aesthetics and psychology but in such diverse areas as mathematics, biology, history, religion, and culture. In the field of consumer research, however, symmetry remains largely understudied.

Definition. Formally, symmetry is defined as self-similarity under a class of transformations such as reflections, rotations, and translations (Wagemans, 1997). In the present research, we restrict our focus to mirror symmetry, or bilateral symmetry, which has been studied extensively in art and is considered the most rapidly detected form of symmetry (Mach, 1893/1986; Palmer & Hemenway, 1978; Rock & Leaman, 1963; Royer, 1981). Mirror Symmetry arises when an object is reflected around the central axis, giving rise to two matching halves. From a strict mathematical point of view, the expression "more or less symmetric" does not have much meaning: a figure is either symmetric or asymmetric. On the other hand, as far as human perception and judgment are concerned, symmetry can be viewed by as a continuous rather than discrete measure. Motivated by this logic, we manipulate symmetry in our lab experiments based on how it is perceived, and not based on any strict mathematical definition. It is important to note that symmetry is distinct from the more abstract concept of balance, which captures the extent to which offsetting figural elements have equal subjective visual weight. For example, a prominent face may be balanced by a distant horizon on the other side of the composition (Arnheim, 1974).

Related Research. The vast majority of research on symmetry in in psychology and sensory marketing has focused on its relationship to affective response. In particular, robust evidence now exists that symmetric stimuli generate a positive aesthetic response and are preferred to asymmetric stimuli (Arnheim, 1974; Berlyne, 1971; Birkhoff, 1933; Fechner, 1876; Pashler, 1990; Pomerantz, 1977; Reber, Schwarz, & Winkielman, 2004). Several explanations have been advanced and tested for this seemingly innate preference for symmetry (e.g., Etcoff, 1999; Pinker, 1997). Evolutionary psychologists claim that symmetry is a reliable indicator of the genetic quality of potential mates, and thus preference for symmetry can be explained as a consequence of selective adaptation (Thornhill & Gangestad, 1993). However, symmetric patterns are preferred even in situations serving no biologically relevant function, and this is true for both human and animal perceivers (e.g., Humphrey, 1997; Rensch, 1957). Another argument, advanced by researchers in psychology and perception, relies on the notion that symmetric stimuli contain less information than asymmetric stimuli, and are therefore easier to process (Garner, 1970). Symmetric stimuli have less informational content than asymmetric stimuli due to the redundancy in their features i.e. one half looks exactly like the other half, so it is redundant in terms of its information content. This redundancy allows greater ease in processing of symmetric stimuli, giving rise to a subjective sense of fluency and a positive aesthetic experience on the part of perceivers (Reber et al., 2004).

In consumer research, symmetry has been investigated primarily in the realm of visual brand elements, such as logos and typefaces. Although the number of relevant studies is small, they have generally shown symmetry in brand elements to produce positive consumer response. For example, Henderson and Cote (1998) demonstrated that affinity for brand logos was positively associated with the design property of harmony, comprised of symmetry and balance. In their research on the design of typefaces such as natural fonts, Henderson, Giese, and Cote (2004), expanded on this definition of harmony and showed that it increased observer impressions such as pleasantness, and reassurance, but decreased impressions such as engagement, and prominence. However, to date, very little research has examined systematically the relationship between symmetry of visual brand elements, and brand personality perceptions (Orth & Malkewitz, 2008; Raffelt, Schmitt, & Meyer, 2013).

Brand Personality

Supplementing existing research on direct affective responses to symmetry, we believe that visual symmetry plays a more subtle role by conveying information about the personality of a brand. A strong brand personality is characterized by favorable, strong, and unique associations in consumers' mental representations of a brand. The advantages of a strong brand personality are well established: compared to other brands, those with strong personalities benefit from greater differentiation, enhance consumer preference, and stronger consumer-brand relationships (Aaker, 1997; Ahluwalia et al., 2000; Fournier, 1998; Keller 1993).

To capture possible effects of symmetry on brand personality, we draw on Aaker's (1997) seminal five-factor model. In order to identify the core factors which capture the human characteristics attributed to brands, Aaker (1997) asked respondents to rate 40 brands on 114 personality traits. A factor analysis of respondent ratings resulted in five significant factors: "sincerity," "excitement," "competence," "sophistication," and "ruggedness." Subsequent investigations by other researchers have confirmed the number and nature of these dimensions, and the 5-factor model has been shown to be generalizable across product categories and cultures (Sweeney & Brandon, 2006).

A number of prominent investigations by consumer researchers examining the process by which brand personality show that people observe brand behaviors and make inferences about underlying personality in the same way that observers attribute personality characteristics to people during everyday interactions (Srull & Wyer, 1989). Under this conceptualization, marketers are able to shape consumer perceptions of brand personality by "transferring cultural meaning" in various ways: e.g., by utilizing communications to associate the brand with an endorser or setting that already possesses the desired personality or meaning (McCracken, 1986). Our research provides further evidence of this transference-of-meaning by showing how personality perceptions associated with an image itself are transferred to the brand.

Symmetry and Arousal

The first of our predictions is that low levels of symmetry (i.e., asymmetry) in the design of visual brand elements leads to perceptions of brand excitement. The second of our two predictions is that high levels of symmetry in the design of visual brand elements leads to perceptions of brand sophistication. Further, we argue that arousal is the primary psychological mechanism driving both effects.

As traditionally defined (Pribram & McGuinness, 1975), arousal occurs when a change in sensory input produces a measurable increment to physiological response (e.g., galvanic skin response) or behavioral response (e.g., frequency of a locomotor activity). In the present research, we focus instead on subjective arousal, defined as the subjective experience of energy mobilization (Mehrabian & Russell, 1974; Russell & Barrett, 1999). Subjective measures of arousal have the advantage of being non-invasive and have been shown to correlate well with physiological measures (e.g., Chartrand, Van Baaren, & Bargh, 2006; Husain, Thompson, & Schellenberg, 2002).

It is generally accepted that asymmetry in a visual stimulus produces high arousal, and conversely, symmetric stimuli should be expected to evoke low arousal or calmness. In a repetitive example, Krupinski and Locher (1988) manipulated the symmetry contained in various examples of non-representational compositions, then asked respondents to judge the aesthetic potential of each composition while measuring their skin conductance. Findings showed that the less complex, symmetric compositions produced less arousal due to the reduced number and variety of unique elements. Using a different approach, Locher and Nodine (1989) recorded eye fixation patterns as participants rated a series of symmetrical and asymmetric paintings. Results revealed that the area of visual exploration was greater for the asymmetrical paintings. Several explanations have been advanced for the link between symmetry and arousal. One oft-cited explanation, is that asymmetry in a stimulus is associated with increased visual complexity which elicits a high uncertainty about the stimulus in the perceiver, leading to a sharp elevation in arousal (Berlyne, 1971).

Consistent with the notion that asymmetric stimuli evoke elevated arousal in perceivers, symmetric stimuli should be expected to evoke low arousal or calmness. Writings dating to classical times have also recognized that symmetry represents harmony, calmness, and stability. In fact, the Roman architect Vitruvius defined symmetry as "the appropriate harmony arising out of the details of the work itself: the correspondence of each given detail to the form of the design as a whole" (Vitruvius, 1970).

Arousal Attribution and Perceptual Spillover

Our research assumes that the high (low) arousal experienced by the perceiver of an asymmetric (symmetric) image is attributed by the perceiver to the image itself. This assumption is based on evidence from prior research most notably that regarding "feelings-as-information," which has shown that contextually induced affective and cognitive responses are treated as relevant input in subsequent target judgments (Schwarz & Clore, 1983). More recently, research by Meyers-Levy, Zhu and Jiang (2010) have shown that bodily sensations influence assessments of a target product viewed simultaneously. In addition, we assume that the high (low) arousal attributed to asymmetric (symmetric) designs "spills-over," or translates onto the perception of the brand itself. This assumption is consistent with recent evidence for the art-infusion phenomenon (Hagtvedt & Patrick, 2008). Work on art-infusion shows that when a product is associated with a work of art, perceptions of luxury evoked by the art are incorporated into the consumer assessments of the product itself.

While the link between arousal and perceptions of brand excitement is intuitive, the link between calmness and brand sophistication is less clear. However, evidence for such a link is apparent in both the brand personality literature and real-world advertisements. Concerning the former, the specific trait "smooth" (a synonym for "calm") is a component of the sophisticated personality dimension within Aaker's (1997) brand personality framework. Concerning the latter, advertisements in luxury-goods categories often adopt a classical style that is characterized by a high degree of symmetry (Messaris, 1997). Art historians associate the classical style with the Greek and Roman periods, the Renaissance, and the Neo-classical era, all of which were characterized by calmness, reason, order, and idealism (Kleiner & Mamiya, 2006). Given that these periods were also characterized by the consolidation of wealth and power (Dressler & Robbins, 1975), it is hardly surprising to see the classical style adopted by purveyors of luxury good themselves associated with exclusion and attainment.

Based on the above, our primary hypothesis can be summarized as follows:

> H1: Symmetry in visual brand elements is negatively (positively) associated with consumer perceptions of brand excitement (sophistication).

Overview of Experiments

We conducted three laboratory experiments to investigate how symmetry in visual design affects consumer perceptions of brand personality. Study 1 tested the proposed relationship between asymmetry (symmetry) and brand excitement (sophistication), by asking participants to choose between promotional materials that varied in symmetry. Study 2 replicated the basic effect using logo designs. Study 3 utilized a more open-ended experimental procedure, in which participants were asked to draw their own logos for exciting and sophisticated brands.

Study 1

Our first study involved a scenario in which participants were acting as brand managers involved in the selection of communication materials for the firm: 118 undergraduates (42% female) from a North American university participated for course credit. The study utilized a within-subjects design in which participants were asked to choose artwork for use by two brands: one positioned as sophisticated and the other positioned as exciting.

Target stimuli for the study consisted of 14 pairs of artwork. The artwork was selected to ensure that the key distinction in each pair was the level of bilateral symmetry (i.e., each pair contained one symmetric artwork and one asymmetric artwork). Symmetric items were high in symmetry (about the y-axis), while asymmetric artwork had little or no symmetry. To construct the stimulus pairs, we consulted online repositories of paintings by Western artists. To ensure consistency and avoid potential confounds, stimuli were selected so that the artwork within each pair was drawn by the same artist, painting in the same style, and using the same predominant colors. For completeness, we included seven pairs of abstract artwork and seven pairs of representational artwork. Broadly speaking, representational art aims to represent actual objects or subjects from reality, whereas abstract art presents objects in way that is different from the way they are viewed in our reality. To disguise the purpose of the study, we also created six filler pairs, comprised of two symmetric or two asymmetric paintings. (Data from fillers was excluded in the analyses.)

On the first screen, participants read the following cover story: "This survey involves an eyewear company, CAHP Limited. The company will soon be introducing two new brands of sunglasses—Audax and Elegans. CAHP is constantly evolving its portfolio of brands, and the launch of Audax and Elegans is aimed at expanding its customer base further. The goal of this survey is to select the promotional material that will be used to represent the two brands. On the following screens, you will be shown information describing the positioning of the two brands. Afterwards, you will be shown various pairs of artwork, and asked to select the artwork that you think fits best with the brand." We selected the sunglasses category because it allowed for the realistic use of both exciting and sophisticated positioning (a survey of the real-world marketplace revealed that both are common). We used unfamiliar brand names to avoid confounds with brand familiarity or preexisting associations.

The second screen presented a brand positioning statement for the first brand of sunglasses (either exciting or sophisticated, counterbalanced). To induce high situational accessibility of the exciting trait, the brand positioning statements included trait-relevant claims from Aaker's (1997) brand personality scale. Thus, in the exciting condition (Audax), participants read: "Audax is designed to be 'fashion' eyewear. Specifically, the company wants to position Audax as a brand that is exciting, up-to-date, daring, spirited, imaginative, youthful, trendy, and cool. Therefore, your goal is to select a logo that will help consumers to perceive the brand as exciting." In the sophisticated condition (Elegans), participants read: "Elegans is designed to be 'luxury' eyewear. Specifically, the company wants to position Elegans as a brand that is sophisticated, glamorous, good looking, premium, upper-class, and prestigious. Therefore, your goal is to select artwork that will help consumers to perceive the brand as sophisticated."

On the following screens, participants viewed 21 pairs (15 target pairs plus 6 fillers), one brand at a time, and made forced-choice decisions about which item in each pair they thought would be most appropriate for use by that brand in its advertising and promotional materials (see Appendix 1 for an example). Participants were instructed to choose based on their natural reaction to the artwork and to not overanalyze the images. In half of the trials, the symmetric artwork appeared on top, and in the other half the symmetric artwork of the pair appeared on the bottom. After completing their choices for the first brand, participants read the positioning statement for the second brand, then again observed the artwork pairs and made their choices. The overall sequence of presentation was counterbalanced between the sophisticated brand and the exciting brand. Next, participants indicated their gender, and rated their interest in the topic of visual art and visual communication on a 7-point scale (1 = not at all interested, 7 = very interested). They also completed an open-ended suspicion probe.

To form the dependent variable in the main analysis, we summed the number of times that symmetric artwork was chosen for each brand. A paired t-test revealed that symmetric artwork was chosen more often for the sophisticated brand

($M = 7.94$) than the exciting brand ($M = 6.64$, $t(118) = -4.264$, $p < 0.01$). Notably, the observed effect of positioning was robust to both representational artwork ($M = 4.03$ vs. 3.31) and abstract artwork ($M = 3.91$ vs. 3.33). In sum, results of the initial study provided initial support for our hypothesis that asymmetry (symmetry) in visual brand elements will strengthen perceptions of a brand as exciting (sophisticated).

Study 2

In our second study, we conducted a replication and extension of Study 1 with one fundamental change: the target stimuli for the study consisted of logos instead of artwork. The key advantage of this approach was that symmetry could be manipulated while holding other design characteristics constant.

Target stimuli included twelve pairs of black and white logos. In keeping with scholars such as Henderson and Cote (1998), we use the term "logo" to refer to the graphic design that a company uses (with or without its name) to identify itself or its products. The logo pairs in the stimulus set were divided into two types: (1) six "basic" logo pairs in which each logo was a geometrical pattern (Jacobsen & Höfel, 2002), and (2) six "realistic" logo pairs which contained more visual detail. The basic logos were created by the researchers by a systematic construction process: elements of the basic logos consisted of simple shapes, and symmetry was operationalized by varying the regularity of these elements around the vertical axis. Care was taken to keep the number of elements in the patterns constant. The realistic logos were created by a professional designer.

One hundred and four undergraduate students (53% females) from a North American university participated in the study for course credit. The procedure was similar to that of Study 1. On the first two screens, participants read the same cover story involving a sunglass manufacturer introducing two new brands. However, instead of artwork, participants were told that they would be choosing between pairs of logos for the two new brands. The brand names (exciting: "Audax"; sophisticated: "Elegans") and positioning statements were the same as those used in the prior study. As before, the order of brands was counterbalanced. After being introduced to the first brand, participants were shown 15 pairs of logos (12 target + 3 filler), one pair at a time, and asked to select from each pair the logo that they considered most appropriate for the brand. Each pair consisted of an asymmetric logo and a symmetric logo; in half of trials, the symmetric logo appeared on the right of the trial pair, and in the other half the symmetric logo appeared on the left. The realistic logo pairs were intermixed with the basic logo pairs.

Finally, participants completed a recognition question to ascertain the success of our manipulation: "Which of the following best describes the positioning of the brand involved in this study? [Exciting, daring, spirited, and imaginative/ Sophisticated, glamorous, and upper-class/ High Quality, and reliable])." They also completed an attention check question which asked them to recall the name of the brand involved in this study.

Analysis of the recognition check measure indicated that three participants could not correctly recall the positioning of the brand, and two participants could not correctly recall the name of the brand. However, no participant failed both checks, so the full sample was retained for the analyses. As the dependent variable in the main analysis, we summed the number of times that symmetric artwork was chosen for each brand. Consistent with our predictions, an independent samples t-test revealed that symmetric logos were chosen more often for the sophisticated brand ($M = 7.21$) than for the exciting brand ($M = 4.25, t(102) = 5.89, p < 0.01$). When the realistic and basic logos were examined separately, results revealed that the effect of symmetry was robust across both types (realistic logos: $M = 3.31$ vs. 2.56; basic logos: $M = 3.90$ vs. 1.69, $ps < .05$). The fact that our prediction was confirmed even for basic logos suggests that it was not simply a result of confounds between symmetry and logo content or other design dimensions.

Study 3

In our third study, we examined the hypothesized relationships in our framework with a substantially different procedure. Our procedure was based on the "method of production" (Fechner 1876), whereby participants create their own aesthetic objects in the laboratory. The primary advantage of the method of production is that it is less likely to be constrained by the experimenter's preconceptions or pre-existing cultural norms. Rather than choosing between competing stimuli, participants in the study were required to manipulate the stimuli themselves by taking part in a "logo design" task. After eliciting a motive to position a brand in a certain way, participants were given the opportunity to draw brand logos for two brands. The dependent measure was the degree of symmetry present in the logos created for each brand. In keeping with our theory and the results of Studies 1–2, we predicted that participant-created logos for sophisticated brands would contain more symmetry than those for exciting brands.

One-hundred and ninety-four students from a North American university participated in the study in exchange for course credit. Participants were seated at individual tables that had a computer and a clipboard with letter size sheets of paper, a pencil, and an eraser. The cover story, which was similar in content to the previous studies, asked participants to design two logos that will be used to represent each of two new brands of sunglasses (Audax and Elegans). Participants were told to draw the two logos using the sheets of paper provided.

Next, participants were given descriptions and positioning statements for the two brands, similar to those in the prior studies, followed by a set of guidelines for drawing logos. The guidelines included a description of what constitutes a log, the different types of logos that exist (font-based, shape-based, etc.), characteristics of a "good" logo (it should be memorable, it should not evoke any negative associations, etc.), and suggested steps for designing logos (which included understanding the personality of the brand and how it is supposed to be perceived). Participants were told that they had to use the pencils and erasers provided. Order was counterbalanced so that half of participants drew the exciting logo (Audax) first and half of participants drew the sophisticated logo (Elegans) first. The design sheets provided a "scratch area" that could be used to sketch different options. Participants were given 10 minutes to draw both logos, and were shown a warning message when 5 minutes had elapsed. Following completion of the drawing task, participants were asked to indicate the extent to which they thought about various aspects of logos during their construction, including representativeness, symmetry, complexity, and proportion (1 = "not important in my design," 7 = "very important in my design"). Next, as an exploratory measure and suspicion probe, they completed an open-ended items asking why they drew the logo that they did.

Seven respondents were excluded from the analyses due to missing data. To form the primary dependent variable, we measured the degree of vertical mirror symmetry present in each of the participant-created logos, as follows. Three independent coders with experience in graphic design assessed each logo, using a 4-point scale (1 = perfectly asymmetrical, 4 = perfectly symmetrical). The coders were instructed to use a mirror image technique, in which an imaginary vertical line was drawn through the middle of each logo, thus dividing the logo into two halves. The coders then compared one half of the logo to the other. A logo was categorized as perfectly symmetrical if one half was the exact mirror image of the other, and a logo was categorized as perfectly asymmetrical if there was no correspondence between the two halves. Disagreements were resolved through discussion.

A paired-samples t-test was conducted to compare the degree of symmetry present in participant-created logos for the two brands. Consistent with our predictions, results indicated that participants drew significantly more symmetrical logos for the sophisticated brand than for the exciting brand ($M = 2.9$ vs. 2.6, $t(179) = -3.926, p < 0.01$). Moreover, results of the follow-up questions revealed a marginally significant interaction effect of self-stated symmetry ($F(1, 179) = 3.2$, $p < 0.07$). Specifically, the difference in symmetry present in the sophisticated vs. exciting logo was greater among participants who stated that they were mindful of symmetry during the construction process.

Implications for Design

Our research offers a number of valuable implications for designers in marketing and related fields. Perhaps most importantly, we demonstrate that the "power of good design" in branding extends beyond simply improving recognition or liking for the brand, but rather can be used to help imbue brands with specifically targeted consumer associations.

Among marketing practitioners, it is generally accepted that they possess deep intuitive understanding of their field, and utilize this understanding to carefully select design elements that elicit desired consumer responses. However, it remains a common belief among laypersons and practitioners alike is that design is an inherently subjective process with limited underlying framework or principles. We believe that our research represents an opportunity to improve the "disconnect" between designers and their clients. Specifically, we offer empirical evidence that can be drawn upon by designers as they explain their choices to audiences lacking training in the field. We look forward to future work addressing this objective.

Finally, for designers involved in brand introductions, brand re-launches, or brand repositioning, our model and findings offer pragmatic implications for determining (a priori) design characteristics that will prove useful in shaping the personality of the brand. The role of symmetry is particularly noteworthy in this regard, as symmetry represents a design characteristic that can be objectively assessed and applied.

Implications for a Theory of Design

The primary goal of the present research has been to provide a theory-based account for the influence of symmetry in visual brand imagery on customer response. Based on an integration of diverse prior literature, we argue that symmetry can play an important role in formulating brand personality perceptions. In particular, we suggest that asymmetry evokes perceptions of brand excitement through high levels of arousal, and symmetry evokes perceptions of brand sophistication through low arousal (calmness). A series of three experimental studies provided initial evidence for these assertions.

Our research contributes broadly to current understanding of the role of visual design in consumer research. First, among the relatively little academic research on visual design in consumer settings, the vast majority has been focused on aesthetic response: i.e., on the characteristics that make a marketing stimulus more attractive or pleasing to the beholder. A common theme across this research has been the value of symmetry for enhancing perceptions of beauty, perfection, etc. Our work is among the first to move beyond the investigation beyond aesthetics and toward an understanding of the specific meanings conveyed by specific design properties.

More broadly, our exploration contributes to the large and growing stream of work on brand personality. In particular, prior research has emphasized the important role of design in shaping brand personality impressions (Johar, Sengupta, & Aaker, 2005). Supplementing this research, our work is the first to demonstrate the influence of a specific and important design characteristic (symmetry) on specific consumer inferences regarding brand personality.

A growing body of research has explored the extent to which consumer perceptions of design are incorporated into judgments regarding products and brands themselves. In particular, recent work on "spill-over effects" has demonstrated that perceptions evoked by product- or brand-related visual elements (e.g., the presence of "high" or "low" art on product packaging) can be assimilated into perceptions of product quality and related judgments (Hagtvedt & Patrick, 2008). Our research extends this line of argumentation to a more nuanced process of consumer inference. Under our approach, salient aspects of visual design, such as symmetry, induce specific and predictable perceptions, which then presumably spill over to perceptions of the associated product. These spillovers are not limited to general connotations such as quality, but may also involve such specific connotations such as excitement or sophistication.

References

Aaker, J. L. (1997). Dimensions of brand personality. *Journal of Marketing Research, 34*, 347–356.

Ahluwalia, R., Burnkrant, R. E., & Unnava, H. R. (2000). Consumer response to negative publicity: The moderating role of commitment. *Journal of Marketing Research, 37*, 203–214.

Arnheim, R. (1974). *Art and visual perception*. Berkeley: University of California Press.

Barlow, H. B., & Reeves, B. C. (1979). The versatility and absolute efficiency of detecting mirror symmetry in random dot displays. *Vision Research, 19*, 783–793.

Berlyne, D. E. (1971). *Aesthetics and psychobiology*. New York, NY: Appleton-Century-Crofts.

Birkhoff, G. (1933). *Aesthetic measure*. Cambridge, MA: Harvard University Press.

Bloch, P. H., Brunel, F. F., & Arnold, T. J. (2003). Individual differences in the centrality of visual product aesthetics: Concept and measurement. *Journal of Consumer Research, 29*(4), 551–565.

Chartrand, T. L., Van Baaren, R. B., & Bargh, J. A. (2006). Linking automatic evaluations to emotion and information processing style: Consequences for experienced affect, impression formation and stereotyping. *Journal of Experimental Psychology: General, 135*, 70–77.

Dressler, W., & Robbins, M. (1975). Art styles, social stratification, and cognition: An analysis of Greek vase painting. *American Ethnologist, 2*, 427–434.

Etcoff, N. (1999). *Survival of the prettiest: The science of beauty*. New York, NY: Anchor Books/Doubleday.

Fechner, G. T. (1876). *Vorschule der aesthetik*. Leipzig: Breitkopf and Haertel.

Fournier, S. (1998). Consumers and their brands: Developing relationship theory in consumer research. *Journal of Consumer Research, 24*(4), 343–373.

Garner, W. R. (1970). Good patterns have few alternatives. *American Scientist, 58*, 34–42.

Gombrich, E. H. (1984). *A sense of order* (2nd ed.). London: Phaidon.

Hagtvedt, H., & Patrick, V. (2008). Art infusion: The influence of visual art on the perception and evaluation of consumer products. *Journal of Marketing Research, 40*, 379–389.

Henderson, P. W., & Cote, J. A. (1998). Guidelines for selecting or modifying logos. *Journal of Marketing, 62*, 14–30.

Henderson, P. W., Giese, J. L., & Cote, J. A. (2004). Impression management using typeface design. *Journal of Marketing, 68*(October), 60–72.

Humphrey, D. (1997). Preferences in symmetries and symmetries in drawings: Asymmetries between ages and sexes. *Empirical Studies of the Arts, 15*, 41–60.

Husain, G., Thompson, W. F., & Schellenberg, E. G. (2002). Effects of musical tempo and mode on arousal, mood, and spatial abilities. *Music Perception, 20*, 151–171.

Jacobsen, T., & Höfel, L. (2002). Aesthetic judgments of novel graphic patterns: Analyses of individual judgments. *Perceptual and Motor Skills, 95,* 755–766.

Johar, V. G., Sengupta, J., & Aaker, J. L. (2005). Two roads to updating brand personality impressions: Trait versus evaluative inferencing. *Journal of Marketing Research, 72*(November), 458–469.

Julesz, B. (1971). *Foundations of cyclopean perception.* Chicago, IL: University of Chicago Press.

Keller, K. L. (1993). Conceptualizing, managing and measuring consumer-based brand equity. *Journal of Marketing, 57,* 1–22.

Keller, K. L., & Lehmann, D. R. (2006). Brands and branding: research findings and future priorities. *Marketing Science, 25*(6), 740–759.

Kleiner, F. S., & Mamiya, C. J. (2006). *Gardner's art through the ages: Western perspective.* Belmont, CA: Thomson Wadsworth.

Krupinski, E., & Locher, P. (1988). Skin conductance and aesthetic evaluative responses to nonrepresentational works of art varying in symmetry. *Bulletin of the Psychonomic Society, 26,* 355–358.

Locher, P., & Nodine, C. (1989). The perceptual value of symmetry. *Computers & Mathematics With Applications, 17*(4), 475–484.

Mach, E. (1986). *On symmetry.* In *Popular scientific lectures.* LaSalle, IL: Open Court. (Original work published 1893)

McCracken, G. (1986). Culture and consumption: A theoretical account of the structure and movement of the cultural meaning of consumer goods. *Journal of Consumer Research, 13*(June), 71–84.

Mehrabian, A., & Russell, J. A. (1974). *An approach to environmental psychology.* Cambridge, MA: MIT Press.

Messaris, P. (1997). *Visual persuasion: The role of images in advertising.* Thousand Oaks, CA: SAGE.

Meyers-Levy, J., Zhu, R., & Jiang L. (2010). Context effects from bodily sensations: Examining bodily sensations induced by flooring and the moderating role of product viewing distance. *Journal of Consumer Research, 37,* 1–14.

Norman, D. A. (2004). *Emotional design: Why we love (or hate) everyday things.* New York, NY: Basic Books.

Orth, U. R., & Malkewitz, K. (2008). Holistic package design and consumer brand impressions. *Journal of Marketing, 72*(May), 64–81.

Palmer, S. E., & Hemenway, K. (1978). Orientation and symmetry: Effects of multiple, rotational, and near symmetries. *JEP:HPP, 4,* 691–702.

Pashler, H. (1990). Coordinate frame for symmetry detection and object recognition. *Journal of Experimental Psychology: Human Perception and Performance, 16*(1), 150–163.

Pinker, S. (1997). *How the mind works.* New York, NY: Norton.

Pomerantz, J. R. (1977). Pattern goodness and speed of encoding. *Memory and Cognition, 5,* 235–241.

Pribram, K., & McGuinness, D. (1975). Arousal, activation and effort in the control of attention. *Psychological Review, 82,* 116–149.

Raffelt, U., Schmitt, B., & Meyer A. (2013). Marketing function and form: How functionalist and experiential architectures affect corporate brand personality. *International Journal of Research in Marketing, 30,* 201–210.

Reber, R., Schwarz, N., & Winkielman, P. (2004). Processing fluency and aesthetic pleasure: Is beauty in the perceiver's processing experience? *Personality & Social Psychology Review, 8*(4), 364–382.

Rensch, B. (1957). Aesthetische Faktoren bei Farb- und Formbevorzugungen von Affen [Aesthetic factors in color and form preferences in monkeys] & [The effects of aesthetic factors in vertebrates]. *Zeitschrift für Tierpsychologie, 14*, 71–99.

Rock, I., & Leaman, R. (1963). An experimental analysis of visual symmetry. *Acta Psychologica, 21*, 171–183.

Royer, F. L. (1981). Detection of symmetry. *JEP:HPP, 7*(6), 1186–1210.

Russell, J. A., & Barrett, L. F. (1999). Core affect, prototypical emotional episodes, and other things called emotion: Dissecting the elephant. *Journal of Personality and Social Psychology, 76*, 805–819.

Schwarz, N., & Clore, G. L. (1983). Mood, misattribution, and judgments of well-being: Informative and directive functions of affective states. *Journal of Personality and Social Psychology, 45*, 513–523.

Srull, T. K., & Wyer, R. S. (1989). Person memory and judgment. *Psychological Review, 96*(1), 58–83.

Sweeney, J. C., & Brandon, C. (2006). Band personality: Exploring the potential to move from factor analytical to circumplex models. *Psychology and Marketing, 23*, 639–663.

Thornhill, R., & Gangestad, S. W. (1993). Human facial beauty: Averageness, symmetry, and parasite resistance. *Human Nature, 4*, 237–269.

Vitruvius. (1970). *On architecture* (F. Granger, Trans.). Cambridge, MA: Harvard University Press. (Originally 1st century BC)

Wagemans, J. (1997). Characteristics and models of human symmetry detection. *Trends in Cognitive Sciences, 1*(9), 346–352.

9

HOW TO USE VISUAL DESIGN TO BOOST BRAND EQUITY

*Antonios Stamatogiannakis
and Jonathan Luffarelli*

IE UNIVERSITY

Haiyang Yang

JOHNS HOPKINS UNIVERSITY

Since the late 1800s, the development of strong brands has been a major objective for organizations (Low & Fullerton, 1994). Having a strong brand offers many competitive advantages such as greater customer loyalty, lower price sensitivity, higher purchase intentions, and more favorable word-of-mouth. These competitive advantages, in turn, can help firms achieve superior economic performances. Put simply, a strong brand provides brand equity (i.e., tangible and intangible value) to organizations.

Brand equity can be created in different ways (Boulding, Lee, & Staelin, 1994; Yoo, Donthu, & Lee, 2000), such as through advertising (Batra, Lehmann, Burke, & Pae, 1995; Chaudhuri, 2002) or sales promotions (Gupta, 1988; Srinivasan & Anderson, 1998). It can also be created through the visual design of elements such as products, packages, and logos (Crilly, Moultrie, & Clarkson, 2004; Hertenstein, Platt, & Veryzer, 2005; Landwehr, McGill, & Herrmann, 2011; Reimann, Zaichkowsky, Neuhaus, Bender, & Weber, 2010; Yamamoto & Lambert, 1994). In fact, visually appealing product designs are perceived to be of higher quality (Page & Herr, 2002) and are more likely to get noticed and chosen (Bloch, 1995; Hoegg & Alba, 2007).

The visual design of products, packages, and logos is a critical aspect of brand-building. Yet, it can involve a substantial amount of resources (e.g., monetary costs associated with designing and implementing the design on all products) and risks (e.g., consumers end up disliking the design). Despite the importance and risks associated with visual design, most marketing managers lack systematic design training and knowledge, and are thus often not closely involved in the design of products, packages, and logos. In a vicious circle, the low involvement of marketing managers in design processes further hampers their abilities to develop thorough understanding of how visual designs can affect consumer behavior and the "bottom-line."

This chapter examines how marketing managers and designers may use product, package, and logo visual design to increase brand equity. We first review the marketing literature and discuss how visual design elements and principles (i.e., rules to arrange and organize the design elements) can influence brand equity. We then draw attention to the often overlooked need for aligning the visual design of products, packages, and logos with other brand elements such as brand personalities, concepts, slogans, and names. We argue that the lack of alignment can negatively affect brand equity, even when the design satisfies the known principles of good design. Specifically, we propose and show that despite the ubiquitous evidence for the positive effects of symmetry on individuals' perceptions and preferences (Reber, 2002; Reber, Schwarz, & Winkielman, 2004; Rhodes, Proffitt, Grady, & Sumich, 1998; Wynn, 2002), symmetrical products, packages, and logos can be detrimental to the equity of certain brands.

Visual Design of Products, Packages, and Logos Can Boost Brand Equity

The role of products, packages, and logos in brand-building and equity creation is well-established. For instance, logos can facilitate the communication of brand attributes (Park, Eisingerich, Pol, & Park, 2013), and influence brand recognition, evaluations (Henderson & Cote, 1998; Henderson, Cote, Leong, & Schmitt, 2003; Van der Lans et al., 2009), as well as customers' self-expressive values and purchase intentions (Wilcox, Kim, & Sen, 2009). Similarly, packages are particularly critical in the creation of brand equity. They can help attract customers' attention (Underwood, Klein, & Burke, 2001), affect product categorization and evaluations (Schoormans & Robben, 1997), influence consumers' perceptions (Deng & Kahn, 2009), and strengthen the brand-consumer relationship (Underwood, 2003). Beyond establishing the general relationship between brand visuals and brand equity, research in marketing has also shed important light on the effects of specific design elements and principles. We review these findings in the sections below.

Visual Design Elements and Brand Equity

Much marketing research has focused on how three visual design elements—size, proportion, and shape—affect brand equity.[1] With regards to size, evidence suggests that large (vs. small) package formats generally promote product usage and consumption (Granger & Billson, 1972; Wansink, 1996), even if the opposite may occur with hedonic products (Coelho do Vale, Pieters, & Zeelenberg, 2008; Scott, Nowlis, Mandel, & Morales, 2008).

With regards to proportions, evidence suggests that package and logo proportions between 1:1 and 1:1.732 are most likely to augment brand equity. For instance, Pittard, Ewing, and Jevons (2007) found that consumers prefer logos with proportions equal to 1:1, except when these logos are inspired from natural forms (e.g., flower, wave). In this case, proportions of 1:1.618 (i.e., "the golden ratio") are preferable. Similarly, Raghubir and Greenleaf (2006) found that customer preferences, purchases intentions, and market shares are higher for less frivolous products sold in square-shaped packages (i.e., ratio of 1:1) and higher for more frivolous products sold in packages with width-to-height ratios between 1:1.414 and 1:1.732.

Finally, even if products, packages, and logos come in many different shapes, only roundedness (vs. angularity) and height have received attention from marketing studies. More precisely, research indicates that more (vs. less) elongated package may negatively (vs. positively) affect product consumption (Wansink & Van Ittersum, 2003) and sales volumes (Yang & Raghubir, 2005). Research also indicates that customers have a general preference for rounded (vs. angular) designs (Bar & Neta, 2006). For example, in two experiments, Westerman et al. (2012) manipulated the roundedness and angularity of chocolate boxes and water and bleach bottles. They found that rounded boxes and bottles are associated with higher aesthetic ratings and purchase intentions. However, this general preference for roundedness seems to be moderated by individual differences such as self-construal (Zhang, Feick, & Price, 2006) and brand commitment. For instance, brands with more (vs. less) committed customer bases should use more angular logos (vs. rounded; Walsh, Winterich, & Mittal, 2010, 2011).

Visual Design Principles and Brand Equity

In marketing research, Henderson and Cote (1998) were among the first to provide a typology of design principles. They suggested that three principles are particularly important in eliciting positive customer responses: elaborateness, naturalness, and harmony. Using, 195 relatively unknown logos, they established that more (vs. less) natural and harmonious logos tend to be preferred, perceived as more distinctive, and generate interest. The effect of elaborateness, however, is not monotonic but rather follows an inverted U-shape pattern with low and high level of elaborateness resulting in less positive responses than a moderate level of elaborateness. The importance of these three design principles has been corroborated using data from numerous countries such as Argentina, China, or Australia (Henderson et al., 2003; Van der Lans et al., 2009) and in the contexts of package (Orth, Campana, & Malkewitz, 2010; Orth & Malkewitz, 2008) and typeface (Grohmann, Giese, & Parkman, 2013) design.

Marketing research has also focused on how three other design principles— prototypicality, unity, and complexity—might affect brand equity. Veryzer and Hutchinson (1998) examined prototypicality and unity by manipulating the contours of different products. They found that higher levels of prototypicality and unity are associated with more favorable responses to product designs. Cox and Cox (2002) examined design complexity and found that moderately complex product designs are usually preferred over less and more complex ones. Thus, prototypicality, unity, and complexity seem to boost product attitudes, hence brand equity. Landwehr, Labroo, and Herrmann (2011) present more direct evidence. They examined how design prototypicality and complexity affected sales for 28 car models in the German market. Their results indicate that both principles might independently, but also conjointly, lead to higher sales, with prototypical but complex car models selling the most. Interestingly, the number of exposures to a given design seems to moderate all these relationships. In fact, as the number of exposures increases, individual preferences for a given typical design decrease and preferences for a given atypical design increase (Landwehr, Wentzel, & Herrmann, 2013). Similarly, as the number of exposures increases, individual preferences for a simple design decrease and preferences for a complex design increase (Cox & Cox, 2002). Therefore, typical and simpler (vs. atypical and complex) designs may hurt (vs. boost) brand equity when a given customer is repeatedly exposed to the same product, package, or logo.

The dominant explanation for the positive effects of these design elements is founded on the concept of perceptual fluency (Reber, 2002; Reber, Schwarz, & Winkielman, 2004; Reber, Winkielman, & Schwarz, 1998; Winkielman, Schwarz, Fazendeiro, & Reber, 2003). Designs which are, for instance, typical, natural, or harmonious are easier and faster to process (i.e., perceptually fluent). In turn, designs which are easier and faster to process elicit positive affect. Processing fluency is also facilitated by other design principles such as symmetry. Not surprisingly then, since it makes a design perceptually more fluent and likeable, symmetry is frequently incorporated in the design of many products, packages, and logos.

The Meanings of Visual Design Elements and Principles

Although, as discussed above, the effects of certain design elements and principles are well-documented, few studies have examined the meanings that these specific design elements and principles evoke in customers' minds (Mick, 1986). We know, for instance, that incompleteness can convey the notion of innovativeness (Hagtvedt, 2011), that roundedness can convey the notion of harmony (Zhang, Feick, & Price, 2006), and that dynamic images can convey the notion of movement (Cian, Krishna, & Elder, 2014). We also know, that colors such as white, red, black, and blue are respectively related to the notion of sincerity, excitement, sophistication (Labrecque & Milne, 2012), and relaxation (Gorn, Chattopadhyay, Sengupta, & Tripathi, 2004). Not surprisingly though, the meanings evoked by color hue may vary across cultures (e.g., brown is associated with "formal" in Colombia but "masculine" in Austria; Madden, Hewett, & Roth, 2000). Beyond color hue, color value (i.e., darkness) and chroma (i.e., saturation) can also bring to mind different meanings. For instance, higher levels of color value (i.e., lighter colors) are associated with relaxation, and higher levels of chroma (i.e., more saturated colors) with excitement (Gorn, Chattopadhyay, Yi, & Dahl, 1997; Gorn et al., 2004). Finally, research also shows that typefaces elicit different meanings. For instance, fonts with heavy lines are associated with masculinity (Henderson, Giese, & Cote, 2004) and serif (vs. sans serif) fonts evoke gentleness (vs. roughness) and honesty (dishonesty) (Tantillo, Di Lorenzo-Aiss, & Mathisen, 1995).

Adding to this emerging stream of literature, we conducted two experiments involving more than 400 participants to examine the meanings evoked by asymmetrical and symmetrical brand logos. In particular, we were interested in determining whether symmetrical versus asymmetrical logos are imbued to different degrees with notions reinforcing different brand personalities (Aaker, 1997). For instance, because asymmetry is more arousing (Krupinski & Locher, 1988; Locher & Nodine, 1989) and hence exciting than symmetry, exposures to asymmetrical (vs. symmetrical) shapes and the accompanying experience of excitement may create associations between excitement and asymmetry in long-term memory. Indeed, our results indicate that compared to symmetrical logos, asymmetrical logos are associated in memory with notions related to excitement and (to a much lesser degree) sophistication. Conversely, compared to asymmetrical logos, symmetrical logos are associated with notions related to sincerity, competence, and ruggedness.

Aligning Visual Designs With Other Brand Elements

The meanings of design elements and principles described in the previous section have been typically examined in isolation from other brand elements. Therefore, whether certain design elements and principles may be beneficial for some brands but detrimental for others is unknown. Since a brand is a holistic concept, such alignment sounds like a natural objective. Yet, to-date, only few empirical studies offer insights on how design elements and principles should be aligned with other brand elements. For instance, Bottomley and Doyle (2006b) established that functional colors (e.g., gray, green) are more appropriate for functional products (e.g., car tires, kitchen roll) while sensory colors (e.g., red, yellow) are more appropriate for sensory products (e.g., perfume, chocolates). Childers and Jass (2002) established that consistency between typeface, ad copy, and ad picture increase ad recall. Finally, Bottomley and Doyle (2006a) established that brand choice can be affected by the level of congruity between font and product category.

An interesting question which remains unanswered is whether visual design should be aligned with other brand elements, even if this alignment requires a violation of the aforementioned principles of good design. To answer this question, we conducted one experiment and one field study. Both studies revealed that aligned meanings (vs. unaligned meanings) evoked by certain design elements and principles (in our case, logo asymmetry vs. symmetry) and those evoked by certain brand elements (in our case, brand personality) results in higher brand equity. Specifically, in our experimental study, we found that because asymmetry evokes the notion of excitement, customers have more favorable brand attitudes when a brand with an exciting brand personality uses an asymmetrical (vs. symmetrical) logo. In our field study, we were interested in replicating this effect outside of the laboratory, using well-known brands. For the 100 brands listed on the 2011 Interbrand ranking (e.g., Coca-Cola, Google, Dell), we obtained a well-established measure of brand equity (i.e., BrandAsset Valuator) and a measure of the personality dimension of excitement from the branding consultancy agency Young & Rubicam. These two measures are constructed by surveying approximately 15,000 U.S. consumers. A separate group of U.S. customers evaluated the asymmetry of the logos of these 100 brands. Results show that asymmetrical logos lead to higher brand equity for brands with exciting brand personalities, and to lower brand equity for those with less exciting brand personalities. To sum up, results of both studies support our broader suggestion: The visual design of products, packages, and logos should be consistent with other brand elements to augment brand equity, even if this implies going against principles of good design.

Implications for a Theory of Design

This chapter highlights a need for a comprehensive theory of design in the field of marketing. The literature and the evidence we presented thus far demonstrate that visual design can benefit brand equity in tangible and intangible ways. Well-designed products, packages, and logos can boost brand equity, whereas poorly designed ones can hurt it. More surprisingly, even simple design elements and principles such as shape, proportion, complexity, or symmetry may affect customer responses and firms' financial performances.

While prior research has shed important light on the effects of product, package, and logo design on brand-building, we suggest that a theory of design should go beyond the sensory aspects of design, and deeper than the downstream consequences of design on customers or firm performance. Specifically, it should incorporate formal hypotheses and propositions regarding the meanings conveyed by design elements and principles. Related to this point, we identify two interesting research avenues. First, there is a need for a systematic examination of the meanings conveyed by design elements and principles in the context of marketing. Second, research needs to explore whether and how the meanings elicited by elements and principles which are conjointly used in a design can interact to affect brand equity. For instance, can the meanings elicited by small versus large package shapes interact with the meanings elicited by package symmetry versus asymmetry? Unfortunately, with the exception of a small number of recent studies (Van Rompay & Pruyn, 2011), the marketing literature has typically not examined interactions between design elements and principles. Consequently, questions like the one above remain largely unanswered.

In the field of marketing, we also put forward that a theory of design should thoroughly examine interaction effects between the meanings evoked by visual designs and other brand elements. In this chapter, we proposed that the meanings elicited by visual design and by brand elements should be aligned to maximize brand equity. In line with this argument we briefly presented evidence that brand equity is higher (vs. lower) when the meanings of design elements and principles are aligned with the meanings (vs. not aligned with the meanings) elicited by brand elements. A series of studies indicates that asymmetry consistently evokes the notion of excitement and, as such, the combination of an asymmetrical logo with an exciting brand personality boosts brand equity. It is worth noting that even if we used brand logos as stimuli in our studies, our propositions and findings are equally relevant to all visual aspects of a brand (e.g., product and package design).

Finally and perhaps most importantly, it seems that a theory of design would be better developed as a set of contingencies than as a set of specific guidelines. In other words, there seem to be no such thing as a good or bad design. The effects of identical product, package, and logo designs on brand equity can be moderated by specific individual or contextual conditions; thus, design recommendations should also vary accordingly. Such moderators of the effects of design on brand equity include brand personality, consumer commitment (Walsh, Winterich, & Mittal, 2010, 2011), individuals' visual aesthetic sensitivity (Bloch, Brunel, & Arnold, 2003; Orth, Campana, & Malkewitz, 2010) and the number of exposures to a given design (Cox & Cox, 2002; Landwehr, Wentzel, & Herrmann, 2013). We also make a powerful demonstration of this suggestion by showing that symmetry—a property habitually proposed to characterize good design (Henderson & Cote, 1998; Reber, 2002; Reber, Schwarz, & Winkielman, 2004)—backfires when designing a logo for an exciting brand. In a different study, we also tested whether individual differences and brand personality would jointly moderate the effect of symmetrical versus asymmetrical designs on brand equity. Participants were presented with one of four descriptions of a fictitious brand. The brand had a symmetrical or asymmetrical logo, and was described as having an exciting or sincere brand personality. We measured brand attitudes, as well as individual differences in the extent to which participants tend to associated asymmetry or symmetry with the notion of excitement. The results indicate that the effect of logo visual design (i.e., symmetrical versus asymmetrical) on brand attitudes is influenced by both brand personality and individual differences. Specifically, participants who tend to associate asymmetry with excitement have more favorable attitudes towards an exciting brand with an asymmetrical logo. Conversely, participants who tend to associate symmetry with excitement have more favorable attitudes towards an exciting brand with a symmetrical logo.

Implications for Designers and Marketers

When it comes to the actual practice of design, the most important implication of our study is that designers should develop a global vision and an understanding of the role that their work plays in marketing and branding. To paraphrase a famous quote by David Packard, *design is too important to be left to the designers.* Indeed, even a well-trained designer cannot anticipate the complexities that can come from the specific use of a design. For example, it would be hard for any designer to predict that as our data consistently shows, the use of symmetry—which is very frequent in logo design and usually associated with good design—could predictably backfire for exciting brands. The field study presented in this chapter supports this assertion. Interestingly, data from this study suggests that the logos of brands with exciting personalities tend to be more symmetrical than the logos of brands with other personalities, showing that at least in this context logo design is not well-aligned with brand personality.

If design is too important to be left to designers, it also seems to be too important to be left to marketers, who are often unfamiliar with the positive and negative effects that design can have on their brands. Therefore, a close cooperation between designers and their clients or marketers seems to be necessary to grasp the potential interplay of brand elements with design elements and principles. Such cooperation can be fostered if, for instance, design schools were to include specific concentrations on branding in their curricula, and if business schools were to do the same with theories of design.

To conclude, the evidence we review and present underscores the need for practitioners to identify the unique meanings evoked by the different elements and principles used in their designs. It also underscores the need to understand how the meanings elicited by different design elements can interact, as well as how these meanings reinforce or conflict with other brand elements. More generally, while past research has typically focused on studying each brand element in isolation, this chapter highlights the need for a more holistic understanding of how different brand elements—especially product, package, and logo visual design—can interact to impact brand equity.

Note

1 Of course, visual design of products, packages, and logos is not limited to shape, size, and proportion. However, relatively few marketing studies have explored the effects of other design elements on brand equity (which is our focus here). For instance, while prior research shows that color (Grossman & Wisenblit,1999; Labrecque, Patrick, & Milne, 2013; Singh, 2006) and typeface (Childers & Jass, 2002; Doyle & Bottomley, 2004; Grohmann, 2014; Henderson, Giese, & Cote, 2004) can convey meanings, less is known about the effects of these visual elements on brand equity.

References

Aaker, J. L. (1997). Dimensions of brand personality. *Journal of Marketing Research, 34*(August), 347–356.

Bar, M., & Neta, M. (2006). Humans prefer curved visual objects. *Psychological Science, 17*(August), 645–648.

Batra, R., Lehmann, D. R., Burke, J., & Pae, J. H. (1995). When does advertising have an impact? A study of tracking data. *Journal of Advertising Research, 35*(September–October), 19–32.

Bloch, P. H. (1995). Seeking the ideal form: Product design & consumer response. *Journal of Marketing, 59*(July), 16–29.

Bloch, P. H., Brunel, F. F., & Arnold, T. J. (2003). Individual differences in the centrality of visual product aesthetics: Concept & measurement. *Journal of Consumer Research, 29*(March), 551–565.

Bottomley, P. A., & Doyle, J. R. (2006a). Dressed for the occasion: Font-product congruity in the perception of logotype. *Journal of Consumer Psychology, 16*(2), 112–123.

Bottomley, P. A., & Doyle, J. R. (2006b). The interactive effects of colors and products on perceptions of brand logo appropriateness. *Marketing Theory, 6*(March), 63–83.

Boulding, W., Lee, E., & Staelin, R. (1994). Mastering the mix: Do advertising, promotion, and sales force activities lead to differentiation? *Journal of Marketing Research, 31*(May), 159–172.

Chaudhuri, A. (2002). How brand reputation affects the advertising-brand equity link. *Journal of Advertising Research, 42*(May–June), 33–43.

Childers, T. L., & Jass, J. (2002). All dressed up with something to say: Effects of typeface semantic associations on brand perceptions and consumer memory. *Journal of Consumer Psychology, 12*(2), 93–106.

Cian, L., Krishna, A., & Elder, R. S. (2014). This logo moves me: Dynamic imagery from static images. *Journal of Marketing Research, 51*(April), 184–197.

Coelho do Vale, R., Pieters, R., & Zeelenberg, M. (2008). Flying under the radar: Perverse package size effects on consumption self-regulation. *Journal of Consumer Research, 35*(October), 380–390.

Cox, D., & Cox, A. D. (2002). Beyond first impressions: The effects of repeated exposure on consumer liking of visually complex and simple product designs. *Journal of the Academy of Marketing Science, 30*(Spring), 119–130.

Crilly, N., Moultrie, J., & Clarkson, P. J. (2004). Seeing things: Consumer response to the visual domain in product design. *Design Studies, 25*(November), 547–577.

Deng, X., & Kahn, B. E. (2009). Is your product on the right side? The location effect on perceived product heaviness and package evaluation. *Journal of Marketing Research, 46*(December), 725–738.

Doyle, J. R., & Bottomley, P. A. (2004). Font appropriateness and brand choice. *Journal of Business Research, 57*(August), 873–880.

Gorn, G. J., Chattopadhyay, A., Sengupta, J., & Tripathi, S. (2004). Waiting for the web: How screen color affects time perceptions. *Journal of Marketing Research, 41*(May), 215–225.

Gorn, G. J., Chattopadhyay, A., Yi, T., & Dahl, D. W. (1997). Effects of color as an executional cue in advertising: They're in the shade. *Management Science, 43*(10), 1387–1400.

Granger, C. W. J., & Billson, A. (1972). Consumers' attitudes toward package size and price. *Journal of Marketing Research, 9*(August), 239–248.

Grohmann, B. (2014). Communicating brand gender through type fonts. *Journal of Marketing Communications.* doi:10.1080/13527266.2014.918050

Grohmann, B., Giese, J. L., & Parkman, I. D. (2013). Using type font characteristics to communicate brand personality of new brands. *Journal of Brand Management, 20*(April–May), 389–403.

Grossman, R. P., & Wisenblit, J. Z. (1999). What we know about consumers' color choices. *Journal of Marketing Practice: Applied Marketing Science, 5*(3), 78–88.

Gupta, S. (1988). Impact of sales promotions on when, what, and how much to buy. *Journal of Marketing Research, 25*(November), 342–355.

Hagtvedt, H. (2011). The impact of incomplete typeface logos on perceptions of the firm. *Journal of Marketing, 75*(July), 86–93.

Henderson, P. W., & Cote, J. A. (1998). Guidelines for selecting or modifying logos. *Journal of Marketing, 62*(April), 14–30.

Henderson, P. W., Cote, J. A., Leong, S. M., & Schmitt, B. (2003). Building strong brands in Asia: Selecting the visual components of image to maximize brand strength. *International Journal of Research in Marketing, 20*(December), 297–313.

Henderson, P. W., Giese, J. L., & Cote, J. A. (2004). Impression management using typeface design. *Journal of Marketing, 68*(October), 60–72.

Hertenstein, J. H., Platt, M. B., & Veryzer, R. W. (2005). The impact of industrial design effectiveness on corporate financial performance. *Journal of Product Innovation Management, 22*(January), 3–21.

Hoegg, J., & Alba, J. W. (2007). A role for aesthetics in consumer psychology. In C. P. Haugvedt, P. M. Herr, & F. R. Kardes (Eds.), *Handbook of Consumer Psychology* (pp. 733–754). Newbury Park, CA: Sage.

Krupinski, E., & Locher, P. (1988). Skin conductance and aesthetic evaluative responses to nonrepresentational works of art varying in symmetry. *Bulletin of the Psychonomic Society, 26*(October), 355–358.

Labrecque, L. I., & Milne, G. R. (2012). Exciting red and competent blue: The importance of color in marketing. *Journal of the Academy of Marketing Science, 40*(September), 711–727.

Labrecque, L. I., Patrick, V. M., & Milne, G. R. (2013). The marketers' prismatic palette: A review of color research and future directions. *Psychology & Marketing, 30*(February), 187–202.

Landwehr, J. R., Labroo, A. A., & Herrmann, A. (2011). Gut liking for the ordinary: Incorporating design fluency improves automobile sales forecasts. *Marketing Science, 30* (May–June), 416–429.

Landwehr, J. R., McGill, A. L., & Herrmann, A. (2011). It's got the look: The effect of friendly and aggressive facial expressions on product liking and sales. *Journal of Marketing, 75*(May), 132–146.

Landwehr, J. R., Wentzel, D., & Herrmann, A. (2013). Product design for the long run: Consumer responses to typical and atypical designs at different stages of exposure. *Journal of Marketing, 77*(September), 92–107.

Locher, P., & Nodine, C. F. (1989). The perceptual value of symmetry. *Computers & Mathematics With Applications, 17*(4–6), 475–484.

Low, G. S., & Fullerton, R. A. (1994), Brands, brand management, and the brand manager system: A critical-historical evaluation. *Journal of Marketing Research, 31*(May), 173–190.

Madden, T. J., Hewett, K., & Roth, M. S. (2000), Managing images in different cultures: A cross-national study of color meanings and preferences. *Journal of International Marketing, 8*(Winter), 90–107.

Mick, D. G. (1986). Consumer research and semiotics: Exploring the morphology of signs, symbols, and significance. *Journal of Consumer Research, 13*(September), 196–213.

Orth, U. R., Campana, D., & Malkewitz, K. (2010). Formation of consumer price expectation based on package design: Attractive and quality routes. *Journal of Marketing Theory and Practice, 18*(Winter), 23–40.

Orth, U. R., & Malkewitz, K. (2008). Holistic package design and consumer brand impressions. *Journal of Marketing, 72*(May), 64–81.

Page, C., & Herr, P. M. (2002). An investigation of the processes by which product design and brand strength interact to determine initial affect and quality judgments. *Journal of Consumer Psychology, 12*(2), 133–147.

Park, C. W., Eisingerich, A. B., Pol, G., & Park, J. W. (2013). The role of brand logos in firm performance. *Journal of Business Research, 66*(February), 180–187.

Pittard, N., Ewing, M., & Jevons, C. (2007). Aesthetic theory and logo design: Examining consumer response to proportion across cultures. *International Marketing Review, 24*(4), 457–473.

Raghubir, P., & Greenleaf, E. (2006). Ratios in proportion: What should be the shape of the package? *Journal of Marketing, 70*(April), 95–107.

Reber, R. (2002). Reasons for the preference for symmetry. *Behavioral and Brain Sciences, 25*(June), 415–416.

Reber, R., Schwarz, N., & Winkielman, P. (2004). Processing fluency and aesthetic pleasure: Is beauty in the perceiver's processing experience? *Personality and Social Psychology Review, 8*(November), 364–382.

Reber, R., Winkielman, P., & Schwarz, N. (1998). Effects of perceptual fluency on affective judgments. *Psychological Science, 9*(January), 45–48.

Reimann, M., Zaichkowsky, J., Neuhaus, C., Bender, T., & Weber, B. (2010). Aesthetic package design: A behavioral, neural, and psychological investigation. *Journal of Consumer Psychology, 20*(October), 434–441.

Rhodes, G., Proffitt, F., Grady, J. M., & Sumich, A. (1998). Facial symmetry and the perception of beauty. *Psychonomic Bulletin & Review, 5*(December), 659–669.

Schoormans, J. P. L., & Robben, H. S. J. (1997). The effect of new package design on product attention, categorization & evaluation. *Journal of Economic Psychology, 18*(April), 271–287.

Scott, M. L., Nowlis, S. M., Mandel, N., & Morales, A. C. (2008). The effects of reduced food size and package size on the consumption behavior of restrained and unrestrained eaters. *Journal of Consumer Research, 35*(October), 391–405.

Singh, S. (2006). Impact of color on marketing. *Management Decision, 44*(6), 783–789.

Srinivasan, S. S., & Anderson, R. E. (1998). Concepts and strategy guidelines for designing value enhancing sales promotions. *Journal of Product & Brand Management, 7*(5), 410–420.

Tantillo, J., Di Lorenzo-Aiss, J., & Mathisen, R. E. (1995). Quantifying perceived differences in type style: An exploratory study. *Psychology & Marketing, 12*(August), 447–457.

Underwood, R. L. (2003). The communicative power of product packaging: Creating brand identity via lived and mediated experience. *Journal of Marketing Theory and Practice, 11*(Winter), 62–76.

Underwoord, R. L., Klein, N. M., & Burke, R. R. (2001). Packaging communication: Attentional effects of product imagery. *Journal of Product and Brand Management, 10*(7), 403–422.

Van der Lans, R., Cote, J. A., Cole, C. A., Leong, S. M., Smidts, A., Henderson, P. W., . . . Moorthy, J. (2009). Cross-National logo evaluation analysis: An individual-level approach. *Marketing Science, 28*(September–October), 968–985.

Van Rompay, T. J. L., & Pruyn, A. T. H. (2011). When visual product features speak the same language: Effects of shape-typeface congruence on brand perception and price expectations. *Journal of Product Innovation Management, 28*(July), 599–610.

Veryzer, R. W., & Hutchinson, J. W. (1998). The influence of unity and prototypicality on aesthetic responses to new product designs. *Journal of Consumer Research, 24*(March), 374–394.

Walsh, M. F., Winterich, K. P., & Mittal, V. (2010). Do logo redesigns help or hurt your brand? The role of brand commitment. *Journal of Product & Brand Management, 19*(2), 76–84.

Walsh, M. F., Winterich, K. P., & Mittal, V. (2011). How re-designing angular logos to be rounded shapes brand attitude: Consumer brand commitment and self-construal. *Journal of Consumer Marketing, 28*(6), 438–447.

Wansink, B. (1996). Can package size accelerate usage volume? *Journal of Marketing, 60*(July), 1–14.

Wansink, B., & Van Ittersum, K. (2003). Bottoms up! The influence of elongation on pouring and consumption volume. *Journal of Consumer Research, 30*(December), 455–463.

Westerman, S. J., Gardner, P. H., Sutherland, E. J., White, T., Jordan, K., Watts, D., & Wells, S. (2012). Product design: Preferences for rounded versus angular design elements. *Psychology & Marketing, 29*(August), 595–605.

Wilcox, K., Kim, H. M., & Sen, S. (2009). Why do consumers buy counterfeit luxury brands. *Journal of Marketing Research, 46*(April), 247–259.

Winkielman, P., Schwarz, N., Fazendeiro, T. A., & Reber, R. (2003). The hedonic marking of processing fluency: Implications for evaluative judgment. In J. Musch & K. C. Klauer (Eds.), *Psychology of evaluation: Affective processes in cognition and emotion* (pp. 189–217). Mahwah, NJ: Erlbaum.

Wynn, T. (2002). Archaeology and cognitive evolution. *Behavioral and Brain Sciences, 25*(June), 389–438.

Yamamoto, M., & Lambert, D. R. (1994). The impact of product aesthetics on the evaluation of industrial products. *Journal of Product Innovation Management, 11*(September), 309–324.

Yang, S., & Raghubir, P. (2005). Can bottles speak volumes? The effect of package shape on how much to buy. *Journal of Retailing, 81*(4), 269–281.

Yoo, B., Donthu, N., & Lee, S. (2000). An examination of selected marketing mix elements and brand equity. *Journal of the Academy of Marketing Science, 28*(Spring), 195–211.

Zhang, Y., Feick, L., & Price, L. J. (2006). The impact of self-construal on aesthetic preference for angular versus rounded shapes. *Personality and Social Psychology Bulletin, 32*(June), 794–805.

10

DOMINANT DESIGNS

The Role of Product Face-Ratios and Anthropomorphism on Consumer Preferences

Ahreum Maeng

UNIVERSITY OF KANSAS

Pankaj Aggarwal

UNIVERSITY OF TORONTO

Anthropomorphism, or seeing the human in non-human objects, things, and entities, is a fairly widespread phenomenon. Marketers frequently encourage consumers to anthropomorphize their products and brands. Brands are often associated with humanlike characters, like the Pillsbury Doughboy and the Michelin Man. Products are shaped like humans, such as the shapely Pom bottle and the smiling face of the Volkswagen Beetle car. One consequence of brand anthropomorphism is that the brand is endowed with human traits and characteristics, which often makes it easier for consumers to relate to them. In fact, consumers are able to form relationships with brands (Fournier, 1998). A related stream of research has noted that brands are often seen to have distinct personality traits, much like the human personality traits, and these brand personalities serve a symbolic and self-expressive function that help consumers express their own identity (Belk, 1989), differentiate the brand (Halliday, 1996), and drive consumer preference (Biel, 1993). Foundational work on brand personality by Aaker (1997) suggests that brands have five different personality dimensions: sincerity, excitement, competence, sophistication, and ruggedness. While marketers often use brand advertising and communication to endow their brands with specific personality traits, there are other factors too, such as product design, and in particular the product face, that affect how consumers perceive the brand. In this chapter, we propose the interesting proposition that products which are anthropomorphized and are associated with a humanlike face (e.g., a car), will also show an association between the width-to-height ratio of the product face and the product's perceived dominance. We further suggest that consumers prefer such dominant products since they allow consumers to achieve a higher status/power, and as such, these products enjoy an advantage over products that show a lower width to height ratio of the product face. We first present a brief literature review of both the anthropomorphism and product design research, and then present evidence from our studies that support the overall premise that we propose.

Anthropomorphism

Anthropomorphism indicates a process of inductive inference about unobservable characteristics of nonhuman agents, that is, imbuing nonhuman agents with humanlike characteristics, intentions, or underlying mental states (Aggarwal & McGill, 2007; Aggarwal & McGill, 2012; Epley, Waytz, & Cacioppo, 2007). These nonhuman agents may include anything that acts like or is believed to have the potential to act with apparent independence, including nonhuman animals, natural forces, religious deities (i.e., gods), and a host of other entities including products and brands. Much research has indicated that anthropomorphic tendency is a fundamental feature of human judgment that occurs automatically (Guthrie 1993; Mitchell, Thompson, & Miles, 1997). Other research provides a psychological explanation of when and why people are likely to anthropomorphize nonhuman agents. It has been suggested that there are two motivational factors that can explain why people tend to anthropomorphize non-human entities. First, people anthropomorphize objects to reduce uncertainty in the environment and to improve predictability about these entities. This explanation is also called the effectance motivation. Second, people like to be socially connected, and are motivated to anthropomorphize non-human entities to be able to fulfil this need. Finally, there is a cognitive explanation according to which people are more likely to anthropomorphize an object if the features of the object activate agent knowledge, that is, that object elicits and activates human schema and when this occurs, that particular object is more likely to be seen as humanlike and hence anthropomorphized (Epley et al., 2007).

This notion of knowledge activation of anthropomorphism posits that people generally project their characteristics or traits onto nonhuman objects when the object that they interact with activates that knowledge. That is, just as people are likely to project their beliefs and desires egocentrically onto people who appear similar to the self (Ames, 2004; Epley, Keysar, Van Boven, & Gilovich, 2004), they are also likely to project their own beliefs and desires anthropomorphically onto stimuli that look humanlike in their characteristics (Guthrie, 1993; Morewedge, Preston, & Wegner, 2007). Thus, anthropomorphism is likely to result when individuals reason about unfamiliar entities, as the self often serves as the default concept for reasoning about unfamiliar agents (e.g., Davis, Hoch, & Ragsdale, 1986; Meltzoff, 2007).

More interestingly, anthropomorphism also occurs due to the attribution of humanlike physical features to another nonhuman agent (Gray, Gray, & Wegner, 2007).

Studies have shown that anthropomorphism increases for stimuli that have a morphological similarity to humans, thereby increasing the accessibility of egocentric or homocentric knowledge (e.g., Eddy, Gallup, & Povinelli, 1993). For instance, research has shown that when human schema is activated, people tend to anthropomorphize a human-resembling product more than when object schema is activated (Aggarwal & McGill, 2007). Further, this anthropomorphic tendency toward products has been shown to influence consumers' evaluation of them. For example, emotional facial expressions influence product liking, such that people prefer products that are more typically humanlike, for example, those resembling smiling faces (Aggarwal & McGill, 2007), slanted headlights (vs. arched headlights), and upturned grilles (vs. downturned grills; Landwehr, McGill, & Herrmann, 2011).

How did such a perceptual bias evolve and persist? Generally speaking, throughout history, humans have been forced to interpret the world primarily in social terms, as the failure to identify agents (e.g., another human, predator, or prey) could be detrimental but less so when accidentally treating a non-agent as an agent (e.g., stone as a human). Such asymmetries in the recurrent costs, or errors in inference, have led to the evolution of biases even when these biases result in greater rates of inferential error and favor the persistence of a hypersensitive agent detection system (Haselton & Buss, 2000). In other words, an overperception error in terms of processing artifacts as agents does no harm at all, whereas a single real encounter that would lack that inference could be lethal. This effect probably forces us to interpret our world primarily in social terms. Guthrie (1993) similarly suggests that anthropomorphizing may be seen as a cognitive and perceptual strategy akin to making a bet that the world is humanlike—a bet that has more upside than downside risks.

Brand Personality, Brand Traits, and Product Design

A brand's personality perceptions are often based on the consumers' direct or indirect contact with the brand (Plummer, 1985). Consumers' direct contact with the brand, its advertising, brand consumption, and other interactions help establish the brand's personality. Furthermore, indirect influences such as the brand name, the packaging design, the pricing, as well as distribution outlets all affect its perceived personality (Batra, Lehmann, & Singh, 1993). Additionally, brands are associated with other traits often associated with people such as gender (masculine vs. feminine), age (young vs. old), as well as ethnicity (Caucasian vs. African American). Thus, it has been suggested that Virginia Slims is a feminine brand while Marlboro is a masculine brand; similarly, Apple is young while IBM is old.

Aaker (1997) did pioneering work in the domain of brand personality and examined the extent to which the different dimensions of brand personality mapped on to the different dimensions of human personality. Her results show that brands are typically associated with five different types of personality traits which she called Sincerity (e.g., typified by Hallmark cards), Excitement (e.g., MTV Channel), Competence (e.g., the Wall Street Journal), Sophistication (e.g., Guess jeans), and Ruggedness (e.g., Nike tennis shoes). While the first three dimensions map on to the human personality traits of Agreeableness, Extraversion, and Conscientiousness, the other two are different from the other two human personality traits of Openness, and Neuroticism. Interestingly, the two key dimensions of brand personality—Sincerity and Competence—also map on to the two universal dimensions of social judgments—warmth and competence—that have been shown to provide fundamental answers about social structures and status (Fiske, Cuddy, & Glick, 2007). In fact, these two dimensions are known to give information about whether the "other" has good intentions (warmth) and whether they have the ability to enact those intentions (competence). More recent research has noted that the two dimensions of warmth and competence are equally applicable in a brand context too (Kervyn, Fiske, & Malone, 2012).

Other research in marketing has examined the role of product and package design in creating and communicating the brand message and impressions to customers (Henderson, Cote, Leong, & Schmitt, 2003; Underwood, 2003), and shown that design helps products gain advantage in the global marketplace (Berkowitz, 1987; Cooper & Kleinschmidt, 1987). Further, package design was seen as over three times more of an important determinant of new product performance than price (Bruce & Whitehead, 1988). Prior research has also documented the immense value of product designs in significantly improving brand strength, liking, and quality perceptions (Page & Herr, 2002), as well as influencing the type of personality the brand is endowed with, such as charming, spirited, and up-to-date, that increase purchase intent (Bourdreaux & Palmer, 2007). In a similar vein, Noble and Kumar (2008) find that product design affects loyalty, joy of use, and passion for the product through emotional value creation.

Recent work has examined the role of design and how they affect consumer impressions about the brand (Orth & Malkewitz, 2008). In particular, this research suggests that package design can be categorized more simply as being of one of five types: massive, contrasting, natural, delicate, and nondescript. Further, this research suggests that sincere brands should have natural package designs, exciting brands should have contrasting designs, competent brands should have delicate designs, sophisticated brands should have natural or delicate designs, and rugged brands should have contrasting or massive designs. While interesting in that this research is able to identify different types of designs with the brand's personality, the focus of this research was on package designs, and the studies did not focus as much on the underlying process mechanism. Other research in this stream of work has found evidence of the effect of product dimensions on user's emotional experience and purchase intentions (Seva, Duh, & Helander, 2007), and of color, shape, and size on product evaluations (Creusen & Schoormans, 2004).

In this chapter, we contribute to this stream of research by examining a particular dimension of product design and highlighting how it relates to a particular dimension of the brand's personality. More specifically, we look at the ratio of the product face and examine the association between the width-to-height ratio of the face and the extent to which the consumers perceive the brand as being endowed with dominance as a personality trait. Further, we suggest that the product's dominance trait results in the product being evaluated more positively due to its perceived higher value as a status product since dominant personalities are seen as being more powerful and high in status.

Face Dominance and *f*WHR

The most fundamental dimensions of making trait inferences from static facial cues are valence and dominance (Oosterhof & Todorov, 2008). Functionally, valence- and dominance-related facial cues give rise to inferences about a person's intentions, that is, whether the person is harmful or harmless, and if the person possesses the ability to implement these intentions, respectively (Keating & Doyle, 2002). In fact, these two cues map almost perfectly on to the judgment of warmth and competence that is seen as universal in social judgments (Fiske, Cuddy, & Glick, 2007). Whereas valence evaluation is an overgeneralization of the perception of facial cues signaling whether to approach or avoid a person, dominance evaluation is an overgeneralization of the perception of facial cues signaling the physical strength/weakness of the person. Thus, since dominance is normally linked to hierarchy in social interactions, and allows people to maintain status in relationships, it forecasts probable success or failure during competitive interactions with others. Hence, the dominance signal from facial structure normally allows others to infer status and/or a dominance hierarchy in others (Keating & Doyle, 2002; Keating, Mazur, & Segall, 1977; Zebrowitz & Montepare, 1989). Dominance is also perceived from emotional expressions, such as anger, and from static facial cues. For instance, baby faces are perceived as weak (Zebrowitz & Montepare, 1989), angry faces are perceived as highly dominant, and sad and fearful faces are perceived as low in dominance (Montepare & Dobish, 2003). Small eyes are perceived as indicators of dominance in contrast to large eyes (Keating & Doyle, 2002). Additionally, non-smiling face has been viewed as a sign of dominance (Halberstadt & Saitta, 1987; Keating et al., 1977).

However, recently, the facial width-to-height ratio (*f*WHR: bizygomatic width divided by upper-face height) has been identified as a facial metric with links to a range of dominant traits and perceived dominance and aggression. Previous research has shown that faces with high *f*WHR are perceived to be more dominant and have a higher potential for aggressiveness. Some institutions still associate muscular and dominant-looking faces with high-ranked male positions (Mazur et al., 1984). Although face ratio is associated with more positive behaviors, such as striving for achievement (Lewis, Lefevre, & Bates, 2012) and

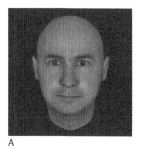 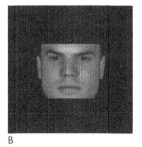 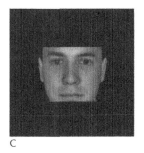

A   B   C

FIGURE 10.1 Panel (A): Measure of *f*WHR: horizontal lines represent the maximum distance between the left and right facial boundary (bizygomatic width), vertical lines represents the upper lip and highest point of the eyelids (upper face height). *f*WHR was calculated as width divided by height $[(a - b)/(c - d)]$. Panel (B): Example of high ratio face (*f*WHR = 2.13). Panel (C): Example of low ratio face (*f*WHR = 1.70).

Source: The face images used in the experiments were created using FaceGen Modeller 3.5 (Singular Inversions, Toronto, ON, Canada, www.facegen.com). Reproduced with permission.

self-sacrifice towards the in-group (Stirrat & Perrett, 2012), high ratio faces are generally less liked by perceivers (Stirrat & Perrett, 2010). Further, individuals with a high *f*WHR have been shown to demonstrate more aggression (Carré & McCormick, 2008; Carré, McCormick, & Mondloch, 2009), deception, and untrustworthiness (Haselhuhn & Wong, 2012). Thus, others generally dislike individuals with high *f*WHR faces (Stirrat & Perrett, 2010). Interestingly, it has been shown that women find men with high *f*WHR more attractive for short-term dates, but because these men are also seen as more dominant, women do not prefer them for long-term relationships (Valentine, Li, Penke, & Perrett, 2014).

This sensitivity towards *f*WHR as a reliable cue of dominance behavior may be a part of an evolved mechanism. Interestingly, non-human primates also use the expressive abilities of the face to communicate social dominance information (e.g., van Hooff, 1967). These facial signals help maintain dominance or status relationships by permitting members of the species to forecast probable success or failure during competitive interactions with others. Evolutionary continuity between the facial expressions of nonhuman primates and humans has been argued by several theorists. Hence, perhaps comparable facial gestures characterize human dominance interactions (e.g., Andrew, 1963; Steklis & Raleigh, 1979).

Dominance relates to the overgeneralization of cues that signal the physical strength to implement the harmful intention (Keating & Doyle, 2002). Thus, this is normally linked to hierarchy as it helps to maintain status relationships. Research suggests that a wide face in men is not only inferred as being dominant and aggressive, but that these men indeed behave more aggressively, whereas narrow faced men are inferred as nice but weak. A person with high *f*WHR demonstrates traits that are more dominant, and this person is perceived as more dominant (Carre & McCormick, 2008). Consistent with the fact that morphological aspects of the face may communicate status information between humans (Guthrie, 1993), high ratio is a reliable marker of a person's dominant trait, and individuals with high ratio faces have been found to behave more competitively and thus achieve more. For instance, US presidents have higher fWHR compared to average people (Lewis et al., 2012), and a significant positive association was found between fWHR and achievement drive, and a negative association between fWHR and "poise and polish." CEOs with a higher fWHR are more successful, having higher ROI (Wong, Ormiston, & Haselhuhn, 2011). Furthermore, fWHR has been found to correlate with professional athletes' performance (Tsujimura & Banissy, 2013).

Consistent with this line of thinking, this inference of dominance from faces with high ratio appears to be adaptive. Detection of the propensity for aggression based on facial structure is irrespective of face race (Short et al., 2012). Furthermore, even when faces were manipulated, such that feature-related cues were eliminated while the facial width-to-height ratio was maintained, the propensity for aggression was detected, suggesting that the ratio guides judgments of aggression (Carré et al., 2009). Additionally, eight-year-old children judged faces with a high ratio to be more dominant and aggressive, suggesting that sensitivity to fWHR may be broadly tuned such that abundant experience is not required to use this ratio as a cue for dominant and aggressive potential (Short et al., 2012). This tendency of perceiving high ratio faces being more dominant is likely to be overgeneralized to anthropomorphized products with morphological similarity to human faces. The ecological theory of social perceptions proposes that innate or well-developed attunements to stimulus information can result in overgeneralized perceptions (e.g., Zebrowitz & Collins, 1997). Thus, when products have 'faces' or features that trigger human face-like processing, products too are likely to follow the same perceptual rule.

Distinct Consequences of fWHR for Product Versus Person Perception

While faces with a high ratio are perceived as dominant and aggressive and tend to be evaluated as less likable, there is much evidence to support our premise that product faces with a high ratio are preferred to those with a low ratio, unlike the interpersonal domain. As dominance and social rank signal wealth and superfluity, research shows that consumers use products to signal dominance and social rank. Indeed, it has been suggested that one of the most important goals of one's social life is to attain status in the groups to which he/she belongs. Status is omnipresent in social life and determines individual personality. For instance, Adler (1930) famously argued that humans are inherently social beings motivated by attaining superiority over others. Hogan (1983) also suggested that people are motivated to get ahead of others. Indeed, hierarchies exist in all social groups

(Eibl-Eibesfeldt, 1989; Mazur, 1985), and striving for status has been suggested to be a key human motive (e.g., Barkow, 1975).

One strategy to achieve superiority or status is through consumption. Much research has demonstrated that status products tap into consumers' heightened need for status. For example, Belk, Bahn, and Mayer (1982) discussed the notion that products can signal one's status. They also reported that with age, consumers tend to gravitate toward high-status items to demonstrate their status to others. Lasswell and Parshall (1961) also supported the proposition that products, such as the clothing consumers choose to wear, signal status to other consumers. Ordabayeva and Chandon (2011) demonstrated that in a competitive environment where people are motivated to compete with others, they tend to display greater conspicuous consumption. Dubois, Rucker, and Galinsky (2012) suggested that relative size of choice options serves as a status-signaling device, increasing preferences and willingness to pay for bigger sized items over smaller sized items.

Much evidence states that status signaling items act as strong social reinforcers and are highly rewarding (Morgan et al., 2002). Reward mechanisms, which are involved in behaviors to meet basic drives, such as buying food and finding attractive mates, are also involved in the regulation of social relations, like dominance and social rank. Indeed, neurological evidence has demonstrated that dominant looking automobiles signal wealth and superfluity, and, like an attractive woman, activate the dopaminergic reward circuitry (Erk et al., 2002). Hence, we suggest that dominant looking products might help consumers feel more empowered themselves, as if they were ranked higher in the social hierarchy, leading them to prefer and be more willing to pay for those items.

Consistent with these findings, researchers recently found that a high width-to-height ratio of product faces leads to an attribution of high dominance characteristics, much in the same way that high width-to-height ratio of human faces are rated high on dominance traits. Specifically, Maeng and Aggarwal (2014) demonstrated that individuals show greater preference for wider product faces but not for human faces and the perceived dominance from the product and human faces respectively mediated these effects. They attributed this seemingly opposite effect to the usage of a product as a signaling device: consumers use highly dominant product to enhance their own status. They further demonstrated that the type of products moderated this effect, the products that are seen as status products (e.g., a car or a house) show this effect while products that are incapable of being used as a signaling device (e.g., a mop) show the opposite effect. Based on the findings, it was argued that the effect of dominance perception on product evaluation is related to consumers leveraging dominant products to signal status, or to elevate their relative rank in a social hierarchy. That is, people react to product faces in much the same way as they react to human faces, in terms of associating fWHR with dominance, and base their evaluation of the products on their impression of the product faces (Maeng & Aggarwal, 2014).

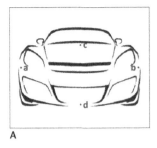
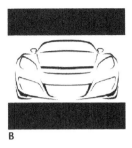
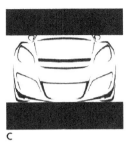

A   B   C

FIGURE 10.2 Measuring points used for morphometric calculations and examples of high and low ratio automobile faces. Panel (A): Measure of fWHR: automobile fWHR was calculated as width divided by height $[(a - b)/(c - d)]$. Panel (B): Example of high ratio automobile face (fWHR = 2.11). Panel (C): Example of low ratio automobile face (fWHR = 1.68).

Source: Ahreum Maeng.

In summary, these findings provide the first demonstration of the influence of fWHR on product preferences while simultaneously providing the underlying conceptual basis for why this effect is observed. Indeed, products that are used to signal status are liked more when they have a high fWHR, unlike human faces that are liked less when they have high fWHR.

General Discussion

In this chapter, we discuss the influence of fWHR on product design preferences, suggesting that product faces may be perceived the same way as human faces, such that the fWHR influences their perceived dominance traits. Further, products that are used to signal status are liked more when they have a high fWHR, unlike human faces that are liked less when they have high fWHR. This research has significant managerial and theoretical implications.

Implications for Designers

Research discussed in this chapter suggests that consumers react to product faces in much the same way as they react to human faces based on its fWHR. Specifically, consumers perceive high ratio faces as dominant and preferable. Furthermore, individuals who are motivated to impress others perceive these products as more dominant but like them more. These findings provide suggestions to product designers on how to utilize fWHR to induce dominance in the appearance of a design and thus systematically trigger preferences and positive responses from consumers. Furthermore, although not directly tested, Maeng and Aggarwal (2014) found some initial evidence that, for some types of products that require warmth and submissiveness as a desirable trait (e.g., mops), low fWHR might lead to greater positive response from consumers. In their experiment, non-status signaling items, such as a mop, are preferred more when the face ratio was low as people infer more submissive personality traits from the low ratio face. As such, product designers might want to utilize fWHR by increasing and decreasing the ratio depending on types of products in order to trigger desired consumer preferences towards products.

Based on these findings, designers can increase the affective value of products by creating dominant looking designs, especially for status signaling products (e.g., by emphasizing or exaggerating width-to-height ratio). By modifying a product's appearance, product designers can use a deeply embedded human perceptual bias due to the evolutionary significance of human features, namely face width-to-height ratio. This universal perceptual bias is especially valuable for product design, as perceivers are highly sensitive to it. This might be most useful for designers of status products, such as automotive and luxury goods.

Overall, the extent to which uniquely humanlike traits are associated with products which then result in human personality dimensions being endowed to products is now being applied to the specific context of face-ratio associations for human as well as product faces. Further, the changes in face-ratios are associated with consumer preferences—a direct outcome of changes in the physical design of the products. Finally, these changes in face-ratios also significantly affect the products being endowed with unique personality traits—which can aid or hurt the marketer's efforts in other aspects of the marketing mix. Going forward, marketers may pause a little before rushing to launch new products—they may wish to examine the very many different aspects of their product designs and what the different characteristics may translate to in the human context to ensure that they fully understand the ramifications of those designs for what it means for the products that they are launching. Without such clarity, it is possible that the products may be endowed with personality traits that may be quite unintended, or worse, counterproductive.

Implications for a Theory of Design

It was demonstrated that fWHR of diverse products such as automobiles and houses elicits dominant perception, yielding greater preferences and WTP (Willingness to Pay). Although there is existing evidence about face-like product designs (people see faces in face resembling products), this research is first to demonstrate that trait inferences from facial structures actually occur from product faces in much the same manner as from human faces. This result is the key, as it supports the theorization that humans' built-in predisposition to respond to facial qualities that reveal these characteristics can be overgeneralized to anthropomorphic products.

Moreover, this research suggests that perceived dominance is the underlying mechanism of the effect of ƒWHR on product liking and WTP. This contributes to the body of research on conspicuous consumption. The existing research on status that signals conspicuous consumption concerns only economic outcomes (i.e., the amount spent). Those studies manipulated status signaling products as types of products that are related to high class versus low class and measured the amount of money spent on each type of products (e.g., Becker, Murphy, & Werning, 2005). However, to our knowledge, not much effort has been put in to test within category effects based on product shapes that can signal status. Here, we demonstrate for the first time the possibility that product shapes can actually signal status and result in conspicuous consumption.

To apply this finding to the practice of product design, it is important to understand how and when such inferences influence explicit behavioral responses, such as purchase. We demonstrate that this dominance inference from high ratio faces is the most beneficial (i.e., greater preferences and WTP) when consumers are motivated to impress others in a competitive setting as the means to gain higher status in the social hierarchy. This effect is maximized when products have the ability to signal status and diminished when the products have no such ability. Along this line, boundary conditions related to these effects should be taken into account. For example, although signaling status, certain product types might not benefit from ƒWHR, as such products are associated with traits contrary to dominance (e.g., warmth). Thus, for the types of products for which warmth is more important than competence, the opposite effect might occur. Furthermore, although having high ratio, a face might be perceived to have childlike traits when it has facial features that are associated with babies such as large eyes, a large and prominent forehead, a small chin, and a curved face. In particular, this face might be perceived as the opposite of a dominant trait such as being more socially dependent, intellectually naïve, and physically weak but warm (Berry & McArthur, 1985; Keating, 1985; McArthur & Apatow, 1984). Thus, this face will be liked more but might not be perceived being high in status, meaning that the opposite effect of ƒWHR might occur.

Similar to this point, previous research has demonstrated that cuteness of product design increases positive affect towards the product (Miesler, Leder, & Herrmann, 2011). Although this finding may seem to contradict our finding, it is actually rather consistent. It cannot be assumed that affective responses always increase individuals' purchase intention. For example, although a cute looking automobile might evoke a quick affective response, people might also like dominant looking automobiles and be willing to pay for them especially when they need to impress others. Likewise, people might smile at a cute looking house, but they might be be willing to pay more for one that signals higher status. In other words, since a baby-face is likely to be seen as being low on dominance, in the domain of products such a baby-faced product is also likely to be seen as less appropriate for high status needs. In any case, as noted in our empirical findings, the context and the goal behind the product purchase (e.g., whether or not it is being purchased to impress others, or to achieve higher status) will determine if a higher or lower fWHR in product faces will be preferred or not.

Finally, future research should test whether and how fWHR can be applied in terms of ergonomics of product design, such as user-interface design. Would users interact with products with wider faces better or worse? Would certain types of products be perceived performing better with high ratio? Would people with certain attributes, age, size, strength, cognitive ability, prior experience, cultural expectations, and goals better interact or use product with high ratio? How could we optimize performance, safety, and comfort using fWHR? All these interesting questions may be considered by future researchers.

On a broader level, this research suggests that product characteristics that remind consumers of human characteristics may also endow on products similar personality dimensions. One may wonder if such an effect would hold true for other characteristics beyond just those related to product faces. For example, people may be seen as tall versus short, masculine versus feminine, muscular versus shapely, tough versus delicate, etc.—traits that may also be imbued on to products. Physical characteristics that allow consumers to perceive products with such personality traits may be worthy of future investigation by researchers to examine the extent to which such product design aspects may be consciously incorporated by marketers to better manage not just the product's design but also its perceived characteristics and personality dimensions.

Conclusion

In summary, this chapter aims to advance our current knowledge in a variety of domains including anthropomorphism, product design, and personality traits. In Particular, we discussed that product fWHR influences preferences toward product design by influencing perceptions of dominance of the product faces. Researchers and practitioners may now examine strategic ways in which they might wish to examine related issues in the future and develop interesting tools to more successfully market their products to us.

References

Aaker, J.L. (1997). Dimensions of brand personality. *Journal of Marketing Research,* *34*(August), 347–356.

Adler, A. (1930). Individual psychology. In C. Murchison (Ed.), *Psychologies of 1930* (pp. 395–405). Worcester, MA: Clark University Press.

Aggarwal, P., & McGill, A. L. (2007). Is that car smiling at me? Schema congruity as a basis for evaluating anthropomorphized products. *Journal of Consumer Research, 34*(4), 468–479.

Aggarwal, P., & McGill, A. L. (2012). When brands seem human, do humans act like brands? Automatic behavioral priming effects of brand anthropomorphism. *Journal of Consumer Research, 39*(2), 307–323.

Ames, D. R. (2004). Strategies for social inference: A similarity contingency model of projection and stereotyping in attribute prevalence estimates. *Journal of Personality and Social Psychology, 87*(5), 573.

Andrew, R. J. (1963). The origin and evolution of the calls and facial expressions of the primates. *Behaviour, 20*(1–2), 1–109.

Barkow, J. H. (1975). Prestige and culture: A biosocial interpretation. *Current Anthropology, 16*, 553–572.

Batra, R., Lehmann, D. R., & Singh, D. (1993). The brand personality component of brand goodwill: Some antecedents and consequences. In D. A. Aaker & A. L. Biel (Eds.), *Brand equity and advertising* (pp. 83–96). Hove: Lawrence Erlbaum Associates.

Becker, G. S., Murphy, K. M., & Werning, I. (2005). The equilibrium distribution of income and the market for status. *Journal of Political Economy, 113*(2), 282–310.

Belk, R. W. (1989). Extended self and extending paradigmatic perspective. *Journal of Consumer Research, 16*, 129–132.

Belk, R. W., Bahn, K. D., & Mayer, R. N. (1982). Developmental recognition of consumption symbolism. *Journal of Consumer Research, 9*(June), 4–17.

Berkowitz, D. (1987). TV news sources and news channels: A study in agenda-building. *Journalism Quarterly, 64*, 508–513.

Berry, D. S., & McArthur, L. Z. (1985). Some components and consequences of a babyface. *Journal of Personality and Social Psychology, 48*, 312–323.

Biel, A. L. (1993). Converting image into equity. In D. A. Aaker & A. L. Biel (Eds.), *Brand equity and advertising: Advertising's role in building strong brands* (pp. 67–81). London: Lawrence Erlbaum Associates.

Boudreaux, C. A., & Palmer, S. E. (2007). A charming little cabernet: Effects of wine label design on purchase intent and brand personality. *International Journal of Wine Business Research, 19*(3), 170–186.

Bruce, M., & Whitehead, M. (1988). Putting design into the picture: The role of product design in consumer purchase behavior. *Journal of the Market Research Society, 30*(2), 147–162.

Carré, J. M., & McCormick, C. M. (2008). Aggressive behavior and change in salivary testosterone concentrations predict willingness to engage in a competitive task. *Hormones and Behavior, 54*(3), 403–409.

Carré, J. M., McCormick, C. M., & Mondloch, C. J. (2009). Facial structure is a reliable cue of aggressive behavior. *Psychological Science, 20*(10), 1194–1198.

Cooper, R. G., & Kleinschmidt, E. J. (1987). New products: What separates winners from losers? *Journal of Product Innovation Management, 4*(3), 169–184.

Creusen, M., & Schoormans, J. (2004). The different roles of product appearance in consumer choice. *Journal of Product Innovation Management, 22*(1), 63–81.

Davis, H. L., Hoch, S. J., & Ragsdale, E. K. E. (1986). An anchoring and adjustment model of spousal predictions. *Journal of Consumer Research*, 25–37.

Dubois, D., Rucker, D. D., & Galinsky, A. D. (2012). Super size me: Product size as a signal of status. *Journal of Consumer Research, 38*(6), 1047–1062.

Eddy, T. J., Gallup, G. G., & Povinelli, D. J. (1993). Attribution of cognitive states to animals: Anthropomorphism in comparative perspective. *Journal of Social Issues, 49*(1), 87–101.

Eibl-Eibesfeldt, I. (1989). *Human ethology*. New York, NY: Aldine de Gruyter.

Epley, N., Keysar, B., Van Boven, L., & Gilovich, T. (2004). Perspective taking as egocentric anchoring and adjustment. *Journal of Personality and Social Psychology, 87*(3), 327.

Epley, N., Waytz, A., & Cacioppo, J. T. (2007). On seeing human: A three-factor theory of anthropomorphism. *Psychological Review, 114*(4), 864.

Erk, S., Spitzer, M., Wunderlich, A. P., Galley, L., & Walter, H. (2002). Cultural objects modulate reward circuitry. *Neuroreport, 13*(18), 2499–2503.

Fiske, S. T., Cuddy, A. J. C., & Glick, P. (2007). Universal dimensions of social cognition: Warmth and competence. *Trends in Cognitive Sciences, 11*(2), 77–83.

Fournier, S. (1998). Consumers and their brands: Developing relationship theory in consumer research. *Journal of Consumer Research, 24*(4), 343–353.

Gray, H. M., Gray, K., & Wegner, D. M. (2007). Dimensions of mind perception. *Science, 315*(5812), 619.

Guthrie, S. (1993). *Faces in the clouds*. Oxford: Oxford University Press.

Halberstadt, A. G., & Saitta, M. B. (1987), Gender, nonverbal behavior, and perceived dominance: A test of the theory. *Journal of Personality and Social Psychology, 53*(2), 257.

Halliday, J. (1996, September 30). Chrysler brings out brand personalities with '97 ads. *Advertising Age*, 3.

Haselhuhn, M. P., & Wong, E. M. (2012). Bad to the bone: Facial structure predicts unethical behavior. *Proceedings of the Royal Society B: Biological Sciences, 279*(1728), 571–576.

Haselton, M. G., & Buss, D. M. (2000). Error management theory: A new perspective on biases in cross-sex mind reading. *Journal of Personality and Social Psychology, 78*(1), 81.

Henderson, P. W., Cote, J. A., Leong, S. M., & Schmitt, B. (2003). Building strong brands in Asia: Selecting the visual components of image to maximize brand strength. *International Journal of Research in Marketing, 20*(4), 297–313.

Hogan, R. (1983). A socioanalytic theory of personality. In M. M. Page (Ed.), *Nebraska symposium on motivation* (Vol. 29, pp. 55–89). Lincoln: University of Nebraska Press.

Keating, C. F. (1985). Human dominance signals: The primate in us. In S. L. Ellyson & J. F. Dovidio (Eds.), *Power, dominance, and nonverbal behavior. Springer Series in Social Psychology* (pp. 89–108). New York, NY: Springer-Verlag.

Keating, C. F., & Doyle, J. (2002). The faces of desirable mates and dates contain mixed social status cues. *Journal of Experimental Social Psychology, 38*(4), 414–424.

Keating, C. F., Mazur, A., & Segall, M. H. (1977). Facial gestures which influence the perception of status. *Sociometry, 40*(4), 374–378.

Kervyn, N., Fiske, S. T., & Malone, C. (2012). Brands as intentional agents framework: How perceived intentions and ability can map brand perception. *Journal of Consumer Psychology, 22*(2), 166–176.

Landwehr, J. R., McGill, A. L., & Herrmann, A. (2011). It's got the look: The effect of friendly and aggressive facial expressions on product liking and sales. *Journal of Marketing, 75*(3), 132–146.

Lasswell, T. E., & Parshall, P. F. (1961). The perception of social class from photographs. *Sociology & Social Research, 45*, 407–414.

Lewis, G. J., Lefevre, C. E., & Bates, T. C. (2012). Facial width-to-height ratio predicts achievement drive in US presidents. *Personality and Individual Differences, 52*(7), 855–857.

Maeng, A., & Aggarwal, P. (2014). Striving for superiority: Face ratio, anthropomorphism, and product preferences. Working paper.

Mazur, A. (1985). A biosocial model of status in face-to-face primate groups. *Social Forces, 64*(2), 377–402.

Mazur, A., Mazur, J., & Keating, C. (1984). Military rank attainment of a West Point class: Effects of cadets' physical features. *American Journal of Sociology*, 125–150.

McArthur, L. Z., & Apatow, K. (1984). Impressions of babyfaced adults. *Social Cognition, 2*, 315–342.

Meltzoff, A. N. (2007). 'Like me': A foundation for social cognition. *Developmental Science, 10*(1), 126–134.

Miesler, L., Leder, H., & Herrmann, A. (2011). Isn't it cute: An evolutionary perspective of baby-schema effects in visual product designs. *International Journal of Design, 5*(3), 17–30.

Mitchell, R., Thompson, N., & Miles, L. (Eds.). (1997). *Anthropomorphism, anecdotes, and animals*. Albany: State University of New York Press.

Montepare, J. M., & Dobish, H. (2003). The contribution of emotion perceptions and their overgeneralizations to trait impressions. *Journal of Nonverbal Behavior, 27*(4), 237–254.

Morewedge, C. K., Preston, J., & Wegner, D. M. (2007). Timescale bias in the attribution of mind. *Journal of Personality and Social Psychology, 93*, 1–11.

Morgan, D., Grant, K. A., Gage, H. D., Mach, R. H., Kaplan, J. R., Prioleau, O., . . . Nader, M. A. (2002). Social dominance in monkeys: Dopamine D2 receptors and cocaine self-administration. *Nature Neuroscience, 5*(2), 169–174.

Noble, C. H., & Kumar, M. (2008). Using product design strategically to create deeper consumer connections. *Business Horizons, 51*(5), 441–450.

Oosterhof, N. N., & Todorov, A. (2008). The functional basis of face evaluation. *Proceedings of the National Academy of Sciences, 105*(32), 11087–11092.

Ordabayeva, N., & Chandon, P. (2011). Getting ahead of the Joneses: When equality increases conspicuous consumption among bottom-tier consumers. *Journal of Consumer Research, 38*(1), 27–41.

Orth, U. R., & Malkewitz, K. (2008). Holistic package design & consumer brand impressions. *Journal of Marketing, 72*(3), 64–81.

Page, C., & Herr, P. M. (2002). An investigation of the processes by which product design and brand strength interact to determine initial affect and quality judgments. *Journal of Consumer Psychology, 12*(2), 133–147.

Plummer, J. T. (1985). How personality makes a difference. *Journal of Advertising Research, 24*(6), 27–31.

Seva, R. R., Duh, H. B.-L., & Helander, M. G. (2007). The marketing implications of affective product design. *Applied Ergonomics, 38*(6), 723–731.

Short, L. A., Mondloch, C. J., McCormick, C. M., Carré, J. M., Ma, R., Fu, G., & Lee, K. (2012). Detection of propensity for aggression based on facial structure irrespective of face race. *Evolution and Human Behavior, 33*(2), 121–129.

Steklis, H. D., & Raleigh, M. J. (1979). Behavioral and neurobiological aspects of primate vocalization and facial expression. *Neurobiology of Social Communication in Primates*, 257–282. doi:10.1016/B978–0–12–665650–3.50015–3

Stirrat, M., & Perrett, D. I. (2010). Valid facial cues to cooperation and trust male facial width and trustworthiness. *Psychological Science, 21*(3), 349–354.

Stirrat, M., & Perrett, D. I. (2012). Face structure predicts cooperation men with wider faces are more generous to their in-group when out-group competition is salient. *Psychological Science, 23*(7), 718–722.

Tsujimura, H., & Banissy, M. J. (2013). Human face structure correlates with professional baseball performance: Insights from professional Japanese baseball players. *Biology Letters, 9*(3). doi:10.1098/rsbl.2013.0140

Underwood, R.L. (2003). The communicative power of product packaging: Creating brand identity via lived and mediated experience, *Journal of Marketing Theory and Practice, 9*(Winter), 62–76.

Valentine, K.A., Li, N.P., Penke, L., & Perrett, D.I. (2014). Judging a man by the width of his face the role of facial ratios and dominance in mate choice at speed-dating events. *Psychological Science, 25*(3), 806–811.

van Hooff, J.A.R.A.M. (1967). The facial displays of catarrhine monkeys and apes. In D. Morris (Ed.), *Primate Ethology* (pp. 7–68). London: Weidenfeld & Nicolson.

Wong, E.M., Ormiston, M.E., & Haselhuhn, M.P. (2011). A face only an investor could love: CEOs' facial structure predicts their firms' financial performance. *Psychological Science, 22*(12), 1478–1483.

Zebrowitz, L.A., & Collins, M.A. (1997). Accurate social perception at zero acquaintance: The affordances of a Gibsonian approach. *Personality and Social Psychology Review, 1*(3), 204–223.

Zebrowitz-McArthur, L., & Montepare, J.M. (1989). Contributions of a baby face and a childlike voice to impressions of moving and talking faces. *Journal of Nonverbal Behavior, 13*, 189–203.

11

HOW CONSUMERS RESPOND TO CUTE PRODUCTS

Tingting Wang and Anirban Mukhopadhyay

HONG KONG UNIVERSITY OF SCIENCE
AND TECHNOLOGY

Cute products are everywhere, and cuteness is big money. For example, Hello Kitty, a global icon for 40 years now, reaps $5 billion annually in profits for her mother-company, Sanrio (Kovarovic, 2011). Another giant company that has mastered the art of capitalizing cuteness, and indeed for many people is synonymous with the concept, is Disney—currently valued at over $23 billion (Forbes, 2013). Countless companies, brands, and their attendant knock-offs rely on cuteness to allure customers. Their reach spans product categories from stuffed toys, cartoons, clothes, household appliance, fast food, and automobiles, to even airlines (Barrett, 2010). The ubiquity and commercial success of corporate behemoths such as Sanrio and Disney proves that cuteness can be a critical element in marketing.

The remarkable success of cuteness in product design makes it a particularly important topic for researchers and practitioners alike; however, in contrast to its ubiquity on store shelves, cuteness is in surprisingly short supply in academic marketing research. This chapter aims to provide a review of the research conducted on cuteness. We propose to span the fields of ethology, neural science, and psychology, to borrow, apply, and adapt what is relevant to marketing. First, we will review cuteness as a construct, and the factors that determine the extent to which people perceive a given stimulus as being cute. We will then elaborate on people's responses to cute objects, cognitive as well as affective, which have developed through the process of evolution and continue to affect consumer decision making in modern times. Following this, we will discuss in detail the downstream influence of cuteness on consumers' behaviors as well as implications for designers and marketers.

Types of Cuteness

Cuteness is ubiquitous in the marketplace, and the word "cute" is equally commonplace in the vernacular. It is therefore important at the outset to provide a clear definition of the concept of cuteness. "Cute" is a frequently used term in daily communication, and it has multiple meanings ranging from "someone that is sweet and nice" to "something that you want to squeeze" and "behaviors that are funny and humorous" (Urban dictionary online, n.d.; Ihara & Nittono, 2012). These various connotations attached to the word "cute" in modern language complicate its definition.

In contrast to these various different meanings of cuteness in colloquial language, however, the academic representation of this construct is reassuringly clear. An object is considered "cute" is it satisfies either of two criteria. The classic criterion is known as *Kindchenschema*, and it assesses the degree to which the object is baby-like in appearance (Hildebrandt & Fitzgerald, 1979; Lorenz, 1943; Sternglanz, Gray, & Murakami, 1977). This is the well-accepted definition of cuteness in the literature: a prototypically cute object possesses a specific configuration of infantile behavioral and physical features (Alley, 1981, 1983; Sherman, Haidt, & Coan, 2009). Recently, Nenkov and Scott (2014) proposed a second dimension of cuteness that focuses on characteristics of whimsical fun and playfulness. These two definitions of cuteness are distinctively different from each other, and in the following paragraphs, we will elaborate on each conceptualization in detail.

Kindchenschema *Cuteness*

First formalized by the German anthropologist Konrad Lorenz (1943), cuteness is defined as the configuration of visually perceived physical and behavioral features, which are characteristically babyish or infantile—hence *Kindchenschema*. Lorenz (1943) suggested that the physical characteristics of infants, such as a relatively big head compared to the body size, round and protruding cheeks, large eyes placed relatively low in the face, and plump and rounded body shape with soft-elastic surface texture, when integrated together, together make a stimulus appear cute. An object that possesses these features, or a large enough proportion of them, can simulate the physical attractiveness of infants and make people perceive it as cute and adorable. In short, cuteness represents infantility.

Since *Kindchenschema* cuteness comprises certain specific physical features, objects that possess greater numbers of these characteristics, and in specific configurations, are more appealing and more attractive than others. For example, some babies are cuter than others. As a consequence, perceived cuteness may be systematically susceptible to changes in physical features, and may be reduced or increased by modifying these physical features. Let us take the shape of the head as an example. The shapes of the heads of human infants, as well as of infants of other mammals, are uniquely different from the corresponding head shapes of mature adults. This suggests that subtle changes in the shape of the head may affect the perceived cuteness of a given individual. Indeed, Alley (1981) found that drawings of babies with more infantile head shapes were judged as cuter than those with less baby-like head shapes, keeping other physical features constant. Similarly, by measuring the perceived cuteness of drawings of objects that varied in these specific physical characteristics, including facial features (e.g., eye size, eye width, shape of cheeks, forehead, head size, head shape) and bodily features (e.g., body shape and surface), researchers have identified these stimulus-based physical determinants of perceived cuteness (Alley, 1981, 1983; Sternglanz et al., 1977). Adopting a different method, other researchers have utilized photos of human babies and animals that differ naturally in their physical features to ascertain the *Kindchenschema* features (e.g., Glocker et al., 2009; Robson & Moss, 1970; Sprengelmeyer et al., 2009). Consistent with Lorenz's (1943) observations, these researchers too arrived at similar sets of the physical characteristics that determine cuteness—cute objects tend to have large round eyes, middle-placed noses, round and protruding cheeks, protruding foreheads, round faces, big heads, and thick extremities.

Research has also established that the effect of these physical characteristics on people's cuteness perceptions is robust and it tends to dominate the effects of other visual cues. For example, facial expressions of positive versus negative emotions are usually found to increase perceived attractiveness (Hildebrandt, 1983; Power, Hildebrandt, & Fitzgerald, 1982). However, perceptions of cuteness driven by *Kindchenschema* characteristics override the effects of facial expressions (Hildebrandt, 1983). Specifically, in the study, participants were shown different sets of photographs of 24 different infants, which varied in their facial expressions, and were instructed to rate the cuteness of each photo. The results showed that although positive facial expressions increased perceived cuteness, the cuteness ratings varied less within each infant than across infants. That is, cute babies were generally rated as looking cute, despite the expressions they conveyed—highlighting the robustness of *Kindchenschema* on the perception of cuteness.

This robust effect of *Kindchenschema* is important because although people's lay beliefs about cuteness may include meanings other than infantility, as per the dictionary meanings listed above, yet, infantility is deemed as cute universally (Golle, Lisibach, Mast, & Lobmaier, 2013; Ihara & Nittono, 2012; Sanefuji, Ohgami, & Hashiya, 2007). For example, Sanefuji et al. (2007) found that preschool children have similar preferences for cute objects, including cute infants and cute animals, as adults. In their studies, Sanefuji et al. (2007) instructed both adults and preschool children to rank order images of human beings, chimpanzees, rabbits, dogs, and cats of different ages, and found that adults and preschool children showed similar patterns in perceptions of cuteness. The finding that children with little cultural experience have similar perceptions of *Kindchenschema* cuteness is consistent with other research evidence (e.g., Montepare & Zebrowitz-McArthur, 1989; Zebrowitz,

1997), suggesting that the perception of *Kindchenschema* cuteness is universal rather than culturally determined. Hence, responses to *Kindchenschema* cuteness are strong, and possibly hard-wired, as we will discuss below. This may explain not only why the lure of cuteness is so strong, but also why *Kindchenschema* cuteness is generalizable to non-human entities such Hello Kitty toasters and Mickey Mouse desk lamps. But first, we address the second dimension of cuteness.

Whimsical Cuteness

Very different from *Kindchenschema* cuteness is "whimsical cuteness." From examinations of the cute products sold in the marketplace, Nenkov and Scott (2014) observed and proposed a novel and ignored dimension of cuteness. They called this "whimsical cuteness," "which is associated with capricious humor and playful disposition." This has nothing to do with infantility. For example, an ice cream spoon shaped like a lady's coiffure is "whimsical cute" because the design is playful. Other examples of whimsical cute products include "an ice-cream scoop shaped like a miniature person or a dress with tropical colors and pink flamingos" (Nenkov & Scott, 2014, p. 327). The French firm Pylones is an excellent example of a marketer capitalizing on whimsical cuteness. As the firm's website says, it specializes in "poetic and colorful objects" with "shapes, often figurative", and promises its customers to "write many beautiful stories together; a smile, a wink, a burst of laughter" (http://www.pylones.com/en/).

The concept of whimsical cuteness is essentially a nod to the vernacular. Although both kinds of cuteness, *Kindchenschema* and whimsical, may be referred to as "cute" by consumers, these two constructs are distinctly different from each other, as suggested by their definitions. Consequently, they exert different influences on consumers' behaviors. In their research, Nenkov and Scott (2014) proposed that the "fun" nature of whimsical cuteness activates consumers' motivation for self-rewarding behaviors, leading them to make more indulgent consumption choices. In contrast, the vulnerability associated with *Kindchenschema* cuteness (infants are vulnerable) leads to more careful and restrained behaviors. For example, in one study, Nenkov and Scott gave participants either a whimsical cute gift card (featuring colorful circular patterns), a *Kindchenschema* cute card (featuring a cute baby), or a neutral (plain) card. Participants were then instructed to choose movies to watch from a list containing movies of which some were relatively more indulgent (i.e., lowbrow movies), while others were less so (i.e., highbrow movies). Participants with a whimsical cute gift card were more likely to choose lowbrow movies to watch than those with a *Kindchenschema* cute (or neutral) gift card, suggesting that exposure to whimsical cuteness rather than *Kindchenschema* cuteness heightens self-indulgent motivations.

Hence, these two types of cuteness have different associations, and consequently, different influences. Both types of cute products are popular in the marketplace, though anecdotal evidence suggests *Kindchenschema* is more widespread. Moreover, since the concept of *Kindchenschema* was proposed by Konrad Lorenz (1943), it has been well studied in the field of ethology and anthropology for over 70 years, exploring its biological basis, physical antecedents, and evolutionary purpose (e.g., Alley, 1981, 1983; Barrett, 2010; Berridge & Kringelbach, 2008; Berry & McArthur, 1985; Brosch, Sander, & Scherer, 2007; Glocker et al., 2009; Golle et al., 2013). Therefore, we focus our subsequent attention in this chapter on *Kindchenschema* cuteness.

Generalizing Cuteness

As mentioned, a major implication of the physical cues associated with *Kindchenschema* cuteness relates to its generalization. Lorenz (1943) observed that similar features characterize infants of different species, and proposed that cuteness is a universal representation of infantility, determined by certain physical infantile feature. Consequently, other entities that have some or all of these characteristics should be able to trigger the perception of cuteness, and indeed, cuteness perceptions are not limited to human infants but are generalized to other stimuli, including other animals, adults, and even non-living objects. For example, other mammalian baby animals (e.g., wild pigs) are perceived as cute although the adults may not be regarded as cute at all (Morreall, 1991). Baby wild pigs are small in size, with big heads and thick and short extremities, but as they reach adulthood, their physical appearance goes through dramatic changes. They gradually lose the *Kindchenschema* features, and therefore, the adults are no longer perceived as being cute. Different from wild pigs, however, some mammalian animals including human beings may preserve some infantile physical features and behavioral characteristics into adulthood—a phenomenon called *neotony* (Ryke, 1986). Therefore, adult animals and human beings who possess infantile features are perceived as cute (Berry & McArthur, 1985). Examples of adult animals that retain neotony include panda bears and koalas; they are very much similar to their offspring in terms of physical appearance and behavioral features, and are regarded as among the cutest animals (Barrett, 2010).

In order to test the generalization of the concept of cuteness from human infants to baby animals, Golle et al. (2013) adopted the perceptual adaptation paradigm. They first exposed participants to either cute human babies or cute puppies, and then measured their perception of cuteness in human infants. They found adaptation to either cute infants or cute puppies leads to similar changes in participants' perception of cuteness in human infants. This finding suggests that people have a universal processing system to code cuteness in both human infants and animals.

As a logical extension, and most directly relevant to marketing, the concept of *Kindchenschema* cuteness is also applicable to non-living commercial products. Marketers design products with exaggerated infantile visual features to make them appear as cute as possible to attract consumers (Barrett, 2010). An analysis of the change in appearance of some products over time clearly reveals a shift in product design towards cuteness. Teddy bears are an excellent exemplification of this shift: A typical teddy bear has an oversized head in proportion to its body, which is similar to human infants; and, its fluffy surface produces a comfortable and pleasant sensation when touched, much like the soft elastic skin of chubby infants. However, the original Teddy Bear produced in 1904 looked very different from the version we currently know it. This original bear looked like an adult bear—it had little if any resemblance to a human infant (Morris, Reddy, & Bunting, 1995). Over time, the teddy bear has evolved to its current cute look, with a larger head, a shorter snout, chubbier body, and shorter and thicker extremities—a far cry from the thin old bear that looked as if it would ask us to get off its lawn at any moment. The evolution of the teddy bear toward extreme cuteness is in fact evolutionary, fueled by consumers' liking for cuteness, such that the *Kindchenschema* features were repetitively selected and reproduced to arrive at the current form (Morris et al., 1995). A similar process of evolution towards *Kindchenschema* cuteness with exaggerated physical cues led to the current form of another commercial icon of cuteness, Mickey Mouse. The original Mickey Mouse looked like an actual mouse, while the current Mickey Mouse is far cuter, with his supernormal large head and big round eyes (Gould, 1979).

These examples, of teddy bears and Mickey Mouse, demonstrate the successful extension of cuteness from human babies to other non-baby objects that possesses infantile features. The generalizability of *Kindchenschema* cuteness is the basis of the popularity of cute products in the market. But if cute products are baby-like, must they necessarily be human? We now turn to the important distinction between cuteness and anthropomorphism.

Anthropomorphism and Cuteness

Anthropomorphism, or humanization, refers to people's tendency to attribute human-like characteristics, intentions, and behaviors to nonhuman objects (Aggarwal & McGill, 2007; Epley, Waytz, & Cacioppo, 2007). Recent research on anthropomorphism has identified two sources of humanization behaviors: cognition-based and motivation-based. Cognition-based anthropomorphism refers to the analogical reasoning of using human schema as a structure to think about nonhuman entities (Morewedge, Preston, & Wegner, 2007). Objects with human-like features are likely to trigger the human schema and consequently to be viewed in an anthropomorphic way. This explains why the Michelin Man can have a personality, and why his personality can be different from that of Miss Piggy. However, motivation-based humanization suggests people may anthropomorphize objects due to specific desires; for example, loneliness and desire for social contact may increase the tendency to humanize nonhuman objects (Epley, Waytz, Akalis, & Cacioppo, 2008). Overall, the accessibility of agentic beliefs increases anthropomorphic thinking. For example, Kim and McGill (2011) found that when playing with a slot machine, high-power participants who win (vs. lose) the game are more likely to humanize the slot machine since the machine is acting like other people would have (i.e., giving the participants what they want), and similarly, low-power people who lose (vs. win) the game tend to humanize the slot machine because the machine winning is again like other people playing against them would behave (i.e., getting what they want).

Thinking about objects as humanlike has specific influences on consumers' behaviors towards the product; as Chandler and Schwarz (2010) say "when people think about objects in anthropomorphic terms, they apply knowledge about the social world to the inanimate world" (p. 139). In other words, consumers tend to interact with humanized products in a social way, which in turn has downstream consequences for their attitudes and behaviors towards the product. For instance, Chandler and Schwarz (2010) found that humanization of products directs consumers' attention away from instrumental attributes such as product quality and performance. Consumers focus instead on relational status and social factors, which result in consumers' reduced intention to replace the products. In one study, the authors primed participants with either social anthropomorphic thinking or impersonal thinking by asking them to evaluate their car on either personality traits (e.g., reserved, quarrelsome, open to new experiences) or mechanical attributes (quiet, responsive, shaky) respectively. They then measured participants' intention to replace their car before graduation. Participants primed with anthropomorphic thinking reported a much lower rate of intention to replace the car compared to those in the mechanical attributes evaluation condition. This suggests the proposition that humanization leads to favorable consumer responses because they are seeing the products as human-like. Similarly, Aggarwal and McGill (2007) found that humanized products cause consumers to show more favorable attitudes.

Anthropomorphism is found to activate favorable consumer reactions because consumers think of and treat humanized products in a social way. Although cuteness refers to configuration of infantile features, which are human-like, these two concepts are meaningfully and significantly different. The human-like features lead to humanization, but only infantile *Kindchenschema* features constitute the concept of cuteness. Put differently, not all cute objects are humanized, and not all humanized objects are cute. For example, Jabba the Hutt, the evil alien from the Star Wars series, is a humanized sloth who is ugly, repulsive, and anything but cute. Humanization is an important and widespread marketing tool, but since cuteness represents particular configurations of physical characteristics with fundamental evolutionary significance for human beings, it elicits unique and distinctive reactions from people. We will now turn to a discussion of how people may differ in their responses to cuteness, and the corresponding consequences for consumer behaviors.

Interpersonal Differences in Cuteness Perceptions

The popularity of cute products in the market implies that at least some consumers have strong preferences for cuteness. But who are these people, and what are their identifying characteristics, if any? Prior research is silent on this question. Might it be gender, age, or something else? Previous research, as described above, has largely focused on stimulus-based characteristics that influence perceived cuteness. These include physical characteristics (Alley, 1981, 1983; Hildebrandt & Fitzgerald, 1979) and emotional expressions (Hildebrandt, 1983; Karraker & Stern, 1990). However, there is little established knowledge regarding individual differences in cuteness perception, and the mechanisms underlying such individual variations. Our research is aimed at filling this gap in the literature.

Cuteness is an evolutionarily important stimulus for human beings, because the cuteness of infants is a primary elicitor of care-giving behaviors from adults (Lorenz, 1943; Morreall, 1991; Robson & Moss, 1970). Ensuring the life of the next generation is vital for the survival of any species; therefore, many animals including human beings have evolved a natural primitive instinct to care for and nurture their offspring (Darwin, 1873). Given this evolutionary role of cuteness, people's perceptions of and responses to cute entities are biologically hardwired rather than acquired by learning (Berridge & Kringelbach, 2008). The ability to recognize and differentiate cute entities from non-cute ones reflects an innate human motive to nurture and care for the offspring. To corroborate this notion, it's found that preschool children perceive cuteness in the same way as mature adults (Sanefuji et al., 2007).

There is a great deal of evidence for the association between infant cuteness and nurturant adult responses. For example, cute infants, compared to less cute ones, receive more affectionate interactions from their mothers (Langlois, Ritter, Casey, & Sawin, 1995). Cute babies attract more attention from adults than the less cute ones (Broch, Sander, & Scherer, 2007). Additionally, cuteness regulates the emotional attachment between parents and their babies; infant cuteness produces social pleasure for parents (Berridge & Kringelbach, 2008), and mobilizes parental love (Parsons, Young, Kumari, Stein, & Kringelbach, 2011). The bottom line is that cuteness in a baby functions as a positive, attractive stimulus that drives people to approach it.

A simple principle of motivated behavior is that people approach rewards and avoid punishments. Rewarding stimuli generate sensory pleasure, prompt approach motivation, and elicit approaching behaviors, fulfilling the purpose of survival (Elliot, 1999). In contrast, punishment-related or aversive stimuli activate avoidance motivation and elicit withdrawing behaviors. Both rewarding stimuli and aversive stimuli elicit responses that serve the Darwinian goal of ensuring survival. Many recent findings from neuroscientific research provide evidence for the relationship between cuteness and approach motivation. For example, maternal love, as an expression of parental instinct, activates brain regions associated with reward-processing (the substantia nigra, the globus pallidus, and the nucleus of Meynert; Bartels & Zeki, 2004). Similarly, when people look at children's faces, brain areas associated with reward processing get activated (Kringelbach et al., 2008; Leibenluft, Gobbini, Harrison, & Haxby, 2004). Glocker et al. (2009) manipulated photos of human infants using morphing techniques to create multiple images of the same baby that varied in degrees of cuteness. They then monitored participants' brain activity while viewing these pictures. Their results showed that the activity of the brain areas associated with the anticipation of reward, altruistic, and affiliative behaviors increased when participants viewed cuter images. Together, these findings show that the rewarding-processing neural system plays a significant role in people's perception of and reaction to cuteness.

Critically, individuals differ in their sensitivity of the neural systems regulating the processing of rewarding (as well as punishing) cues (Gray, 1981). Thus, individual differences in the sensitivity of the reward-processing neural system may well determine individual differences in perceptions of, and responses to, the primitive reward offered by cuteness. Much research has shown that people's affective, motivational, and behavioral reactions to incentives and punishments are driven by two independent motivational systems: the behavioral approach system (BAS), which regulates the processing of rewarding stimuli, appetitive motivation, and approach behaviors, and the behavioral inhibition system (BIS), which regulates the processing of punishment-related stimuli, avoidance motivation, and avoidance behavior (Gray, 1981). BAS is involved in processing of and responding to rewarding stimuli; it organizes, motivates, and guides behaviors in response to positive incentives. In contrast, BIS is activated in processing of and responding to negative incentives. It motivates and regulates reactions to negative cues for punishment or pain (Gray, 1981, 1990). So, as motivational orientation systems, the BAS (vs. BIS) regulates people's appetitive (vs. aversive) motivations and their corresponding behaviors.

BAS and BIS are fundamental "biobehavioral" systems as distinct from social-cognitive models of human psychology (such as regulatory focus theory; see Strauman & Wilson [2010] for an extensive discussion of the similarities and differences between the two). Moreover, BAS and BIS are independent of each other rather than correlated. People differ in the sensitivity of their BAS and BIS; some people have highly sensitive reward-processing neural system and highly sensitive punishment-processing neural system at the same time. Others may have relatively insensitive reward-processing systems and punishment-processing systems at the same time. These two systems regulate, organize, motivate, and guide their approach (avoidance) behaviors in response to rewarding (aversive) stimuli. Thus, the characteristics of these two systems determine people's processing of rewarding (and punishing) stimuli, and subsequently shape their sensitivity, behavioral responsiveness, and affect (Gray, 1981; Sutton & Davidson, 1997). In particular people with relatively strong systems are more sensitive and responsive to positive incentives (cues of danger). For example, people with clinical depression, which is linked with deficient BAS and overactive BIS (Kasch, Rottenberg, Arnow, & Rotlib, 2002), exhibited reduced sensitivity to rewards but similar responsiveness to punishments compared to non-depressed people (Henriques & Davidson, 2000).

As the processing of rewarding stimuli and punishing stimuli is linked with approaching behaviors and avoiding behaviors respectively, the sensitivity of BAS and BIS can shape people's approach and avoidance tendencies (Gray, 1981; Carver, 2006). Carver and White (1994) created the Behavioral Approach Scale and Behavioral Inhibition Scale (BIS/BAS scales) to measure an individual's general approach and avoidance tendencies through self-report indicators of the sensitivity of their behavioral approach and behavioral inhibition systems. In particular, people scoring high on the BAS subscale of BIS/BAS scales should have a highly sensitive behavioral approach system (BAS), and thus would exhibit stronger approach motivation towards rewarding incentives than those who score low on the BAS subscale, that is, having a relatively insensitive behavioral approach system. The BAS/BIS scale is the standard measure of individual differences in approach and avoidance. Using this scale, Simon et al. (2010) found that in receipt of rewards, people scoring high on BAS showed heightened activity in the ventral striatum, the neural substrate of the approach motivational system (Smillie, 2008). Similarly, Desjardins, Zelenski, and Coplan (2008) found that mothers who scored high on BAS were more nurturing than those who scored low on BAS, and Wadhwa, Shiv, and Nowlis (2008) found that high-BAS participants were more sensitive to rewarding drinks. Indeed, much research suggests that people who are higher in BAS are more sensitive to rewarding stimuli in general (Revelle, 1995).

Building on the foregoing discussions, we propose that people's motivational approach orientation influences their processing of, and their reactions to, cute entities. Thus, we propose that in addition to the relationship between *Kindchenschema* features and perceived cuteness, a person's general approach tendencies (i.e., BAS) can moderate their responses to cute stimuli. Specifically, given a stimulus with *Kindchenschema* features, people exhibiting strong approach motivation (i.e., high-BAS), compared to those with weak approach motivation (low-BAS), should perceive this stimulus as being "cuter" and should like it more.

These propositions are supported in a couple of studies we conducted (Wang & Mukhopadhyay, 2014a). In one study, we showed participants picture of either cute stimuli or non-cute stimuli (which included products, animals, and human infants), and asked them to rate their cuteness on a Likert scale (1 = not cute at all, 100 = extremely cute). After a filler task, we asked them to respond to the BAS/BIS scale. As predicted, a regression analysis of perceived cuteness on stimulus type, participants' BAS, and their interaction revealed a main effect of stimulus type and a significant interaction effect. The positive effect of *Kindchenschema* on perceived cuteness was stronger for people scoring high on BAS than for those with low-BAS. Similarly, in another study, high-BAS people reported higher liking for cute animals and cute products in general more than low-BAS people. These results supported our proposition that people's approach motivation regulates their processing of and reaction to cute objects.

Complex Consequences of Cuteness: Opposing Factors

Kindchenschema cuteness elicits an approach motivation, as discussed, but also carries several other rich connotations, including cognitive, motivational, affective, inferential, and behavioral aspects. Two of these, cognition and affect, have important consequences for product and promotion design. In this section, we discuss the research investigating responses to cute entities, and highlight how there may be opposing influences of cognition and affect, with significant downstream effects on consumers' decision making.

Inferential Responses to Cute Objects

One important mechanism by which cuteness in an infant stimulates the interaction between an adult and the infant is via activating inferential responses from the adult. People make inferences about traits and qualities from the physical appearance of other people because these inferences are valuable for survival and social interaction (Haselton & Buss, 2000). For example, males infer a female's reproductive fertility from her body shape (Singh, 1993). Correspondingly, cuter infants are believed to be more sociable, active, competitive, and likable (Karraker & Stern, 1990; Stephan & Langlois, 1984), and are more likely to elicit adults' intention to interact with them (Maier, Holmes, Slaymaker, & Reich, 1984). Such inferences are relatively stable and override other characteristics such as facial expression and gender (Karraker & Stern, 1990).

The primary inference that cuteness triggers is vulnerability, which stimulates nurturing responses (McDougall, 1908). Infants are cute, and they are at the most vulnerable stage of life; consequently, people tend to associate cuteness with physical weakness and vulnerability (Berry & McArthur, 1985; Lorenz, 1943). Traits and qualities inferred from physical appearance can provide useful information, and hence the generalization of such associations is often adaptive (McArthur & Baron, 1983). When people encounter cuteness, they make these inferences spontaneously (Berry & McArthur, 1985; Gorn, Jiang, & Johar, 2008; Keating, Randall, Kendrick, & Gutshall, 2003; Nenkov & Scott, 2014; Zebrowitz, Kendall-Tackett, & Fafel, 1991). However, people overgeneralize the traits associated with infants, including the trait of vulnerability, to baby-faced adults. For example, baby-faced adults tend to be evaluated as more dependent, naive, submissive, warm, kinder, more honest, and more trustworthy than mature-faced ones (Berry & McArthur, 1985; Friedman & Zebrowitz, 1992; Keating et al., 2003; Gorn et al., 2008; Zebrowitz et al., 1991). Gorn et al. (2008) found that participants tend to trust cute baby-faced CEOs more than mature-faced CEOs of a company facing a product harm crisis, perhaps because belief in honesty is triggered by facial cuteness cues.

As discussed above, such inferences of vulnerability from cuteness can generalize even further; specifically, to cute stimuli that are not even human, such as cute products. In line with the discussion on anthropomorphization above, people make inferences from the physical appearance of commercial products. For example, Windhager et al. (2008) found that consumers draw similar inferences about car front ends as they do from human faces when evaluating the cars on certain traits. Cars with a large windshield and a small size, which resemble the big forehead and small size of human infants, are judged as more submissive, more friendly, and more agreeable. Cute products are purposefully designed with exaggerated infantile features so that consumers are likely to make similar inferences from products' cute appearance (Nenkov & Scott, 2014).

Making inferences has long been documented as affecting people's decisions and behaviors by changing their cognition and evaluation (e.g., Dick, Chakravarti, & Biehal, 1990). The vulnerability inferred from cuteness can exert a strong attraction for consumers. However, the same vulnerability inferences from cute products can have serious adverse effects. In a series of studies, we tested consumers' reactions to the malfunction of products that were *Kindchenschema* cute. As we expected, the inferences about vulnerability that consumers made from cute products—which initially attracted them to the product, especially if they were high in BAS—also discouraged them from repairing and reusing these same products when they malfunctioned. In this case, the vulnerability inferences turned against the cute product because they functioned as a diagnostic signal of inferior quality. As another example, the vulnerability inferences generated by cuteness may have a negative implication on consumers' perception of brand personality; specifically, the dimension of ruggedness (Aaker, 1997). Inferences of high vulnerability from a cute brand may well lead to the perception of low ruggedness in the brand.

Affective Responses to Cute Objects

Apart from the automatic inferential responses from cuteness, people simultaneously experience positive emotions at the sight of cute entities (Hildebrandt & Fitzgerald, 1978; Sherman & Haidt, 2011). Cuteness arouses positive feelings as a basic sensory pleasure (Berridge & Kringelbach, 2008; Hildebrandt & Fitzgerald, 1978; Lorenz,

1943; Zebrowitz, 1997). For example, Hildebrandt and Fitzgerald (1978) found that when people look at infants, the facial muscles related with positive emotions are automatically activated. Moreover, seeing cute animals makes people experience positive moods and helps them to better deal with stress (Rossbach & Wilson, 1992). Not only can cute infants and cute animals activate positive feelings, even cute products can make people feel happy (Miesler, Leder, & Herrmann, 2011). Based on the fact that people tend to view the front of cars in a similar way as they perceive human faces, Miesler et al. (2011) manipulated the fronts of cars to be either more or less baby-like and then measured participants' micro-level facial expressions using facial electromyograms when they viewed pictures of these cars. They found that participants who viewed cute baby-faced car fronts showed stronger activation of facial muscles related with positive emotions than those who viewed pictures of the original cars, in a similar manner to when they viewed infants' faces. These positive emotional reactions to cuteness are initiated very quickly, indicating their automaticity and the fact that they appear to require no cognitive appraisals (Miesler et al., 2011).

The affective reactions to cuteness are more complex than mere positive mood: Cuteness also triggers specific hardwired emotions. In particular, cuteness elicits the emotion of tenderness (Batson, Lishner, Cook, & Sawyer, 2005; Kalawski, 2010; Lishner, Oceja, Stocks, & Zaspel, 2008; Sherman & Haidt, 2011). Ethnologists and psychologists have long proposed that human beings experience tenderness towards cute entities (McCabe, 1988; McDougall, 1908; Sherman et al., 2009). William McDougall (1908) suggested that people naturally experience tender feelings at the sight of human infants. The emotion of tenderness is a strong, stable, and robust affective reaction to cuteness, and is the direct emotional elicitor of adults' parental instinct. Corroborating McDougall's argument, Kalawski (2010) demonstrated that the emotion of tenderness is one of the basic emotions, which are defined as "emotions that have been characterized as having evolutionarily old neurobiological substrates, as well as an evolved feeling component and capacity for expressive and other behavioral actions of evolutionary origin" (Izard, 2007, p. 261).

According to appraisal theories of emotion, every emotion arises from specific patterns of cognition (Han, Lerner, & Keltner, 2007; Lazarus, 1991). People make cognitive appraisals of a situation along certain dimensions, such as certainty, agency, and valence, and these cognitive appraisals combine to create specific emotions. Recent research has identified the appraisal of vulnerability as the core cognitive appraisal antecedent of the emotion of tenderness (Lishner, Oceja, Stocks, & Zaspel, 2008). That is, people experience feelings of tenderness when they see cute infants and cute animals because the baby-like physical and behavioral features displayed by these cute infants and animals are heuristic cues of vulnerability (Lorenz, 1943). As discussed, people infer vulnerability not just from human infants and baby animals, but also from products with *Kindchenschema* features. As a result, in addition to their general positive affective response, consumers may also experience tender emotions when they see cute products (Miesler et al., 2011).

Miesler et al. (2011) found that positive affective responses to cute products are only initiated when the situation requires response to cuteness, but this may be due to their subtle manipulation of product cuteness. Particularly, in the car images they used, they enlarged the headlights to make the car appear more infantile. This is a subtle manipulation, and it is possible that their participants were unable to recognize and appreciate the car's cuteness. However, in the market, companies create many commercial products of readily recognizably cute appearance, such as the Volkswagen Beetle and the Mini Cooper (keeping with the same category), or decorate products with cute images and cartoon characters. Consumers should be more likely to appreciate the cuteness of these products given their highly salient cues.

Emotions motivate people to behave in ways consistent with the cognitive appraisal underlying them (Han et al., 2007), and hence tenderness motivates nurturing and care-giving behaviors (Frijda, 1986; McDougall, 1908). Therefore, the tenderness elicited by cuteness has important consequences in motivating people's prosocial behaviors. Apart from the prevalent use of cuteness in commerce, cuteness also frequently appears in charitable appeals that aim to elicit prosocial behaviors, such as the donation of money, time, effort, or blood. For example, the World Wildlife Fund frequently puts images of cute animals on their advertisements that request attention and care to the living conditions of animals. Similarly, charity advertisements concerning the living conditions of children in underdeveloped countries frequently display photos of cute smiling children. This is presumably because charity organizations believe that cute images can enhance people's prosocial behaviors. Considering the role of tenderness in activating caregiving behaviors, it is likely that images of cute victims may elicit stronger prosocial intentions from potential donors than other images. This is exactly what we found across several studies (Wang & Mukhopadhyay, 2014b). Specifically, victims' cuteness, together with the perceived danger to them, enhances people's prosocial donations. Likewise, in a large-scale field study, we found that cute images, when combined with slogans that prompt activity (i.e., high BAS), increase the quantity of material that people recycle.

Implications for Designers

Cuteness is ubiquitous, but should it be? It is a common lay theory that cute products are designed for female consumers only, or for young people. However, an extensive review of the literature suggests otherwise, as does our data. In fact, there are no clear findings regarding sex differences in perception of and responses to cute objects (e.g., Hildebrandt & Fitzgerald, 1978; Karraker & Stern, 1990; Parsons et al., 2011; Power et al., 1982). Some researchers find age and gender effects, whereas others don't. In our research, we have found no consistent effect of either. As Phyllis Berman (1980) suggested, any observed gender differences in responses to cute objects may result from participants' expectation "to present themselves in what they assume to be a socially appropriate manner" (p. 10), which vary depending on the norms of the individual's culture and the extent to which he/she has adopted the norm.

More importantly, research has shown that even within each gender, people's general approach motivation matters; for example, as mentioned, mothers who were high in approach motivation (BAS) are more nurturing to their babies than mothers who score low on BAS (Desjardins et al., 2008). Across our studies, we also found that people with a strong approach motivation perceive cute objects as cuter and report higher liking for cute objects, even after controlling for gender differences. These findings suggest to designers that cute products with *Kindchenschema* features should be targeted at people with high BAS.

But how can this be done? We suggest three methods that designers can employ. The simplest is to use surveys. Designers can identify consumers high in BAS by conducting consumer surveys, and then promote cute products with cute advertisements for them. Instead of formal consumer surveys, it should be possible to introduce a couple of BAS-related questions in membership sign-up forms or other such instruments. Secondly, designers in specific product categories may be able to identify specific correlates of BAS. For example, people high in BAS are generally more active, and hence may be more into adventure sports, and more likely to try stimulating products, new experiences, etc. And finally, as our research shows, it is also possible to momentarily stimulate consumers' BAS using messages and slogans that cue activity. Such messages may well increase people's liking for cute objects. Therefore, another approach that designers may adopt is to include BAS features when designing product package or commercial advertisements for the cute products to appeal to the more responsive consumer segment.

Implications for a Theory of Design

Overall, this chapter aims to provide a better understanding of the concept of cuteness, including the two types of stimulus-based determinants of cuteness—*Kindchenchema* and whimsicality. We found evidence for individual differences in perceptions of and reaction to cute entities, and for the multidimensionality of reactions to cuteness. These factors are important for theories of design because of the potential downstream consequences of cuteness perception for consumers' behaviors. Understanding each of these factors can improve our understanding of product and promotion design. The fact that people have multiple reactions to cute objects suggests that designers should selectively stimulate the relative strength or salience of these individual "levers," as appropriate. To summarize, cuteness is an important marketing tool that is worthy of more future research exploring its role in design and consumer decision making.

References

Aaker, J. L. (1997). Dimensions of brand personality. *Journal of Marketing Research, 34*(3), 347–356.

Aggarwal, P., & McGill, A. L. (2007). Is that car smiling at me? Schema congruity as a basis for evaluating anthropomorphized products. *Journal of Consumer Research, 34*(4), 468–479.

Alley, T. R. (1981). Head shape and the perception of cuteness. *Developmental Psychology, 17*(5), 650–654.

Alley, T. R. (1983). Age-related changes in body proportions, body size, and perceived cuteness. *Perceptual and Motor Skills, 56*(2), 615–622.

Barrett, D. (2010). *Supernormal stimuli: How primal urges overran their evolutionary purpose.* New York, NY: W. W. Norton.

Bartels, A., & Zeki, S. (2004). The neural correlates of maternal and romantic love. *Neuroimage, 21*(3), 1155–1166.

Batson, C. D., Lishner, D. A., Cook, J., & Sawyer, S. (2005). Similarity and nurturance: Two possible sources of empathy for strangers. *Basic & Applied Social Psychology, 27*(1), 15–25.

Berman, P. W. (1980). Are women more responsive than men to the young? A review of developmental and situational variables. *Psychological Bulletin, 88*(3), 668–695.

Berridge, K., & Kringelbach, M. (2008). Affective neuroscience of pleasure: Reward in humans and animals. *Psychopharmacology, 199*(3), 457–480.

Berry, D. S., & McArthur, L. Z. (1985). Some components and consequences of a babyface. *Journal of Personality and Social Psychology, 48*(2), 312–323.

Brosch, T., Sander, D., & Scherer, K. R. (2007). That baby caught my eye . . . attention capture by infant faces. *Emotion, 7*(3), 685–689.

Carver, C. S. (2006). Approach, avoidance, and the self-regulation of affect and action. *Motivation & Emotion, 30*(2), 105–110.

Carver, C. S., & White, T. L. (1994). Behavioral inhibition, behavioral activation, and affective responses to impending reward and punishment: The BIS/BAS scales. *Journal of Personality and Social Psychology, 67*(2), 319–333.

Chandler, J., & Schwarz, N. (2010). Use does not wear ragged the fabric of friendship: Thinking of objects as alive makes people less willing to replace them. *Journal of Consumer Psychology, 20*(2), 138–145.

Cute. (n.d.). In Urban Dictionary online, Retrieved September 24, 2014, from http://www.urbandictionary.com/define.php?term=cute

Darwin, C. (1873). *The expression of emotions in man and animals.* New York, NY: Appleton.

Desjardins, J., Zelenski, J. M., & Coplan, R. J. (2008). An investigation of maternal personality, parenting styles, and subjective well-being. *Personality and Individual Differences, 44*(3), 587–597.

Dick, A., Chakravarti, D., & Biehal, G. (1990). Memory-based inferences during consumer choice. *Journal of Consumer Research, 17*(1), 82–93.

Elliot, A. J. (1999). Approach and avoidance motivation and achievement goals. *Educational Psychologist, 34*(3), 169–189.

Epley, N., Waytz, A., Akalis, S., & Cacioppo, J. T. (2008). When we need a human: Motivational determinants of anthropomorphism. *Social Cognition, 26*(2), 143–155.

Epley, N., Waytz, A., & Cacioppo, J. T. (2007). On seeing human: A three-factor theory of anthropomorphism. *Psychological Review, 114*(4), 864.

Forbes. (2013). The world's most valuable brands. Retrieved from http://www.forbes.com/powerful-brands/list/

Friedman, H., & Zebrowitz, L. A. (1992). The contribution of typical sex differences in facial maturity to sex role stereotypes. *Personality and Social Psychology Bulletin, 18*(4), 430–438.

Frijda, N. H. (1986). *The emotions.* Cambridge: Cambridge University Press.

Glocker, M. L., Langleben, D. D., Ruparel, K., Loughead, J. W., Gur, R. C., & Sachser, N. (2009). Baby schema in infant faces induces cuteness perception and motivation for caretaking in adults. *Ethology, 115*(3), 257–263.

Golle, J., Lisibach, S., Mast, F. W., & Lobmaier, J. S. (2013). Sweet puppies and cute babies: Perceptual adaptation to babyfacedness transfers across species. *PloS One, 8*(3), e58248.

Gorn, G. J., Jiang, Y., & Johar, G. V. (2008). Babyfaces, trait inferences, and company evaluations in a public relations crisis. *Journal of Consumer Research, 35*(1), 36–49.

Gould, S. J. (1979). Mickey Mouse meets Konrad Lorenz. *Natural History, 88*(5), 30–36.

Gray, J. A. (1981). A critique of Eysenck's Theory of Personality. In H. J. Eysenck (Ed.), *A Model for Personality* (pp. 246–276). Berlin: Springer-Verlag.

Gray, J. A. (1990). Brain systems that mediate both emotion and cognition. *Cognition and Emotion, 4*(3), 269–288.

Han, S., Lerner, J. S., & Keltner, D. (2007). Feelings and consumer decision making: The appraisal-tendency framework. *Journal of Consumer Psychology, 17*(3), 158–168.

Haselton, M. G., & Buss, D. M. (2000). Error management theory: A new perspective on biases in cross-sex mind reading. *Journal of Personality and Social Psychology, 78*(1), 81–91.

Henriques, J. B., & Davidson, R. J. (2000). Decreased responsiveness to reward in depression. *Cognition & Emotion, 14*(5), 711–724.

Hildebrandt, K. A. (1983). Effect of facial expression variations on ratings of infants' physical attractiveness. *Developmental Psychology, 19*(3), 414–417.

Hildebrandt, K. A., & Fitzgerald, H. E. (1978). Adults' responses to infants varying in perceived cuteness. *Behavioural Processes, 3*(2), 159–172.

Hildebrandt, K. A., & Fitzgerald, H. E. (1979). Facial feature determinants of perceived infant attractiveness. *Infant Behavior and Development, 2,* 329–339.

Ihara, N., & Nittono, H. (2012). Cute things are not always infantile: A psychophysiological study on the feeling of cuteness. *International Journal of Psychophysiology, 85*(3), 404.

Izard, C. E. (2007). Basic emotions, natural kinds, emotion schemas, and a new paradigm. *Perspectives on Psychological Science, 2*(3), 260–280.

Kalawski, J. P. (2010). Is tenderness a basic emotion? *Motivation & Emotion, 34*(2), 158–167.

Karraker, K. H., & Stern, M. (1990). Infant physical attractiveness and facial expression: Effects on adult perceptions. *Basic and Applied Social Psychology, 11*(4), 371–385.

Kasch, K. L., Rottenberg, J., Arnow, B. A., & Gotlib, I. H. (2002). Behavioral activation and inhibition systems and the severity and course of depression. *Journal of Abnormal Psychology, 111*(4), 589.

Keating, C. F., Randall, D. W., Kendrick, T., & Gutshall, K. A. (2003). Do babyfaced adults receive more help? The (cross-cultural) case of the lost resume. *Journal of Nonverbal Behavior, 27*(2), 89–109.

Kim, S., & McGill, A. L. (2011). Gaming with Mr. Slot or gaming the slot machine? Power, anthropomorphism, and risk perception. *Journal of Consumer Research, 38*(1), 94–107.

Kovarovic, S. (2011). Hello Kitty: A brand made of cuteness. *Journal of Culture and Retail Image, 4*(1). Retrieved from http://www.library.drexel.edu/publications/dsmr/kovarovic%20final.pdf

Kringelbach, M. L., Lehtonen, A., Squire, S., Harvey, A. G., Craske, M. G., Holliday, I. E., . . . Stein, A. (2008). A specific and rapid neural signature for parental instinct. *PLoS One, 3*(2), e1664.

Langlois, J. H., Ritter, J. M., Casey, R. J., & Sawin, D. B. (1995). Infant attractiveness predicts maternal behaviors and attitudes. *Developmental Psychology, 31*(3), 464–472.

Lazarus, R. S. (1991). Cognition and motivation in emotion. *American Psychologist, 46*(4), 352–367.

Leibenluft, E., Gobbini, M. I., Harrison, T., & Haxby, J. V. (2004). Mothers' neural activation in response to pictures of their children and other children. *Biological Psychiatry, 56*(4), 225–232.

Lishner, D. A., Oceja, L. V., Stocks, E. L., & Zaspel, K. (2008). The effect of infant-like characteristics on empathic concern for adults in need. *Motivation and Emotion, 32*(4), 270–277.

Lorenz, K. (1943). Die angeborenen Formen möglicher Erfahrung [The innate forms of potential experience]. *Zeitschrift für Tierpsychologie, 5*, 233–519.

Maier, R. A., Jr., Holmes, D. L., Slaymaker, F. L., & Reich, J. N. (1984). The perceived attractiveness of preterm infants. *Infant Behavior and Development, 7*(4), 403–414.

McArthur, L. Z., & Baron, R. M. (1983). Toward an ecological theory of social perception. *Psychological Review, 90*(3), 215.

McCabe, V. (1988). Facial proportions, perceived age, and caregiving. In T. R. Alley (Ed.), *Social and applied aspects of perceiving faces* (pp. 89–95). Mahwah, NJ: Erlbaum.

McDougall, W. (1908). *An introduction to social psychology.* London: Methuen.

Miesler, L., Leder, H., & Herrmann, A. (2011). Isn't it cute: An evolutionary perspective of baby-schema effects in visual product designs. *International Journal of Design, 5*(3), 17–30.

Montepare, J. M., & Zebrowitz-McArthur, L. (1989). Children's perceptions of babyfaced adults. *Perceptual and Motor Skills, 69*(2), 467–472.

Morewedge, C. K., Preston, J., & Wegner, D. M. (2007). Timescale bias in the attribution of mind. *Journal of Personality and Social Psychology, 93*(1), 1.

Morreall, J. (1991). Cuteness. *British Journal of Aesthetics, 31*(1), 39–47.

Morris, P. H., Reddy, V., & Bunting, R. C. (1995). The survival of the cutest: Who's responsible for the evolution of the teddy bear? *Animal Behaviour, 50*(6), 1697–1700.

Nenkov, G. Y., & Scott, M. L. (2014). "So cute I could eat it up": Priming effects of cute products on indulgent consumption. *Journal of Consumer Research, 41*(2), 326–341.

Parsons, C. E., Young, K. S., Kumari, N., Stein, A., & Kringelbach, M. L. (2011). The motivational salience of infant faces is similar for men and women. *PLOS One, 6*(5), e20632.

Power, T. G., Hildebrandt, K. A., & Fitzgerald, H. E. (1982). Adults' responses to infants varying in facial expression and perceived attractiveness. *Infant Behavior and Development, 5*(1), 33–44.

Revelle, W. (1995). Personality processes. *Annual Review of Psychology, 46*(1), 295–328.

Robson, K. S., & Moss, H. A. (1970). Patterns and determinants of maternal attachment. *Journal of Pediatrics, 77*(6), 976–985.

Rossbach, K. A., & Wilson, J. P. (1992). Does a dog's presence make a person appear more likable? Two studies. *Anthrozoös, 5*(1), 40–51.

Ryke, P. (1986). Neotony and evolution. *South African Journal of Science, 82*(8), 426–431.

Sanefuji, W., Ohgami, H., & Hashiya, K. (2007). Development of preference for baby faces across species in humans (*Homo sapiens*). *Journal of Ethology, 25*(3), 249–254.

Sherman, G. D., & Haidt, J. (2011). Cuteness and disgust: The humanizing and dehumanizing effects of emotion. *Emotion Review, 3*(3), 245–251.

Sherman, G. D., Haidt, J., & Coan, J. A. (2009). Viewing cute images increases behavioral carefulness. *Emotion, 9*(2), 282–286.

Singh, D. (1993). Adaptive significance of female physical attractiveness: Role of waist-to-hip ratio. *Journal of Personality and Social Psychology, 65*(2), 293.

Smillie, L. D. (2008). What is reinforcement sensitivity? Neuroscience paradigms for approach-avoidance process theories of personality. *European Journal of Personality, 22*(5), 359–384.

Sprengelmeyer, R., Perrett, D. I., Fagan, E. C., Cornwell, R. E., Lobmaier, J. S., Sprengelmeyer, A., . . . Young, A. W. (2009). The cutest little baby face: A hormonal link to sensitivity to cuteness in infant faces. *Psychological Science, 20*(2), 149–154.

Stephan, C. W., & Langlois, J. H. (1984). Baby beautiful: Adult attributions of infant competence as a function of infant attractiveness. *Child Development, 55*(2), 576–585.

Sternglanz, S. H., Gray, J. L., & Murakami, M. (1977). Adult preferences for infantile facial features: An ethological approach. *Animal Behaviour, 25*, 108–115.

Strauman, T. J., & Wilson, W. A. (2010). Individual differences in approach and avoidance: Behavioral activation/inhibition and regulatory focus as distinct levels of analysis. In R. H. Hoyle (Ed.), *Handbook of personality and self-regulation* (pp. 447–473). New York, NY: Wiley-Blackwell.

Sutton, S. K., & Davidson, R. J. (1997). Prefrontal brain asymmetry: A biological substrate of the behavioral approach and inhibition systems. *Psychological Science, 8*(3), 204–210.

Wadhwa, M., Shiv, B., & Nowlis, S. M. (2008). A bite to whet the reward appetite: The influence of sampling on reward-seeking behaviors. *Journal of Marketing Research, 45*(4), 403–413.

Wang, T., & Mukhopadhyay, A. (2014a). The cuteness paradox: How approach motivation enhances responses to cute products but worsens reactions if they malfunction. Unpublished manuscript.

Wang, T., & Mukhopadhyay, A. (2014b). The effect of cuteness on motivating prosocial behavior. Unpublished manuscript.

Windhager, S., Slice, D. E., Schaefer, K., Oberzaucher, E., Thorstensen, T., & Grammer, K. (2008). Face to face. *Human Nature, 19*(4), 331–346.

Zebrowitz, L. A. (1997). *Reading faces: Window to the soul?* Boulder, CO: Westview Press.

Zebrowitz, L. A., Kendall-Tackett, K., & Fafel, J. (1991). The influence of children's facial maturity on parental expectations and punishments. *Journal of Experimental Child Psychology, 52*(2), 221–238.

12

CUTENESS, NURTURANCE, AND IMPLICATIONS FOR VISUAL PRODUCT DESIGN

He (Michael) Jia and C. Whan Park

UNIVERSITY OF SOUTHERN CALIFORNIA

Gratiana Pol

UNITED TALENT AGENCY, BEVERLY HILLS

Product designers and marketers have long acknowledged the value of endowing products with a physical appearance that elicits immediate pleasure in consumers (Norman, 2004). Consistent with this view, consumer psychology research has experienced great interest in examining the consumer appeal of products whose appearance can be best classified as beautiful or high-aesthetics (meaning that it incorporates aesthetic design principles such as symmetry, unity, proportion; Kumar & Garg, 2010). Yet, pleasure in product design can also come from a very different source—namely, from the presence of one or more "babyish" or infantile features, which together are part of a baby schema (Hellén & Sääksjärvi, 2013). Products whose appearance conforms to such a baby schema (usually referred to as "cute" products), yet which are targeted at adult consumers (Marcus, 2002), often do surprisingly well in the marketplace. The Volkswagen Beetle, the Mini Cooper, or the Roomba vacuum cleaner exemplify this popular "cute" trend. Moreover, merchandise adorned with images of cute characters such as Hello Kitty or Boo the Dog enjoys a fiercely loyal, cult-like following among adult consumers.

With cuteness becoming an increasingly alluring theme in product design in recent years, academic research on cute-looking product designs has also emerged (Cho, Gonzalez, & Yoon, 2011; Hellén & Sääksjärvi, 2013; Miesler, Leder, & Herrmann, 2011; Nenkov & Scott, 2014). Although this literature is still in its infancy, and our understanding of the role of cuteness in product design is still very limited, several studies have shown that cuteness-induced responses can be generalized from the domain of human infants to the domains of baby-faced adults (Berry & McArthur, 1985; Gorn, Jiang, & Johar, 2008; Keating, Randal, Kendrick, & Gutshall, 2003; Livingston & Pearce, 2009) and even inanimate objects (Miesler et al., 2011). These findings imply that, by understanding how people respond to the cuteness of animate beings (i.e., human newborns or animals), marketing researchers and managers can gain insights into the various consequences of endowing an inanimate object (such as product) with a cute-looking appearance. In this chapter, we conduct a comprehensive review of research on people's responses toward cute-looking animate beings, use an evolutionary perspective to integrate these various research findings, and discuss the implications for developing a theory of visual product cuteness and for managing cute-looking products.

Cuteness in Animate Beings and Products

Cuteness derives from "babyishness" and is usually defined descriptively as a set of attractive infantile features (Alley, 1981; Hildebrandt & Fitzgerald, 1978; Morreall, 1991; Saunders, 1992; Sprengelmeyer et al., 2009). Typical features that define cuteness in animate beings include a relatively small size, soft skin, a plump body with short limbs and a large head, a short face in relation to a high and protruding forehead, large eyes placed in the middle of the face, rounded cheeks, and a small nose, mouth, and chin (Berry & McArthur, 1985; Hildebrandt & Fitzgerald, 1978). As a visual design theme, cuteness can be incorporated into a product at different levels of the product's design. It can be used as an individual visual element that is inserted into the product's layout (e.g., a T-shirt featuring a cute dog image), or it can be integral to the overall shape of a product (e.g., Sephora's Hello Kitty Palette that is holistically shaped like the head of Hello Kitty). Additionally, a product design can appear cute-looking because of some less evident babyish features, such as a small size, soft color, or rounded shape (Cho et al., 2011; Hellén & Sääksjärvi, 2013), although this type of cuteness is less typical than the cuteness that stems from more obvious babyish features (Nenkov & Scott, 2014). At whichever level these pleasurable babyish features are made salient in a product's design, the product will appear to look cute, and such cuteness perceptions have important marketing-related consequences.

The Nurturance-Eliciting Function of Cuteness

Since the concept of cuteness derives from people's perception and evaluation of mammalian babies or infants (Morreall, 1991), there is an automatic and firm link between cuteness and its prototype—babyishness or baby schema (Glocker et al., 2009; Lobmaier, Sprengelmeyer, Wiffen, & Perrett, 2010; Sprengelmeyer et al., 2009). This firm link suggests that, in order to understand how consumers respond to a cute-looking product design, we can start off by exploring how infants benefit from a cute-looking physical appearance.

The evolutionary perspective is particularly helpful in this respect. It postulates that since mammalian infants—particularly human infants—are incapable of taking care of themselves for quite some time after birth, cuteness evolved as an adaptive mechanism for attracting nurturant, protective, and caregiving behaviors from adults, which increase the infants' chance of survival (Glocker et al., 2009; Lorenz, 1971; Morreall, 1991). More broadly, cuteness serves as an elicitor of social affiliation and engagement and triggers adults' social interactions with babies (Sherman & Haidt, 2011). In these processes, cuteness evokes a set of *cognitive appraisals, affective responses,* and *behavioral tendencies,* which together play an important role in serving the nurturance-eliciting function of cuteness.

Cognitive Appraisals of Cuteness

Cognitive appraisals of cuteness result from stereotypes about infants and babies and can be either positive or negative. Irrespective of their valence, these cuteness-related cognitive appraisals help induce and sustain nurturing behaviors from caregivers toward infants. Research on adult baby-facedness provides a good demonstration of the positive and negative perceptions associated with cuteness and baby schema, and clearly suggests that these cognitive appraisals associated with cuteness can transfer from the domain of infants to other domains.

Weakness/Vulnerability

On the negative side, infants are usually perceived as submissive, helpless, incompetent, vulnerable, and physically weak. By association, baby-faced adults are typically also perceived as possessing those qualities (Berry & McArthur, 1985; Gorn et al., 2008; Livingston & Pearce, 2009). However, these negative associations may sometimes have positive consequences. Perceptions of vulnerability and weakness are important elicitors of protection. As a consequence, baby-faced adults are more likely to receive help from others since submissiveness and helplessness invite prosocial behaviors (Keating et al., 2003).

Innocence/Sincerity

On the positive side, cuteness and baby schema are associated with innocence, sincerity, honesty, kindness, warmness, and trustworthiness. Consequently, baby-faced adults also frequently benefit from those positive associations (Berry & McArthur, 1985; Gorn et al., 2008; Livingston & Pearce, 2009). While the negative associations of cuteness (e.g., vulnerability and helplessness) play an important role in *eliciting* nurturing behaviors from caregivers, the positive associations of cuteness (e.g., innocence and sincerity) might be more crucial for *sustaining* nurturing behaviors because the presence of these features are conducive to gaining caregivers' forgiveness and suppressing their aggression when infants commit faults.

In a similar manner, due to its association with innocence or warmth, baby-facedness can benefit adults in terms of eliciting trust and social approval from others (Gorn et al., 2008; Livingston & Pearce, 2009). For instance, Gorn, Jiang, and Johar (2008) showed that, because of their perceived honesty and trustworthiness, baby-faced (as opposed to mature-looking) CEOs can more easily win back customers in a public relations crisis. Moreover, baby-faced out-group members are regarded as less threatening (Livingston & Pearce, 2009). Finally, due to the association with innocence, the presence of baby-related cues can prime people to behave more ethically and pro-socially (Gino & Desai, 2012).

Affective Responses Toward Cuteness

According to Lorenz (1971), cuteness evokes positive affect, a finding recently confirmed using physiological measurements (Miesler et al., 2011). However, given that all visually appealing stimuli typically induce positive affect, it is important to identify the specific affective reactions that are related to cuteness. This argument is particularly important in light of the notion that different types of visually attractive appearances may lead to different kinds of affective responses in viewers. For example, a beautiful object can trigger admiration (Walton, 1993), while an attractive mate can trigger sexual desire (Griskevicius, Goldstein, Mortensen, Cialdini, & Kenrick, 2006). The extant literature suggests that cuteness, on the other hand, triggers compassion and amusement.

Compassion

Since vulnerability and helplessness are important drivers of compassionate feelings (Oveis, Horberg, & Keltner, 2010), it is very natural to expect that, by association, cuteness would induce a strong feeling of compassion. With cuteness serving as a prototypical elicitor of compassion, thinking about a pet, a baby, or a child can all make people feel compassionate (Griskevicius, Shiota, & Neufeld, 2010; Shiota, Keltner, & John, 2006). Consistent with this view, recent research in neuroscience has shown that cuteness-induced feelings of compassion boost parents' nurturing behaviors toward their offspring (Shiota et al., 2006). Relatedly, sympathy has been identified as an important dimension of cuteness in product designs (Hellén & Sääksjärvi, 2013).

Amusement

Caregiving behaviors are highly effortful and require a great investment of time and attention. Since infants are not able to provide any immediate functional benefits to their caregivers (Morreall, 1991), they need to offer some other type of rewards to their caregivers in exchange for the constant and effortful investments they require (Sprengelmeyer et al., 2009). While cute beings are typically characterized by having infantile features, they are often also associated with displaying certain behaviors—such as awkward movements—that are funny to behold (Hildebrandt & Fitzgerald, 1978). From an evolutionary perspective, such an association between cuteness and amusement can be easily conceived, since the entertainment value provided by an infant's amusing behavior can serve to focus the caregiver's attention, promote interactions with the infant, and provide the caregiver with an immediate reward.

Consistent with this view, Griskevicius et al. (2010) showed that participants felt more funny and giggly after they read a scenario depicting a little girl than those reading other scenarios unrelated to cute beings. More recent research has further demonstrated that the whimsically cute features of a product design make the concepts of fun and playfulness more accessible in people's minds, and thus activate a reward-seeking motive which drives indulgent consumption behaviors (Nenkov & Scott, 2014). These findings all suggest that cuteness can induce a feeling of amusement, which has the adaptive value to attract and reward caregivers and, in a product context, consumers.

Behavioral Tendencies Toward Cuteness

Both cognitive appraisals associated with and affective responses elicited by cuteness induce and sustain caregivers' nurturing behaviors, which ultimately manifest in a set of behavioral tendencies towards cute-looking beings. Based on the extant findings, we categorize cuteness-induced behavioral tendencies into three broad categories: attention, approach, and care. While attention and approach are more automatic responses, caretaking necessarily requires more effort.

Attention

Since it takes a long time before newborns mature enough to live on their own completely, cuteness should act as a cue to automatically capture and consequently sustain constant attention from caregivers over an extended period (Glocker et al., 2009; Morreall, 1991). Consistent with this view, research has shown that people tend to look longer at pictures of cute versus less cute babies (Hildebrandt & Fitzgerald, 1978), have an attentional bias toward infant versus adult faces (Cárdenas, Harris, & Becker, 2013), and allocate more attentional resources when viewing images of babies versus adults (Brosch et al., 2007). Furthermore, Borgi, Cogliati-Dezza, Brelsford, Meints, and Cirulli (2014) have demonstrated that the attention-getting advantage of cuteness and baby schema can be extended from viewing human faces to viewing animal faces.

Approach

Because infants are incapable of taking care of themselves after birth, a crucial task for them is to attract and elicit the closeness of adult caregivers (Hildebrandt & Fitzgerald, 1979). To fulfill such a function, cuteness is believed to have evolved as a cue to automatically elicit approaching behaviors from adults toward infants (Hildebrandt & Fitzgerald, 1979) and prompt spontaneous social interactions (Sherman & Haidt, 2011). That cuteness is able to elicit approach is also consistent with the argument that cuteness represents a type of visual attractiveness (Glocker et al., 2009; Hellén & Sääksjärvi, 2013; Hildebrandt & Fitzgerald, 1978; Nenkov & Scott, 2014), given that, by definition, attractiveness implies the ability of an object to incentivize viewers to move in closer (e.g., Pol, Park, & Reimann, 2013; Winkielman & Berridge, 2003).

Care

The purpose of cute beings attracting a caregiver to be close is to further invite protective and caretaking behaviors. In an observational study, Langlois, Ritter, Casey, and Sawin (1995) found that parents of cuter infants exhibit a higher frequency of routine caregiving behaviors and played more with the infants than did parents of less cute infants. Relatedly, Glocker et al. (2009) showed experimentally that babyishness induces both cuteness perceptions and motivation to care. Cuteness and baby schema can also increase behavioral carefulness in different domains. For instance, Nittono, Fukushima, Yano, and Moriya (2012) and Sherman, Haidt, and Coan (2009) showed that viewing pictures of cute animals versus neutral pictures not only improved participants' performance in a subsequent fine-motor dexterity task, but also narrowed their attentional focus down to local rather than global features. Relatedly, even thinking about a kid can lead to more elaborate information processing of written materials, which represents another type of carefulness (Griskevicius et al., 2010).

Summary

As illustrated in this section, the nurturing responses elicited by cuteness have a somewhat complex structure, which includes various cognitive, affective, and behavioral components. These components appear to be interrelated, such that the cognitive appraisals (i.e., vulnerability and sincerity) would drive the corresponding affective responses (i.e., compassion and amusement), which together further activate or sustain certain behaviors (i.e., attention, approach, and care). The findings regarding these different components have clear implications for designers and consumer researchers who are interested in creating cute-looking product designs. We will discuss these implications in more detail in the following sections.

Implications for Designers

For product designers and marketers, two important issues are when to adopt cuteness as a design theme in product design and marketing communications, and how to leverage the positive effects of cuteness. Understanding the cognitive appraisals, affective responses, and behavioral tendencies evoked by cuteness enables us to offer prescriptive suggestions regarding these issues and provide implications for using cuteness as a tool for improving the effectiveness of marketing efforts.

Conveying a Warm Brand Identity

In consumers' minds, different brands have different personalities (Aaker, 1997). From a firm's standpoint, creating and communicating a desirable brand personality or strengthening consumers' perceptions of the intended brand personality are crucial for brand identification and commercial success. Aaker, Vohs, and Mogilner (2010) broadly distinguish between two conceptual bases that can be used for creating desirable brand identities: competence and warmth. We suggest that firms such as health insurance companies, food manufacturers, or charities, for which warmth or trustworthiness represent the basis for a desirable identity, could greatly benefit from incorporating cute-looking elements into their logos, ads, and product designs, or from using cute-looking mascots in their consumer communications. Environmentally friendly products, for example, represent a fertile area for the use of cuteness as a design element. In recent years, many firms have introduced eco-friendly products to the market, from 100% recycled towel papers to all-electric cars. Given that the ethical or pro-environmental attributes of eco-friendly products are often associated with high gentleness and low strength, experts have suggested that eco-friendly products are best introduced to product categories in which safety and gentleness are highly valued, such as skin care products (Luchs, Naylor, Irwin, & Raghunathan, 2010). In such cases, product designers can use cute-looking images as central visual elements in packaging, or incorporate them into the overall package shape in order to enhance the perceived gentleness and warmness of the product and brand.

Building Brand Attachment

In an increasingly competitive market, fostering strong brand attachment (i.e., developing a strong psychological connection between consumers and a brand) has become a key strategic device for a firm to achieve success. Strong brand attachment has been shown to invite effortful purchase behaviors and increase brand purchase shares (Park, Eisingerich, & Park, 2013; Park, MacInnis, Priester, Eisingerich, & Iacobucci, 2010). Given that people are likely to anthropomorphize or personify an entity associated with a cute-looking image (Sherman & Haidt, 2011) and that the evolutionary function of cuteness is to elicit a desire to be close (Hildebrandt & Fitzgerald, 1979), a cute-looking mascot, logo, or product design can be a very powerful tool for fostering consumers' personal connection with and reducing the psychological distance to a brand, thus contributing to the development of strong brand attachment.

Increasing the Effectiveness of Cause-Related Promotions

Cause-related marketing, in which firms make a donation to a cause when consumers buy a product or unit of a product (Winterich & Barone, 2011), has become a widely used tool to communicate firms' social responsibility and promote product sales. We propose that cute-looking products can be used to increase the effectiveness of cause-related marketing campaigns. This argument relies on the finding that, when the source of one's feelings is not clearly defined, consumers can easily misattribute the source of their feelings (Schwarz & Clore, 1983). Given that the sight of a cute-looking product can create a strong compassionate feeling, consumers may misattribute the elicited compassion to the focal cause, and thus exhibit a higher tendency to support the cause by purchasing the product. From such a perspective, cause-related marketing efforts should benefit from being paired with a cute-looking product.

In the context of marketing promotions, we would like to offer some cautionary advice with regard to price discounts. Compared with cause-related marketing efforts, a price discount is a more popular type of sales promotion. However, we do not recommend marketers to run price-based promotions when they are selling cute-looking products, particularly when performance or functionality is an important consideration criterion for such products. Prior research has associated cuteness with submissiveness, incompetence, and weakness (Berry & McArthur, 1985; Gorn et al., 2008; Livingston & Pearce, 2009), and, consequently, with certain negative inferences with regard to consumer products (Cho et al., 2011). At the same time, the literature has shown that monetary discounts may make consumers especially suspicious of the quality of the focal product (Chandran & Morwitz, 2006). Consequently, in the presence of a monetary discount, consumers are likely to make a particularly negative quality or performance inference from a cute-looking product design, which would reduce their purchase intention for the cute product.

Implications for a Theory of Design

Although research on people's responses to cuteness dates back to several decades ago, marketing researchers have not systematically examined cuteness in product design until very recently (Cho et al., 2011; Hellén & Sääksjärvi, 2013; Miesler et al., 2011; Nenkov & Scott, 2014), and our understanding of how consumers respond to cute-looking product designs is still very limited. A systematic review of the relevant literatures reveals several research avenues for broadening the theory of cute-looking product designs.

Interplay Among Cuteness-Induced Responses

The evolutionary function of cuteness is to elicit nurturing responses from caregivers, and we expect that cuteness in product design will induce similar nurturing responses. A review of relevant research suggests that a set of cognitive appraisals, affective responses, and behavioral tendencies underlie cuteness-induced nurturing responses. We suggest two research directions for examining the interplay among these different components. First, we encourage future survey-based research to (a) develop a multi-dimensional scale to capture consumers' nurturing responses toward visual product cuteness and (b) explore the interrelationships of the cognitive, affective, and behavioral components of cuteness-induced nurturing responses. Second, since cuteness is linked to several cognitive appraisals (e.g., warmness and innocence on the positive side, and vulnerability and weakness on the negative side) and to a distinctive set of emotions (e.g., amusement and compassion), an interesting issue is whether the priming of these concepts and emotions can increase the perceived cuteness of a product. Research in this direction will help us better understand whether and how one could use multi-sensory cues to enhance the cuteness factor of an otherwise affect-poor product design.

Cuteness Versus Other Types of Attractiveness

Extant research on product aesthetics has placed a primary emphasis on consumers' responses toward attractive product designs (Hoegg, Alba, & Dahl, 2010; Townsend & Shu, 2010; Townsend & Sood, 2012), whereby the type of visual product attractiveness examined in this literature can be mostly categorized as elegance-based attractiveness (Coates, 2003; Crilly, Moultrie, & Clarkson, 2004). Nevertheless, elegance is not the sole source of visual attractiveness, as such attractiveness perceptions can also be derived from cuteness (Hellén & Sääksjärvi, 2013; Nenkov & Scott, 2014). Several important questions remain unanswered, such as whether elegance-based and cuteness-based visual product attractiveness will have differential effects on different aspects of consumer behavior, from product purchase, use, and retention to product disposal. Relatedly, advertisements featuring an elegant- versus a cute-looking theme may also have differential effects on consumers' response towards the ad, depending on product-specific characteristics, situational factors, and individual differences. Future research can explore these important issues.

Individual Differences in Responses Toward Cuteness

Since females typically need to invest greater resources to reproduce and raise offspring than males (Dahl, Sengupta, & Vohs, 2009; Lobmaier et al., 2010; Sengupta & Dahl, 2008), cuteness should be adaptively suited to more effectively entertain females and sustain their caregiving behaviors. According to such a parental investment perspective (Sundie et al., 2011), females should be more responsive to cuteness than males (Glocker et al., 2009; Lobmaier et al., 2010). Relatedly, responses toward cuteness also appear to be determined by cultural differences, as suggested by the finding that consumers in South Korea display a greater sensitivity to cute-looking product designs than do their American counterparts (Cho et al., 2011). It is possible that certain psychological constructs, such as an interdependent versus independent self-construal, may underlie and parsimoniously explain the apparent relationship between cuteness and both gender and culture. Identifying these latent psychological constructs will deepen our knowledge of individual differences in responses toward cute-looking products.

Concluding Remarks

While consumer researchers have recently begun to examine visual cuteness in product design (Cho et al., 2011; Hellén & Sääksjärvi, 2013; Miesler et al., 2011; Nenkov & Scott, 2014), we are still a long way from having attained a comprehensive understanding of how consumers interpret and respond to product cuteness. We are also missing rich insights into what exactly drives the phenomenal success of various cute-looking products in the marketplace, and under what circumstances cuteness would make for a truly effective product design theme. By providing an integrative review of the research on cuteness in both the psychology and marketing literatures, the present chapter aims to develop the basis for the creation of a theory of product cuteness. We hope that this chapter will generate valuable future research that will enhance our understanding of the cuteness concept and its important role in the context of product design.

References

Aaker, J. L. (1997). Dimensions of brand personality. *Journal of Marketing Research, 34*, 347–356.

Aaker, J., Vohs, K. D., & Mogilner, C. (2010). Nonprofits are seen as warm and for-profits as competent: Firm stereotypes matter. *Journal of Consumer Research, 37*, 224–237.

Alley, T. R. (1981). Head shape and the perception of cuteness. *Developmental Psychology, 17*, 560–654.

Berry, D. S., & McArthur, L. Z. (1985). Some components and consequences of a babyface. *Journal of Personality and Social Psychology, 48*, 312–323.

Borgi, M., Cogliati-Dezza, I., Brelsford, V., Meints, K., & Cirulli, F. (2014). Baby schema in human and animal faces induces cuteness perception and gaze allocation in children. *Frontiers in Psychology, 5*, 411.

Brosch, T., Sander, D., & Scherer, K. R. (2007). That baby caught my eye . . . Attention capture by infant faces. *Emotion, 7*, 685–689.

Cárdenas, R. A., Harris, L. J., & Becker, M. W. (2013). Sex differences in visual attention toward infant faces. *Evolution and Human Behavior, 34*, 280–287.

Chandran, S., & Morwitz, V. (2006). The price of "free"-dom: Consumer sensitivity to promotions with negative contextual influences. *Journal of Consumer Research, 33*, 384–392.

Cho, S., Gonzalez, R., & Yoon, C. (2011). *Cross-cultural difference in the preference for cute products: Asymmetric dominance effect with product designs.* Paper presented at the 4th World Conference on Design Research, Delft, Netherlands.

Coates, D. (2003). *Watches tell more than time: Product design, information and the quest for elegance.* London: McGraw-Hill.

Crilly, N., Moultrie, J., & Clarkson, P. J. (2004). Seeing things: Consumer response to the visual domain in product design. *Design Studies, 25,* 547–577.

Dahl, D. W., Sengupta, J., & Vohs, K. D. (2009). Sex in advertising: Gender differences and the role of relationship commitment. *Journal of Consumer Research, 36,* 215–231.

Gino, F., & Desai, S. (2012). Memory lane and morality: How childhood memories promote prosocial behavior. *Journal of Personality and Social Psychology, 102,* 743–758.

Glocker, M. L., Langleben, D. D., Ruparel, K., Loughead, J. W., Gur, R. C., & Sachser, N. (2009). Baby schema in infant faces induces cuteness perception and motivation for caretaking in adults. *Ethology, 115,* 2257–2263.

Gorn, G. J., Jiang, Y., & Johar, G. V. (2008). Babyfaces, trait inferences, and company evaluations in a public relations crisis. *Journal of Consumer Research, 35,* 36–49.

Griskevicius, V., Goldstein, N. J., Mortensen, C. R., Cialdini, R. B., & Kenrick, D. T. (2006). Going along versus going alone: when fundamental motives facilitate strategic (non) conformity. *Journal of Personality and Social Psychology, 91,* 281–294.

Griskevicius, V., Shiota, M. N., & Neufeld, S. L. (2010). Influence of different positive emotions on persuasion processing: A functional evolutionary approach. *Emotion, 10,* 190–206.

Hellén, K., & Sääksjärvi, M. (2013). Development of a scale measuring childlike anthropomorphism in products. *Journal of Marketing Management, 29,* 141–157.

Hildebrandt, K. A., & Fitzgerald, H. E. (1978). Adults' responses to infants varying in perceived cuteness. *Behavioural Processes, 3,* 159–172.

Hildebrandt, K. A., & Fitzgerald, H. E. (1979). Facial feature determinants of perceived infant attractiveness. *Infant Behavior and Development, 2,* 329–339.

Hoegg, J., Alba, J. W., & Dahl, D. W. (2010). The good, the bad, and the ugly: Influence of aesthetics on product feature judgment. *Journal of Consumer Psychology, 20,* 419–430.

Keating, C. F., Randal, D. W., Kendrick, T., & Gutshall, K. A. (2003). Do babyfaced adults receive more help? The (cross-cultural) case of the lost resume. *Journal of Nonverbal Behavior, 27,* 89–109.

Kumar, M., & Garg, N. (2010). Aesthetic principles and cognitive emotion appraisals: How much of the beauty lies in the eye of the beholder. *Journal of Consumer Psychology, 20,* 485–494.

Langlois, J. H., Ritter, J. M., Casey, R. J., & Sawin, D. B. (1995). Infant attractiveness predicts maternal behaviors and attitudes. *Developmental Psychology, 31,* 464–472.

Livingston, R. W., & Pearce, N. A. (2009). The teddy bear effect: Does having a baby face benefit black chief executive officers? *Psychological Science, 20,* 1229–1236.

Lobmaier, J. S., Sprengelmeyer, R., Wiffen, B., & Perrett, D. I. (2010). Female and male response to cuteness, age and emotion in infant faces. *Evolution and Human Behavior, 31,* 16–21.

Lorenz, K. (1971). *Studies in animal and human behaviour* (Vol. 2; R. Martin, Trans.). Cambridge, MA: Harvard University Press. (Original work published 1950)

Luchs, M. G., Naylor, R. W., Irwin, J. R., & Raghunathan, R. (2010). The sustainability liability: Potential negative effects of ethicality on product preference. *Journal of Marketing, 74,* 18–31.

Marcus, A. (2002). The cult of cute: The challenge of user experience design. *Interactions, 9,* 29–34.

Miesler, L., Leder, H., & Herrmann, A. (2011). Isn't it cute: An evolutionary perspective of baby-schema effects in visual product designs. *International Journal of Design, 5*, 17–30.

Morreall, J. (1991). Cuteness. *British Journal of Aesthetics, 31*, 39–47.

Nenkov, G., & Scott, M. L. (2014). "So cute I could eat it up": Priming effects of cute products on indulgent consumption. *Journal of Consumer Research, 41*, 326–341.

Nittono, H., Fukushima, M., Yano, A., & Moriya, H. (2012). The power of Kawaii: Viewing cute images promotes a careful behavior and narrows attentional focus. *PLoS ONE, 7*, e46362.

Norman, D. A. (2004). *Emotional design: Why we love (or hate) everyday things.* New York, NY: Basic Books.

Oveis, C., Horberg, E. J., & Keltner, D. (2010). Compassion, pride, and social intuitions of self-other similarity. *Journal of Personality and Social Psychology, 98*, 618–630.

Park, C. W., Eisingerich, A. B., & Park, J. W. (2013). Attachment–aversion (AA) model of customer–brand relationships. *Journal of Consumer Psychology, 23*, 229–248.

Park, C. W., MacInnis, D. J., Priester, J., Eisingerich, A. B., & Iacobucci, D. (2010). Brand attachment and brand attitude strength: Conceptual and empirical differentiation of two critical brand equity drivers. *Journal of Marketing, 74*, 1–17.

Pol, G., Park, C. W., & Reimann, M. (2013). *The power of beauty: How aesthetically appealing products drive behavioral effort in consumers.* Paper presented at the Anthropology of Consumption and Markets Conference, Irvine, CA.

Saunders, J. T. (1992). On "cuteness". *British Journal of Aesthetics, 32*, 162–165.

Schwarz, N., & Clore, G. L. (1983). Mood, misattribution, and judgments of well-being: Informative and directive functions of affective states. *Journal of Personality and Social Psychology, 45*, 513–523.

Sengupta, J., & Dahl, D. W. (2008). Gender-related reactions to gratuitous sex appeals in advertising. *Journal of Consumer Psychology, 18*, 62–78.

Sherman, G. D., & Haidt, J. (2011). Cuteness and disgust: The humanizing and dehumanizing effects of emotion. *Emotion Review, 3*, 245–251.

Sherman, G. D., Haidt, J., & Coan, J. A. (2009). Viewing cute images increases behavioral carefulness. *Emotion, 9*, 282–286.

Shiota, M. N., Keltner, D., & John, O. P. (2006). Positive emotion dispositions differentially associated with big five personality and attachment style. *Journal of Positive Psychology, 1*, 61–71.

Sprengelmeyer, R., Perrett, D. I., Fagan, E. C., Cornwell, R. E., Lobmaier, J. S., Sprengelmeyer, A., . . . Young, A. W. (2009). The cutest little baby face: A hormonal link to sensitivity to cuteness in infant faces. *Psychological Science, 20*, 149–154.

Sundie, J. M., Kenrick, D. T., Griskevicius, V., Tybur, J., Vohs, K. & Beal, D. J. (2011). Peacocks, Porsches, and Thorsten Veblen: Conspicuous consumption as a sexual signaling system. *Journal of Personality and Social Psychology, 100*, 664–680.

Townsend, C., & Shu, S. B. (2010). When and how aesthetics influences financial decisions. *Journal of Consumer Psychology, 20*, 452–458.

Townsend, C., & Sood, S. (2012). Self-affirmation through the choice of highly aesthetic products. *Journal of Consumer Research, 39*, 415–428.

Walton, K. L. (1993). How marvelous! Toward a theory of aesthetic value. *Journal of Aesthetics and Art Criticism, 51*, 499–510.

Winkielman, P., & Berridge, K. C. (2003). Irrational wanting and subrational liking: How rudimentary motivational and affective processes shape preferences and choices. *Political Psychology, 24*, 657–680.

Winterich, K. P., & Barone, M. J. (2011). Warm glow or cold, hard cash? Social identity effects on consumer choice for donation versus discount promotions. *Journal of Marketing Research, 48*, 855–868.

13

THE AESTHETICS OF BRAND NAME DESIGN

Form, Fit, Fluency, and Phonetics

Sarah Roche

TEXAS WESLEYAN UNIVERSITY

L. J. Shrum and Tina M. Lowrey

HEC PARIS

The scope of product design is far-reaching. Although product design may most readily bring to mind issues related to functionality and tangible, concrete attributes that meet explicit needs of consumers, research is making it increasingly apparent that intangible, aesthetic product design features can also influence consumer perceptions. These perceptions include basic emotions that may be induced by various sensory perceptions (e.g., visual, aural, olfactory) and operate independently from and interactively with each other.

Several other chapters in this volume focus on the power of physical and visual design attributes to shape perceptions and evaluations of products. In this chapter, we shift focus to the sensory perceptions induced by auditory signals and their implications for consumer perceptions of the product. Specifically, we address the implications of sound for the design of brand and product names. Although brand and product name designs are not generally associated with product design, we argue that this view is short-sighted. We propose that in fact the product and its associated names are inextricably entwined (or at least should be for maximum effectiveness), and that the mere sound of the brand or product name (and its associated symbolism) drives consumer perceptions of the physical, tangible, and functional aspects of the product, which in turn influence expectations, attitudes, and beliefs about the product.

We begin by providing an overview of general phonetic effects. We then review research that links phonetic effects to various aspects of brand and product perceptions, preferences, and attitudes. In doing so, we introduce our own research on phonetic effects in designing stock ticker symbols and how the sound of tickers can affect the initial performance of new IPOs (initial public offerings).

We conclude with a discussion of the implications of this body of research for theories of design and for designers. We focus primarily on the effects of phonetic symbolism, which refers to the notion that sound conveys meaning.

Phonetic Symbolism: The Meaning of Sounds

Phonetic symbolism refers to the notion that the mere sound of a word, whether verbally pronounced or rehearsed mentally, communicates information to the receiver (French, 1977). These sounds derive from phonemes, which are the smallest units of sound and form the basic building blocks of language, and particular sounds are associated with distinct perceptions related to size, shape, speed, luminosity, and motion, to name just a few aspects (Shrum & Lowrey, 2007). Moreover, when these sounds are present in brand names, the sound connotations (sound symbolism) influence perceptions of the brand names themselves, perceptions of the product and its associated attributes, perceptions of the product performance, brand attitudes, fluency, and construal level (among others).

Both vowel and consonant sounds convey information. For example, one way of classifying vowel sounds is whether they are *front* or *back* vowel sounds. The distinction refers to the position of the tongue during pronunciation: For front vowel sounds, the position of the tongue is toward the front of the mouth (e.g., the vowel sound in *tee*), whereas for back vowel sounds, the position of the tongue is more toward the back of the mouth (e.g., the vowel sound in *too*). The different positions produce sounds that vary in pitch, frequency, and volume of the vocal tract (Shrum & Lowrey, 2007; Spence, 2012). Research has consistently shown that these variations in sounds are associated with a variety of dimensions or meanings (size, speed, power, hardness, sharpness, etc.; for reviews, see Klink, 2000; Nichols, 1971; Shrum & Lowrey, 2007). Relative to front vowel sounds, back vowel sounds connote larger, duller, slower, more powerful, and so forth. Moreover, these effects appear to operate along a continuum, such that as the sounds progress from front to back (e.g., the progression of vowel sounds in *tee, tin, too, ton*), so too do the connotations (e.g., from smaller to larger; Newman, 1933; Thompson & Estes, 2011).

Consonants also have their own classifications. For example, consonants can be classified as stops versus fricatives. Stop consonant sounds are formed through complete closure of the articulators (tongue, lips, or teeth) so that air cannot escape the mouth. The letters *b*, (hard) *c*, *d*, *g*, *k*, *p*, and *t* are considered stops. In contrast, fricatives do not have complete closure of the articulators and sounds are created by forcing air through constrictions in the vocal tract. The letters *f*, *s*, *v*, and *z* are fricatives (Ladefoged, 1975). Like the front and back vowel sounds, the physical aspects of pronunciation (closure vs. openness of the articulators) produce sounds with varying frequencies, and the differences in sounds are perceived to have different connotations. For example, relative to fricatives, stops imply larger, heavier, harder, and more masculine. These effects are pervasive, consistent, and appear to have similar effects across almost all languages (Ullmann, 1966; Ultan, 1978).

The notion that sounds convey meaning may seem unremarkable. However, it is one thing to show that different sounds have different connotations, but it is quite another thing to link the sounds of *words* themselves to meaning. Although perhaps intuitive, the question of whether the link between the sounds of words and their meaning is systematic or arbitrary has been debated since ancient times. For example, Plato contrasts the two positions in *Cratylus* (Plato, 1892), in which Socrates and Hermogenes debate the issue. Hermogenes argues that the relation between the sounds of words and their meaning is arbitrary, whereas Socrates argues the contrary. The debate was also a central issue in contemporary linguistics. Saussure declared that "the sign is arbitrary," (1959; p. 67), and other prominent linguistic theorists held similar views (e.g., Chomsky & Halle, 1968).

That said, the empirical evidence for phonetic symbolism is vast, including both lab studies and analyses of natural language (for a review, see Shrum & Lowrey, 2007). In one of the first experimental studies on phonetic symbolism, Sapir (1929) presented participants with pairs of artificial words that differed only in their middle vowel (e.g., *mil* vs. *mal*), and asked them to indicate which was large and which was small, with respect to an arbitrary referent (e.g., Which is the large table?). Across a large number of words and referents, participants associated the back vowel words with a large referent and front vowel sound words with a small referent, about 80% of the time. This finding has been replicated across numerous age groups and languages. Consistent sound symbolism relations, and particularly the front/back distinction, have been documented in natural languages as well. For example, in an analysis across 136 languages, 83% showed the predicted relation between size and vowel sound (Ultan, 1978). Analyses of natural languages also show relations between consonant sounds and perceptions. For example, approximately half of all English words that begin with *gl* have a visual connotation (e.g., *gleam*, *glitter*, etc.), a disproportionate number of words beginning with *sl* have a negative connotation (*slander, slouch, slime, sloven*), and certain back vowel sounds are often associated with sounds of disgust or dislike, at least in the English language (*yuck, bung, muck, blunder*; Jespersen, 1922).

Although the research on phonetic symbolism is compelling, it is not without its critics. Some suggest that the effects may be simple methodological artifacts. For example, some researchers suggest that the effects do not necessarily occur spontaneously, but only when specific dimensional judgments (size, shape, brightness, etc.) are elicited (Bentley & Varon, 1933). Other researchers question the generalizability of the findings across languages. For example, the effects that have been obtained in determining the meaning of foreign words (e.g., matching pairs of antonyms in a foreign language with comparable English antonyms; Brown, Black, & Horowitz, 1955) are eliminated if both sets of stimulus words are in languages foreign to the participants (Maltzman, Morrisett, & Brooks, 1956). Still other critics suggest that the effects may be orthographic (rather than acoustical), in which the shape of the letters may be the driver of perceptions (cf. Atzet & Gerard, 1965; Brackbill & Little, 1957; Brown et al., 1955). Finally, even if the effects are valid, it is still not clear how these sound symbolism effects may translate into perceptions, attitudes, and behaviors associated with the particular word. The latter is particularly crucial in arguing that phonetic symbolism has useful applications to marketing practice.

In the next sections, we review research that addresses these issues. Because of space constraints, this review is far from exhaustive, but rather is intended to highlight specific issues, with attention placed on the most recent research. In particular, we highlight research that shows that phonetic properties of words spontaneously elicit the predicted perceptions, that these perceptions are in fact acoustical, and that the phonetic symbolism of words affects not just perceptions, but also preferences, attitudes, and behavior across a wide variety of contexts. Interestingly, a substantial portion of this research has used marketing and other business contexts to demonstrate these effects. Moreover, this research adds to the growing literature on nonconscious and non-rational influences on economic judgments (Kahneman, 1994, 2003).

Phonetic Symbolism Effects Across Contexts

Surname Effects

Perhaps one of the more provocative (and potentially disconcerting) examples of phonetic symbolism effects is research linking the phonetic symbolism or meanings associated with surnames with perceptions and behaviors towards individuals. One example pertains to the relation between the names of political candidates and election outcomes. Smith (1998) coded the surnames of all of the U.S. presidential candidates since 1824 (when the popular vote was first recorded) in terms of their "comfort index" across three phonetic dimensions (consonant sound, vowel sound, and rhythm), each of which had several sub-dimensions. The index ranged along a continuum from positive (more comfort) to negative (less comfort). He then correlated these numerical comfort ratings with the actual election outcomes. Consistent with predictions that the positivity of the phonetic ratings of the candidates' names would be associated with more winning outcomes, in 35 of the 42 elections (83%) the candidate with the better-sounding name won the election. Of course, a sample size of 42 is a small one and also is just one isolated example. However, Smith also extended this same analysis to local (county) elections in Spokane County, Washington (U.S.). In this analysis, 73% of the winning candidates had a better sounding name. In yet a third demonstration, Smith showed that the results also held for the 1996 U.S. congressional elections (Senate and House of Representatives) in which 59% of the House winners and 65% of the Senate winners had more favorable sounding names.

Although not directly related to phonetic symbolism, a similar surname effect was observed within the context of want ads. Guéguen and Pascual (2011) placed an ad in local French newspapers offering services as a math tutor and manipulated whether the surname of the tutor was described as a professor of mathematics named Mr. Py, Mr. Rie, or Mr. Le Gal. Because Py is pronounced the same way as Pi (the famous mathematical symbol), it was expected to be more effective than either Rie (rhymes with Py, has the same vowel sound and frequency, but has no association with mathematics) or Le Gal (the most frequently used surname in the geographical area of the study). This was the case: Mr. Py received a substantially larger proportion of telephone inquiries in response to the ad (45%) than Mr. Rie (25%) or Mr. Le Gal (29%).

Price Perceptions

Phonetic symbolism can also affect price perceptions. In a clever set of experiments, Coulter and Coulter (2010) demonstrated that not only does phonetic symbolism affect price perceptions, but that these perceptions in turn can distort perceptions of the magnitude of a sales discount, and ultimately can lead to inaccurate perceptions of value. To test for phonetic symbolism effects, they manipulated (between-subjects) whether the numbers in the cents position contained fricatives or stops and front or back vowels, holding the dollar position constant (e.g., $7.66 vs. $7.22). They then asked participants to judge the magnitude of a discount that manipulated the vowel and consonant sounds. Front vowels and fricative consonants within a price were expected to make the price seem smaller, and thus the discount larger, than when the price contained back vowels and stop consonants. This was in fact the case. Participants who saw prices with front vowels and fricative consonants in the cents position judged a price reduction ($10.00 to $7.66) to be larger than those who saw prices with back vowels and stop consonants in the cents position ($10.00 to $7.22), even though the actual discount is greater in the latter (27.8%) than in the former (23.4%). This difference presumably occurred because the numbers with small-connoting phonemes in the cents position ($7.66) were perceived as smaller than the large-connoting phonemes in the cents position ($7.22), thus distorting perceptions of the discounts. Moreover, the effects were observed only under rehearsal conditions, further supporting the sound symbolism explanation. The findings provide a vivid demonstration of how seemingly small phonetic effects can override objective calculations.

The research just reviewed clearly suggests that the meaning of sounds—phonetic symbolism—is evident across many everyday contexts. The next question we address is whether the phonetic symbolism associated with a *brand name* affects perceptions of the brand, and if so, whether and how these perceptions may influence brand attitudes and behavior. This is a critical question that has important implications for marketing strategy. Upwards of 25,000 nonfood and 20,000 food and beverage consumer packaged goods are released each year (United States Department of Agriculture, 2010), providing at least 45,000 instances in which brand name design may potentially utilize phonetic symbolism to enhance and support new product performance. In the following sections, we discuss recent research on phonetic symbolism and brand names, discuss the processes underlying these effects, and suggest ways in which marketers can leverage this research to design optimal brand names for their products.

What's in a Brand Name?

It is perhaps tempting to say that brand names do not matter or influence consumers. After all, as Juliet remarks in Shakespeare's *Romeo and Juliet*, "What's in a name? That which we call a rose by any other name would smell as sweet," and consumers are presumably rational decision makers in most situations (Hastie & Dawes, 2010). Yet the research often tells another story, one in which consumers appear to be influenced by subtle, non-obvious factors on a daily basis (Kahneman, 2003).

The current section is concerned with the question of "What's in a name?" and how brand names influence brand perceptions, expectations, attitudes, and behaviors. We argue that brand name design and product design are inextricably linked, and in particular, the mere sound of the brand name plays an important role in consumer decision-making.

Sound Symbolism and Brand Name Perceptions

One of the first demonstrations of the link between phonetic symbolism and brand name perceptions was provided by Heath, Chatterjee, and France (1990). Using artificial words as hypothetical brand names to avoid semantic associations with existing brands or words, they systematically varied whether the brand names began with a stop or fricative consonant and whether the vowel sounds contained front or back vowels (e.g., Kuge, Kige, Suge, Sige), and they also varied whether the product category was a kitchen paper towel or kitchen cleaner. They then asked participants to indicate their perceptions of the hardness of the hypothetical brand, their brand attitudes, and their purchase intentions, The results showed a general (although sometimes only marginally significant) effect of both the consonant and vowel sounds on perceptions of hardness: Brand names with stop consonants and with front vowels were rated as harder relative to brand names with fricative consonants and back vowels. However, these perceptions did not appear to translate into brand attitudes or purchase intentions in any meaningful way.

Although the findings of Heath et al. (1990) were suggestive of a phonetic symbolism effect on brand name perceptions, they were far from conclusive. A more systematic demonstration of phonetic symbolism effects was provided by

Klink and his colleagues (Athaide & Klink, 2013; Klink, 2000; Klink & Wu, 2014; Wu, Klink, & Guo, 2013). In one study, 124 artificial words (hypothetical brand names) were constructed so that they differed only on one phonetic dimension (e.g., fricative vs. stop consonant; front vs. back vowel). Participants were then asked to provide their perceptions of the brands across several dimensions within a particular product category (e.g., "Which ketchup seems thicker?"). The findings were clear and consistent with predictions: Brands whose names contained front vowel sounds were judged to be smaller, milder, colder, softer, more feminine, thinner, colder, more bitter, lighter in weight, lighter in color, and prettier than brands whose names contained back vowel sounds. Similar results were observed for stops versus fricatives (Klink, 2000).

Although a substantial body of research attests to phonetic symbolism effects on consumer perceptions, the literature just covered does not establish the relation between brand name phonetic symbolism and consumer *preferences*. This is a crucial link in arguing that phonetic symbolism can play an important role in brand name design. For phonetic symbolism to be effective, the perceptions generated by the brand name must be managed and maximized in the design of the brand name. The following sections address this proposition, and provides support for the link between phonetic symbolism and, not only consumer perceptions, but preferences as well.

Phonetic Symbolism, Brand Names, and Consumer Preferences

If sounds do convey certain types of meaning, and the sounds of brand names in turn influence consumer perceptions, the question then is how these perceptions can be managed to generate positive reactions to the brand that translate into actual brand preferences. One strategy, which we term the *fit strategy*, is to maximize the fit between the sound symbolism and the product attributes. Research suggests that the fit between aspects of a brand name and its associated product category positively affects such variables as recall, preference, and inference. These aspects include semantic relations (Keller, Heckler, & Houston, 1998; Lowrey, Shrum, & Dubitsky, 2003; Meyers-Levy, Louie, & Curren, 1994), meaningfulness (Childers & Houston, 1984; Lutz & Lutz, 1977; Saegert & Young, 1983), and perceptions generated by numerical brand names (Pavia & Costa, 1993). Research also shows that consumers indeed have a general, albeit often poorly defined and articulated, perception that certain brand names fit with their product category but that some do not (Zinkhan & Martin, 1987).

Phonetic symbolism effects of brand names may work in the same way. That is, the favorability of consumer judgments in general should be maximized when the fit between the attributes connoted by the sound of the brand name (e.g., small/large, fast/slow, crisp/mellow) and the design and function of the product itself is maximized. Much like "regulatory fit" and "feeling right" effects (Higgins, 2000), fit influences favorability judgments, and increasing feelings of fit leads to more favorable evaluations. Consumers appreciate the experience of harmony, consistency, and sameness within concepts or products, as opposed to contradictions (lack of fit).

Yorkston and Menon (2004) provided evidence that fit interacts with phonetic symbolism to influence brand attitudes. They constructed two artificial brand names for ice cream that differed only on whether the vowel sound was front (Frish) or back (Frosh). They hypothesized that the back vowel sound in Frosh would result in perceptions that the ice cream is smoother, creamier, and richer compared to perceptions generated by the front vowel sound in Frish. Because the attributes of smoother, creamier, and richer are preferred in ice creams, they therefore expected that the ice cream whose brand name was Frosh should also be preferred over the ice cream whose brand name was Frish. Their expectations were confirmed. Frosh was indeed perceived to be smoother, creamier, and richer, and was evaluated more favorably, than Frish. They also showed that these phonetic symbolism effects are relatively automatic (as opposed to controlled).

Research by Lowrey and colleagues provided additional support for the fit hypothesis, and showed that the effects generalize across vowel sounds, languages, and developmental age groups. For example, Lowrey and Shrum (2007) manipulated the product category to show that phonetic symbolism effects are indeed a function of fit. They presented pairs of fictitious brand names that differed only on whether the vowel sound in the brand name was front or back (e.g., gimmel vs. gommel, nillen vs. nallen, etc.), and asked participants to indicate which brand name they preferred. However, they also manipulated the type of product so that in some cases a front vowel sound should be preferred but in other cases a back vowel sound should be preferred. For example, some participants were asked to indicate which brand name they preferred for an SUV and others were asked to indicate which brand name they preferred for a two-seater convertible. Because front vowel sounds connote attributes such as smaller, quicker, faster, and back vowel sounds connote attributes such as bigger, stronger, more powerful, brand names with front vowel sounds were expected to be preferred over brand names with back vowel sounds for the two-seater convertible, but just the opposite was expected when the product was an SUV. These expectations were confirmed, by about a 2–1 margin (see top portion of Table 13.1). A second experiment provided convergent results, but in this case, the product was held constant (beer) and the attributes were manipulated. Participants preferred the brand name with the front vowel sound over the brand name with the back vowel sound when the beer was described as cool, clean, and crisp, again by about a 2–1 margin, but the opposite was true when the beer was described as smooth, mellow, and rich (attributes similar to those used by Yorkston & Menon, 2004).

TABLE 13.1 Brand Name Preference as a Function of Vowel Sounds and Product Category (adapted from Lowrey & Shrum, 2007)

	Front vs. back vowel sound dimension	
	% front vowel	% back vowel
Product category	words preferred	words preferred
Convertible	63%	37%
SUV	30%	70%
Knife	66%	34%
Hammer	34%	66%
	Positive vs. negative vowel sound dimension	
	% positive vowel	% negative vowel
Product category	words preferred	words preferred
Convertible	61%	39%
SUV	71%	29%
Knife	59%	41%
Hammer	71%	29%

Note: All contrasts between % front and back vowel words preferred are significant at $p < .001$ (one-tailed), and all contrasts between % positive and negative words preferred are significant at $p < .04$ (one-tailed).

In addition to the front/back vowel sound distinction, Lowrey and Shrum (2007) also investigated the conjecture made by Jespersen (1922; see also Smith, 1998) that certain sounds in the English language are associated with sounds of disgust. If so, then brand names with those vowel sounds should be evaluated more negatively than brand names with vowel sounds associated with more positive emotions. Their results showed that indeed brand names with vowel sounds often associated with disgust (e.g., fewtip, which has the same [yoo] vowel sound as *puke*) were [less preferred compared to] brand names with more favorably associated sounds (e.g., fawtip) apart from the front/back distinction (see bottom portion of Table 13.1). Moreover, the general effects associated with the front/back distinction have since been replicated across multiple languages (French, Spanish, Chinese alphabetic, and Chinese logographic; Shrum, Lowrey, Luna, Lerman, & Liu, 2012) and young age groups (Baxter & Lowrey, 2011, 2014), and these fit effects for vowel sound phonetic symbolism have also been replicated for consonant sounds (cf. Kuehnl & Mantau, 2013).

Thus, the research on the effects of phonetic symbolism on brand name preferences and brand attitudes is consistent and convincing. The general pattern of findings is important in at least two respects. First, as we discuss in more detail presently, the research suggests that consideration of the phonetic symbolism associated with a potential brand name can be a useful strategy, at least under some conditions. Second, this research is also the first to provide clear evidence that phonetic symbolism perceptions are spontaneous, and not a function of the research method. In previous research on phonetic symbolism, effects were generally observed only when people's perceptions were guided toward relevant contrasts (e.g., Which table is larger?; Which ketchup is thicker?). However, in the research just described, the spontaneous nature of the perceptions is implicit. That is, implicit fit effects can only be explained by the application of particular attributes (smooth, fast, powerful, crisp) that spontaneously result from the manipulation of one particular phonetic attribute.

One question that has not yet been addressed is the extent to which the effects of phonetic symbolism generalize across decision making contexts. For example, the research we have reviewed shows that phonetic symbolism effects hold at least for judgments of consumer products. However, the nature of the designs, such as using fictitious brand names in an effort to maximize internal validity, necessarily suggests that these are low involvement decisions that are made in the absence of any other individuating information about the brand or product. Given this context, it is understandable that phonetic symbolism effects might be observed, given the substantial body of research on nonconscious effects of contextual variables and frequent demonstrations of violations of expected utility theory and principles of rational choice (Kahneman, 1994, 2003).

In the next section, we detail research that explores the possible effects of phonetic symbolism in high-stakes environments. In particular, we look at the possible effects of phonetic symbolism that derives from the mere sound of a stock's ticker symbol on stock trading and financial performance.

Phonetic Symbolism Influences on Stock Performance

Stock investment involves high-stakes decisions that are high involvement and presumably follow rational choice processes. Investors (traders) are presumed to have a wealth of diagnostic information with which to make investment decisions. Consequently, investment decisions are arguably the least likely venue for finding effects of supposed irrational, nonconscious inputs. However, contrary to classical economic theory, a growing body of research suggests that the choice of in which stocks to invest is influenced by decidedly non-economic factors. For example, decreased cloud coverage in New York City predicted higher returns for stocks (Saunders, 1993), and other research has shown similar seasonal patterns, across countries and regions, in which stock performance is positively correlated with the amount of daylight through fall and winter (Kamstra, Kramer, & Levi, 2003). Essentially, the effect of weather on mood leads to lower trading and returns on stocks on gloomy versus sunny days. Even negative feelings induced from the loss of a favorite sports team can negatively impact stock returns. During the elimination stage of the World Cup series, a loss by one's home team was associated with a next-day market loss of 49 basis points (Edmans, García, & Norli, 2007). Cultural biases for one's domestic stocks also influence trading decisions. They result in expectations of higher returns for these stocks and consequently reduce diversification of portfolios, regardless of more objective data such as historical standard returns that might indicate otherwise (French & Poterba, 1991). As one last remarkable example of the impact of non-economic factors on stock performance, higher ratings of CEO attractiveness are associated with higher company stock returns during a CEO's first days on the job (Halford & Hsu, 2013).

Recent research has even shown that the processing fluency of ticker names, reflected in the degree of pronounceability of a ticker symbol (e.g. POV vs. PFV), is related to short-term stock performance. Stocks with more pronounceable ticker symbols outperformed those that were less pronounceable, one day and one week after initial listing, but these differences disappeared at longer terms (6 mo. and 1 yr.; Alter & Oppenheimer, 2006; see also Durham & Santhanakrishnan [2014] for a review of similar effects). Presumably, more objective economic indicators such as company performance eventually erased fluency effects, but in the short-term, the fluency or ease with which the stock name could be pronounced significantly predicted stock performance. In addition, the memorability of ticker symbols (e.g., ones that relate to company's business in a witty or clever way, such as Southwest's LUV) is positively related to stock performance (Head, Smith, & Wilson, 2009).

If performance is influenced by the name of a stock, the cleverness of its symbol, and its mere pronounceability, it seems plausible that the phonetic symbolism associated with the sound of the ticker symbol might also have effects on perceptions of the stocks themselves, much like the effects noted with consumer products. In the next section, we describe a series of studies we recently conducted to test this proposition.

Stock Ticker Design, Phonetic Symbolism, and Performance of IPOs

Given the research showing various linguistic effects of stock ticker symbols on stock performance, we were interested in testing whether phonetic symbolism also plays a role in perceptions of stocks and consequent effects of these perceptions on stock trading decisions. To test this proposition, we conducted a series of studies utilizing both historical stock trading data and a lab experiment. Specifically, we tested the proposition that the same types of effects noted earlier regarding the effects of vowel sounds (front/back) and consonant sounds (fricatives/stops) may influence the decisions stock traders make. To reiterate, back (vs. front) vowel sounds are associated with perceptions of bigger, stronger, and more powerful. The same is true for stop (vs. fricative) consonants.

Thus, we predicted that companies whose (pronounceable) ticker symbols were composed of back vowel sounds would be perceived to be stronger and more powerful relative to companies whose ticker symbols were composed of front vowel sounds, and that ticker symbols beginning with stops would show the same effects relative to those beginning with fricatives. Consequently, we expected that tickers with back vowel sounds would command higher prices than those with front vowel sounds, and that tickers beginning with stop consonants would likewise command higher prices than those beginning with fricative consonants.

In the first study, we tested these propositions using the data from Alter and Oppenheimer (2006; thanks to those authors for promptly sharing their data). We first reduced the set of ticker symbols to include only those that were pronounceable. Phonetic symbolism effects are predicated on the notion that the sounds of the words (tickers) convey meaning, and these phonetic effects can occur directly through auditory channels (hearing the word spoken aloud) or indirectly through subarticulation (saying the word to oneself; Baddeley, 1986). Two coders blind to the hypothesis coded each pronounceable ticker symbol as a fricative or stop consonant sound and as a front or back vowel sound, with a high level of agreement. We then correlated the phonetic properties with stock performance (calculated as % change in price relative to the original offer price at the initial public offering (IPO)) at various points in time (1 day, 1 wk., 6 mo., 1 yr.) after the IPO.

The results of this analysis showed that tickers with stop consonants consistently outperformed tickers with fricatives consonants at each time period. However, no effects of vowel sounds (front vs. back) were observed. Although the results just described are suggestive of phonetic symbolism effects of stock ticker symbols on stock performance, the sample size was small (only 208 pronounceable ticker symbols). To test the robustness of this effect, we developed a larger data set consisting of a randomly drawn subset of IPOs from the New York and American stock exchanges from 1980 to 2004. Again, tickers were coded by an individual blind to the hypotheses, first for pronounceability and then based on consonant sounds (fricatives vs. stops). Stock performance was calculated as the percent change in stock price compared to the price at IPO at 1 day, 2 days, 1 week, 1 month, 1 quarter, 2 quarters, 3 quarters, and 1 year after the IPO. We then correlated the presence of fricative vs. stop consonants with stock performance. Again, the results indicated that stops generally outperformed fricatives on the first day, second day, first quarter, two quarters, three quarters, and 1-year after the IPO (no effects were noted for stock performance after 1 wk. or 1 mo. after trading).

Although the first two studies attempted to control or co-vary out other-variable effects such as the size of the initial capitalization, available data were limited. Consequently, it is possible that some other unmeasured variable(s) may be driving the effects. To address this issue, we conducted a laboratory study to enhance internal validity. Business school undergraduates were recruited to participate in a study ostensibly about financial analyses. Participants read a description of an IPO and were then asked to make predictions about the potential of the company. Real IPO offering descriptions were used, but the phonetic properties of the ticker symbols were systematically manipulated within the IPO descriptions. Some participants read about a stock whose ticker symbols began with a stop consonant (BIF), whereas other participants read about a stock whose ticker symbol began with a fricative consonant (VIF), and all other information (e.g., vowel sound, valuation data) was held constant. After reading the IPO announcement, participants indicated how well they thought the stock would be doing 1 month and 1 year later. The results were consistent with predictions. Performance expectations for the stop sound ticker were significantly greater than those for the fricative ticker at 1 month after trading, and marginally greater after 1 year of trading.

This composite set of findings suggests that even in high-stakes, high-involvement contexts such as financial decision making, relatively subtle, nonconscious factors can influence judgments. These findings not only provide additional evidence of phonetic symbolism effects, but also add to the growing body of work attesting to the limits of expected utility theory and the assumptions of rational choice.

Implications for a Theory of Design

In this chapter, we have presented evidence that the sounds of words convey meaning apart from their actual definitions. We have also discussed research that shows that such phonetic symbolism can shape perceptions, preferences, and attitudes. More importantly, we have demonstrated how these effects apply specifically to brand naming in multiple contexts, from simple brand associations to high-involvement financial decision-making.

The implications for product design are clear. Given the pervasive effects of phonetic symbolism, the effectiveness of brand name design can be enhanced by consideration of how a brand name sounds. We have also detailed the conditions and processes that enhance brand name effectiveness. Specifically, the favorability of consumer judgments in general is maximized when the fit between the attributes connoted by the sound of the brand name (e.g., size, speed, texture, etc.) and the design and function of the product itself are congruent.

That said, we do not want to overstate this proposition. Clearly, there are factors other than phonetic symbolism that impact brand name perceptions. Prominent examples include semantic connotations that refer to specific product attributes (Mr. Clean disinfectant; Mop & Glo floor wax), metaphorical references (Midas automobile mufflers; Amazon internet retailer), and puffery claims (Burger King fast food chain; Best Buy consumer products retailer), just to name a few. Moreover, we are not suggesting that successful brand names should be changed simply to leverage phonetic symbolism effects. However, just as most of the research we have detailed uses artificial, fictitious words as stimuli, so too do companies. There are numerous examples of brand names that are non-words (Kodak, Exxon, Lexus, etc.). It is in these instances that we argue that attention to phonetic symbolism and other linguistic properties may be particularly useful.

We also discussed research showing that (artificial) brand names whose sounds are associated with sounds of disgust (such as the vowel sounds in words such as *yuck*, *phew*, *ugh*) are perceived negatively. From a marketing perspective, one might argue that this proposition is obvious and marketers would always avoid such words. Yet many supportive examples come to mind (*Smuckers* jelly, *Edsel* and *Yugo* automobiles). Of course, only the last two failed, and perhaps not only because of the brand name (although the pervasive dislike for the *Edsel* brand name has been suggested as a contributing reason for its failure; Hartley, 1992; Klink, 2000). But apparently *Smuckers*, which is named after the founder of the company, understood the symbolism imbedded in the name: Their slogan at least at one time was "With a name like Smucker's, it's got to be good."

We also acknowledge that there are always exceptions or counter-examples to the predictions of almost any behavioral theory. Phonetic symbolism is no exception (e.g., the words *big* and *small* are counter-examples to predictions of phonetic symbolism in natural languages). To this point, it may be instructive to recall Socrates's argument for phonetic symbolism. He acknowledged in some cases the relation between the sound of a word and its meaning may be arbitrary, and that not all words reflect phonetic symbolism. However, he argued that *good* words show congruency between their sound and their meaning. We are simply suggesting that when possible, brand names should be good words.

Our contention that the proper use of phonetic symbolism in brand name design enhances consumer evaluations is consistent with general principles of product design. One principle of product design (or any design) is harmony, or the extent to which individual elements complement the whole. To date, the focus has been on elements such as color, smell, shape, and texture. We argue that the sound of a brand name should also harmonize with other aspects of the product to achieve maximal effectiveness.

Implications for Designers

In sum, the research we have outlined in this chapter provides a resounding message that should not be ignored by product, stock, and brand managers. Names matter. The name of a brand or product communicates information to consumers. The good news is that the name is generally in the company's control. This presents the opportunity to design brand names that communicate the best message, and it is particularly pertinent for new products. In addition, the design of stock names and ticker symbols offers the opportunity for managers to enhance the initial appeal of their stock without any additional costs.

Stock names that are designed to be more pronounceable and can be translated into ticker symbols that start with stop sounds are an easy way for managers to enhance the chances of positive stock performance in the first year of trading.

Consumers lack experience with such products, services, and stocks, so they must make initial judgments about whether to trial the offering or buy the stock, without getting to experience or learn more objective information about it first. Therefore, a brand name and its matchup to the desired product attributes, packaging, and logos can serve as a positive cue to potential consumers. In the same way, stock tickers with stop sounds can be used to connote larger gains and stronger performance at the subliminal level, and this information can be used in the early days of trading when less objective records of performance are available. In sum, if product designers understand the basic rules of phonetic symbolism, they can easily apply such concepts to their new product names and stock IPOs. No extra money is needed to design a better or worse name, but knowledge of such effects is essential to recognizing how to capitalize on such associations and how a lack of sound symbolism—product, attribute match— might negatively affect initial evaluations and experience evaluations (because expectations are not met during actual consumption). Therefore, we propose that name choice, whether in the form of brand name, product line name, offering name, stock name, or ticker symbol, should not be an afterthought but instead another important factor to be incorporated into the product design process.

References

Alter, A. L., & Oppenheimer, D. (2006). Predicting short-term stock fluctuations by using processing fluency. *Proceedings of the National Academy of Sciences, 103*, 9369–9372.

Athaide, G. A., & Klink, R. R. (2013). Creating global brand names: The use of sound symbolism. *Journal of Global Marketing, 25*, 202–212.

Atzet, J., & Gerard, H. B. (1965). A study of phonetic symbolism among native Navaho speakers. *Journal of Personality and Social Psychology, 1*, 524–528.

Baddeley, A. D. (1986). *Working memory*. Oxford: Oxford University Press.

Baxter, S., & Lowrey, T. M. (2011). Phonetic symbolism and children's brand name preferences. *Journal of Consumer Marketing, 28*, 516–523.

Baxter, S., & Lowrey, T. M. (2014). Examining children's preference for phonetically manipulated brand names across two English accent groups. *International Journal of Research in Marketing, 31*, 122–124.

Bentley, M., & Varon, E. J. (1933). An accessory study of "phonetic symbolism." *American Journal of Psychology, 45*(January), 76–86.

Brackbill, Y., & Little, K. B. (1957). Factors determining the guessing of meanings of foreign words. *Journal of Abnormal and Social Psychology, 54*, 312–318.

Brown, R. W., Black, A. H., & Horowitz, A. E. (1955). Phonetic symbolism in natural languages. *Journal of Abnormal & Social Psychology, 50*, 388–393.

Childers, T. L., & Houston, M. J. (1984). Conditions for a picture superiority effect on consumer memory. *Journal of Consumer Research, 11*, 551–563.

Chomsky, N., & Halle, M. (1968). *The sound pattern of English*. New York, NY: Harper & Row.

Coulter, K. S., & Coulter R. A. (2010). Small sounds, big deals: Phonetic symbolism effects in pricing. *Journal of Consumer Research, 37*, 315–328.

Durham, G., & Santhanakrishnan, M. (2014). *Do fluent tickers attract sentimental investors?* Unpublished manuscript.

Edmans, A, García, D., & Norli, Ø. (2007). Sports sentiment and stock returns. *Journal of Finance, 62*, 1967–1998.

French, K. R., & Poterba, J. M. (1991). Investor diversification and international equity markets. *American Economic Review, 81*, 222–226.

French, P. L. (1977). Toward an explanation of phonetic symbolism. *Word, 28*, 305–322.

Guéguen, N., & Pascual, A. (2011). Mr. "Py" is probably a good mathematician: An experimental study of the subjective attractiveness of family names. *Names, 59*, 52–56.

Halford, J. T., & Hsu, S. H. C. (2013). Beauty is wealth: CEO appearance and shareholder value. Available at http://ssrn.com/abstract=2357756

Hartley, R. F. (1992). *Marketing mistakes* (5th ed.). New York, NY: Wiley.

Hastie, R., & Dawes, R. M. (2010). *Rational choice in an uncertain world: The psychology of judgment and decision making* (2nd ed.). Thousand Oaks, CA: Sage.

Head, A., Smith, G., & Wilson, J. (2009). Would a stock by any other ticker smell as sweet? *Quarterly Review of Economics and Finance, 49*, 551–561.

Heath, T. B., Chatterjee, S., & France, K. R. (1990). Using the phonemes of brand names to symbolize brand attributes. In W. Bearden & A. Parasuraman (Eds.), *The AMA educator's proceedings: Enhancing knowledge development in marketing* (pp. 38–42). Chicago, IL: American Marketing Association.

Higgins, E. T. (2000). Making a good decision: Value from fit. *American Psychologist, 55*, 1217–1230.

Jespersen, O. (1922). *Language: Its nature, development and origin*. London: Allen & Unwin.

Kahneman, D. (1994). New challenges to the rationality assumption. *Journal of Institutional and Theoretical Economics, 150*, 18–36.

Kahneman, D. (2003). A perspective on judgment and choice: Mapping bounded rationality. *American Psychologist, 58*, 697–720.

Kamstra, M. J., Kramer, L. A., & Levi, M. D. (2003). Winter blues: A SAD stock market cycle. *American Economic Review, 93*, 324–343.

Keller, K. L., Heckler, S. E., & Houston, M. J. (1998). The effects of brand name suggestiveness on advertising recall. *Journal of Marketing, 62*, 48–57.

Klink, R. R. (2000). Creating brand names with meaning: The use of sound symbolism. *Marketing Letters, 11*, 5–20.

Klink, R. R., & Wu, L. (2014). The role of position, type and combination of sound symbolism imbeds in brand names. *Marketing Letters, 25*, 13–24.

Kuehnl, C., & Mantau, A. (2013). Same sound, same preference? Investigating sound symbolism effects in international brand names. *International Journal of Research in Marketing, 30*, 417–420.

Ladefoged, P. (1975). *A course in phonetics*. New York, NY: Harcourt Brace Jovanovich.

Lowrey, T. M., & Shrum, L. J. (2007). Phonetic symbolism and brand name preference. *Journal of Consumer Research, 34*, 406–414.

Lowrey, T. M. Shrum, L. J., & Dubitsky, T. M. (2003). The relation between brand-name linguistic characteristics and brand-name memory. *Journal of Advertising, 32*, 7–17.

Lutz, K. A., & Lutz, R. J. (1977). Effects of interactive imagery on learning: Application to advertising. *Journal of Applied Psychology, 62*, 493–498.

Maltzman, I., Morrisett, L., Jr., & Brooks, L. O. (1956). An investigation of phonetic symbolism. *Journal of Abnormal & Social Psychology, 53,* 249–251.

Meyers-Levy, J., Louie, T. A., & Curren, M. T. (1994). How does the congruity of brand names affect evaluations of brand name extensions? *Journal of Applied Psychology, 79,* 46–53.

Newman, S. S. (1933). Further experiments in phonetic symbolism. *American Journal of Psychology, 45*(January), 53–75.

Nichols, J. (1971). Diminutive consonant symbolism in Western North America. *Language 47,* 826–848.

Pavia, T. M., & Costa, J. A. (1993). The winning number: Consumer perceptions of alpha-numeric brand names. *Journal of Marketing, 57,* 85–88.

Plato. (1892). Cratylus. In B. Jowett (Ed.), *The dialogues of Plato* (Vol. 1, pp. 253–289). Oxford: Clarendon.

Saegert, J., & Young, R. K. (1983). Levels of processing and memory for advertisements. In L. Percy & A. G. Woodside (Eds.), *Advertising and consumer psychology* (pp. 117–131). Lexington, MA: Lexington Books.

Sapir, E. (1929). A study in phonetic symbolism. *Journal of Experimental Psychology, 12,* 225–239.

Saunders, E. M. (1993). Stock prices and Wall Street weather. *American Economic Review, 83,* 1337–1345.

Saussure, F. (1959). *Course in general linguistics.* (W. Baskin, Trans.). New York, NY: Philosophical Library.

Shrum, L. J., & Lowrey, T. M. (2007). Sounds convey meaning: The implications of phonetic symbolism for brand name construction. In T. M. Lowrey (Ed.), *Psycholinguistic phenomena in marketing communications* (pp. 39–58). Mahwah, NJ: Lawrence Erlbaum.

Shrum, L. J., Lowrey, T. M., Luna, D., Lerman, D., & Liu, M. (2012). Sound symbolism effects across languages: Implications for global brand names. *International Journal of Research in Marketing, 29,* 275–279.

Smith, G. W. (1998). The political impact of name sounds. *Communication Monographs, 65,* 154–172.

Spence, C. (2012). Managing sensory expectations concerning products and brands: Capitalizing on the potential of sound and shape symbolism. *Journal of Consumer Psychology, 22,* 37–54.

Thompson, P. D., & Estes, Z. (2011). Sound symbolic naming of novel objects is a graded function. *Quarterly Journal of Experimental Psychology, 64,* 2392–2404.

Ullmann, S. (1966). Semantic universals. In J. H. Greenberg (Ed.), *Universals of language* (pp. 217–264). Cambridge, MA: MIT Press.

Ultan, R. (1978). Size-sound symbolism. In J. H. Greenberg, C. A. Ferguson, & E. A. Moravcsik (Eds.), *Universals of human language: Vol. 2: Phonology* (pp. 525–568). Stanford, CA: Stanford University Press.

United States Department of Agriculture. (2010). *New products. Economic research service.* Retrieved from http://www.ers.usda.gov/topics/food-markets-prices/processing-marketing/new-products.aspx#.U5i42I1dXJc

Wu, L., Klink, R. R., & Guo, J. (2013). Creating gender brand personality with brand names: The effects of phonetic symbolism. *Journal of Marketing Theory and Practice, 21,* 319–329.

Yorkston, E. A., & Menon, G. (2004). A sound idea: Phonetic effects of brand names on consumer judgments. *Journal of Consumer Research, 31,* 43–51.

Zinkhan, G. M., & Martin, C. R., Jr. (1987). New brand names and inferential beliefs: Some insights on naming new products. *Journal of Business Research, 15,* 157–172.

14

THE DESIGN OF EXPERIENCE

Bernd Schmitt

COLUMBIA UNIVERSITY AND ACI SINGAPORE

In this chapter I will discuss how experiences are shaped by design—for brands as well as other domains, such as architecture. I will argue that there may be general principles of how specific dimensions of design relate to specific types of experiences and object perceptions. I will provide examples and empirical findings to illustrate my point. I will conclude with a request to develop a general consumer-driven "theory of design."

First, though, we need some conceptual clarity and common ground. Let me explain how I will use the terms "experience" and "design."

Definitions

"Experience" is associated with sensory components—the color scheme of an ad, the feeling of the materials used in a product, the sound environment of a hotel lobby. Two or more of these physical design components may also come together or interact in a manner that may create a more complex multi-sensory experience.

The word "experience" also captures a broader range of meanings: people may describe a particularly moving book as an emotional experience, an engaging lecture as a learning experience, testing a new vehicle as a driving experience, sharing a meal with neighbors as a community experience. Experience is a complex word and refers not only to the here-and-now of experiencing an event, phenomenon, or design, but also to accumulated knowledge over time. Though the latter meaning may relate to design, typically referring more to knowledge about design, experience in the present is the more relevant definition to use in considering how people experience design.

Design is likewise a complex word with varied meaning. Design goes beyond sensory elements people often describe in areas such as product, graphic, or architectural design. Design is used in the context of "course design," "strategy design," or the "design of an organization." The design field has moved into the direction of design as a way of thinking ("design thinking," as it is called) and thus beyond tangible elements.

Given these definitions, let's look at some good examples of the use of design to create experiences.

Some Examples

In considering the impact of design on the customer experience, it's helpful to consider real-world examples of successful experiential design and marketing. Perhaps one of the most common examples of great design is Apple. Apple is well known for their exceptional attention to detail in the design of products with sensory design components (such as bright colors, unique functionality, and tactile and sound elements) but the experience of their brand goes well beyond the products themselves. Apple's skillful management of the design experience can be seen in their stores in elements but also in small elements that appear in those spaces, such as their logo, the language used (e.g., the genius bar), and the dress of their employees, and even in intangible elements such as the service design. In sum, Apple creates experiences through both tangible and intangible design elements.

Starbucks is another common example of skillful customer experience management through design. The Starbucks experience is broad reaching and involves far more than coffee; it's the design of the cup, the coffee shop environment, and the special language around coffee, turning their customers into coffee "experts."

Other companies, too, are increasingly recognizing the importance of how consumers experience and respond to design. Samsung was able to dramatically transform their brand and improve their global standing by focusing first on improving the quality of their products, then developing their brand image through design, and finally putting the user experience at the center of their design (Schmitt, 2010).

The Process of Using Design to Create Targeted Experiences

Over the years, I have served as a consultant to numerous companies trying to target and improve their customers' experience. Using customer experience models that I have developed, I advise companies on how to create attractive experiences by using design. One recent project involved an international beauty products company looking to improve their standing in Asian markets. Their research included attempts to understand what beauty means, both to females and males, using ethnography, lab studies, and a broad examination of changing consumer lifestyles. Their efforts were focused on how to create the right experience for Asian consumers in particular by understanding what they consider beautiful, not only as it related to consumers' practices of making themselves beautiful, but to other things in their surroundings that they associate with beauty in order to utilize these things in their marketing.

In another consulting work, again in the beauty business, the company identified their target customer as a young, professional, cosmopolitan woman, and I conducted several research studies in order to better understand the customer in terms of her lifestyle and the design elements that she prefers. The customer research revealed that women in this demographic segment struggle with issues related to energy, balance between work and personal life, and the fact that they may live in large, often dirty, cities but still want to feel fresh and beautiful. Based on this information, the company selected "energy" as the core experience concept to guide multiple design aspects of their product and communication: the product designs (including ginseng in their products, an ingredient often associated with energy), packaging, marketing messages, graphic design, and store interiors.

Designing Brand Experiences

In terms of academic contributions, in my 2012 article "The Consumer Psychology of Brands," published in the *Journal of Consumer Psychology*, which draws on academic and consumer literature on brands and brand differentiation, I developed a model that identified various levels and processes on how consumers can relate to brands (Schmitt, 2012). My work suggests there are three distinct forms of "levels of engagement": object-centered, when consumers are engaged by an object they find attractive or exciting; engagement as it relates to the self, a deeper form of engagement in which consumers associate the brand with themselves; and social, an even deeper level of engagement in which consumers associate the brand as a part of a community. In this chapter, I also identify five processes of brand engagement: identifying, experiencing, integrating, signifying, and connecting. The three levels of engagement may subdivide all of these processes, and I argue that this model is more circular (rather than linear or hierarchical) because consumers are likely to encounter a brand from multiple perspectives over time. The key insight of the model for experience is that an experience does not stand alone as a process of engaging with a brand. Experience can be both an input and output to other processes occurring in consumer psychology. In the most successful brands the brand experience often becomes the anchor of a rich brand: that is, the brand experience relates to other processes (such as identifying, integrating, signifying or connecting) and affects product perceptions, the self, and community levels.

Moreover, the process of experiencing a brand is not strictly rational or cognitive, but rather driven by emotions. I was part of a team that demonstrated this using an fMRI study. We displayed brand logos (the logos of strong and weak brands, and entirely new logos for new brands) to participants to observe their subsequent brain activity. The fMRI revealed that much of the differential effect of strong brands could be seen in areas of the brain associated with emotion rather than rational thought, suggesting brands are differentiated based on the emotional experiences that they evoke in consumers (Esch et al., 2012).

In other work, done alone or with co-authors, I have identified five broad dimensions of experiences, or Strategic Experiential Modules: sense, feel, think, act, and relate. Let me illustrate these five dimensions with examples from the alcoholic beverage category.

1) Sense refers to sensory experiences: for example, tasting a particular beverage, noting the flavor, smell, feel, and finish of the drink. There are countless wine, beer, and even vodka tastings that highlight the sensory elements of the experience of drinking.

2) Feel refers to affective experiences: for example, sharing a drink in an intimate moment. In these cases, while people are still likely to use their senses, the taste of the beverage may be far less relevant than the emotions experienced in the moment.

3) Think refers to an experience where consumers evaluate the beverage, or use their imagination, and thereby learn more about the beverage. Wine tasting is a prime example of this: there is a highly specialized language and culture around wine tasting when describing a wine's characteristics.

4) Act refers to experiencing one's body in the context of an action. Some individuals consume alcohol in some situations strictly for the purpose of getting drunk, perhaps quickly drinking shots of liquor. While there is a sensory experience in this act, it's secondary to the act or goal of becoming intoxicated.

5) Relate refers to an experience with others. This experience may occur in social or community settings, when people toast to celebrate an occasion or spend time with friends in a local pub.

These five different types of experiences seem intuitive and individuals are able to distinguish easily between them. The types are also relevant to companies in planning their communications to consumers: what sort of experience do they wish to create with their brands? What type of experience are they currently creating? What type are their competitors creating? What type of experience do they aspire to create?

In Brakus, Schmitt, and Zarantonello (2009), we created a brand experience scale to capture the various dimensions of experience. To do this we first conducted an extensive literature review to select initial items along the five proposed types of experiences and asked study participants to rate the extent to which the various items described their experiences with brands. After eliminating those items that were not very strongly associated with participants' brand experiences, we asked participants to indicate which items described their experiences with various brands. Several rounds of surveys and factor analysis resulted in a short scale that is able to reliably capture consumers' sensory, affective, intellectual, and behavioral experiences as related to various brands. It's worth noting that the brand scale lacks the "relate" experience I described previously. The relate items loaded mostly on the affective factor. The scale items divided by experience type (as determined through factor analysis) are as follows:

Sensory:

1) This brand makes a strong impression on my visual sense.
2) I find this brand interesting in a sensory way.
3) This brand does NOT appeal to my senses. (Reverse-coded)

Affective:

4) This brand induces feelings and sentiments.
5) I do NOT have strong emotions for this brand. (Reverse-coded)
6) This brand is an emotional brand.

Intellectual:

7) I engage in a lot of thinking when I encounter this brand.
8) This brand does NOT make me think. (Reverse-coded)
9) This brand stimulates my curiosity and problem solving.

Behavioral:

10) I engage in physical actions and behaviors when I use this brand.
11) This brand results in bodily experiences.
12) This brand is NOT action oriented. (Reverse-coded.)

These types of experiences can happen in either an individual or social context. And the experiences seem to be related to various outcomes, such as customer satisfaction or loyalty, and it seems that an experience is also the input to another brand process: an inference process about brand personality. In Brakus, Schmitt, and Zarantonello (2009), we found that brand experience had direct effects on customer satisfaction and loyalty, and there is an indirect link from brand experience through brand personality to loyalty and satisfaction. These findings speak to the importance of brand experience as an isolated factor as well as a starting point for a variety of cognitive or inferential processes that can ultimately lead to satisfaction and loyalty.

The idea of different types of brand experiences that can be measured by a scale may prove useful to an advertising agency trying to create different types of messages as well as media with a range of experiential impacts. By doing a correspondence analysis, I could show that one can plot where different types of media are perceived to fall in relation to the type of experience. For example, internet media are closely associated with intellectual and relating experiences, television or radio are more closely associated with a sensory or affective experience, and a sponsored event is a type of media more closely associated with behavioral experience.

Experiences via Architectural Design

In recent work (Raffelt, Schmitt, & Meyer, 2013), we examined the relation between architectural design and experience. People not only notice individual design elements of a building, but evaluate the experience of a building (either inside or outside) as a whole. Corporate architecture thus creates an impression on the people who see or interact with the architecture. Culture and personality are conveyed by what we call "functionalist" and "experiential architectural design."

Functionalist architecture is influenced by the Bauhaus school of thought, which argued that form follows function and focused on extremely functional architectural designs. Functionalist architecture is characterized by simplified forms with many horizontal and vertical lines. It can be described as a stark, rational, industrial look. Examples of functionalist architecture include those stemming from the aforementioned Bauhaus school (such as Walter Gropius and Mies van der Rohe), the International Style seen in the work of Le Corbusier and Phillip Johnson, and more modern works by I. M. Pei and Richard Meier that maintain functional simplicity but have a bit more modern personality.

Experiential architecture goes beyond the functional and is becoming increasingly common in corporate architecture. It is characterized by symbolism and plurality of forms, eclectic forms, and complex, ornamental, and playful design elements. It can be seen in the Postmodern and Deconstructivist movements, exemplified by the works of Frank Gehry, Rem Koolhass, Zaha Hadid, and Daniel Libeskind. (It is worth noting that while the word "experiential" is used to describe this styles of architecture, all types of architecture can and does create an experience.)

In this research, we asked ordinary people and experts (architects) to rate actual buildings on a number of specific design elements. We found five broad dimensions of architectural design: elaborateness, harmony, natural feel, transparency, and colorfulness. The non-expert consumers were asked to assess the same buildings on a brand personality trait scale. A factor analysis of consumer's ratings resulted in four broad brand personality dimensions: excitement, competence, stylishness, and naturalness.

A two-step cluster analysis was then performed in an effort to identify architectural design types based on similarities in design attributes and to assess if these design types align with a functionalist/experiential classification or if there are further subtypes. The analysis revealed four clusters of architectural design types:

Cluster 1: "Disruptive": This cluster is differentiated by below-average harmony scores and were perceived as "dissonant, confusing, clumsy, improvised, and faddish." Examples of disruptive architecture design can be seen in the Deconstructivist movement.

Cluster 2: "Expressive": Cluster 2 is differentiated by above-average elaborateness scores and below-average natural feel and slightly below-average harmony. These buildings are imaginative with a free-flowing form. These buildings are described as "artificial, reflective, smooth, bright, and refined." Examples of buildings in the expressive cluster can be seen in the Postmodernist movement.

Cluster 3: "Balanced": Cluster 3 is differentiated from the other clusters by above-average elaborateness, natural feel, transparency, and harmony, which is particularly highly rated. Buildings in this cluster are characterized as "harmonious, comforting, and coherent and is clear, elegant, planned, timeless, and protective." Contemporary Bauhaus style architecture, such as the work of Richard Meier, provides an example of balanced design.

Cluster 4: "Solid": Cluster 4 is differentiated from the other clusters by below-average elaborateness values. These buildings typically have flat facades and do not usually possess much color or ornamentation. The design of buildings in cluster is described as "impersonal, common, unimaginative, banal, ordinary, and monotonous." "Solid" design is seen in many traditional Bauhaus buildings, with an emphasis on function over form.

The next step of the study examined consumers' ratings of brand personality based on the corporate architecture compared with the four clusters of architectural design types to determine broad trends in how large-scale design influences perceptions of brand personality. There were several interesting trends that emerged: Cluster 1 and Cluster 2 buildings were negatively related to consumer perceptions of competence, but highly correlated with perceptions of excitement (particularly in the case of Cluster 2 buildings). Buildings in Cluster 4, on the other hand, have a strong negative correlation with perceptions of excitement but the strongest positive relationship to perceptions of competence.

Implications for Design

Brand personality is indeed conveyed through a company's building. Companies must be strategic in selecting what brand personality dimensions they wish to express through its building design because a building cannot be associated at the same time both with competence and excitement.

Implications for Theories of Design

It seems to me that there is some type of uniformity in design elements from small to large: people use certain dimensions, perhaps four as found in the architecture study or perhaps more, to judge all designs. And underlying these dimensions may be a well-defined set of design elements. These dimensions of designs, which are based on design elements and are similar for products, packaging, interiors, and even architecture, may then result in similar experiences (similar to the sense, feel, think, act and relate, which I distinguished) as well as similar consumer inferences, for example, in terms of brand personality. This may then form the basis of a general understanding of design from a consumer perspective. I see it as a key task of consumer psychology to develop such a theory that may illuminate not only design as such, but also the design of experience.

References

Brakus, J. J., Schmitt, B., & Zarantonello, L. (2009). Brand experience: What is it? How is it measured? Does it affect loyalty? *Journal of Marketing, 73*(3), 52–68.

Esch, F. R., Möll, T., Schmitt, B., Elger, C. E., Neuhaus, C., & Weber, B. (2012). Brands on the brain: Do consumers use declarative information or experienced emotions to evaluate brands? *Journal of Consumer Psychology, 22*(1), 75–85.

Raffelt, U., Schmitt, B. H., & Meyer, A. (2013). Marketing function and form: How functionalist and experiential architectures affect corporate brand personality. *International Journal of Research in Marketing, 30*, 201–210.

Schmitt, B. (2010). Samsung's next frontier, *Columbia CaseWorks. #100505,* Columbia University Business School, New York, NY.

Schmitt, B. (2012). The consumer psychology of brands. *Journal of Consumer Psychology, 22*, 7–17.

PART III
Underlying Processes

15

THE INHERENT PRIMACY OF AESTHETIC ATTRIBUTE PROCESSING

Claudia Townsend

UNIVERSITY OF MIAMI

Sanjay Sood

UNIVERSITY OF CALIFORNIA: LOS ANGELES

While there has certainly always been an inherent understanding that the look of a product contributes to its success in the marketplace, increasingly the business community's appreciation for product aesthetics and its impact on the bottom line has grown. The success of companies across multiple industries, such as Apple, Target, Nike, and OXO, has been attributed to a focus on aesthetics. Moreover, it has been argued that as product quality parity has become the norm in many categories, manufacturers have looked to aesthetics as a way of differentiating their goods knowing that an attractive product is difficult to pass over (Bloch, 1995; Bloch, Brunel, & Arnold, 2003; Hoegg & Alba, 2008; Patrick & Peracchio, 2010; Schmitt & Simonson, 1997). This ability for aesthetics to influence evaluations and perceptions has been well-documented, even in circumstances beyond consumer products and where one might not expect to see such effects. For example, Yamamoto and Lambert (1994) found that, despite managers claiming otherwise, appearance influenced their choice of industrial products. In the context of financial decision-making, Townsend and Shu (2010) found that the aesthetics of annual reports affected evaluations of companies by experienced investors. These two examples suggest that the influence of aesthetics on evaluation and choice may not be a straightforward deliberative process.

In this chapter, we examine aesthetics in the setting of consumer products, where its value is well-established. However, this is not a review of the importance of product appearance. Instead, we consider how the basic evaluation and processing of aesthetics differs from that of other, more functional, attributes. In doing so, we reveal something about aesthetics that is universal and likely extends beyond this domain of consumer products to any situation where the appearance of something is presented in an image.

While aesthetics can refer to an appreciation of any of the senses, we focus on the visual and consider aesthetics to be the beauty, or lack thereof, of the product. We consider it as separate from function, though in some product categories such as art, clothing, or furniture, aesthetics is central to an option's functionality. It is plausible that some of our discussion and findings may be applied to other senses when not central to a product's functionality (e.g., the sound associated with using a kitchen appliance product). We discuss such applications in the last section of this chapter. Before that, first we briefly summarize relevant research on the presentation of product attribute information, the differences in processing of images versus text, as well as work on dual process models of thinking. Together these various areas of research lead us to suggest that consumers respond differently to aesthetics versus more functional attributes because the former is processed quickly and with less deliberation by the visual system whereas the latter is processed more slowly and with greater deliberation regardless of whether presented visually or in text. In fact, in the section on dual process models we describe the results of a study that corroborates this idea. The chapter then concludes with a discussion of implications for practitioners and researchers.

Product Attribute Presentation and Comprehension

The Processing of Aesthetics in Images Versus Other Attributes in Text

Typically marketing materials such as packaging and advertisements tend to present most product attributes in text, while aesthetics is usually displayed visually. Thus the differences in the processing of images versus text are relevant. Images are processed more quickly than words and the connection between an image and its meaning is more direct than the connection between a word and its meaning (Luna & Peracchio, 2003; Sholl, Sankaranarayanan, & Kroll, 1995). Carr, McCauley, Sperber, and Parmelee (1982) investigated the use of images and words as primes and found that images offer faster access to their meanings than to their names while words offer faster access to their names than their meanings. Moreover, while words must be processed sequentially, an image can be processed all at once (Hart, 1997). In other words, as described by Paivio (1986), the system used to process images is able to work on multiple aspects in parallel, while the verbal system of reading must work serially requiring more time.

The processing of images, and aesthetics more specifically, has also been found to be associated with increased affect. Veryzer and Hutchinson (1998) found aesthetic product design characteristics positively influence affective responses while Kawabata and Zeki (2004) used brain imaging to show that high aesthetics activates the reward center of the brain. In the realm of web design, related work has found that positive responses to high aesthetics occur virtually instantaneously (Lindgaard, Fernandes, Dudek, & Brown, 2006).

The processing of aesthetics can be so quick that we may not be aware of its effects. There is evidence of automatic processing of aspects of aesthetics that influence perceptions of attractiveness even without awareness of them (Arnheim, 1974; Birkhoff, 1933; Fechner, 1871). For example, the golden ratio is a specific ratio of length to height (1.618 to 1) that occurs naturally in the structure of crystals and even aspects of the human body. The ratio is often employed by artists precisely because it arouses a subconscious feeling of beauty. Without any understanding of the existence of the golden ratio, viewers admire works of art such as the Parthenon and the Mona Lisa that employ it. In fact, when looking at an object or artwork that varies slightly from this ratio, viewers often sense that something is not right (Berlyne, 1970). Similarly, in consumer behavior, people prefer products with dimensions that adhere to the golden ratio (Veryzer, 1993). Though somewhat different from product perceptions, studies using images of facial expressions reveal a similar automaticity in that the meaning and emotion expressed in a face depicted in an image seem to be involuntarily processed and understood. The effect is strong enough as to interfere with the more deliberate process of reading text (Stenberg, Wiking, & Dahl, 1998). In the context of evaluating product attributes, the implication is that aesthetics, when presented in image form, will be quickly and automatically processed, in contrast to and perhaps even to the detriment of, the processing of other attributes presented in text.

The Processing of Other Attributes in Images and Aesthetics in Text

Of course, there are instances when attributes, besides aesthetics, might be presented visually. However, in such instances, the processing is not necessarily quick nor without deliberation. For example, brand is one attribute that is often communicated using an image. However, unlike aesthetics, a brand name requires some sort of previous learning to comprehend its meaning. Similarly, the softness of a tissue might be indicated through an image of a kitten (Scott, 1994). However, understanding that the picture of a kitten indicates softness requires "reading" of the image in the same manner that a sentence is read (Scott & Vargas, 2007). Indeed, just as one learns to read writing (Sampson, 1985), meanings of logos (Pimentel & Heckler, 2003) and images (Scott, 1994) must be learned. A logo or other brand image is symbolic; the meaning and value it implies is a learned relationship and not as automatic as an image is to appearance (van Osselaer & Janiszewski, 2001). A functionality may also be depicted visually, for example, in a graph. However, understanding of such a representation requires interpretation, is not automatic, and is vastly different from the experience of using the functionality. This is unlike the experience of viewing aesthetics which does not differ between evaluation and use. The process of viewing an image of a product is an exact simulation of what that experience will be like at the time of consumption and ownership. Thus, utility need not be predicted as it is concurrently experienced at the time of processing. In other words, while other attributes must be effortfully understood (read) and then effortfully evaluated (utility prediction), when presented visually, aesthetics is immediately and automatically understood and the utility is actually experienced.

It also follows that when aesthetics is presented in text, the slow deliberate process of reading comes into play as well as the effort of predicting preference. In fact, evaluating aesthetics when presented in text is a particularly time and cognition intensive process as it requires reading about the various attributes (color, shape, size, etc.), holding them in working memory, and then integrating them into a mental visual model. Research using functional magnetic resonance imaging (fMRI) reveals that, while many of the same neural machinery are used in visual mental imagery as in visual perception, more time (Denis & Kosslyn, 1999) and mental resources are used (Ganis, Thompson, & Kosslyn, 2004). Thus, the quick and automatic nature of processing aesthetics in images does not hold when the attribute is described in text.

Dual Process Models and Aesthetics

This delineation between slower and more effortful processing versus faster, more automatic, and affective processing finds a congruence in the dual process models proposed by many (Epstein, 1990; Kahneman & Frederick, 2005; Sloman, 1996; Stanovich & West, 2002). Researchers have identified two distinct yet parallel modes of thought (Epstein, 1990; Kahneman & Frederick, 2005; Sloman, 1996; Stanovich & West, 2002). The models generally describe an associative (Sloman, 1996) and experiential (Epstein, 1990) system 1 (Stanovich & West, 2002), which involves intuitive thinking that operates quickly and automatically. It is holistic, more emotional, and encodes information using images (Epstein, 1991). In contrast, the rule-based (Sloman, 1996) system 2 processing is slower, serial rather than parallel, and deliberately controlled (Stanovich & West, 2002). System 2 is reason-oriented and encodes information using abstract symbols such as words and numbers (Epstein, 1991). System 2 can override the quick and more impulsive thought rendered by system 1.

Given this distinction, we propose that aesthetics presented visually is processed in a quick system 1-like manner whereas functional attributes, regardless of visual or textual presentation, are likely processed in a more deliberate system 2-like manner.

Study on the Impact of Cognitive Load on Aesthetic Choice

We tested this proposition by using an intervention that influences the relative impact of the two modes of processing. Specifically, prior research reveals that the addition of a cognitively loading task decreases the relative influence of system 2 by limiting the necessary cognitive resources available (Shiv & Fedorikhin, 1999). For choice options that varied on aesthetics, when consumers were cognitively loaded we found that aesthetics was weighed more heavily in the choice decision and respondents were more likely to select the better looking option, even when there was a price premium. Thus, with high aesthetics paired with a higher price, cognitive load *decreased* price sensitivity. System 2 thought was inhibited under load, so the choice was based primarily on system 1 thought (Shiv & Fedorikhin, 1999). Accordingly, we did not predict the same effect of cognitive load on choice when there was no aesthetic variation. In fact, because selecting on price is likely a default choice technique, with no aesthetic variation, cognitive load *increased* price sensitivity. Therefore, we found the influence of cognitive load on price sensitivity reversed depending on the presence of aesthetic variation. Below are further details on the study.

Method

Three hundred ninety eight (398) UCLA students were randomly assigned to one of four conditions in a 2 (Aesthetic Variation or No Aesthetic Variation) X 2 (Cognitive Load or No Cognitive Load) between-subjects design.

In all four conditions participants made four hypothetical purchase decisions with a choice between two products represented by a black and white photograph of the product, its price, and its level on four functional attributes. The directions asked participants to assume that the two options were identical on all information not presented. In selecting the product categories, prices, and attribute levels several pretests were conducted to rule out alternative explanations related to attribute importance and issues of self-presentation. The product categories used were computer monitors, pens, trashcans, and water bottles.

The first independent variable was whether the two choices varied on aesthetics or not—whether the photograph of the product was the same for both choices or different. In the Aesthetic Variation conditions, the high aesthetic option had a higher price and was superior on two functional attributes while the low aesthetic option had a lower price and was superior on the other two functional attributes. Therefore, the two options were balanced in terms of functionality, as confirmed in pretests. In the No Aesthetic Variation conditions, one option was superior on three of four attributes and had a higher price while the other option was superior on only one attribute and had a lower price while the photos for both options were the same. See Figure 15.1 for sample stimuli.

The other independent variable was whether participants were given a cognitively loading task to perform while making the purchase decisions. The cognitive load task consisted of presenting participants with an eight-digit number sequence before the choices and explaining that they would be asked to recall the sequence after the intervening task.

FIGURE 15.1 Example stimuli by condition. Top: No Aesthetic Variation Condition. Bottom: Aesthetic Variation Condition.

Source: Claudia Townsend.

Results and Discussion

There was an interaction of presence or absence of cognitive load and presence or absence of aesthetic variation (across categories) ($\chi^2(1, N = 398) = 26.46$, $p < .001$) (see Figure 15.2). As predicted, when the choice options varied on aesthetics, respondents were more price sensitive without cognitive load than with it. With no load 41% selected the more expensive more aesthetic option, while with load 50% selected this option ($\chi^2(1, N = 198) = 5.46$, $p = .019$). When participants were cognitively loaded and, thus deciding based on predominantly system 1 thought, they were more likely to favor the aesthetically pleasing option.

In contrast, when there was no aesthetic variation, respondents were significantly more price sensitive when cognitive load was present than when it was not present. In the No Aesthetic Variation No Load condition, across product

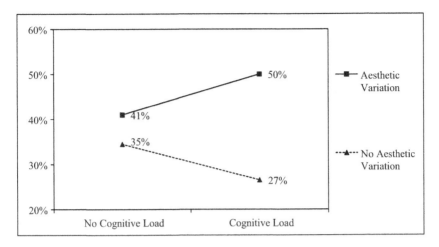

FIGURE 15.2 Impact of cognitive load on choice share of the more expensive option.

Note: Interaction of presence or absence of cognitive load and presence or absence of aesthetic variation $\chi^2(1, N = 398) = 26.46, p < .001$.

Source: Claudia Townsend.

categories 35% of respondents selected the more expensive option, while only 27% selected the more expensive option in the No Aesthetic Variation Load condition ($\chi^2(1, N = 200) = 4.99, p = .025$). Overall, these results were robust and consistent across product categories with a reversal in the impact of cognitive load when aesthetic variation was or was not present.

This study revealed aesthetics plays a *greater* role in the choice decision, even greater than price, when cognitive resources are depleted. This offers evidence for our proposition that an underlying difference between aesthetics and more functional attributes is that consumers naturally consider aesthetics using the more automatic and less effortful system 1 processing while they use the effortful and deliberate system 2 processing for other more functional attributes. Evidently the amount of mental resources available moderates the impact of design on choice. The opposing behavioral response to cognitive load when aesthetics is and is not present reveals the extent of the difference between aesthetics and more functional attributes. When options vary on design, consumers under cognitive load are *less price sensitive* (and more design sensitive) than consumers not under cognitive load. In contrast, when options vary only on function, consumers under cognitive load are *more price sensitive* than consumers not under cognitive load. The increased price sensitivity that occurs with cognitive load in the absence of design variation may be the result of the implementation of a select-the-cheapest heuristic, given all information is more system 2-oriented and therefore difficult to process.

Discussion

Practically every consumer product competes on the attribute of aesthetics; it is typically the first aspect of a product the shopper encounters and, unlike more functional attributes, its evaluation at the time of choice is the same experience it provides after purchase. While previous research has sought to uncover why one design is preferred over another, we sought to understand the consequences of such a preference. The discussion of related research as well as the results of the study suggest that because design is presented visually and because its visual presentation does not require any interpretation, it is processed more quickly and less deliberately than other attributes—requiring fewer cognitive resources.

Implications for Designers

Beyond the academic applications, this differential processing of aesthetics from other product attributes has significant implications in marketing practice. Particularly with today's fast-paced lifestyle where multi-tasking has become the norm, it is important to understand how people make decisions when their attention is divided. For example, aesthetically appealing packaging may lead to greater market share, particularly in situations where consumers are rushed or cognitively loaded.

Moreover, as implied by the research on the golden ratio whereby consumers react to it without knowledge of its existence (Berlyne, 1970; Veryzer, 1993), consumers may not be entirely aware of the impact of aesthetics on their choice decision. In fact, for the study we ran numerous pretests including one on the relative importance of the attributes. Participants consistently rated aesthetics as less important than price and equally or less important than the functional attributes. The implication is that participants were not entirely aware of how important aesthetics would be in their choice decision, particularly choice with minimal cognitive resources. This offers a note of caution for researchers or practitioners seeking to understand consumer preferences; outright probes on the importance of design may not reveal the full significance of this attribute and tools with real choice, such as conjoint analysis, are likely more appropriate.

Most broadly, this research confirms that the appreciation for aesthetics and the work of designers in the marketplace is appropriate. The way a product looks is central to consumers' first impressions as well as choice decisions. But also it seems that aesthetics must be considered as different from other, more functional attributes. What designers produce seems to be processed differently from that of engineers and others. That visual elements seem to be innately important and that aesthetics, when presented visually, seems to be more automatically and quickly processed suggests that, even the consumers making the purchase decision, while deeply influenced by designers, may not fully comprehend this. Evidently more research is needed and the likely outcome is a greater and deeper appreciation for what designers do.

Implications for a Theory of Design

By considering some of the unique qualities and effects of aesthetics in choice, this chapter suggests that aesthetics may not always be comparable to other more functional attributes and may even require new methodological approaches for its study. For example, the study revealed that the influence of limiting cognitive resources on price response depends upon aesthetic variation. This is intriguing as it reveals just how context-dependent price sensitivity is. This has obvious implications for marketers but it also suggests that a theory of design can be far-reaching with input on discussions in seemingly unrelated areas of consumer psychology such as pricing.

While in our discussion and study we were careful to consider aesthetics as separate from function, this is not always the case and when aesthetics does impart important functionality, the way it is considered may also differ. For example, in the study we used non-badge product categories so as to minimize the impact that self-presentation motives might have on choice. The goal was to unearth findings about aesthetics that might be applied to as wide a range of situations and product categories as possible. In effect, we were trying to minimize the boundary conditions to our results. Presumably, the findings presented here also apply, and may even be magnified, when the product is a badge product that is publicly displayed and consciously or unconsciously chosen in an effort to reveal something about its owner. But the product categories we used were also more utilitarian in nature and whether these findings apply to more hedonic categories is also worth investigating. It seems likely that when making a choice in a more hedonic category such as clothing or a restaurant, the decision-maker is primed to realize the impact of more hedonic attributes on his choice. Because our explanation of design's impact has little to do with its hedonic nature, we suspect that more automatic and effortless processing occurs regardless of product category.

However, in considering a psychological theory of design, models such as that of Leder, Belke, Oeberst, and Augustin (2004) suggest multiple levels of design analysis. Thus, while this chapter focuses on the most basic level there are, no doubt, more deliberate levels of design appreciation such as recognizing the style of an article of clothing or piece of furniture. Likely with product categories where aesthetics is inherently tied to function, analysis at this later stage is more important and has a recognized greater impact on choice than for other product categories.

A natural next step for a larger and more all-encompassing theory of design is to look beyond aesthetics and consider whether there are other attributes that may share this same fundamental difference from function. Design as it relates to others senses, such as sound, may be a candidate for examination. While eating at a restaurant, the background music being played may be automatically taken into account in product evaluation and, like aesthetics, it is likely processed more quickly and automatically. Similarly, any attribute that might be presented in the form in which it is later appreciated (e.g., seeing the picture quality of a television) could reveal the same system 1-type processing. Another avenue to consider is whether this system 1-like nature of aesthetics may be relevant to many experienced-based goods.

References

Arnheim, R. (1974). *Art and visual perception: A psychology of the creative eye.* Berkeley: University of California Press.

Berlyne, D. E. (1970). The golden section and hedonic judgments of rectangles: A cross-cultural study. *Sciences del Art/Scientific Aesthetics, 7,* 1–6.

Birkhoff, G. D. (1933). *Aesthetic measure.* Cambridge, MA: Harvard University Press.

Bloch, P. H. (1995). Seeking the ideal form: Product design and consumer response. *Journal of Marketing, 59*(July), 16–29.

Bloch, P. H., Brunel, F., & Arnold, T. J. (2003). Individual differences in the centrality of visual product aesthetics: Concept and measurement. *Journal of Consumer Research, 29*(March), 551–565.

Carr, T. H., McCauley, C., Sperber, R. D., & Parmelee, C. M. (1982). Words, pictures, and priming: On semantic activation, conscious identification, and the automaticity of information processing. *Journal of Experimental Psychology: Human Perception and Performance, 8*(6), 757–777.

Denis, M., & Kosslyn, S. M. (1999). Scanning visual images: A window on the mind. *Current Psychology of Cognition, 18,* 409–465.

Epstein, S. (1990). Cognitive-experiential self-theory. In L. A. Pervin (Ed.), *Handbook of personality: Theory and research* (pp. 165–192). New York, NY: Guilford Press.

Epstein, S. (1991). Cognitive-experiential self-theory: An integrative theory of personality. In S. Epstein (Ed.), *The relational self: Theoretical convergences in psychoanalysis and social psychology* (pp. 111–137). New York, NY: Guilford.

Fechner, G. T. (1871). *Zur experimentalen Aesthetik.* Leipzig: Hirzl.

Ganis, G., Thompson, W. L., & Kosslyn, S. M. (2004). Brain areas underlying visual mental imagery and visual perception: An fMRI study. *Cognitive Brain Research, 20,* 226–241.

Hart, R. P. (1997). Analyzing media. *Modern rhetorical criticism* (2nd ed., pp. 177–208). Boston: Allyn and Bacon.

Hoegg, J., & Alba, J. W. (2008). A role for aesthetics in consumer psychology. In C. P. Haugtvedt, P. M. Herr, & F. R. Kardes (Eds.), *Handbook of consumer psychology* (pp. 733–754). New York, NY: Psychology Press.

Kahneman, D., & Frederick, S. (2005). A model of heuristic judgment. In K. J. Holyoak and R. G. Morrison (Eds.), *The Cambridge handbook of thinking and reasoning* (pp. 267–293). Cambridge: Cambridge University Press.

Kawabata, H., & Zeki, S. (2004). Neural correlates of beauty. *Journal of Neurophysiology, 9*(4), 1699–1705.

Leder, H., Belke, B., Oeberst, A., & Augustin, D. (2004). A model of aesthetic appreciation and aesthetic judgments. *British Journal of Psychology, 95,* 489–508.

Lindgaard, G., Fernandes, G. J., Dudek, C., & Brown, J. (2006). Attention web designers: You have 50 milliseconds to make a good first impression! *Behaviour and Information Technology, 25*(2), 115–126.

Luna, D., & Perrachio, L. A. (2003). Visual and linguistic processing of ads by bilingual consumers. In L. M. Scott & R. Batra (Eds.), *Persuasive imagery: A consumer response perspective* (pp. 153–175). Mahwah, NJ: Lawrence Erlbaum Associates.

Paivio, A. (1986). *Mental representations: A dual-coding approach.* New York, NY: Oxford University Press.

Patrick, V. M., & Peracchio, L. A. (2010). Curating' the JCP special issue on aesthetics in consumer psychology: An introduction to the special issue. *Journal of Consumer Psychology, 20*(4), 393–397.

Pimentel, R. W., & Heckler, S. (2003). Changes in logo designs: Chasing the elusive butterfly curve. In L. M. Scott & R. Batra (Eds.), *Persuasive imagery: A consumer response perspective* (pp. 105–127). Mahwah, NJ: Lawrence Erlbaum Associates.

Sampson, G. (1985). *Writing systems* (2nd ed.). London: Hutchinson.

Schmitt, B. H., & Simonson, A. (1997). *Marketing aesthetics: The strategic management of brands, identity and image.* New York, NY: Free Press.

Scott, L. M. (1994). Images in advertising: The need for a theory of visual rhetoric. *Journal of Consumer Research, 21*(2), 252–273.

Scott, L. M., & Vargas, P. (2007). Writing with pictures: Toward a unifying theory of consumer response to images. *Journal of Consumer Research, 34*(3), 341–356.

Shiv, B., & Fedorikhin, A. (1999). Heart and mind in conflict: The interplay of affect and cognition in consumer decision making. *Journal of Consumer Research, 26*(December), 278–292.

Sholl, A., Sankaranarayanan, A., & Kroll, J. K. (1995). Transfer between picture naming and translation: A test of the asymmetries in bilingual memory. *Psychological Science, 6*, 45–49.

Sloman, S. A. (1996). The empirical case for two systems of reasoning. *Psychological Bulletin, 119*(1), 3–22.

Stanovich, K. E., & West, R. F. (2002). Individual differences in reasoning: Implications for the rationality debate. *Behavioral and Brain Sciences, 23*, 645–726.

Stenberg, G., Wiking, S., & Dahl, M. (1998). Judging words at face value: Interference in a word processing task reveals automatic processing of affective facial expressions. *Cognition and Emotion, 12*(6), 755–782.

Townsend, C. & Shu, S. B. (2010). When and how aesthetics influences financial decisions. *Journal of Consumer Psychology, 20*(4), 452–458.

van Osselaer, S. M. J., & Janiszewski, C. (2001). Two ways of learning brand associations. *Journal of Consumer Research, 28*(September), 202–223.

Veryzer, R. W., Jr. (1993). Aesthetic response and the influence of design principles on product preferences. In L. McAlister & M. L. Rothschild (Eds.), *Advances in consumer research* (Vol. 20, pp. 224–228). Provo, UT: Association for Consumer Research.

Veryzer, R. W., Jr., & Hutchinson, J. W. (1998). The influence of unity and prototypicality on aesthetic response to new product designs. *Journal of Consumer Research, 24*(March), 374–399.

Yamamato, M., & Lambert, D. R. (1994). The impact of product aesthetics on the evaluation of industrial products. *Journal of Product Innovation Management, 11*, 309–324.

16

PROCESSING FLUENCY OF PRODUCT DESIGN

Cognitive and Affective Routes to Aesthetic Preferences

Jan R. Landwehr

GOETHE UNIVERSITY FRANKFURT

In recent years, the famous quote of Louis Sullivan (1896), "form ever follows function," has continuously lost its practical significance. Companies are increasingly facing mature markets in which products differ only slightly in their functionality, and investments in truly functional innovations are decreasing (Cooper, 2011). When functionality no longer differs among products and brands, it would be unwise in terms of market differentiation to equip products with a form that merely follows a product's functionality. Instead, the exterior design—in addition to branding—has become a crucial marketing instrument to differentiate a company's product in a competitive market of functionally homogenous products (Bloch, 1995). An example of the increased importance that firms assign to the aesthetic appeal of their products comes from one of Germany's most successful car companies: Audi. In 2006, Audi introduced the new Audi TT Coupé 8J (see Figure 16.1), a new version of the iconic sports car with its unique design characterized by round geometric shapes. However, they did not go to one of the large motor shows but instead introduced the car at a design fair—the Design Annual in Frankfurt, Germany. Given Audi's key brand claim "Vorsprung durch Technik" (i.e., Truth in Engineering), this example illustrates the special weight that even technologically driven companies currently assign to the visual appearance of their products.

The increased importance of design for a company's market success is, however, not only acknowledged by practitioners (e.g., Audi estimates that aesthetic appeal accounts for 60% of an individual's buying decision; Kreuzbauer & Malter, 2005) but has also entered the scientific discourse on key marketing instruments (e.g., Bloch, 1995). Recent research has begun to systematically determine the relative importance of product design compared to more traditional marketing instruments, such as price, promotion, and branding.

FIGURE 16.1 In 2006, Audi introduced the new Audi TT Coupé 8J, characterized by round geometric shapes.

Source: Jan Landwehr.

In one study of actual sales in the German car market (Landwehr, Labroo, & Herrmann, 2011a), measures of a car's visual aesthetics accounted for 19% of the variance in a sales forecasting model. An additional analysis of the published data revealed that the Delta-R^2 for the design measures was higher than that of any other marketing instrument (price = 18.4%; brand strength = 17.7%; technological sophistication = 11.7%; all other considered instruments < 10%), supporting the intuitive hypothesis of design practitioners that design has become one of the most important marketing instruments. Recent research suggests that the importance of design may even increase when the functional attributes of a product offer a sufficient level of utility and, hence, a low level of functional risk (Chitturi, Raghunathan, & Mahajan, 2007), i.e., increasing trust in a product's functionality (for example, by building a strong brand) further increases the importance of a product's visual aesthetics for consumers' willingness-to-buy (Landwehr, Wentzel, & Herrmann, 2012).

Given the importance of a product's visual appearance for consumers' preferences, the following questions addressed by the present chapter call for further clarification: What concrete design features exert a systematic effect on consumers' aesthetic experience, and for what reason? That is, would it be useful to understand which objective design characteristics can be linked to aesthetic pleasure and which psychological mechanisms establish this link? Knowledge of these objective design characteristics would allow for systematic, straightforward design management; knowledge of the theoretically relevant psychological mechanisms would allow for generalizing empirical findings beyond a given research context and beyond a given product category.

To these ends, the present chapter intentionally considers only those visual determinants of product design preferences that can be measured/operationalized in an objective manner and that can be deductively derived from a coherent theoretical framework of the psychological antecedents of aesthetic preferences. In this respect, the processing fluency account of aesthetic pleasure (Reber, Schwarz, & Winkielman, 2004) offers a parsimonious explanation of the psychological process underlying aesthetic experiences (i.e., the experience of cognitive ease when processing a visual stimulus triggers aesthetic pleasure), and it proposes a limited set of well-defined visual characteristics (i.e., simplicity, prototypicality, symmetry, and contrast/clarity) that determine the amount of processing fluency and, thereby, an aesthetic experience. Hence, this chapter will exclusively adopt a processing fluency perspective on the determinants of aesthetic preferences in product design.

The key tenets of the processing fluency framework are presented in the first part of the present chapter. The second part of the chapter is dedicated to a summary of empirical studies examining one or more of the four aforementioned visual characteristics. Due to the focus of this volume, this summary focuses exclusively on studies in the domain of product design and does not cover other types of aesthetic stimuli. Based on a recent extension of the processing fluency framework called the "Pleasure-Interest Model of Aesthetic Liking" (PIA-Model; Graf & Landwehr, 2015), the third part of this chapter introduces the idea that the valence of fluency may change, conditional on the processing mode (affective/automatic vs. cognitive/controlled processing). This new perspective allows the integration of some contradictory empirical findings, which indicate positive effects of disfluent visual characteristics. The fourth and fifth parts finally offer implications for designers and a theory of design, respectively.

Processing Fluency and Aesthetic Pleasure

In 2004, Reber et al. published a seminal review paper on the determinants of an aesthetic experience. The authors reviewed a number of empirical studies to ultimately integrate them into a processing fluency model of aesthetic pleasure. The model's key proposition is that certain visual stimulus characteristics vary in their processing demand for the perceptual system. That is, stimulus characteristics such as high visual contrast/clarity facilitate processing in comparison to low visual contrast/clarity, which impedes processing (see Figure 16.2). This processing ease or difficulty is further proposed to be metacognitively monitored by the observer and to be experienced as a feeling of processing fluency. Importantly, processing fluency has been shown to feel inherently good (Winkielman & Caccioppo, 2001). Hence, on a merely affective level, ease of processing is immediately experienced as pleasurable. Unless a person has a

Kids and grown-ups love it so – the happy world of HARIBO

Kids and grown-ups love it so – the happy world of HARIBO

FIGURE 16.2 An advertising slogan printed in an easy-to-read contrast (upper box) should aesthetically be preferred when compared to a more difficult-to-read print (lower box).

Source: Jan Landwehr.

reason to call the diagnosticity of the fluency experience into question, the gut-level pleasure triggered by fluency is directly attributed to aesthetic liking of the eliciting stimulus (Reber et al., 2004). Based on the previously described mechanism, the fluency framework proposes that greater processing ease of a (visual) stimulus leads to greater aesthetic liking of that stimulus (Reber et al., 2004). Hence, the exemplary advertising slogan depicted in Figure 16.2 should aesthetically be preferred when printed in an easy-to-read contrast (upper box) compared to a difficult-to-read contrast (lower box).

In the current literature on the relationship between fluency and aesthetic liking, four core visual stimulus characteristics that facilitate perceptual processing are discussed: simplicity (i.e., amount of information), prototypicality, symmetry, and contrast/clarity (Reber et al., 2004). Merely based on the key tenets of Fluency Theory, one would predict that simpler, more typical, more symmetric, and higher-contrast/clarity stimuli would garner greater aesthetic liking. Although there is substantial empirical evidence for each of the four stimulus characteristics in isolation (for a review see Reber et al., 2004), studies that consider more than one stimulus characteristic at a time sometimes fail to support a mere fluency-based explanation. That is, once the joint influence of more than one stimulus characteristic is taken into account, the positive effect of simplicity, for instance, vanishes and, instead, complexity becomes the preferred end of the continuum (e.g., Landwehr et al., 2011a). Moreover, sometimes a non-linear, inverted u-shaped relationship between a fluency-related stimulus characteristic (i.e., complexity) and preference has been found (Berlyne, 1970, 1971), which also contradicts the monotonic prediction of the pure fluency framework. Finally, mere exposure has been shown to decrease liking of fluent stimuli (e.g., simple or typical stimuli) and to increase liking of disfluent stimuli (e.g., complex or atypical stimuli; Cox & Cox, 2002; Landwehr, Wentzel, & Herrmann, 2013), although the fluency account would predict that mere exposure increases fluency and, hence, liking of all types of stimuli.

Currently, the processing fluency framework addresses these challenging empirical findings by proposing two different psychological responses to visual stimuli: on the one hand, a stimulus can trigger an actual fluency experience with the usual effect on aesthetic liking; on the other hand, it can trigger a processing expectation in terms of fluency that determines whether the actual fluency experience is expected or comes as a surprise (Landwehr et al., 2011a). Moreover, only when the fluency experience comes as a surprise is it assumed to be sufficiently salient to be included in a liking judgment (Hansen & Wänke, 2013). In contrast, when an experience is expected, the intensity of the experience is too weak to enter the judgment or may even be consciously discounted as being uninformative (Hansen & Wänke, 2013; Schwarz, 2004). In particular, visual simplicity has been proposed to be one key stimulus characteristic that may trigger a processing expectation such that a simple (complex) stimulus is expected to be easy (difficult) to process (Landwehr et al., 2011a). When, for instance, a stimulus is simple and prototypical, the fluency experience of prototypicality has been expected and does not surpass the threshold of being considered (see Figure 16.3; left: Suzuki Swift). However, when the stimulus is complex and prototypical, the fluency experience of prototypicality comes as a surprise and is accordingly experienced as quite intense, which is transferred into an accordingly positive judgment (see Figure 16.3; right: Opel Corsa).

Although this explanation is able to account for a positive interaction of complexity and prototypicality and may also explain inverted u-shaped relationships, it cannot explain a positive main effect of complexity. Moreover, the fluency framework does not specify which stimulus characteristics are expected to trigger an expectation rather than an actual experience. That is, the framework does not provide a rationale for what makes simplicity different from the other

FIGURE 16.3 On left, the Suzuki Swift, illustrating a stimulus where the fluency experience of prototypicality is due to design's simplicity. On right, the Opel Corsa provides a complex yet prototypical stimulus, so that the fluency experience of prototypicality comes as a surprise. As a result, the experience is more intense, which is transferred into an accordingly positive judgment.

Source: Jan Landwehr.

visual characteristics nor why simplicity triggers a processing expectation instead of a processing experience. Before a dual-process perspective on the effects of processing fluency (Graf & Landwehr, 2015) is adopted to resolve these two issues, the next section reviews further empirical findings on the four key visual characteristics in the domain of product design that call for a refinement of the fluency framework to fully explain aesthetic preferences.

The Processing of Product Design

There is much empirical evidence for the processing fluency framework of aesthetic pleasure provided by basic research, using well controlled but often artificial stimuli, such as random dot patterns (e.g., Winkielman, Halberstadt, Fazendeiro, & Catty, 2006) or abstract shapes (e.g., Reber & Schwarz, 2006). These studies have been crucial in terms of theory building and are comprehensively reviewed elsewhere (Reber et al., 2004). The aim of the present literature review is to focus exclusively on articles that examine core visual fluency determinants (i.e., prototypicality, simplicity, symmetry, and contrast/clarity) in product design.

Prototypicality

Among the aforementioned visual characteristics, prototypicality is probably the best examined visual characteristic and the one that has shown the most robust positive relationships with both fluency and aesthetic liking. Halberstadt (2006), for instance, reviews an impressive set of empirical studies on the positive relationship between subjectively perceived prototypicality and attractiveness for such diverse product categories as eyeglasses, handguns, rings, watches, and cars. Experimental evidence for the positive link between visual prototypicality and aesthetic liking comes from Veryzer and Hutchinson (1998) for telephones and refrigerators as well as from Kumar and Garg (2010) for DVD players. Empirical evidence for an effect of visual prototypicality on real sales data was provided by Landwehr and colleagues (2011a) for the German automotive market, who also showed that this effect is mediated by processing fluency and who established an objective measure for visual prototypicality of product design (a measure of the visual distance of characteristic features of a design from the average position of these features within a category).

Although the general effect of prototypicality on aesthetic liking has been shown to be robust, a special type of atypicality—namely novelty—has also been shown to have positive effects on aesthetic liking. This contradiction is best illustrated in a series of studies by Hekkert, Snelders, and van Wieringen (2003), who showed positive effects of both perceived prototypicality and perceived novelty on aesthetic preferences for sanders, telephones, teakettles, and cars. To reconcile the finding that two opposing visual properties have positive effects on the same outcome, a study by Carbon and Leder (2005) suggests that novelty (i.e., innovativeness) of car interiors becomes more favorable by means of multiple exposure and, hence, by the opportunity to familiarize oneself with a novel/innovative design. This interpretation is also in accordance with a recent study by Landwehr and colleagues (2013), who studied sales in the German car market; they found that at the time of market introduction, prototypical designs are preferred over atypical designs—a pattern that is reversed over the course of a car's lifetime cycle and, hence, by means of multiple exposure.

In sum, the results regarding prototypicality suggest that there is a strong link between prototypicality and aesthetic liking. Furthermore, there is also evidence that—in perfect accordance with fluency theory—this positive effect is mediated by processing fluency. However, novelty/innovativeness, which is by definition atypical and hence disfluent, has also been shown to trigger aesthetic liking— especially after sufficient exposure. This finding cannot easily be integrated into the present fluency framework of aesthetic pleasure.

Simplicity

Considering an additional visual characteristic discussed in the fluency literature— simplicity (often times in the literature denoted by the opposite end of the continuum: complexity)—a similar interactive pattern with mere exposure as was described for prototypicality has been observed. Cox and Cox (2002) showed that simple designs are initially preferred over complex designs for female fashion apparel—a pattern that is reversed by multiple exposure. Other studies that did not consider such temporal dynamics found contradictory evidence either in favor of simplicity (i.e., low complexity) of VHS video recorders (Creusen, Veryzer, & Schoormans, 2010) or in favor of complexity in car designs (Landwehr et al., 2011a). Additionally, the study by Landwehr and colleagues (2011a) established an objective measure for the visual complexity of product design (a measure of the non-redundant information contained by a stimulus indicated by the file size of a compressed digital image).

In sum, the evidence regarding simplicity is again mixed such that it seems to be sometimes positive and sometimes negative in terms of aesthetic liking— especially after prolonged exposure. Hence, the fluency framework is partially supported but also challenged by the empirical evidence unless it relies on additional constructs, such as processing expectation triggered by complexity (Landwehr et al., 2011a). However, a more parsimonious way of integrating these findings into the fluency framework would be preferable.

Symmetry

The third dimension proposed by the fluency framework is visual symmetry, which is only examined by very few studies in the domain of product design. One of these studies is the previously described study by Creusen and colleagues

(2010), which showed that people prefer symmetric video recorders to asymmetric ones. Mayer and Landwehr (2014) developed an objective measure of vertical symmetry (a measure of the pairwise correlation of digital image pixels mirrored on the vertical axis). They showed that symmetry increased aesthetic liking of artworks and that this effect is mediated by processing fluency. I am not aware of any convincing study in the domain of product design that shows a negative effect of symmetry on aesthetic outcome variables; the lack of negative effects of symmetry is in perfect accordance with the fluency framework.

Contrast and Clarity

Finally, the fourth visual characteristic discussed by the fluency framework— contrast and clarity—has, to my knowledge, not been examined in a product design context and, hence, offers an important gap in the scientific literature that has yet to be filled by future research. Given the capabilities of digital image processing software, it would be straightforward to develop an objective measure for this visual characteristic and to examine downstream effects on consumers' aesthetic responses.

Preliminary Conclusion

In sum, the empirical evidence regarding fluency-related visual characteristics of product design is mixed. Prototypicality and symmetry seem to have robust effects on aesthetic liking due to their fluent processing. However, novelty—a special type of atypicality—also increases consumers' aesthetic preferences, a finding that cannot easily be integrated into a fluency perspective. Furthermore, the dimension of visual simplicity-complexity also seems to be a double-edged sword: sometimes one and sometimes the other endpoint of the continuum is aesthetically preferred.

An Extended Cognitive-Affective Perspective on Processing Fluency

As the previous literature review shows, the processing fluency framework of aesthetic pleasure by Reber and colleagues (2004) constitutes a theoretical basis to examine aesthetic responses to product design. The framework allows for the derivation of a limited set of visual characteristics (prototypicality, simplicity, symmetry, and contrast/clarity) that presumably influence aesthetic preferences, and it offers a parsimonious explanation for the responsible psychological mechanism: processing fluency. However, some of the empirical findings (positive effects of complexity and atypicality/novelty) contradict the basic processing fluency account of aesthetic pleasure (Reber et al., 2004) or can only be integrated into the framework by intricate additional assumptions (such as processing expectations).

The Pleasure-Interest Model of Aesthetic Liking

To resolve the problems with the fluency framework, the Pleasure-Interest Model of Aesthetic Liking (PIA-Model) has recently been proposed by Graf and Landwehr (2015). The key idea of this model is to extend the mere affective, automatic response level proposed by Reber and colleagues (2004) that may lead to aesthetic pleasure by a deliberate, controlled response level, potentially leading to aesthetic interest. That is, the PIA-Model adopts a dual-system perspective (e.g., Strack & Deutsch, 2004) of the fluency-liking link and predicts different preference patterns for processing fluency determinants within the respective systems. While the automatic system prefers fluent stimuli that feel familiar and pleasing, the controlled system rather prefers disfluent stimuli with a sufficient (but not overtaxing) potential to stimulate cognitive engagement with the stimulus (cf. Nakamura & Csikszentmihalyi, 2002). Evident from the empirical results, the automatic processing level is perfectly sufficient to explain preferences for prototypicality, simplicity, and symmetry. However, the preferences for novelty and complexity are captured by the additional controlled level of processing proposed by the PIA-Model.

Moreover, by taking the basic principle of common dual-system theories (e.g., Strack & Deutsch, 2004) into account, according to which the affective system always produces a response and the cognitive system may only produce an additional, supplementary response, one may propose that the combination of visual characteristics with fluent and disfluent elements may trigger the strongest preferences. That is, designs that feel pleasurable due to fluent visual elements but are simultaneously cognitively considered to be interesting due to other disfluent visual elements should lead to the strongest consumer preferences (see, for instance, the right car in Figure 16.3: the Opel Corsa combines prototypicality [a fluent design element] with complexity [a disfluent design element] and should hence be aesthetically liked). Importantly, this notion would also allow for an integration of the finding that the combination of friendly (i.e., pleasurable) and aggressive (i.e., stimulating) design elements in anthropomorphic designs has been proven to be preferred by consumers and is bestselling in the market (Landwehr, McGill, & Herrmann, 2011b).

Activation of Controlled, Cognitive Processing

A crucial question that results from the general idea of an affective and a cognitive route to aesthetic preferences asks for the circumstances under which consumers take each route. As previous research has shown, one immediate determinant is the stimulus characteristic itself; while fluent stimulus processing triggers low processing motivation, disfluent stimulus processing triggers high processing motivation (Alter, Oppenheimer, Eyre, & Eply, 2007). That is, prototypical, simple, and symmetric stimuli are only processed on an affective level and preferred due to their fluency. Novel and complex stimuli are processed on a cognitive level and are preferred due to their potential to stimulate the cognitive system.

Another potential determinant of cognitive processing is simply the number of presented opportunities to consider the stimulus. That is, more opportunities for an individual to perceive a stimulus provide a greater likelihood that he or she will begin to think about the stimulus and, hence, to process the stimulus on a cognitive level. This idea is in perfect accordance with the empirical findings in the domain of product design reviewed previously. For both simplicity/complexity (Cox & Cox, 2002) and prototypicality/atypicality (Landwehr et al., 2013), it has been shown that products with simple/prototypical designs are initially preferred. However, after sufficient exposure to the stimuli, a preference shift towards complex/atypical designs occurs. Given these consistent empirical findings, it is even reasonable to propose that exposure (i.e., the opportunity to invest cognitive energy) is a requirement for the engagement of the cognitive processing of aesthetic stimuli. That is, atypicality or complexity can only trigger liking when consumers have had prolonged prior exposure to a stimulus and, hence, the opportunity to invest sufficient cognitive energy in processing the stimulus' atypical/complex visual features.

Discussion of the PIA-Model

The proposed application of the PIA-Model (Graf & Landwehr, 2015) to aesthetic preferences for product designs is depicted in Figure 16.4. As seen from the figure, the four discussed visual determinants of processing fluency are conceptualized as continuous dimensions with fluent (lower end) and disfluent (upper end) endpoints. While the fluent visual characteristics are processed on an affective level and preferred due to their fluency, the disfluent visual characteristics are processed on a cognitive level—given sufficient exposure—and are preferred due to their potential to stimulate. As outlined in the review of empirical studies in the domain of product design, there is, to my knowledge thus far, no study examining the effect of contrast/clarity of design on aesthetic liking and no study showing a positive effect of asymmetry. It would, therefore, be very interesting to see whether the predictions regarding high and low contrast/clarity provided by Figure 16.4 hold and whether asymmetry can lead to liking when processed on a cognitive level.

A crucial question regarding the functional relationship between disfluent stimulus characteristics and aesthetic liking is posed by a model put forward by one of the most influential researchers in the history of empirical aesthetics: Daniel E. Berlyne (1970, 1971, 1974). The present application of the PIA-Model (Graf & Landwehr, 2015) proposes, in accordance with the empirical findings on product design, that on a cognitive level, potential for stimulation monotonically increases aesthetic liking. Both considered disfluent stimulus variables (i.e., novelty and complexity) show a perfect overlap with the *collative variables* already proposed

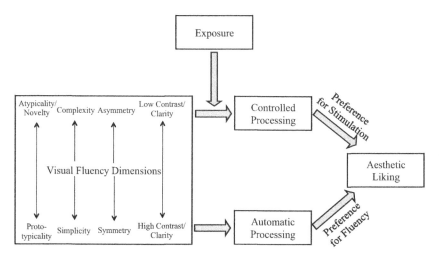

FIGURE 16.4 The proposed application of the PIA-Model (Graf & Landwehr, 2015) to aesthetic preferences for product designs.

Source: Jan Landwehr.

by Berlyne (1970, 1971). The key idea of Berlyne's model is that the beholder of a visual stimulus assesses the *arousal potential* of these collative variables and that people prefer a medium level of arousal potential. That is, because arousal potential is assumed to increase monotonically with increasing novelty and complexity, respectively, individuals will exhibit an inverted u-shaped relationship between the intensity of the collative variables and their aesthetic liking.

When comparing the fluency approach and the arousal potential approach, it is important to note that there is an inverse relationship between fluency and arousal potential such that those collative variables that monotonically increase arousal potential monotonically decrease fluency, and vice versa. Hence, although the key mediating constructs of both approaches substantially differ in terms of their conceptualization, they can be inversely mapped onto each other and predict similar visual characteristics as important determinants of an aesthetic liking experience, though with different functional relationships: linear vs. inverted u-shaped. Most evidence for inverted u-shaped relationships is based on artificial stimuli (e.g., Berlyne, 1970) and has not been replicated in the domain of product design (e.g., Landwehr et al., 2011a).

It would, therefore, be pertinent to examine whether this relationship is due to a fundamental difference in the way product designs and abstract stimuli are psychologically evaluated or simply occurs because, in product design research, only acceptable but not extreme levels of novelty or complexity are implemented. The latter explanation would suggest that only the increasing side of the inverted "u" is considered in product design research, and the decreasing side is ignored by means of the available stimulus material. The exact functional relationship between cognitively processed visual determinants of processing fluency and aesthetic liking remains an open question for future research—for market-ready product designs the assumption of a monotonic relationship is, however, at least heuristically sufficient.

Implications for Designers

Based on the PIA-Model (Graf & Landwehr, 2015) and its application to the visual characteristics of product design, several practical implications can be derived. First, the key challenge for product designers lies in the identification of the "sweet spot" of visual aesthetics, where the visual design characteristics combine in a way that they are both pleasing and interesting. A heuristic recommendation would be to balance fluency and disfluency across different visual characteristics. For instance, a high level of prototypicality in the overall shape of a product (= high fluency) could be combined with a low level of simplicity of the product's surface or features (= low fluency), as it is suggested by Landwehr and colleagues (2011a) and exemplified in the Opel Corse in Figure 16.3. If the balance of fluency and disfluency is maintained, the opposite pattern may also work: a design based on simple elements that are combined in an unusual way. The global form of the original Audi TT from 1998—and to some extent also its successor depicted in Figure 16.1—distinctively violated existing norms for the design of a sports car by having rounded instead of streamlined shapes and rather plain instead of segmented surfaces. In this sense, the global form of the car is atypical, but the geometric shapes that build the body of the car are plain and simplistic and, hence, visually simple. With more than 500,000 sold units since 1998, this design strategy for the Audi TT was obviously successful.

Second, the notion that exposure may change whether fluent or disfluent design characteristics are preferred by consumers is also noteworthy for product designers (see Figure 16.4). As empirical studies have convincingly shown (Cox & Cox, 2002; Landwehr et al., 2013) cognitive processing and a preference for disfluent design features increases over the course of multiple exposures. Hence, design features that are aesthetically disliked when introduced into the market can become highly preferred over the lifetime cycle of a product. An impressive example for this notion can again be found in the car industry. When BMW introduced its new 7 series in 2001, the rather atypical and unusual design of the trunk lid—which sits on the body of the car (see Figure 16.5)—confused both car critics and consumers, resulting in low sales figures. When Mercedes introduced the new S-Class four years later (2005) with an almost visually identical trunk lid design, the car was highly praised by design critics and became very successful in the market. This anecdotal example illustrates the power of exposure in making initially disfluent design characteristics accessible to consumers' perceptions, which may ultimately lead to a preference reversal. Ironically, in this example, BMW

FIGURE 16.5 BMW's 7 series (2001) had a rather atypical and unusual design of the trunk lid, which sits on the body of the car (right). Mercedes introduced the S-Class (2005) with an almost visually identical trunk lid design (left). The unsuccessful BMW prepared the eye of the consumer for the new Mercedes.

Source: Jan Landwehr.

prepared the eye of the consumer for the new Mercedes—something that was certainly not intended by designers and managers at BMW.

Finally, although a fluency-based explanation of aesthetic preferences allows clear identification of visual design characteristics that must be considered when trying to optimize consumers' processing experience, it does not provide any guidance on how the available design dimensions should be combined because several combinations of affectively fluent and cognitively disfluent design elements are expected to lead to beneficial outcomes. Hence, although the presented model allows for understanding of the roots of given design preferences and to derive abstract recommendations for product design, it does not replace the creative genius of product designers who manage to combine visual design dimensions in such a way that great designs emerge.

Implications for a Theory of Design

The proposed application of the PIA-Model (Graf & Landwehr, 2015) to aesthetic liking of product design seeks to fulfill three major aims that are crucial for any consumer behavior theory on product design: (1) identification of objectively measurable design characteristics; (2) understanding of psychological processes that connect stimulus characteristics with an aesthetic experience/judgment; (3) empirical validation in the context of real products and real consumption behavior. Of course, there may be other interesting aspects of product design, such as an understanding of the creative act of designing a product or the impact of the general zeitgeist on design trends. However, once a theory of product design is concerned with an understanding of consumers' responses towards design, I regard the previously mentioned points as essential. In addition, at least from a marketing or business perspective, an understanding of consumers' aesthetic preferences is of primary interest for economic success.

My first claim is based on a position paper by Fiedler (2014), who proposed ecological functionalism as a guideline for valuable theory building in social psychology. His main point is that the explanatory value of a theory tends to be greater as the distance between the explanatory variable (independent variable) and the explained outcome (dependent variable) increases. This tendency is, however, not limited to theories in social psychology but can easily be extended to psychological theories in general, such as a psychological theory of design. In particular, Fiedler (2014) calls for an objective measurement of theoretical constructs instead of a mere focus on intrapsychic processes to enable impactful theoretical claims. Applied to the given context, this perspective suggests that any valuable theory of product design should strive for the identification of objective visual stimulus properties that can be linked to psychological processes (i.e., aesthetic experience) and behavioral outcomes (i.e., buying behavior). In this sense, it would not be sufficient to collect subjective perceptions of stimulus properties (e.g., subjectively experienced complexity of a design), but it would be preferable to measure objective properties of the design (e.g., the amount of information within a visual stimulus as a measure of complexity, see Landwehr et al., 2011a).

My second claim is based on a position paper by Strack (2012), who called for the importance of understanding the underlying mechanism of an effect over and above merely showing an effect. That is, a good theory of design must understand not only how design variables are related to aesthetic experiences but also why they are related. I regard fluency as a parsimonious yet very powerful theoretical construct to explain the causal mechanism responsible for explaining aesthetic experiences, and I would like to stress the importance of the seminal paper by Rolf Reber, Norbert Schwarz, and Piotr Winkielman (2004) for the field of empirical aesthetics in general and a theory of design in particular. The theoretical extension of the processing fluency framework presented in this chapter can be seen as a rough sketch of the empirical challenges of the original model in the domain of product design and potential modifications that may improve the predictive strength. From the reading of the chapter, it is likely evident that the idea of conceiving fluency both from an affective and a cognitive perspective is only a preliminary attempt to integrate findings from product design into an overarching framework. Readers interested in a detailed analysis of the underlying psychological mechanisms of a dual-process perspective on aesthetic preferences are referred to "The Pleasure-Interest Model of Aesthetic Liking" (PIA Model; Graf & Landwehr, 2015).

Finally, my third claim is substantiated by the fact that product design is an applied discipline. Many studies in the field of aesthetics have been conducted with rather artificial stimuli, such as random dot patterns (e.g., Winkielman et al., 2006) or abstract shapes (e.g., Reber & Schwarz, 2006). While such stimulus material can be highly valuable for the formulation of generic aesthetic theories, it is crucial to provide evidence that these theories also hold in an applied setting with real products. Therefore, the review of extant empirical findings in this chapter had a clear focus on studies that examine the effect of visual design characteristics on aesthetic outcome variables in an applied product design context. Some of these studies even analyzed the market success of product designs (Landwehr et al., 2011a, 2011b, 2013), which I would regard as the ultimate validity test of any theory on product design.

References

Alter, A. A., Oppenheimer, D. M., Eyre, R. N., & Eply, N. (2007). Overcoming intuition: Metacognitive difficulty activates analytic reasoning. *Journal of Experimental Psychology: General, 136*(4), 569–576.

Berlyne, D. E. (1970). Novelty, complexity, and hedonic value. *Perception and Psychophysics, 8,* 279–286.

Berlyne, D. E. (1971). *Aesthetics and psychobiology.* New York, NY: Appleton-Century-Crofts.

Berlyne, D. E. (1974). *Studies in the new experimental aesthetics: Steps toward an objective psychology of aesthetic appreciation.* Washington, DC: Hemisphere.

Bloch, P. H. (1995). Seeking the ideal form: Product design and consumer response. *Journal of Marketing, 59*(July), 16–29.

Carbon, C. C., & Leder, H. (2005). The repeated evaluation technique (RET): A method to capture dynamic effects of innovativeness and attractiveness. *Applied Cognitive Psychology, 19*(5), 587–601.

Chitturi, R., Raghunathan, R., & Mahajan, V. (2007). Form versus function: How the intensities of specific emotions evoked in functional versus hedonic trade-offs mediate product preferences. *Journal of Marketing Research, 44,* 702–714.

Cooper, R. G. (2011). Perspective: The innovation dilemma: How to innovate when the market is mature. *Journal of Product Innovation Management, 28*(S1), 2–27.

Cox, D., & Cox, A. D. (2002). Beyond first impressions: The effects of repeated exposure on consumer liking of visually complex and simple product designs. *Journal of the Academy of Marketing Science, 30*(2), 119–130.

Creusen, M.E.H., Veryzer, R. W., & Schoormans, J.P.L. (2010). Product value importance and consumer preference for visual complexity and symmetry. *European Journal of Marketing, 49*(9/10), 1437–1452.

Fiedler, K. (2014). From intrapsychic to ecological theories in social psychology: Outlines of a functional theory approach. *European Journal of Social Psychology, 44*(7), 657–670.

Graf, L.K.M., & Landwehr, J.R. (2015). A dual-process perspective on aesthetic response formation: The pleasure-interest model of aesthetic liking. Manuscript submitted for publication. *Personality and Social Psychology Review.* doi:10.1177/1088868315574978

Halberstadt, J. (2006). The generality and ultimate origins of the attractiveness of prototypes. *Personality and Social Psychology Review, 10*(2), 166–183.

Hansen, J., & Wänke, M. (2013). Fluency in context: Discrepancy makes processing experiences informative. In C. Unkelbach & R. Greifeneder (Eds.), *The experience of thinking: How the fluency of mental processes influences cognition and behavior* (pp. 70–84). London: Psychology Press.

Hekkert, P., Snelders, D., & van Wieringen, P. C. W. (2003). Most advanced, yet acceptable: Typicality and novelty as joint predictors of aesthetic preference in industrial design. *British Journal of Psychology, 94,* 111–124.

Kreuzbauer, R., & Malter, A. J. (2005). Embodied cognition and new product design: Changing product form to influence brand categorization. *Journal of Product Innovation Management, 22*(March), 165–176.

Kumar, M., & Garg, N. (2010). Aesthetic principles and cognitive emotion appraisals: How much of the beauty lies in the eye of the beholder?. *Journal of Consumer Psychology, 20*, 485–494.

Landwehr, J. R., Labroo, A. A., & Herrmann, A. (2011a). Gut liking for the ordinary: Incorporating design fluency improves automobile sales forecasts. *Marketing Science, 30*(3), 416–429.

Landwehr, J. R., McGill, A. L., & Herrmann, A. (2011b). It's got the look: The effect of friendly and aggressive "facial" expressions on product liking and sales. *Journal of Marketing, 75*(May), 132–146.

Landwehr, J. R., Wentzel, D., & Herrmann, A. (2012). The tipping point of design: How product design and brands interact to affect consumers' preferences. *Psychology & Marketing, 29*(6), 422–433.

Landwehr, J. R., Wentzel, D., & Herrmann, A. (2013). Product design for the long run: Consumer responses to typical and atypical designs at different stages of exposure. *Journal of Marketing, 77*(5), 92–107.

Mayer, S., & Landwehr, J. R. (2014). When complexity is symmetric: The interplay of two core determinants of visual aesthetics. *Advances in Consumer Research, 42*, 608–609.

Nakamura, J., & Csikszentmihalyi, M. (2002). The concept of flow. In C. R. Snyder & S. J. Lopez (Eds.), *Handbook of positive psychology* (pp. 89–105). Oxford: Oxford University Press.

Reber, R., & Schwarz, N. (2006). Perceptual fluency, preference, and evolution. *Polish Psychological Bulletin, 37*(1), 16–22.

Reber, R., Schwarz, N., & Winkielman, P. (2004). Processing fluency and aesthetic pleasure: Is beauty in the perceiver's processing experience? *Personality and Social Psychology Review, 8*(4), 364–382.

Schwarz, N. (2004). Metacognitive experiences in consumer judgment and decision making. *Journal of Consumer Psychology, 14*(4), 332–348.

Strack, F. (2012). The wow and how of research in social psychology: Causes and consequences. *European Bulletin of Social Psychology, 24*(2), 4–8.

Strack, F., & Deutsch, R. (2004). Reflective and impulsive determinants of social behavior. *Personality and Social Psychology Review, 8*(3), 220–247.

Sullivan, L. H. (1896). The tall office building artistically considered. *Lippincott's Magazine, 57*, 403–409.

Veryzer, R. W., & Hutchinson, J. W. (1998). The influence of unity and prototypicality on aesthetic responses to new product design. *Journal of Consumer Research, 24*, 374–394.

Winkielman, P., & Cacioppo, J. T. (2001). Mind at ease puts a smile on the face: Psychophysiological evidence that processing facilitation leads to positive affect. *Journal of Personality and Social Psychology, 81*, 989–1000.

Winkielman, P., Halberstadt, J., Fazendeiro, T., & Catty, S. (2006). Prototypes are attractive because they are easy on the mind. *Psychological Science, 17*(9), 799–806.

17

AESTHETIC PRINCIPLES OF PRODUCT FORM AND COGNITIVE APPRAISALS

Predicting Emotional Responses to Beauty

Minu Kumar

SAN FRANCISCO STATE UNIVERSITY

Product design is one of the core elements of a product and is defined as the discrete properties of a product's form (i.e., the aesthetics of the tangible good and/or service) and its function (i.e., its capabilities) together with the holistic properties of the integrated form and function (Luchs & Swan, 2011; Noble & Kumar, 2010). Often the first point of contact for consumers, in retail aisles or on websites, the product's design can create a lasting impression that affects whether the product is actively considered for purchase (Bloch, 1995). It can have a pervasive effect on the desirability of a good, its sales, its fit with the parent brand, and, eventually, the satisfaction consumers derive from its use (Kumar, Townsend, and Vorhies 2014; Landwehr, Labroo, & Hermann, 2011; Noble & Kumar, 2008). To name just a few examples, products such as the iPod, the Volkswagen Beetle, and the Dyson vacuum cleaner have succeeded in large part due to their design (Nussbaum, 2004).

In marketing and consumption, Bloch (1995) presented a broad conceptual framework on how consumers cognitively and affectively respond to product form. In his framework Bloch identified design goals and constraints (e.g. designer factors, performance goals, ergonomic, regulatory/legal factors among others), individual tastes and preferences, and situational factors as playing a major role in the cognitive and affective responses consumers have to product form. Since then many research articles have approached product form from the vantage of product development managers, marketers, and consumers. Although these research articles bring tremendous value to our understanding of how product form shapes consumer behavior, very few of these in Marketing and Consumer Behavior have provided the exposition for the neural and biological mechanisms behind the connections between Product Form and Emotional Responses. One facet of product form, aesthetics, is a particularly rich area for investigation because it has previously been singled out as evoking emotional responses (e.g., Creusen & Schoormans, 2005; Holbrook & Hirschman, 1980).

Aesthetics[1] is an inherent part of the form of a product (Veryzer & Hutchinson, 1998). This book chapter adopts Baumgarten's definition of aesthetics as sensory feelings (as defined in his book *Aesthetica* in 1750). This definition is more appropriate for this chapter because pleasure or displeasure resulting from the overall appraisal of visual cues can be subjective (Coates, 2003; Kringelbach & Berridge, 2009) and can account for variations in aesthetic response. In marketing and consumer behavior, aesthetics has most often been connected to emotional responses (e.g., Bloch, 1995; Creusen & Schoormans, 2005; Holbrook & Hirschman, 1980). However, one of the factors that Bloch included as having moderating influence between product form and consumers' psychological responses to product form is "Innate Design Preferences." Although a few research papers in the Marketing and Consumer Behavior study aesthetic factors such as unity and proportionality on consumer preference (e.g., Veryzer & Hutchinson, 1998; Raghubir & Greenleaf, 2006) and offer us an understanding of what happens under various conditions, a more fundamental exposition of what the innate preferences are and how they contribute in creating an emotional response is lacking.

The theoretical underpinnings marketing customer behavior literature uses to explain the connection between the aesthetics and emotional response falls into one or both of the following approaches: (a) the properties of the product's composition (e.g., Orth & Malkewitz, 2008; Ragubhir & Greenleaf, 2006), (b) the cognitive the processes involved in engagement with the product (e.g., Kumar & Garg, 2010). Yet, any scientific theory of aesthetics and its influence on human behavior would be incomplete without including, at the very least, the following three theoretical components: (a) the universality of aesthetics: whether common rules apply to consumer responses to aesthetic principles; (b) the evolutionary rationale: why these rules evolved and why they take the form that they do; and (c) the physiological and neurological mechanisms of consumer responses to aesthetic information (Chatterjee, 2014).

The primary goal of this review is to use these three theoretical underpinnings to develop a deeper and more fundamental understanding of why consumers have similar responses to designs rooted in aesthetic principles. Further, it explores the connections between aesthetic principles and the cognitive appraisals they may evoke as a way of explaining "visceral" emotional reactions to the aesthetic properties of a product. This type of understanding is particularly important because of the critical role that emotions play in consumers' purchase decision making (Cohen & Areni, 1991; Westbrook & Oliver, 1991) and the demonstrable effect product design has on the sales of a product (Landwehr et al., 2011). Furthermore, a better-developed theoretical base can provide researchers, product designers, and product development managers a more fundamental understanding of the mechanisms through which aesthetics affect consumer reactions and behavior such that they can design products more effectively. Moreover, several experts have called for the need for a more fundamental understanding of consumer responses to product form.[2]

This chapter breaks aesthetics down to its more objective components and emotions are decomposed into their component cognitive appraisal structures and, based on a review of empirical research from a variety of fields (including art, anthropology, neuroaesthetics, cognitive psychology, consumer behavior, marketing, and new product development, among others), their relevant interconnections are explored. Further, the review presents a schematic model of how consumers process aesthetic information and presents several propositions connecting *aesthetic principles* and *cognitive appraisals*.

In the ensuing pages, this chapter will explore how aesthetics can evoke cognitive appraisals that can elicit a variety of emotions. Taking the decompositional approach it will break down aesthetics and emotion into universal design principles and conitive appraisal dimensions respectively. Based on a review of literature from marketing, psychology, anthropology, and neuroaesthetics, it will put forth propositions that connect aesthetic principles and cognitive appraisals. Finally it will propose a rich and radical set of research ideas with implications for practice.

Theoretical Background

The Logic of Aesthetics: Aesthetic Principles

Through the centuries, and through a multitude of artistic movements, ranging from classicism to post-modernism, artists have continually explored aesthetic principles. The term "aesthetic principles" refers to the compositional strategies used to logically organize the structural elements of a product's form to achieve universal appeal (Coates, 2003). The following seven principles are often used as the principles of aesthetics: *balance, emphasis, movement, pattern, proportion, harmony,* and *variety* (Arnheim, 1974; Kim, 2006). This research focuses on aesthetic principles (as opposed to other more subjective elements, such as the meanings associated with elements of design). The responses to products can be "visceral," behavioral, and reflective (Norman, 2004). Consumers tend to be "reflective" when they choose products that are used in public view, often drawing symbolic meanings from this type of stimuli (apparel, fashion accessories, cars, etc.); they often see products as an extension of themselves and want to be self-expressive in their product choices. Therefore the multiple symbolic meanings associated with a single stimulus are usually at the reflective level rather than at the visceral level. While the influence of meaning on aesthetic experiences is an area of active study in neuroaesthetics and clearly relevant to product design and their associated brands, for the time being, since this chapter is more focused on the visceral reaction to aesthetic properties, it is set aside. Furthermore, aesthetic principles lend themselves to being more easily manipulated and studied in a more systematic manner (Ramachandran & Hirstein, 1999).

According to Kim's (2006) definitions, *balance* is defined as the equalization of visual weight in a composition such that its artistic elements appear stable. *Emphasis,* or focal point, is defined as the first place one's eyes land in a composition. *Rhythm* is caused by the repetition of an element in a composition. *Harmony* is defined as the degree to which the visual resources of a composition's design form a coherent unified pattern. Notably, some of these aesthetic principles lend themselves to be measured numerically more easily than others. For example, proportion and balance, which are inherently relative and involve ratios, can be more easily measured and used in empirical studies (cf. Raghubir & Greenleaf, 2006; Wilson & Chatterjee, 2005) than rhythm and emphasis, which are more often used to highlight a composition's metaphoric (e.g., drawing attention to a religious or cultural artifact in a composition) or functional meaning (e.g., drawing a user's attention to a switch or button or control or to signal direction of motion). Such meanings create a high degree of subjectivity in how it drives preference for the form (Hagtvedt & Patrick, 2008; Peracchio & Meyers-Levy, 2005). For example, one can objectively assess the compositional balance of the iconic design of the Alessi Juicy Salif citrus juicer along various axes, using light meters and other instruments (Coates, 2003). By contrast, the potential metaphorical meaning of its bulbous head is more subjective; it can be interpreted simply as a futuristic-looking juicer or compared to a menacing spider or alien (Noble & Kumar, 2010).

One goal of this review is to advance several testable propositions, each of which will require reliably measurable variables. For this reason, this review will omit the aesthetic principles of emphasis and rhythm from discussion. This chapter will also omit the principle of proportion because the preference for the "universally-preferred" ratios (Phi ratio, golden ratio) have been disputed and do not appear to be universal (Höge, 1997).

Aesthetic Principles and Cognitive Appraisals

Dating back to Fechner's (1876) landmark work and Berlyne's (1971) work on aesthetics, psychology has had a long tradition of experimentally studying the preferences, evaluations, and feelings related to aesthetics. Previous work has shown that aesthetics predominantly creates emotional reactions (Frijda & Schram, 1995). As a subfield of psychology, emotion research has enjoyed a long history that has generated many theories and theoretical traditions (cf. Silvia & Warburton, 2006). In recent years, cognitive appraisal theories of emotion have emerged as one leading perspective on the underlying processes creating emotions (e.g. Ellsworth & Scherer, 2003; Lerner & Keltner, 2000). Cognitive appraisal is a process in which individuals evaluate whether an encounter with the environment is relevant to their well-being (Lazarus, 1991). The cognitive appraisal view posits that emotions are evolved, pan-cultural psychological mechanisms for dealing with "fundamental life tasks" (Ekman, 1992). Many researchers have suggested that cognitive appraisals are part of the emotions evoked by product aesthetics (e.g., Desmet & Hekkert, 2007; Silvia & Warburton, 2006).

Smith and Ellsworth (1985), in their experimental study of cognitive appraisal and emotions, identified six orthogonal cognitive-appraisal dimensions that combine to form several commonly experienced emotions: pleasantness, responsibility, certainty, attentional activity, effort, and situational control. Subsequent research using this model has shown that each emotion has a distinct appraisal structure composed of varying levels of each of the six appraisal dimension. This enables researchers to compare and contrast discrete emotions (e.g., Ellsworth & Scherer, 2003; Han, Lerner, & Keltner, 2007). Given the extensive use of these six appraisal dimensions of emotions, Smith and Ellsworth's (1985) appraisal set is often referred to as the "dimensions of emotions" (Han et al., 2007). Smith and Ellsworth's (1985) work is noteworthy for associating emotions (largely subjective in experience) with relatively more objective, measurable cognitive appraisals, making it particularly helpful in investigative efforts that seek to examine emotional response to aesthetics.

Desmet (2002) found that product design can create 14 different emotional reactions: desire, inspiration, admiration, amusement, satisfaction, fascination, pleasant surprise, disgust, indignation, contempt, unpleasant surprise, dissatisfaction, disappointment, and boredom. In a series of experiments involving a broad variety of products, he showed that consumers' perceptions of a product's design can trigger four of the six appraisals from Smith and Ellsworth's (1985) framework: pleasantness, attentional activity, certainty (in using the product), and anticipated effort (in using the product). It is important to underscore that while Desmet's (2002) work explored the overall impact of product design on cognitive appraisals (including aesthetics, kinesthetics, and functional elements of the design). By contrast, this review explores relationships among aesthetic principles and relevant cognitive appraisals that are known to be closely associated with emotions.

Subconscious and Conscious Appraisals in Aesthetic Evaluations

To understand the relationship between aesthetic principles and cognitive appraisals, we must first explore the neurophysiological processes through which aesthetic information is processed. Norman (2004) identifies three levels of processing of aesthetic information: a first subconscious fast "visceral level" response that appraises the attractiveness of the design; a second more cognitive "behavioral-level" response that appraises the mode of use and functionality of the design; and a third more "reflective-level" response that is more self-expressive that appraises the personal and social significance attached to the design. This chapter will focus on the first "visceral-level" response on the first few seconds after being exposed to the stimuli because neuroimaging data shows that evaluations of the aesthetics elements are organized at this early stage (Cela-Conde et al., 2013). Figure 17.1 (adapted from Leder, Belke, Oeberst, & Augustin, 2004) depicts a schematic of the

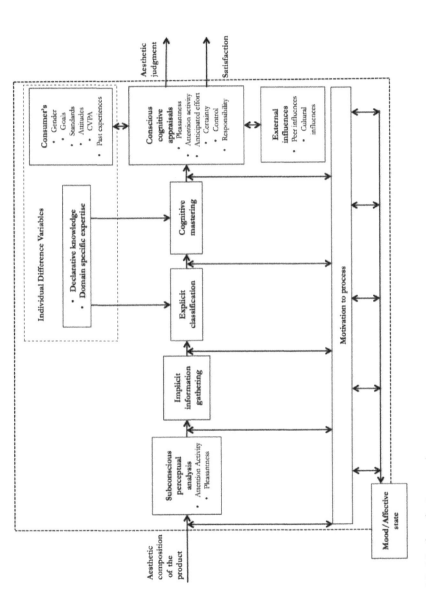

FIGURE 17.1 Model of aesthetic experience.

Source: Adapted from Leder et al. (2004).

underlying processes through which aesthetics can create an emotional response. As Figure 17.1 shows, there is a temporal sequencing to the appraisals that are elicited to an aesthetic stimulus. Research in neural correlates of aesthetics has shown that in the initial reaction stage, appraisals of attention activity and pleasantness are activated (Nadal, Munar, Capó, Rosselló, & Cela-Conde, 2008). If necessary, consumers then engage in a more conscious and more self-aware appraisal on all six dimensions of cognitive appraisals (Leder et al., 2004). Figure 17.1 also depicts the possibility that, during this second stage, consumers may revise or augment their initial reaction, leading to the eventual overall evaluation of the aesthetic merit of the product. This review focuses more on consumers' initial reaction to product aesthetics, as it is expected to be more universal in nature.

As an illustration of the aesthetic experience of a new product, consider a consumer shopping for a juicer on a major e-tailer's website. She pulls up the iconic Alessi Juicy Salif, along with a list of other juicers in her search results. As she views the Juicy Salif for the first time, visual information is captured on her retina, then sent for processing through the optic nerve to the visual cortex. This region of the brain is made up of more than two-dozen visual areas that analyze different visual attributes, such as motion, color, depth, and form (Chatterjee, 2004, 2011; Nolte, 2008). Here correlations between the visual data are computed, and mental maps of this information are created and stored (Barlow, 1986; Cela-Conde et al., 2013).

Often this processing is accompanied by the determination of the novelty of the stimulus using structures in the limbic system such as hippocampus (Squire, 1992). If she is unfamiliar with the Alessi Juicy, the brain will devote more attentional resources to studying it (Norman & Shallice, 1986). Attentional input is maximized by orienting sensitive receptors in regions such as locus coeruleus toward the stimulus, or by some internal means, such as a "spotlight" (e.g., Crick & Koch, 1990). More often the processes involved in determining the novelty of the information are implicit and are not consciously experienced (Kringelbach & Berridge, 2009). Cela-Conde et al. (2013) used magnetoencephalography (which detects changes in the magnetic fields generated by the postsynaptic activity of neurons) to study differences in the patterns of brain activity of 24 individuals in three intervals after being exposed to two types of stimuli (beautiful and non-beautiful): an artifact-free time window of 500 milliseconds before stimuli projection (T0); 250–750 milliseconds after exposure to stimuli (T1); and 1000–1500 milliseconds after exposure (T2). The differences in patterns of brain activity for both beautiful and non-beautiful were not very different from each other immediately after exposure (250–750 millisecond interval). They identified a specific pattern of brain activity, which they called "sensu-stricto," that can be interpreted as the initial appraisal of attentional activity at this point, the consumer may further subconsciously process the aesthetic information and quickly appraise the pleasantness of the product's design depending on the salience attached to the information and attach a valence to it (Schachter & Singer, 1962). Cela-Conde et al. (2013) term this stage (1000–1500 milliseconds after exposure) as "sensu-lato" with distinct activities involving connectivity with the orbitofrontal cortex. Cela-Conde et al. (2013) and others (e.g. Brown et al., 2011: Ishizu & Zeki, 2011) find greater activity involving the medial orbitofrontal cortex (mOFC), ventral striatum, and nucleus accumbens in the beautiful condition during this stage. Here again they identify a very specific pattern of brain activity that can be interpreted as the appraisal of pleasantness and is characterized by networks involving the visual cortex and OFC. The aesthetic properties of designs that follow the aesthetic principles can be viewed as reliant on innate, universally shared aesthetic preferences that have evolved over thousands of years of human history (Ramachandran & Hirstein, 1999) and can be considered as an inseparable component of universal human *aesthetic values* (Chatterjee, 2014). Compositions consistent with aesthetic principles are likely to be appraised as pleasant and a positive valence attached in the sensu lato stage of neural response. On the other hand and consistent with Berlyne's (1971) work, if the stimulus requires extreme levels of attention to the extent that the system is overwhelmed, the task is more likely to be abandoned and a negative valence will be attached to it.

Although compositions that are consistent with aesthetic principles may be viscerally appraised as pleasant, this may not be the final word on the preference for the composition. As Figure 17.1 shows, the various stages have the potential to create and modify the consumer's affective state (e.g., mood) and influence the ensuing more conscious processing (Dijksterhuis & Bargh, 2001). This can be viewed as a bootstrapping mechanism the system undergoes (Keltner, Ellsworth, & Edwards, 1993) to create a blend of simultaneous appraisals. If the subconscious appraisals determine a need for conscious cognitive involvement, the consumer engages in activities such as gathering more information, classifying product information, and interpreting and evaluating this information, resulting in aesthetic judgment and an emotion. When using higher-order cognitive abilities, consumers draw on information from their long- or short-term memory and use the structures and pathways (involving the anterior cingulate and orbifrontal cortex) to appraise and attach meaning to the incoming aesthetic information (Kirk et al., 2009a, 2009b; Leder et al., 2004) that can be interpreted as belonging to the "behavioral" and "reflective" realm (Norman, 2004). Several individual difference factors (gender, expertise, knowledge, goals, standards, and attitudes) play a role in assessing the product's aesthetic properties at this stage. Notably, Centrality Visual Product Aesthetic (CVPA), or the level of significance that visual aesthetics hold for a particular consumer in his/her relationship with products, has been shown to have an important role in consumers' evaluation of aesthetics (Bloch, Brunel, & Arnold, 2003). As shown in Figure 17.1, external factors such as peer influence and culture can also affect consumers' judgment of the aesthetic qualities of a design. A greater variation in appraisals is expected at the second stage of increased conscious processing of aesthetic information.

Proposition Development

Balance and Cognitive Appraisals

According to an evolutionary, *prägnanz*-based, and gestalt notion of psychological response to visual stimulus (Koffka, 1922), our sensory systems must detect order in chaos or unity in variety (Hekkert, 2006). Balance in a composition helps the visual cortex derive correlations among the elements of a design. Early studies in brain activity showed that balance is extracted and sent to the limbic system very early in the visual processing cycle (Julesz, 1971). Studies have shown that humans are sensitive to balance in visual compositions (Locher, Gray, & Nodine, 1996). Moreover, people tend to perceive perfect symmetry, an extreme form of balance, as pleasant. This may be because symmetrical compositions lend themselves to be perceptually analyzed and correlated more easily than asymmetrical compositions as suggested by research on perceptual fluency (Reber, Schwarz, & Winkielman, 2004). Moreover, anthropological studies have found that symmetry is often seen as an indicator of good health in the opposite sex (Enquist & Arak, 1994; Grammer et al., 2003; Zaidel, 2005).

As mentioned earlier, it is expected that consumers will devote more attentional resources on unbalanced objects as they try to make sense of the imbalance in the "sensu stricto" stage (Cela-Conde et al., 2013). The balance principle also has boundary conditions. First, perfect symmetry can be perceived as boring and dysfunctional, as in the case of a car that is designed to have a perfectly symmetrical side view (Coates, 2003). By contrast, asymmetry signifies that a car moves in the direction of the greater compositional weight. Asymmetry may also make sense when it conveys other types of meanings. For example, asymmetry along the horizontal axis of the Volkswagen Beetle's face creates the perception of a bug-like design and exaggerated smile that evokes amusement. Typically, consumers prefer to see meaning attached to any form of imbalance in a product's design that allows it to "make sense"; imbalance for the sake of imbalance tends to be unappealing. Therefore a consumers will need to involve reward circuitry (e.g., mOFC, nucleus accumbens, and ventral striate) that attach valence to the information in a stage that Cela-Conde et al. (2013) call "sensu stricto." Therefore, it is expected that the sensu stricto patterns for an unbalanced condition will be characterized by more intense brain activity and connections with the mOFC. In other words, the process checks with the OFC if the imbalance "makes sense."

Second, if the imbalance in a product's composition is typical to its product category, then consumers come to expect this imbalance in new products and will not devote added attentional resources to it. Any deviations from the typical can potentially gain the attentional resources of the consumer. A symmetrically designed car (in lateral view), for example, may capture unfavorable attention because of the meanings derived from atypicality. At the other end of the spectrum, if a product is extremely atypical, then consumers' informational processing apparatus will not recognize it (Oppenheimer, 2005). For example, consumers who fail to recognize the atypical Alessi juicer, may not dedicate further attentional resources to process the stimulus and may see it as irrelevant. This more cognitively involved determination also happens at the sensu lato stage. Therefore, under these boundary conditions, it is hypothesized that:

> P1: *Symmetrical product forms will require less attentional activity*
> *Sensu Stricto (0–250ms) brain network synchronization will be less robust for less symmetrical Product Forms and will involve connections with mOFC*
>
> *Sensu Stricto (0–250ms) brain network synchronization will be more robust for more symmetrical Product Forms and* will not *involve connections with mOFC*
> P2: *Consumers will appraise product forms that are more symmetrical as more pleasant*
> *Sensu Lato (500–750ms) brain network synchronization will be more robust for less symmetrical Product Forms*

Harmony and Cognitive Appraisals

A number of studies have found that consumers generally prefer harmony to disharmony, even in a composition with a variety of elements (Lennon 1990; Locher, Stappers, & Overbeeke, 1999). In the consumption realm using a variety of products, Veryzer and Hutchinson (1998) found that as the harmony (used interchangeably with unity) in the design of products increased, there was a corresponding non-linear super-additive increase in aesthetic preference for the product. According to the gestalt tradition of cognitive psychology, humans tend to see things that are close together or that look, sound, or feel the same as belonging together (Wertheimer, 1925). Consumers use principles of *prägnanz,* or "good form," to generate such perceptions of harmony. High levels of perceived harmony in the design of products such as the Volkswagen beetle and the iPod make them inherently attractive (Coates, 2003). Neuroscience research has shown that the different extrastriate visual areas of the visual cortex may have evolved specifically to extract correlations in different domains (e.g., form, depth, color) and to discover and link multiple features ("grouping") into unitary clusters (Zaidel, 2005). This process is facilitated and reinforced by direct connections from these extrastriate visual areas to the limbic structures. Moreover, there is an evolutionary advantage to grouping and discovering relations, as doing so allows us to detect objects or meaningful wholes. This ability may have developed from the ability to detect a threat, such as a tiger that is partially hidden behind a tree (Hekkert, 2006). Humans tend to expect such unified visual patterns, to the extent that any deviation from harmony can evoke subconscious appraisals of attention.

Recent studies have shown that humans are born with aesthetic predispositions that develop spontaneously into sophisticated knowledge bases and procedures about aesthetics. For example, studies of congenital amusia, a music processing disorder, have shown that infants process consonant music intervals better than dissonant intervals and detect mistuning to invented musical scales, among other musical capabilities (Peretz & Hyde, 2003; Zaidel, 2005, p. 109). Such connections offer a clear neuropsychological advantage. Given that the brain constantly tries to maximize efficiency in the allocation of attentional resources, such connections help it categorize, classify, and process more efficiently (Hekkert, 2006). Making correlations and unifying elements of a composition is inherently rewarding and satisfying in itself (Ramachandran & Blakeslee, 1998). When a product's composition is unified, it is more perceptually fluent, and consumers can devote fewer attentional resources to it (Reber et al., 2004). It is posited here that the subconscious process of deriving correlations among the various would aesthetic elements will happen at the sensu stricto stage.

Similar to the balance principle, the principle of harmony has boundary conditions. If deviations from harmony are typical of a product category or signify functional or emotional meaning, the consumer may appraise them as pleasant. Kumar and Garg (2010) showed that typicality plays a moderating role in consumers' attention and pleasantness appraisals of the design. Returning to the Alessi Juicy Salif example, some consumers may find its harmonious design to be atypical or even alien and thus unattractive (Noble & Kumar, 2010). Here again it is expected that the conscious attachment of valence to the pleasantness appraisal will happen at the second sensu lato stage. Hence:

> P3: Harmonious product forms will require less attentional activity
>
> Sensu Stricto (0–250ms) brain network synchronization will be more robust for less harmonious Product Forms and will involve connections with mOFC
>
> Sensu Stricto (0–250ms) brain network synchronization will be less robust for more harmonious Product Forms and will not involve connections with mOFC
>
> P4: Consumers will generally appraise product forms that are more harmonious as more pleasant
>
> Sensu Lato (500–750ms) brain network synchronization will be more robust for less harmonious Product Forms

Interactions Among Aesthetic Principles

Gestalt psychologists argue that the perception of an entity's whole differs from a sum of the perceptions of its individual parts (Katz, 1950). The notion of *prägnanz,* or "good form," includes several aesthetic principles and how they can act together to influence the perception of an individual (Fisher, 1951). Several of the seven aesthetic principles are often grouped together and viewed as having a synergistic effect on consumers' appraisals of the aesthetic merit of a product (Kim, 2006). Based on these observations, it is posited that:

P5: *Interactions among the aesthetic principles will have a synergistic effect on the appraisals of pleasantness during the sensu lato stage.*

As these discussions show, anthropological and neuroscientific findings help to explain why the use of aesthetic principles in a composition can affect sub-conscious cognitive appraisals and perhaps influence emotional response.

Neuroscientists are slowly but surely piecing together the neural networks and activation patterns in response to aesthetic stimuli (Chatterjee, 2011). Previously, research in design and psychology has shown that specific emotions that are evoked by design are characterized by distinct cognitive appraisal structures (Desmet, 2002; Smith & Ellsworth, 1985). This chapter attempts to connect the neural networks activated inside the brain apparatus to specific cognitive appraisals in such a way that that specific brain activity patterns can be associated with a distinct cognitive appraisal. The chapter makes the case that the "sensu stricto" and "sensu lato" brain activity patterns are key to explaining visceral response to the aesthetic properties of a product in that they characterize the attentional activity and pleasantness appraisals. According to Smith and Ellsworth (1985) framework, the emotions that are characterized primarily by these two appraisals (high and low attention, and high and low pleasantness) are: interest, surprise, happiness, boredom, and disgust. It is argued here that during the visceral response to product design (during first 1500 milliseconds of exposure to a design) these are the emotions that are more likely to be evoked. It is argued here that marketers should use aesthetic elements that are more attuned to the aesthetic principles in order to evoke favorable attentional activity and pleasantness appraisals that result in emotional reactions such as interest, happiness, and pleasant surprise.

This chapter helps provide a more fundamental understanding of the underlying mechanisms through which design and aesthetics create emotional response by exploring the connections between aesthetic principles and their related cognitive appraisals. While review research papers on aesthetics and the response to it exist in other literature streams (e.g., Chatterjee, 2011), this chapter is unique in exploring the connections between aesthetic principles and consumer cognitive appraisals in a marketing and consumer behavior context. The propositions in this review, when empirically validated, can pave the way to connect the aesthetic principles to cognitive appraisals and emotions. These connections offer a host of avenues for research that some marketers are calling *buyology* and *neuromarketing* (Lindstrom, 2008). Based on systematic study using data (using technology such as fMRI) researchers in the future may be able to identify the signature neural activity patterns associated with all of the dimensions of cognitive appraisals. When our understanding about brain activity develops to this level of sophistication, based on already well developed knowledge about the distinctive cognitive appraisal structures characterizing each emotion type, marketers will likely be able to predict the visceral emotional response to their product designs. Next, the chapter explains some of these possibilities.

Implications for Design

As stated earlier, the feasibility of a model that can predict the emotions developed through specific design types can be explored. Since we know the different emotions product design can elicit and their underlying appraisal structures (Desmet & Hekkert, 2007), future researchers can perhaps explore the aesthetic elements that drive these appraisals and connect these dots and can explore the feasibility of a predictive model. To be provocative and even futuristic, such predictive models can potentially offer a set of rules of thumb that are linked to predictable appraisals and emotions that can later be linked to the downstream perceptions of personality of the brand (Aaker, 1997). These thumb rules, when developed, can be very valuable to the designer and for the manager.

It has been often said that attractive objects work better (Norman, 2002). This is however yet to be proven conclusively through empirical testing. This work can help throw light on how such a perception can develop. It is plausible that when a product is built in accordance with the design principles, the probability that it will evoke moderate levels of appraisals of attention activity and high levels of appraisals of pleasantness, increases. This in turn can increase appraisals of certainty and reduce appraisals of anticipated effort leading to the user being confident about using the product. Such halo effects of some design elements on seemingly unrelated benefits have been found in recent studies (Hoegg, Alba, & Dahl, 2010). A confident user is often prone to fewer user errors. This stream of research can have major implications for devices used in high-risk situations. A potential area of study could be in medical devices where deaths related to incorrect use of medical devices have been extensively reported.

Coates (2003) talks of two main factors that contribute to the aesthetics of a product: *information* and *concinnity*. He defines information as a perceivable variation, difference or change of something (Coates, 2003, p. 123). He identifies two dimensions of information (contrast and novelty) and two dimensions for concinnity (objective and subjective concinnity). A concinnuous design is driven by aesthetic principles that have a universal appeal whereas contrast and novelty are the properties of the design that create the most subjectivity. Coates (2003) posits that the objective concinnity in a product can be measured using instruments such as light meters; however, the subjective component is less quantifiable. Perhaps future research can validate this theory in a cross-cultural setting.

Implications for Theories of Design

Figure 17.1 presents a schematic that could potentially be tested in a series of future studies. For example, the notion that the aesthetic principles actually evokes implicit subconscious appraisals can be tested. Further, the role of individual difference variables such as prior experience and CVPA and how they would influence the appraisals can be explored. The role of culture and how it can affect the individual appraisals or appraisal structures can be explored. Figure 17.1 shows that the aesthetic experience can constantly modify the affective state of the consumer and can create a blend of emotions. Researchers could examine this dynamic process and provide more explanations of how and why this might happen. Further, researchers can explore the conditions under which consumers who have a favorable initial appraisal of a product will continue to like a product after their subsequent more conscious appraisal is negative.

This review has shown that the two subconscious appraisals (attention activity and pleasantness) from the set of six (Smith & Ellsworth, 1985) are triggered in an initial visceral response to aesthetic principles (Cupchik & Gebotys, 1990). This chapter also argues that the strictu stage and sensu lato brain activity patterns represent these two "visceral" appraisals. Future research can investigate if signature neural activity patterns for the remaining appraisals perhaps "reflect" on the aesthetic properties of a product design. Conditions under which designs that are viscerally appraised as pleasant are eventually appraised as unpleasant can be explored.

As stated earlier, in most cases these aesthetic principles coexist in a composition and interact with one another. The interaction between the principles and their effect on the appraisals can be studied. However, it needs to be noted here that isolating such effects will remain a challenging task in an experimental setting because the manipulation of the stimulus will be fraught with confounds from other compositional elements. Therefore, researchers may find it easier to study gestaltic impressions (such as unity and contrast) of the design (e.g., Orth & Malkewitz, 2008; Veryzer & Hutchinson, 1998).

Conclusion

This review explored how product design can evoke cognitive appraisals that can elicit a variety of emotions. It then took a decompositional approach to break product design to the aesthetics, ergonomics, and functional elements. Following this, the review showed that aesthetics is primarily responsible for the emotional reaction to products. Taking the decompositional approach again it broke aesthetics and emotion into universal design principles and appraisal dimensions respectively. Based on Leder et al.'s (2004) work, a schematic of consumers' aesthetic experience is offered that highlights the subconscious appraisals that are activated by the principles of design. While Leder et al. (2004) imply that appraisals of all design elements and strategies are subjective in nature, this review argues that some compositional strategies will elicit universally consistent appraisals. These subconscious appraisals can be thought of as the "hardwired" response of every consumer to universal "human aesthetic values" passed down through thousands of years of human evolution.

Acknowledgements

The author is immensely grateful to Anjan Chatterjee (Department of Neurology, University of Pennsylvania) for his extensive feedback and his contribution to the development of this manuscript. The author is also grateful to Dahlia W. Zaidel (Brain Research Institute at UCLA) for her friendly review of the chapter.

Notes

1 Please note that this article is concerned with aesthetics of products and not art for the sake of self-expression and art itself.
2 See conclusions of the Association of Consumer Research session in San Francisco in 2009.

References

Aaker, J.L. (1997). Dimensions of brand personality. *Journal of Marketing Research, 34*(August), 347–356.

Arnheim, R. (1974). *Art and visual perception, The new version.* London: Faber & Faber.

Barlow, H. B. (1986). Why have multiple cortical areas? *Vision Research, 26*(1), 81–90.

Berlyne, D. E. (1971). *Aesthetics and psychobiology.* New York, NY: Appleton-Century-Crofts.

Bloch, P. H. (1995). Seeking the ideal form: Product design and consumer response. *Journal of Marketing, 59*(July), 16–29.

Bloch, P. H., Brunel, F. B., & Arnold, T. A. (2003). Individual differences in the centrality of visual product aesthetics: Concept and measurement. *Journal of Consumer Research, 29*, 551–565.

Brown, S., Gao, X., Tisdelle, L., Eickhoff, S. B., & Liotti, M. (2011). Naturalizing aesthetics: Brain areas for aesthetic appraisal across sensory modalities. *NeuroImage, 58*(1), 250–258.

Cela-Conde, C. J., García-Prieto, J., Ramasco, J. J., Mirasso, C. R., Bajo, R., Munar, E., & Maestú, F. (2013). Dynamics of brain networks in the aesthetic appreciation. *Proceedings of the National Academy of Sciences, 110*, 10454–10461.

Chatterjee, A. (2004). Prospects for a cognitive neuroscience of visual aesthetics. *Bulletin of Psychology and the Arts, 4*(2), 55–60.

Chatterjee, A. (2011). Neuroaesthetics: A coming of age story. *Journal of Cognitive Neuroscience, 23*(1), 53–62.

Chatterjee, A. (2014). *The aesthetic brain: How we evolved to desire beauty and enjoy art.* New York, NY: Oxford University Press.

Coates, D. (2003). *Watches tell more than time.* New York, NY: McGraw-Hill.

Cohen, J. B., & Areni, C. S. (1991). Affect and consumer behavior. In A. Robertson & H. Kassarjian (Eds.), *Handbook of Consumer Behavior* (pp. 188–240). Englewood Cliffs, NJ: Prentice-Hall.

Creusen, M.E.H., & Schoormans, J.P.L. (2005). The different roles of product appearance in consumer choice. *Journal of Product Innovation Management, 22*(January), 63–81.

Crick, F.H.C., & Koch, C. (1990). Towards a neurobiological theory of consciousness. *Seminars in the Neurosciences, 2,* 263–275.

Cupchik, G. C., & Gebotys, R. J. (1990). Interest and pleasure as dimensions of aesthetic response. *Empirical Studies of the Art, 8*(1), 1–14.

Desmet, P.M.A. (2002). *Designing emotions.* Delft: Delft University of Technology.

Desmet, P.M.A., & Hekkert, P. (2007). Framework of product experience. *International Journal of Design, 1*(1), 57–66.

Dijksterhuis, A., & Bargh, J.A. (2001). The perception-behavior expressway: Automatic effects of social perception on social behavior. *Advances in Experimental Social Psychology, 33,* 1–40.

Ekman, P. (1992). An argument for basic emotions. *Cognition and Emotion, 6,* 169–200.

Ellsworth, P. C., & Scherer, K. R. (2003). Appraisal processes in emotion. In R. J. Davidson, K. R. Scherer, & H. H. Goldsmith (Eds.), *Handbook of affective sciences* (pp. 572–595). New York, NY: Oxford University Press.

Enquist, M., & Arak, A. (1994). Symmetry, beauty and evolution. *Nature, 372,* 169–172.

Fechner, G. T. (1876). *Vorschule der Ästhetik* [Elementary aesthetics]. Leipzig: Breitkopf & Härtel.

Fisher, J., (1951). The memory process and certain psychosocial attitudes with special reference to law of *prägnanz. Journal of Personality, 19,* 406–420.

Frijda, N. H., & Schram, D. (Eds.). (1995). *Emotions and cultural products. Special Issue, Poetics,* Vol. 23.

Grammer, K., Fink, B., Moller, A. P., & Thornhill, R. (2003). Darwinian aesthetics: Sexual selection and the biology of beauty. *Biological Review, 78,* 385–407.

Hagtvedt, H., & Patrick, V. M., (2008). Art infusion: The influence of visual art on the perception and evaluation of consumer products. *Journal of Marketing Research, 45*(June), 379–389.

Han, S., Lerner, J. S., & Keltner, D. (2007). Feelings and consumer decision making: The appraisal-tendency framework. *Journal of Consumer Psychology, 17*(3), 158–168.

Hekkert, P. (2006). Design aesthetics: Principles of pleasure in product design. *Psychology Science, 48,* 157–172.

Hoegg, J., Alba, J., & Dahl, D. (2010). The good, the bad, and the ugly: Aesthetic influence on information processing. *Journal of Consumer Psychology, 20*(October), 419–430.

Höge, H. (1997). The golden section hypothesis: Its last funeral. *Empirical Studies of the Arts, 15*(2), 233–255.

Holbrook, M., & Hirschman, E. (1980). Symbolic consumer behavior: An introduction. In E. Hirschman & M. Holbrook (Eds.), *Proceedings of the conference on consumer esthetics and symbolic consumption* (pp. 1–2). New York, NY: Association for Consumer Research.

Ishizu, T., & Zeki, S. (2011). Toward a brain-based theory of beauty. *PLoS ONE, 6*(7), e21852.

Julesz, B. (1971). *Foundations of cyclopean perception.* Chicago, IL: University of Chicago Press.

Katz, D. (1950). *Gestalt psychology, its nature and significance.* New York, NY: Ronald Press.

Keltner, D., Ellsworth, P. C., & Edwards, K., (1993). Beyond simple pessimism: Effects of sadness and anger on social perception. *Journal of Personality & Social Psychology, 64,* 740–752.

Kim, N. (2006). A history of design theory in art education. *Journal of Aesthetic Education, 40*(2), 12–28.

Kirk, U., Skov, M., Christensen, M. S., & Nygaard, N. (2009a). Brain correlates of aesthetic expertise: A parametric *f* MRI study. *Brain and Cognition, 69,* 306–315.

Kirk, U., Skov, M., Hulme, O., Christensen, M. S., & Zeki, S. (2009b). Modulation of aesthetic value by semantic context: An *f*MRI study. *Neuroimage, 44*, 1125–1132.

Koffka, K. (1922). Perception: An introduction to the gestalt-theories. *Psychological Bulletin, 19*(October), 531–585.

Kringelbach, M., & Berridge, K. C. (2009). Towards a functional neuroanatomy of pleasure and happiness. *Trends in Cognitive Sciences, 13*, 479–487.

Kumar, M., & Garg, N. (2010). Aesthetic principles and cognitive emotion appraisals: How much of the beauty lies in the eye of the beholder? *Journal of Consumer Psychology, 20*(4), 485–494.

Kumar M., Townsend J., & Vorhies D. W., (2014) "Enhancing relationship with brands using product design." *Journal of Product Innovation Management.* DOI: 10.1111/jpim.12245

Landwehr, J. R., Labroo, A. A., & Herrmann, A. (2011). Gut liking for the ordinary: Incorporating design fluency improves automobile sales forecasts. *Marketing Science, 30*(3), 416–429.

Lazarus, R. S. (1991). *Emotion and adaptation.* New York, NY: Oxford University Press.

Leder, H., Belke, B., Oeberst, A., & Augustin, D. (2004). A model of aesthetic appreciation and aesthetic judgments. *British Journal of Psychology, 95*, 489–508.

Lennon, S. J. (1990). Effects of clothing attractiveness on perceptions. *Home Economics Research Journal, 18*(4), 303–310.

Lerner, J. S., & Keltner, D. (2000). Beyond valence: Toward a model of emotion-specific influences on judgment and choice. *Cognition and Emotion, 14*, 473–493.

Lindstrom, M. (2008). *Buyology: The truth and lies of why we buy.* New York, NY: Doubleday.

Locher, P., Gray, S., & Nodine, C. (1996). The structural framework of pictorial balance. *Perception 25*(12), 1419–1436.

Locher, P., Stappers, P. J., & Overbeeke, K. (1999). An empirical evaluation of the visual rightness theory of pictorial composition. *Acta Psychologica, 103*, 261–280.

Luchs, M. G., & Swan, S. (2011). The emergence of product design as a field of marketing inquiry. *Journal of Product Innovation Management, 28*(3), 327–345.

Nadal, M., Munar, E., Capó, M. A., Rosselló, J., & Cela-Conde, C. J. (2008). Towards a framework for the study of the neural correlates of aesthetic preference. *Spatial Vision, 21*, 379–396.

Noble, C. H., & Kumar, M. (2008). Using product design strategically to create deeper consumer connections. *Business Horizons, 51*(5), 441–450.

Noble, C. H., & Kumar, M. (2010). Exploring the appeal of product design: A grounded, value-based model of key design elements and relationships. *Journal of Product Innovation Management, 27*, 640–657.

Nolte, J. (2008). *The human brain: An introduction to its functional anatomy.* Philadelphia, PA: Mosby.

Norman, D. A. (2002). Emotion and design: Attractive things work better. *Interactions Magazine, 9*(4), 36–42.

Norman, D. A. (2004). *Emotional design: Why we love (or hate) everyday things.* New York, NY: Basic Books.

Norman, D. A., & Shallice, T. (1986). Attention to action: Willing and automatic control of behavior. In R. J. Davidson, G. E. Schwartz, & D. Shapiro (Eds.), *Consciousness and self-regulation* (Vol. 4, pp. 1–18). New York, NY: Plenum Press.

Nussbaum, B. (2004, May 17). The power of design. *Business Week*, 64.

Oppenheimer, A. (2005). From experience: Products talking to people—Conversation closes the gap between products and consumer. *Journal of Product Innovation Management, 22*(January), 82–91.

Orth, U. R., & Malkewitz, K. (2008). Holistic package design and consumer brand impressions. *Journal of Marketing, 72*(May), 64–81.

Peracchio, L. A., & Meyers-Levy, J. (2005). Using stylistic properties of ad pictures to communicate with consumers. *Journal of Consumer Research, 32*(June), 1–29.

Peretz, I., & Hyde, K. L. (2003). What is specific to music processing? Insights from congenital amusia. *Trends in Cognitive Sciences, 7*(8), 362–367.

Raghubir, P., & Greenleaf, E. (2006). Ratios in proportion: What should be the shape of the package? *Journal of Marketing, 70*(April), 95–107.

Ramachandran, V. S., & Blakeslee, S. (1998). *Phantoms in the brain.* New York, NY: William Morrow.

Ramachandran, V. S., & Hirstein, W. (1999). The science of art: A neurological theory of aesthetic experience, *Journal of Consciousness Studies, 6*, 15–51.

Reber, R., Schwarz, N., & Winkielman, P. (2004). Processing fluency and aesthetic pleasure: Is beauty in the perceiver's processing experience? *Personality and Social Psychology Review, 8*, 364–382.

Schachter, S., & Singer, J. (1962). Cognitive, social, and physiological determinants of emotional state. *Psychological Review, 69*, 379–399.

Silvia, P. J., & Warburton, J. B. (2006). Positive and negative affect: Bridging states and traits. In D. L. Segal & J. C. Thomas (Eds.), *Comprehensive handbook of personality and psychopathology: Vol. 1. Personality and everyday functioning* (pp. 268–284). New York, NY: Wiley.

Smith, C. A., & Ellsworth, P. C. (1985). Patterns of cognitive appraisals in emotions. *Journal of Personality and Social Psychology, 48*(4), 813–838.

Squire, L. R. (1992). Memory and the hippocampus: A synthesis from findings with rats, monkeys, and humans. *Psychological Review, 99*(2), 195–231.

Veryzer, R., & Hutchinson, W. J. (1998). The influence of unity and prototypicality on aesthetic responses to new product designs. *Journal of Consumer Research, 24*(March), 374–394.

Wertheimer, M. (1938). Gestalt theory (1925). In W. D. Ellis (Ed.) *A source book of gestalt psychology.* London: Routledge and Kegan Paul.

Westbrook, R. A., & Oliver, R. L. (1991). The dimensionality of consumption emotion patterns and consumer satisfaction. *Journal of Consumer Research, 18*(1), 84–91.

Wilson, A., & Chatterjee A. (2005). The assessment of preference for balance: Introducing a new test. *Empirical Studies of the Arts, 23*(2), 165–180.

Zaidel, D. W. (2005) *Neuropsychology of art: Neurological, cognitive, and evolutionary perspectives.* Hove: Psychology Press.

18

GOOD AESTHETICS IS GREAT BUSINESS

Do We Know Why?

Ravindra Chitturi

LEHIGH UNIVERSITY

All firms are in the business of improving cash flow because it leads to greater shareholder wealth. Apple has been one of the highest valued firms for the past decade, and most would agree that Apple products have developed a reputation for offering products with superior design. This research discusses the role of design—more specifically aesthetics—in improving cash flow by improving profit margin per unit. This chapter considers aesthetics as artistically beautiful or pleasing appearance. It explores and identifies why aesthetics leads to greater willingness to pay (i.e., profit margin per unit) on the part of the consumer. What motivates the consumer to pay a higher price, and is the motivation due to aesthetics?

The purpose of this research is to show that aesthetics increases willingness to pay by improving three types of perceived benefits—functional, experiential, and self-expressive. The research explores the role of visual aesthetics in evoking certain types of positive promotion and prevention emotions leading to greater willingness to pay. Specifically, the research focuses on the role of superior aesthetics in evoking the positive promotion emotions of excitement and pride, resulting from improved perceived experiential and self-expressive benefits respectively. Further, the research focuses on how superior aesthetics evoke positive prevention feelings of confidence, resulting from improved perceptions of a product's functionality. In summary, the research shows that good aesthetics improves the anticipated promotion and prevention emotions of functional confidence, experiential excitement, and self-expressive pride, and, how these emotions make different levels of contribution to consumers' willing to pay more.

Background

What is design? It has been defined differently by different academic specializations to fulfill their respective needs. Chitturi (2009) offers a definition that is relatively more generalizable. It defines design as a planned organization of elements in a domain, interconnected with a specific purpose. According to this definition, design must have a plan and a purpose (i.e., a goal) and must involve interconnection of elements. Elements could be things (real or imagined as in movies or video games), people, organizations, etc. Design is complete when these elements are interconnected according to a plan that successfully fulfills the purpose. The purpose of any design is to create benefits to fulfill the consumption wants and needs of the customer. Over the years, there have been a variety of theoretical frameworks for design benefits. One of the frameworks proposes that all consumer benefits offered by a design can be categorized as hedonic or utilitarian (Batra & Ahtola, 1990; Higgins, 1997). Hedonic benefits offer fun, pleasure, excitement (Holbrook & Hirschmann, 1982). They are associated with wants and/or luxury (Shiv & Fedorikhin, 1999; Kivetz & Simonson, 2002a). Chitturi, Raghunathan, and Mahajan (2007) define hedonic benefits as those that fulfill goals of increasing pleasure (Higgins, 1997, 2001). On the other hand, utilitarian benefits primarily serve instrumental purpose. They are associated with needs and necessities (Kivetz & Simonson, 2002b; Wertenbroch, 1998). Chitturi et al. (2007) define utilitarian benefits as those that fulfill the goals of decreasing pain. Chernev (2004) and Higgins (1997) define hedonic attributes as those that fulfill aspirational goals whereas utilitarian attributes as those that fulfill goals of safety and security. Further, hedonic benefits have also been defined as those that fulfill promotion goals (increasing pleasure), and utilitarian benefits as those that fulfill prevention goals (decreasing pain) (Chernev, 2004; Chitturi et al., 2007; Higgins, 2001).

For the purposes of this research, this chapter uses a relatively more appropriate framework offered by Park, Jaworski, and MacInnis (1986) and Aaker (1992). It proposes three types of benefits—functional benefits, experiential benefits, and self-expressive benefits. The framework defines functional benefits as those that offer problem solving capabilities. The experiential benefits are defined as those that offer sensory and/or cognitive stimulation. And, lastly self-expressive benefits are defined as those that offer reference group or ego enhancement association. This framework lends itself better to managerial applications, especially if we want actionable conclusions with greater precision. Therefore, this chapter adopts the framework proposed by Park et al. (1986) to design our studies and measure the emotions of confidence, excitement, and pride along with consumers' willingness to pay.

Hypotheses Development

Previous research has shown that customers are willing to pay more for hedonic benefits than for utilitarian benefits. Chitturi et al. (2007) find that consumers are willing to pay more for an aesthetically superior car over a functionally superior one. For example, they show that adding a panoramic sunroof and a 12-speaker audio system motivates greater willingness to pay compared to improving mileage. However, previous research does not address the question of why. This research answers the question by using the framework proposed by Park et al. (1986) and

Aaker (1992) involving three benefit categories—functional, experiential, and self-expressive. All products offer one or more of these benefits at different levels. Would willingness to pay for any or all of these benefits significantly change due to aesthetics, and why?

Functional Benefits, Visual Aesthetics, and Confidence

Chitturi et al. (2007) show that in a tradeoff situation involving style and attractiveness and functionality, consumers feel a variety of positive and negative emotions depending on the direction of tradeoff—favoring functionality over style and attractiveness, or vice versa. Specifically, they found that greater style and attractiveness are associated with positive emotions of excitement whereas greater functionality is associated with positive feelings of confidence. Recently, Landwehr, Wentzel, and Herrmann (2012) successfully tested the principle of hedonic dominance using secondary data from the automobile industry. However, their work does not break down interaction effects of visual aesthetics with other types of benefits. In this research, the focus is more on how changes in visual aesthetics—i.e., style and attractiveness of a car—influence customer perceptions of a car's functional, experiential, and self-expressive benefits. Is superior visual aesthetics likely to improve perceptions of anticipated functional performance by improving overall feelings of confidence in the product? Prior research has shown that people anticipate or believe that better looking products are more likely to be superior in usability (Sonderegger & Sauer, 2009; Tractinsky, Katz, & Ikar, 2000; Tuch, Roth, Hornbæk, Opwis, & Bargas-Avila, 2012). Prior work also shows that greater functionality makes people more confident (Chitturi, 2009). Therefore, it is expected that improving visual aesthetics would lead to greater feelings of confidence in the functional capabilities of the product. On the contrary, negative visual aesthetics should have the opposite effect of decreasing functional confidence. Therefore, it is expected that poor visual aesthetics are likely to significantly lower confidence in the functional benefits offered by the product.

> H1a: Superior visual aesthetics are likely to increase feelings of confidence in the functional benefits offered by a product
> H1b: Inferior visual aesthetics are likely to decrease feelings of confidence in the functional benefits offered by a product

Experiential Benefits, Visual Aesthetics, and Excitement

Prior work has shown that hedonic attributes fulfill promotion goals and utilitarian attributes fulfill prevention goals (Chernev, 2004; Higgins, 1997). In the case of cars, a panoramic sunroof and a 12-speaker audio system that enhances pleasure would be considered hedonic attributes, whereas anti-lock brakes and greater mileage would be considered utilitarian/functional attributes. According to the framework proposed by Park et al. (1986), experiential benefits are defined as those that offer sensory and/or cognitive stimulation leading to a state of higher arousal (Lazarus 1991). Therefore, a panoramic sunroof and a 12-speaker audio system, both offering visual and auditory sensory stimulation, would be categorized as attributes that offer experiential benefits. Prior work has shown that hedonic attributes enhance feelings of excitement (Chitturi et al., 2007). What would be the effect of superior visual aesthetics on the feelings of excitement evoked by a panoramic sun roof and a 1-speaker audio system? Superior visual aesthetics should further enhance the feeling of excitement from experiential benefits by adding to them. Therefore, it is expected that greater visual aesthetics are likely to enhance the feelings of excitement offered by experiential benefits. On the contrary, inferior visual aesthetics should reduce the feeling of excitement from experiential benefits.

> H2a: Superior visual aesthetics are likely to increase feelings of excitement with the experiential benefits offered by a product
> H2b: Inferior visual aesthetics are likely to decrease feelings of excitement with the experiential benefits offered by a product

Self-Expressive Benefits, Visual Aesthetics, and Pride

As discussed so far, it is expected that visual aesthetics would significantly impact perceived functional and experiential benefits offered by a product as measured by the feelings of confidence and excitement respectively. What about the third dimension of self-expressive benefits proposed by Park et al. (1986) and Aaker (1992)? Would visual aesthetics significantly impact perceptions of consumers' self-expression, and which emotion is most relevant and therefore likely to be evoked?

Self-expressive benefits are defined as those that offer reference group and/or ego-enhancement benefits Park et al. (1986). One of the primary motivations for offering novel, stylish, and attractive visual aesthetics is to help the consumer develop a "cool image" by reference group association as well as ego-enhancement or sense of self-worth (Lazarus, 1991). When the benefits offered to the consumer are goal relevant and congruent, and offer enhancement of self and social esteem with an opportunity for full or partial credit to oneself, then the consumer is likely to experience the feelings of pride (Lazarus, 1991; Roseman, 1991). While "cool image" is one source of self-expressive pride, environmentally responsible consumption or sustainable consumption could be another source of pride. For some consumers, sustainable consumption is a matter of great importance because it demonstrates a willingness to sacrifice one's instant gratification goals in favor of resource preservation for future generations—a noble cause evoking a sense of pride. Therefore, if a product offers green technology—a type of self-expressive benefit, then it offers consumers an opportunity for self-credit for sustainable consumption leading to feelings of pride.

Additionally, when a product is combined with stylish and attractive visual aesthetics leading to "cool image"—another type of self-expressive benefit, the feeling of pride is further strengthened because of reference group association with people who aspire to a "cool image." For example, Apple iPhone users consider themselves to be a superior reference group compared to Nokia cell phone users because of superior "cool image" factor. It is very likely that there is relatively less ego-enhancement from owning a Nokia cell phone because the reference group lacks a "cool image" due to average or poor visual aesthetics. It is expected that pride resulting from the self-expressive benefit of green technology/sustainable consumption would be further enhanced if accompanied by attractive visual aesthetics that offer "cool image" enhancement. Perhaps, one could argue that feelings of pride resulting from sustainable consumption are tempered in the absence of stylish and attractive visual aesthetics. Therefore, the greater the attractiveness of visual aesthetics, the greater the feeling of pride evoked due to consumption of self-expressive benefits such as green technology. Further, it is expected that poor visual aesthetics would reduce the feeling of pride from green technology consumption.

> H3a: Superior visual aesthetics are likely to increase feelings of pride with the self-expressive benefits offered by a product
>
> H3b: Inferior visual aesthetics are likely to decrease feelings of pride with the self-expressive benefits offered by a product

Visual Aesthetics, Emotions, and Willingness to Pay

Chitturi, Raghunathan, and Mahajan (2008) and Chitturi (2009) show that behavioral consequences of trade-offs between functional benefits and experiential benefits follow directly from emotional consequences. Consumers are much more loyal to experientially superior products than they are to functionally superior products when they have a positive consumption experience. In addition, they are much more likely to say negative things about the functionally superior product than they are about the experientially superior product if they have a negative consumption experience. However, at the time of purchase, consumers report significantly greater willingness to pay for experientially superior product than for functionally superior product (Chitturi et al., 2007). As discussed earlier, by offering self-expressive benefits such as green technology leading to sustainable consumption, designers could evoke feelings of pride in consumers. Additionally, the feelings of functional confidence and experiential excitement result from superior functionality and experiential benefits respectively. Further, as discussed earlier, the addition of superior visual aesthetics to existing functional, experiential, and self-expressive benefits offered by the product is likely to increase the feelings of confidence, excitement, and pride respectively. The increased feelings of confidence, excitement, and pride will motivate greater willingness to pay for aesthetically superior option. This is because confidence with functionality, excitement with experiential benefits, and pride due to self-expressive benefits are significantly higher in positive arousal, and moreover strongly associated with willingness to pay (Lazarus & Folkman, 1984; Roseman, 1991; Wegener & Petty, 1994). Therefore, it is predicted that improving visual aesthetics of products will lead to greater willingness to pay for the product.

> H4: Superior visual aesthetics are likely to increase consumers' willingness to pay for functional benefits, experiential benefits, and self-expressive benefits offered by a product

Methodology and Results

The research used cars as stimuli for data collection and hypotheses testing. There were two levels of visual aesthetic manipulation (good and poor), and one control group without any visual picture of the car. Two different pictures were used to manipulate visual aesthetics of car. One with good visual aesthetics showed a light grey, two-door coupe with hatchback, notable for its angled windows and curved corners. The second with poor visual aesthetics showed a white, boxy four-door sedan. The benefits were also manipulated across four conditions—i.e., only functional information (F), functional and experiential information (FE), functional and self-expressive information (FS), and functional, experiential and self-expressive information (FES) were provided. It was a (Type of Benefits (F, FE, FS, FES) (4) x (No visual aesthetics, Good visual aesthetics, Poor visual aesthetics) (3) between-group design. The data was collected with undergraduate students of a medium sized university in North America. A total of 367 students participated in this study. Consumers' feelings of confidence, excitement, and pride were measured on Likert scale of 0 (Not at all likely) to 10 (Extremely likely). Consumers' willingness to pay was also measured on a scale of 0 (Low) to 10 (High). The results of the analysis are summarized in Table 18.1.

The results show that visual aesthetics significantly changes the feelings of confidence with functional benefits, the feelings of excitement with experiential benefits, and the feelings of pride with self-expressive benefits offered by the car. As hypothesized, the good visual aesthetic condition significantly enhances and poor visual aesthetic condition significantly reduces the feelings of confidence, excitement, and pride. Further, the presence of visual aesthetic (good versus poor) significantly alters (increases or decreases) consumers' willingness to pay.

Specifically, in this experiment, consumers reported significantly greater levels of confidence when the same functional information about the car was combined with a stylish and attractive looking picture of the car compared to

TABLE 18.1 A Comparison of Post-consumption Customer Emotions Based on Types of Benefits and Aesthetics

Post-consumption Customer Emotions	No Visual Aesthetics (Control)	Good Visual Aesthetics	Poor Visual Aesthetics
Functional Benefits Condition			
Confidence	3.2	5.2*	1.9*
Excitement	1.1	4.9**	1.1
Pride	1.2	5.1**	1.1
Willingness-to-pay	2.5	4.9*	2.1
Functional and Experiential Benefits Condition			
Confidence	3.3	5.5*	1.8*
Excitement	4.1	6.2*	3.1
Pride	1.4	6.1*	1.4
Willingness to pay	3.6	5.9*	2.5*
Functional and Self-Expressive Benefits Condition			
Confidence	3.0	5.1*	1.7*
Excitement	1.3	4.8*	1.1
Pride	4.2	6.7*	2.5
Willingness to pay	3.2	5.2*	2.0
Functional, Experiential, and Self-Espressive Benefits Condition			
Confidence	3.6	5.6*	2.1*
Excitement	4.4	6.1*	2.9*
Pride	3.7	7.2**	1.6*
Willingness to pay	4.0	8.8**	2.6*

Note: * indicates significant at $p < .05$; ** indicates $p < .01$.

the control group without any visuals of the car (n = 61; $p < 0.05$). In the condition where only functional information was provided and no experiential and self-expressive attributes were described, the addition of a good-looking picture of the car significantly increased anticipatory excitement and pride felt by the subjects (n = 61; $p < 0.01$). In fact, improvement in experiential excitement and self-expressive pride was stronger than functional confidence in this condition. This implies that design managers can use style and attractiveness as a substitute, at least until they are fully production ready with other experiential and self-expressive benefits such as panoramic sunroof and green technology. On the other hand, when functional information was combined with a poor looking picture of the car, consumers' functional confidence significantly reduced, and there was no improvement in experiential excitement and self-expressive pride.

Further, increases in the feelings of confidence, excitement, and pride translated into significantly greater willingness to pay, whereas decrease in functional confidence significantly lowered consumers' willingness to pay ($n = 60$; $p < 0.05$). However, compared to control, poor visual pictures did not have a statistically significant negative impact on willingness to pay. Perhaps this is because functional information on mileage and anti-lock brakes was considered basic with minimal willingness to pay, and was therefore not impacted by a poor looking picture of the car. This implies that for low priced purely functional products, design managers should invest in improving the functional capabilities of the product over visual aesthetics. However, in conditions where experiential and self-expressive attribute information (such as a 12-speaker audio system or green technology) was included in the description of the product, a good looking picture of the car had a major positive impact on experiential excitement and self-expressive pride leading to significantly larger increases in willingness to pay ($n = 123$; $p < 0.01$). When the same information was combined with a poor looking picture of the car, the willingness to pay significantly dropped except in the functional plus self-expressive benefits condition. It seems that self-expressive benefits of green technology were relatively immune to poor visual aesthetics. This finding implies that poor visual aesthetics may not hurt profit margin per unit for a product primarily positioned as a green technology product, but good visual aesthetics have a strong positive impact on the profit margin per unit in all conditions. This unequivocally demonstrates that good visual aesthetics is great business because it significantly improves willingness to pay—i.e., profit margin per unit. And, it does so by improving consumers' feelings of functional confidence, experiential excitement, and self-expressive pride.

Implications for Design

As discussed earlier in this chapter, design is a planned organization of elements in a domain, interconnected with a specific purpose (Chitturi, 2009). The design manager is responsible for understanding and supporting the fulfillment of the business objective or purpose by selecting the right elements and interconnecting them optimally. Therefore, to be a successful design manager one must understand the psychology of each element and its interactions with other elements. The results from this research significantly improve designers' understanding of the interaction between the elements of visual aesthetics, functionality, experiential attributes, and self-expressive attributes (Norman, 2004).

The title of this chapter claims that good aesthetics is great business. The research successfully tests the statement for the product category of cars. It shows that good visual aesthetics can: (1) improve consumers' confidence in the functional capability of the product, such as anti-lock brakes (ABS); (2) enhance excitement with experiential benefits of the product, such as panoramic sunroof; (3) increase pride in the ownership of the product with green technology; and (4) significantly increase consumers' willingness to pay for the product when functional confidence, experiential excitement, and self-expressive pride are delivered to the consumer with an integrated design strategy. These are significant conclusions for a design manager. The design manager can use results to more effectively allocate time, effort, and money towards improving the element of visual aesthetics or towards improving functional, experiential, and self-expressive benefits offered by the product. As our understanding of the interaction between visual aesthetics and product benefits improves, the design manager would be able to design more successful products with lower investments of time, effort, and money, thereby improving return on investment (ROI). The results also show that neglecting visual aesthetics is a risky strategy. Poor visual aesthetics significantly hurt consumers' anticipatory feelings of functional confidence, experiential excitement, and self-expressive pride as an owner of the product.

Implications for Theories of Design

It is surprising that there has been little or no empirical research in the premier journals of marketing on the topic of design as it relates to marketing. The topic of design seems like a natural fit with marketing, and perhaps marketing strategy can greatly benefit by improving our understanding of design, product, and customer interactions. However, there was only one conceptual *Journal of Marketing* article, by Bloch (1995), until the year 2007 that pushed for more empirical research to understand design and its role in product and marketing strategy. Perhaps due to a lack of theory of design, the scholars were unable to get their work published in the premier marketing journals. This was a gap in the theory of design that was waiting to be addressed.

More than the operational aspects of design management, the real challenges in developing the theory of design are in improving our understanding of the psychology of design. We proposed a psychological theory of design based upon how consumers interacted and valued the hedonic and utilitarian attributes of a product at the time of purchase and before consumption (Chitturi et al., 2007). Another article focused on how hedonic and utilitarian benefits of a product influence consumer behavior such as customer word of mouth and repurchase intentions after experiencing the consumption of the product (Chitturi et al., 2008). Collectively, the two papers proposed and tested a theoretical model for the psychology of design at the time of purchase, after purchase, during consumption, and post-consumption behavior from the consumers' perspective. A more comprehensive extension of the work was meant to encourage design researchers to explore challenging research questions at the interface of design and marketing (Chitturi, 2009).

A similar approach to improving our understanding of the psychological theory of design was also demonstrated by Luchs, Brower, and Chitturi (2012). They studied trade-off emotions involving green attributes with sustainability benefits and functional benefits. Chitturi et al. (2007) proposed and tested two guiding principles to add to the theory of design—the principle of functional precedence and the principle of hedonic dominance. The first principle, the principle of functional precedence, states that when the choice is between two products, and neither product adequately fulfills consumers' requirement for functional and hedonic (i.e., experiential) benefits, consumers are more likely to choose a functionally superior product over a hedonically superior product. The second principle, the principle of hedonic dominance, states that when the choice is between two products, and both products meet or exceed consumers' requirement for functional and hedonic benefits, consumers are more likely to favor a hedonically superior product over a functionally superior product.

This chapter primarily focuses on advancing our understanding of the principle of hedonic dominance. Specifically, with respect to the principle of hedonic dominance, Chitturi et al. (2007) showed that consumers are willing to pay more for increases in hedonic benefits than for increases in functional benefits when both product choices meet or exceed their minimum needs for hedonics and functionality. However, Chitturi et al. (2007) did not break down the types of hedonic benefits and did not study the interaction effects of visual aesthetics with the three types of design benefits—functional, experiential, and self-expressive (Park et al., 1986). The research in this chapter significantly improves our understanding of the principle of hedonic dominance—i.e., it identifies experiential and self-expressive benefits as key contributors to hedonic dominance as measured by customers' willingness to pay. It further shows that increasing willingness to pay is associated with increasing feelings of experiential excitement and self-expressive pride. The research also identifies a strong interaction between visual aesthetics and perceived functional benefits as measured by feelings of confidence. While loss in functional confidence can significantly decrease willingness to pay, the increase in willingness to pay was primarily influenced by experiential excitement and self-expressive pride. The results help explain how functional, experiential, and self-expressive benefits via feelings of confidence, excitement, and pride respectively impact consumers' willingness to pay—thereby advancing our understanding of the principle of hedonic dominance and the psychological theory of design.

This chapter successfully tests the statement in the title, "Good Aesthetics Is Great Business." It accomplishes this by studying the interaction effects of good and poor visual aesthetics on consumers' willingness to pay for a car's functional benefits, experiential benefits, and self-expressive benefits. The research explains how visual aesthetics enhances consumers' functional confidence, experiential excitement, and self-expressive pride leading to a greater willingness to pay—i.e., greater profit margin per unit for the manufacturer. In the process of testing the claim that good aesthetics is great business, this research further improves our understanding of the principle of hedonic dominance at a higher granularity—experiential versus self-expressive benefits—thereby adding to our knowledge of the theory of design.

References

Aaker, D. (1992). *Building strong brands.* New York, NY: Free Press.

Batra, R., & Ahtola, O. T. (1990). Measuring the hedonic and utilitarian sources of consumer attitudes. *Marketing Letters, 2*(2), 159–170.

Bloch, P. (1995). Seeking the ideal form: Product design and consumer response. *Journal of Marketing, 59*(3), 16–29.

Chernev, A. (2004). Goal-attribute compatibility in consumer choice. *Journal of Consumer Psychology, 14*(1–2), 141–150.

Chitturi, et al., (2007). *The idea of luxury.* Cambridge: Cambridge University Press.

Chitturi, R. (2009). Emotions by design: A consumer perspective. *International Journal of Design, 3*(2), 7–17.

Chitturi, R., Raghunathan, R., & Mahajan, V. (2007). Form versus function: How the intensities of specific emotions evoked in functional versus hedonic trade-offs mediate product preferences. *Journal of Marketing Research, 44*(4), 702–714.

Chitturi, R., Raghunathan, R., & Mahajan, V. (2008). Delight by design: The role of hedonic versus utilitarian benefits. *Journal of Marketing, 72*(3), 48–63.

Higgins, E. T. (1997). Beyond pleasure and pain. *American Psychologist, 52*(12), 1280–1300.

Higgins, E. T. (2001). Promotion and prevention experiences: Relating emotions to non-emotional motivational states. In Joseph P. Forgas (Ed.), *Handbook of affect and social cognition* (pp. 186–211). London: Lawrence Erlbaum.

Holbrook, M. B., & Hirschman, E. C. (1982). The experiential aspects of consumption: Consumer fantasies, feelings, and fun. *Journal of Consumer Research, 9*(September), 132–140.

Kivetz, R., & Simonson, I. (2002a). Self-control for the righteous: Toward a theory of pre-commitment to indulgence. *Journal of Consumer Research, 29*(2), 199–217.

Kivetz, R., & Simonson, I. (2002b). Earning the right to indulge: Effort as a determinant of customer preferences toward frequency program rewards. *Journal of Marketing Research, 39*(2), 155–170.

Landwehr, J. R., Wentzel, D., & Herrmann, A. (2012). The tipping point of design: How product design and brands interact to affect consumers' preferences. *Psychology & Marketing, 29*(6), 422–433.

Lazarus, R. S. (1991). *Emotion and adaptation.* New York, NY: Oxford University Press.

Lazarus, R. S., & Folkman, S. (1984). *Stress, appraisal, and coping.* New York, NY: Springer.

Luchs, M. G., Brower, J., & Chitturi, R. (2012). Product choice and the importance of aesthetic design given the emotion-laden trade-off between sustainability and functional performance. *Journal of Product Innovation Management, 29*(6), 903–916.

Norman, D. A. (2004). *Emotional design.* New York, NY: Basic Books.

Park, C. W., Jaworski, B., & MacInnis, D. (1986). Strategic brand concept-image management. *Journal of Marketing, 50*(October), 135–145.

Roseman, I. J. (1991). Appraisal determinants of discrete emotions. *Cognition and Emotion, 5*(3), 161–200.

Shiv, B., & Fedorikhin, A. (1999). Heart and mind in conflict: The interplay of affect and cognition in consumer decision making. *Journal of Consumer Research, 26*(December), 278–292.

Sonderegger, A., & Sauer, J. (2009). The influence of design aesthetics in usability testing: Effects on user performance and perceived usability. *Applied Ergonomics, 41*(3), 403–410.

Tractinsky, N., Katz, A. S., & Ikar, D. (2000). What is beautiful is usable. *Interacting with Computers, 13*(2), 127–145.

Tuch, A. N., Roth, S. P., Hornbæk, K., Opwis, K., & Bargas-Avila, J. A. (2012). Is beautiful really usable? Toward understanding the relation between usability, aesthetics, and affect in HCI. *Computers in Human Behavior, 28*(5), 1596–1607.

Wegener, D. T., & Petty, R. E. (1994). Mood management across affective states: The hedonic contingency hypothesis. *Journal of Personality and Social Psychology, 66,* 1034–1044.

Wertenbroch, K. (1998). Consumption self-control by rationing purchase quantities of virtue and vice. *Marketing Science, 17*(4), 317–337.

19

CHANGE IS THE ONLY CONSTANT

Advertising, Design, and the Effects of Nonconscious Change

James A. Mourey

DEPAUL UNIVERSITY

Ryan S. Elder

BRIGHAM YOUNG UNIVERSITY

Companies spend exorbitant amounts of time and money on iterations of product designs, with many of the implemented changes possibly going unnoticed by consumers. Take, for example, the changes made to the product design between the first iPhone and the iPhone 6 over the course of seven years. While the size is markedly different and salient, consumers may fail to consciously recognize changes such as the rounded edges, the different shaped buttons for volume, or even the weight of the product in their hands. Despite the consumers' obliviousness to these changes, the subtle experience of change may impact their evaluations through a process we refer to as Dynamic Transference (Mourey & Elder, 2015). Dynamic Transference is built on the theoretical foundation of the change blindness (e.g., Simons & Rensink, 2005), inattentional blindness (e.g., Simons & Chabris, 1999), and visual sensing (e.g., Rensink, 2004) literatures, and proposes that changes in one domain, although not consciously attended to, can impact evaluations in a subsequent domain.

In this chapter, we provide an overview of change blindness, emphasizing recent findings regarding the consequences of change blindness within an advertising and design context. We first focus our attention on the prior literature within change blindness. We then move to literature on visual sensing, or the feeling that one is experiencing change without being able to visually identify it. Finally, we show how this feeling of change impacts consumer evaluations of advertising and design. We extend these implications into domains particularly relevant for designers and conclude with implications for a broader theory of design.

Change and Inattentional Blindness

Sunday comics usually have a section wherein children are asked to spot the difference between two scenes. It is a surprisingly difficult task, even for adults. It largely requires working memory of the initial image in order to compare it to the second image. Take, for example, Figure 19.1, which shows two images. As quickly as you can, identify the difference between the two images. It's likely that you will have to go back and forth several times before you can spot the difference.

Even in a task such as the one above, wherein you are specifically looking for changes, they can go unnoticed. Indeed, in our everyday environment we have a difficult time of consciously recognizing change (Simons & Rensink, 2005). This inability to identify changes between two stimuli has been labeled "change blindness" within the fields of visual cognition and cognitive psychology and has received considerable empirical support. A related construct, inattentional blindness, refers to the failure to recognize a stimulus that is present in an environment. So if Mona Lisa's smile were to change from a bemused smirk to an unhappy frown when you blink and you do not notice the change, this is change blindness. If a fly is crawling along the famous painting while you are viewing the art and you never consciously notice the fly, this is inattentional blindness. We discuss findings across these bodies of literature prior to highlighting the implications for advertising and design.

Experimental Examples of Change and Inattentional Blindness

The bulk of the initial research within change blindness has focused on establishing conditions for its existence. A common manipulation to study change blindness experimentally is a minor adaptation of the task previously presented regarding the Chicago skyline. In what is called the "flicker task" (e.g., Rensink, O'Regan, & Clark, 1997), participants are shown an original image, followed by

FIGURE 19.1 Examples of images used for the flicker task. The image is of the Chicago skyline. Note, the third building from the left is missing in the image on the right.

Source: Wikimedia Commons.

a blank display, which is then followed by a modified version of the original image containing a change (e.g., something missing from the original image). Thus, using the Chicago pictures in Figure 19.1 as an example, participants would first view the image on the left, then a blank grey screen serving as a visual distractor, followed by the image on the right. Participants would see this cycle of images until they noticed the change, at which point they would press a key stopping the cycle. This simple yet effective experimental task serves as the primary method for exploring change blindness.

If you participated in the mental exercise involving Figure 19.1 earlier, you may have failed to notice the change on your 1st, 2nd, or even 10th time. Perhaps, therefore, it is not surprising to note that participants in the change blindness studies are very poor at identifying changes. Using the flicker task manipulation, Rensink and colleagues (1997) found that participants had to view the images over 17 times before they were able to identify changes to non-focal points of the pictures, which equated to more than 10 seconds. Even when the changes were made to the focal points of the picture (e.g., the central Trump International Hotel and Tower in Figure 19.1), it still took participants over seven rounds to identify the changes.

The robustness of the change blindness effects is shown across multiple stimuli, including motion pictures (Levin & Simons, 1997). In this series of studies, the authors had participants view a film wherein changes were made between each cut. In one study, changes were made to focal points (e.g., the clothing of a main character) or non-focal points (e.g., the color of the plates on the table) of the scenes. Across participants, only *one* out of 90 changes was noticed—stated differently, 99% of the changes went unnoticed. When the main character was replaced between scenes, the numbers were significantly better, but even then only 33% of participants identified this change, meaning 67% of people did not notice a change.

Failing to notice actors changing within a video is surprising, but failing to notice changes to actual people with whom one is interacting is markedly more astonishing. Simons and Levin (1998) had one experimenter engage a participant in conversation and then created a distraction by having a door carried in between the participant and experimenter. Following the distraction, the participant was speaking to a new experimenter. Similar to the motion picture results mentioned earlier, only about one third of participants realized they were speaking with an entirely new individual.

Inattentional blindness is a similar construct to change blindness, as discussed earlier. The primary inattentional blindness manipulation is similarly simplistic in its design as the change blindness flicker task (see Mack & Rock, 1998). Participants in inattentional blindness studies are told to look at a fixation cross and judge which of its arms are longer. This screen is presented for a set period of time (e.g., 200 msec.). On one of the trials an additional stimulus (e.g., a small square) is presented simultaneously in one of the quadrants of the screen.

Immediately following the presentation of the new stimulus, participants are asked if they were aware of anything on the last screen that was not on the previous screens. The number of participants that fail to notice the objects depends largely on the additional stimulus but can be as high as 40%.

Participants also fail to notice the presence of more complex stimuli than simple shapes and figures. For example, in the oft-noted "invisible gorilla" task, participants are instructed to count the number of times players pass a ball. While attention is directed to this effort, an individual in a gorilla suit walks right through the middle of the scene.[1]

Researchers have clearly established that humans are often inept at identifying change. Therefore, the next crucial topic to understand is why we fail to notice these changes. We now move our attention to the causes of change blindness.

Causes of Change Blindness

The primary cause of change blindness has been proposed to be differences in attention (Rensink et al., 1997; Simons & Ambinder, 2005; Simons & Levin, 1998). Specifically, changes may go unnoticed when attention is distracted away from the change, when other items in the scene are more distinctive, when the amount of attention is simply not enough to detect the change, or when the objects do not receive any attention at all (Simons & Ambinder, 2005). Several of the key additional insights into how and why change blindness occurs, as well as an elaboration of these proposed processes, have been discovered using neuroscience methodologies.

How visual stimuli are processed tells us much about the factors that lead to change blindness, especially the level of conscious processing involved. The stimuli themselves, as well as the changes involved, impact this level of processing. Specifically, Dehaene, Changeux, Naccache, Sackur, and Sergent (2006) propose that within subliminal processing, the bottom-up information input does not reverberate within one's neuronal networks enough to register. Within preconscious processing, the bottom-up information would be consciously processed, but there is not enough top-down attentional amplification. Thus, the researchers propose that change and inattentional blindness occur largely because of a lack of attentional resources devoted to the stimulus and provide neuroscience support for this proposition.

Additional work provides further clarification for the distinction between attention and consciousness. Lamme (2003) proposes that we may actually be conscious of a stimulus, but due to a lack of attention, we are unable to report the conscious experience. Certain characteristics of a visual stimulus may garner attention (e.g., focal characteristics like color and shape), while other characteristics may only be preconsciously processed and attended to (e.g., background visual cues).

These findings on conscious processing of visual stimuli are in reference to visual stimuli in general, but can be extended to instances of change. Whether changes are discrete or relative (i.e., gradual) impacts how they are perceived and the conscious identification of change. Relative changes are more likely than discrete changes to go unnoticed, but can also lead to a "feeling of knowing that something changed, but with little to no ability to identify what the change was" (Aly, Ranganath, & Yonelinas, 2014, p. 792; see also Aly & Yonelinas, 2012). This neuroscience research shows that discrete changes lead to greater parietal activation and are more likely to be consciously reported, whereas relative and subtle changes lead to weaker occipito-temporal activation and are less likely to be consciously reported (Aly et al., 2014; see also Aly & Yonelinas, 2012). Taken as a whole, the brain is designed to perceive changes but not necessarily to consciously identify these changes. Both stimulus properties and the level of top-down attentional amplification are core elements in change blindness and change detection.

The Feeling of Change

While there is considerable evidence for the existence of change and inattentional blindness, prior literature also shows that the brain perceives the change at a level below consciousness (Beck, Rees, Frith, & Lavie, 2001). This perceptual activity may have a residual effect, such that changes may be felt even when they cannot be consciously identified. Indeed, research on visual sensing and "mindsight" would suggest that these changes can lead to feelings of change.

The subjective experience or feeling of change can occur even in the absence of change recognition (Rensink, 2004). Using the flicker task described earlier, Rensink (2004) had participants indicate as soon as they felt that a change occurred between the stimuli, and indicate as well when they could visually identify the change. For roughly one third of participants, this feeling of change existed, suggesting that there are separate processes for feeling or sensing change and consciously identifying change. Participants could sense that a change was present before they could visually locate the change.

We propose that it may be possible to qualify this feeling of conscious visual identification of a change. Prior literature suggests that one of the primary resulting emotions from change is arousal (Pribram & McGuinness, 1975). In everyday life, changes to stimuli either in intensity or in timing lead to arousal. Thus, when changes are visually sensed, we propose that this will be felt as arousal.

Consequences of Change Blindness in Advertising and Design

The bulk of the prior literature has been focused on establishing the existence of change blindness, inattentional blindness, and visual sensing or mindsight. Very little research has explored what being blind to a change may mean downstream. Advertising and design presents an attractive substantive domain in which to explore change blindness given the importance of the downstream consequences of affect, persuasion, and ultimately behavior. One recent piece of research has begun this exploration. Specifically, Shapiro and Nielsen (2013) show how a logo that changes location across advertisements increased its familiarity, which in turned facilitated processing and led to processing fluency effects, such that the brand evaluations were more positive and choice of the brand increased. This surprising effect of processing fluency suggests there may be broader consequences that experiences of subtle change could have on behavior and attitude.

Dynamic Transference

Our own research has begun to further the exploration of the consequences of change blindness. We examine the impact of change blindness on evaluations through visual sensing and a misattribution paradigm (Mourey & Elder, 2015). We draw upon much of the literature already discussed to derive our hypotheses. The "visual sensing" or "mindsight" research we highlighted earlier suggests that although the changes in stimuli go consciously unnoticed, they are felt (Rensink, 2004). Since the visual source of the change is not identified, the consequential feelings of change are not correctly attributed to the source stimulus, making it possible that they get misattributed to another source. Specifically, we propose that the feeling of change, qualified as physiological arousal, will ultimately be misattributed to evaluations of objects, and in the context of marketing, to product evaluations. We label this misattribution Dynamic Transference as the consequences of change within one set of stimuli are transferred to another stimulus.

We propose that the misattribution of physiological arousal is most likely to impact evaluations when objective answers do not exist and consumers are relying on how they feel at the moment to make their judgments. Constructed preference, wherein we form our evaluations on the spot, occurs largely when we are in an unfamiliar context, when we have to make tradeoffs, or when we have difficulty quantifying how we feel (Lichtenstein & Slovic, 2006). When in this frame of mind, numerous additional factors come into play and affect our evaluations, such as contextual factors, metacognitions, or feelings (Reber, Schwarz, & Winkielman, 2004; Schwarz, 2004; Schwarz & Clore, 1996). Thus, we propose that the misattribution of arousal from change will differentially impact subjective and objective evaluations, with the greatest impact on the subjective evaluations.

The impact of arousal on evaluations should be a bolstering effect. That is, if participants have a positive evaluation of the product, it will become more favorable with increased arousal. Prior research supports this process, as arousal, in general, and not the valence of the arousal, affects evaluations of stimuli (Gorn, Tuan Pham, & Yatming Sin, 2001). For example, if participants are asked to evaluate a chocolate chip cookie (a positively valenced stimulus), increased arousal will likely make these evaluations more positive. In contrast, if participants are asked to evaluate raisin pie or Brussels sprout pie (seemingly negatively valenced stimuli), increased arousal will likely make these evaluations more negative. This is important in our research as we present different directionalities of stimuli change (e.g., increases or decreases in size, increases or decreases in color saturation). Although it is tempting to assume that the direction of the experienced change will influence the direction of the subsequent ratings (i.e., changes in an increasing direction will lead to higher ratings, changes in a decreasing direction will lead to lower ratings), prior research would suggest that the arousal itself is the driving force, and not the valence or directionality of the arousal (Gorn et al., 2001).

We are currently exploring Dynamic Transference, explicating the process and establishing the robustness of the effects across different contexts (Mourey & Elder, 2015). While we will not go into full detail on the studies, we will highlight a few key findings that provide support for our hypotheses and will hopefully spur future research in this area and provide implications for designers.

To demonstrate initial support for the proposed Dynamic Transference hypothesis, we had participants answer a series of 10 questions regarding their Starbucks habits (e.g., "What do you typically order when you go to Starbucks?"). Each question was presented on its own screen, with a visual picture of a Starbucks cup of hot chocolate above the question prompt. This picture served as our manipulation of change. We had three conditions: increasing, decreasing, and control. In the increasing condition, the cup presented on the first screen was small and increased by 10% on each subsequent screen (see Figure 19.2 for examples of

FIGURE 19.2 Examples of stimuli used in Mourey and Elder's (2015) experiments.

Note: The top series of cups shows the ordering from smallest to largest. The bottom set of cups shows the smallest and largest cups next to each other.

Source: Ryan Elder.

the stimuli). In the decreasing condition, the cup presented on the first screen was the largest cup from the increasing condition and decreased in size by 10% on each screen. In the control condition, the cup remained the same size, which was the average size of the cups used in the other two conditions. Despite the dramatic change in size between the first and last cups in the increasing and decreasing conditions, no participants noticed the change.

Upon answering the questions about their Starbucks habits, we had participants answer five questions about Starbucks. Three of these questions were subjective (e.g., "How likely would you be to buy hot chocolate from Starbucks right now?") and two of the questions were objective (e.g., "How hot (in degrees Fahrenheit) do you think Starbucks hot chocolate is served?"). These five questions served as our dependent measures. In support of our Dynamic Transference hypothesis, change, whether increasing or decreasing, had a significant impact on subjective but not objective ratings.

We replicated the findings from this study using color as the manipulation of change instead of size, as well as dynamic video instead of static visual cues. We also explored the mediating effect of arousal within this process. Our preliminary findings provide compelling support for our Dynamic Transference hypothesis. Changes, even those that go consciously unnoticed by participants, impact evaluations. While our findings contribute theoretically to literature on change blindness, visual sensing, and constructed preference, perhaps the biggest impact will be on the practical utilization of our research. Two direct areas that will benefit from this research are advertising and design. We discuss actionable implications from this research, and highlight how our understanding of Dynamic Transference can inform design theory.

Implications for Designers

The finding that exposure to subtle change systematically influences subjective ratings is not just interesting with respect to theory, but the finding also has numerous practical applications in advertising and design. In our studies, we relied on very subtle manipulations of size and color, two types of stimuli changes that can be seamlessly made within television advertisements. In fact, we used a real television commercial to demonstrate the Dynamic Transference effect. We also relied on interesting marketing questions—e.g., How likely are you to purchase Starbucks? How much do you like Anheuser-Busch products?—that could have an effect on actual consumer behavior. Interestingly, a dish detergent brand has a recent commercial in which the main characters change clothes between scenes. The impact of these changes may be unknown to the advertiser, but our findings would suggest that subsequent evaluations should be affected.

Although we limit our manipulations to visual changes, it is likely that the Dynamic Transference effects occur with other sensory experience (i.e., sound, smell, taste, or touch). This possibility greatly expands the relevant contexts in which advertisers and designers can utilize Dynamic Transference. For example, advertisers that have the ability to engage multiple sensory modalities within a particular medium (e.g., television with vision and sound) can change stimuli in one or all modalities. It is possible that the interactive effects between sensory modalities would lead to even larger consequences on behavior and evaluations. Additionally, it is likely that when one sensory modality is engaged, change is less likely to be detected in another sensory modality.

Several examples within advertising and design exhibit the intuition of subtle change. For example, package design changes rarely entail complete overhauls, but rather only a few changes are made. These changes, although noticeable to the designer and brand manager, may go consciously unnoticed by the consumer. However, given that the change may be felt, even subtle changes could have noticeable impacts. Within logo design the implications are similar. Take, for example, the evolution of Google's logo from 1999 to the most recent change in 2013. The initial removal of the drop shadow behind the letters, as well as the subsequent removal of the bevel and shading on the letters may have gone consciously unnoticed by consumers, yet the changes may have been felt. These changes could have implications not only for the search engine giant but also for general search behavior, as well.

In sum, Dynamic Transference presents numerous, directly applicable implications for advertising and design. Our theoretical framework, as well as our findings, contribute to building a more detailed theory of design that relies less on conscious attention to detail and more on the importance of nonconscious influence.

Implications for a Theory of Design

Our research on Dynamic Transference provides a better understanding of the implications of change. Prior research in art and design has explored the construct of dynamism, or perceived movement, as an element of visual grammar (Leborg, 2006). However, incorporating actual change into different versions of the stimuli, be it immediate as with a scene change or gradual within a movie, presents important implications for design theory. The resulting increase in physiological arousal from change may be a critical component of aesthetic appreciation for product form or graphic design as the arousal is misattributed to elements of design.

Another important implication for design theory involves the role of misattribution. Effects like Dynamic Transference are possible because individuals, consciously unaware of their exposure to change, have no ability to link the change to its source. As a result, the arousal associated with the change is misattributed to the task that *is* consciously accessible: the subjective questions being asked. Coupling this with the neuroscience work suggesting two distinct neural processes for state-based change and strength-based change, designers would be wise to consider whether changes in color, shape, size, or layout are obvious or relative.

Large, state-based changes may not produce effects like Dynamic Transference whereas subtler, relative changes (e.g., gradually increasing cup size, changing color saturation) should. Whether designing various rooms in a hotel, packaging for a company's different product lines, or the frame-by-frame storyboard of an advertisement, designers would be wise to keep in mind that all changes are not created equal and that these important differences in "change" can have profound implications on subjective ratings, attitudes, and consumer behavior.

Note

1   See https://www.youtube.com/watch?v=IGQmdoK_ZfY for a video. Within this video, however, there is also another change that the viewer may fail to notice, which is described at the end of the video.

References

Aly, M., Ranganath, C., & Yonelinas, A. P. (2014). Neural correlates of state- and strength-based perception. *Journal of Cognitive Neuroscience, 26*(4), 792–809.

Aly, M., & Yonelinas, A. P . (2012). Bridging consciousness and cognition in memory and perception: Evidence for both state and strength processes. *PLoS One, 7*, e30231, 1–16.

Beck, D. M., Rees, G., Frith, C. D., & Lavie, N. (2001). Neural correlates of change detection and change blindness. *Nature Neuroscience, 4*, 645–650.

Dehaene, S., Changeux, J. P., Naccache, L., Sackur, J., & Sergent, C. (2006). Conscious, preconscious, and subliminal processing: A testable taxonomy. *Trends in Cognitive Science, 10*(5), 204–211.

Gorn, G., Tuan Pham, M., & Yatming Sin, L. (2001). When arousal influences ad evaluation and valence does not (and vice versa). *Journal of Consumer Psychology, 11*(1), 43–55.

Lamme, V.A.F. (2003). Why visual attention and awareness are different. *Trends in Cognitive Science, 7*(1), 12–18.

Leborg, C. (2006). *Visual grammar.* New York, NY: Princeton Architectural Press.

Levin, D. T., & Simons, D. J. (1997). Failure to detect changes to attended objects in motion pictures. *Psychonomic Bulletin & Review, 4*(4), 501–506.

Lichtenstein, S., & Slovic, P. (Eds.). (2006). *The construction of preference.* Cambridge: Cambridge University Press.

Mack, A., & Rock, I. (1998). *Inattentional blindness.* Cambridge, MA: MIT Press.

Mourey, J. A., & Elder, R. S. (2015). Change blindness and the consumer: The evaluative consequences of dynamic transference. Working paper.

Pribram, K. H., & McGuinness, D. (1975). Arousal, activation, and effort in the control of attention. *Psychological Review, 82*(2), 116.

Reber, R., Schwarz, N., & Winkielman, P. (2004). Processing fluency and aesthetic pleasure: Is beauty in the perceiver's processing experience? *Personality and Social Psychology Review, 8*(4), 364–382.

Rensink, R. A. (2004). Visual sensing without seeing. *Psychological Science, 15*(1), 27–32.

Rensink, R. A., O'Regan, J. K., & Clark, J. J. (1997). To see or not to see: The need for attention to perceive changes in scenes. *Psychological Science, 8*(5), 368–373.

Schwarz, N. (2004). Metacognitive experiences in consumer judgment and decision making. *Journal of Consumer Psychology, 14*(4), 332–348.

Schwarz, N., & Clore, G. L. (1996). Feelings and phenomenal experiences. *Social Psychology: Handbook of Basic Principles, 2*, 385–407.

Shapiro, S. A., & Nielsen, J. H. (2013). What the blind eye sees: Incidental change detection as a source of perceptual fluency. *Journal of Consumer Research, 39*(6), 1202–1218.

Simons, D. J., & Ambinder, M. S. (2005). Change blindness theory and consequences. *Current Directions in Psychological Science, 14*(1), 44–48.

Simons, D. J., & Chabris, C. F. (1999). Gorillas in our midst: Sustained inattentional blindness for dynamic events. *Perception-London, 28*(9), 1059–1074.

Simons, D. J., & Levin, D. T. (1998). Failure to detect changes to people during a real-world interaction. *Psychonomic Bulletin & Review, 5*(4), 644–649.

Simons, D. J., & Rensink, R. A. (2005). Change blindness: Past, present, and future. *Trends in Cognitive Sciences, 9*(1), 16–20.

20

ERGONOMIC DESIGN AND CHOICE OVERLOAD

Matteo Visentin, Samuel Franssens, and Simona Botti

LONDON BUSINESS SCHOOL

Companies develop new products with several strategic objectives in mind—establish competitive differentiation, communicate quality, satisfy customer needs, attract new customers, and retain old ones. Because product design is an important step in product development (Ulrich & Eppinger, 2012, p. 15), the aforementioned objectives are greatly influenced by the work of designers who are trained to be attentive to aesthetic appeal, usability, and the creation of innovative solutions to customer needs. In this chapter, we investigate how the design of product features that were intended to deliver a benefit during usage may have unintended negative consequences during purchase. The focus of our research is on consumer confidence in and satisfaction with choices made from large versus small product assortments that include products with either high- or low-usability designs. In our experimental work we use programmable thermostats as a product category for which usability can be an important aspect of the purchase decision. We find that consumers are less satisfied with and less confident of choices made from large versus small assortments when thermostats are characterized by a high-usability design, but not when they are characterized by a low-usability design. That is, in large assortments, high-usability designs appear to exacerbate feelings of choice overload and can be detrimental to post-choice evaluations of the outcome, relative to low-usability designs.

We believe these findings are important for two reasons. First, manufacturers need to be aware that the ergonomics of a product may affect post-purchase satisfaction. Paradoxically, a company may design products with the intention of improving comfort during usage, but this design may actually lower satisfaction before usage even begins. Second, retailers need to be aware of the potential effect of perceived usability on purchase decisions. We argue that insights into choice overload can tell retailers how to optimally assemble their assortments, especially in product categories where usability is a key desired quality.

In the following sections we review the choice overload literature, introduce the novel construct of design scripts, and summarize the evidence from our experimental work. We conclude by discussing the implications of our results for a theory of design and for designers.

Choice Overload

Choice overload refers to a situation in which consumers exposed to a large set of options are less likely to buy than those exposed to a small set of options (Iyengar & Lepper, 2000). This phenomenon contradicts the regularity principle of rational economic theory, according to which the addition of an option to a choice set should never increase the probability of selecting an option from the original set (Lancaster, 1990).

Literature on choice overload has also shown that, even when consumers manage to overcome their resistance to purchase, selecting an option from a large set makes them less happy with their choice than selecting an option from a small set (Iyengar, Wells, & Schwartz, 2006). This finding is explained by the fact that perusing and comparing options requires more intense mental effort when the number of options is large than when it is small (Malhotra, 1982; Tversky & Shafir, 1992). Given that consumers are cognitive misers (Simon, 1955), the increased mental effort needed to process information in the case of large sets generates a host of negative psychological and behavioral consequences. Specifically, research has documented that choosing from large assortments is likely to cause greater regret (Carmon, Wertenbroch, & Zeelenberg, 2003; Sagi & Friedland, 2007), lower decision confidence (Chernev, 2003), and lower satisfaction with the chosen option (Brenner, Rottenstreich, & Sood, 1999).

Obviously, large assortments do not always reduce purchase likelihood and satisfaction with the choice outcome compared with small assortments. The choice overload literature has identified two categories of moderators of the choice overload effect: one category pertains to the characteristics of the chooser and the other to the characteristics of the assortment. Within the first category of moderators—individual characteristics—the degree to which choosers have clear preferences (Chernev, 2003), expect to find the ideal match (Diehl & Poynor, 2010; Iyengar et al., 2006), tend to be maximizers (Schwartz et al., 2002), and their cultural values (Markus & Schwartz, 2010), have been shown to reduce the choice overload effect. Within the second category of moderators— assortment characteristics—organizing and categorizing the items within the assortment (Kahn & Wansink, 2004; Mogilner, Rudnick, & Iyengar, 2008) also reduces the choice overload effect. This is in part because the organization and categorization of the items makes it easier to compare the different attributes of the options included in the assortment (Gourville & Soman, 2005) and to identify their ideal option (Chernev, 2005; Sagi & Friedland, 2007). Thus, changes in the structure of the assortment allow consumers to enjoy the greater variety offered by large choice sets without their having to bear the associated information-processing costs.

We aim to contribute to this literature by identifying a new moderator of choice overload: the design of the options constituting the assortment. Research on ergonomics has shown that product design can simplify the processing of information regarding the usability of the assortment options (Karwoski, 2012). Simplification reduces choice overload (Kahn & Wansink, 2004; Mogilner et al., 2008); hence, it is plausible to predict that consumers will be less likely to experience choice overload when choosing from an assortment characterized by high-usability designs relative to low-usability designs.

Our results suggest, however, that choosing from high-usability designs is harder than choosing from low-usability designs. We found that this increase in choice difficulty occurs because, relative to low-usability designs, high-usability designs decrease the level of perceived variety within an assortment and make it more difficult for consumers to identify their preferred option. As a result, we observe a mitigation of choice overload for assortments that include low-usability designs, which allow consumers to better discriminate between more and less preferred options.

Design Scripts

In our studies, we vary the perceived usability of products by manipulating the presence of design elements that we call design scripts. Based on literature on ergonomics, we define a design script as a design characteristic that informs consumers about how to use a product and that works as a shortcut for evaluating the usability dimension.

The concept of design script borrows from the fields of ergonomics, which is concerned with the information-processing capabilities of the human mind. This discipline hinges on the premise that human behavior is predictable and that this predictability can be exploited to design the most efficient human–product interactions in order to reduce the potential for error. The design of any product interface addresses how to transfer information from the product to the user and vice versa. Control mechanisms (e.g., levers, buttons, switches, keyboards) deliver information from the user to the product as well as from the product to the user (e.g., computer screen, control panel, display, and LED indicators). The extent to which the information-transfer process is fast and easy will determine the efficiency of the human–product interaction. A necessary condition for an efficient human–product interaction is to design a product interface that is easy to read and to interpret, such that the possibility of user error or injury is minimized (Karwoski, 2012).

The idea of design scripts is closely related to that of population stereotypes within the field of human factors and ergonomics (Bergum & Bergum, 1981; Wiebe & Vu, 2009). A population stereotype is a form of expectation about how a product reacts to certain user actions (e.g., if the volume controller of my stereo is rotated clockwise, the volume will increase—the clockwise-to-increase principle). This concept is based on the premise that users expect products to behave in certain ways given a certain type of control device or environment. Examples of population stereotypes include color-coding (e.g., red signifies "stop" or "danger"; yellow signifies "warning," "slow," or "caution"; green signifies "go") and direction coding (e.g., the "up" position of a switch signifies "on"; the "down" position of a switch signifies "off"; rotary controls are expected to turn clockwise for "on" positions and counterclockwise for "off" positions).

The main difference between the concept of design scripts proposed in the present research and that of population stereotypes proposed in ergonomics research is that the former does not require the usability enhancement to be an adopted norm. For our theory development, it is sufficient to assume that a design script provides a clearer expectation about how a product works, either because this expectation is based on an established norm or because it is intuitive.

We predict that, even though design scripts simplify information processing with regard to usability when consumers are faced with a single option, they exacerbate, rather than mitigate, choice overload when consumers are faced with a large number of high-usability designs. Research has shown that consumers who are presented with an assortment in which alternatives are close substitutes for each other on one dimension (e.g., quality) find it harder to discriminate between options (Diehl, Kornish, & Lynch, 2003). Similarly, dense assortments, in which the attribute-by-attribute distance between one product and its closest competitors is small, have been found to reduce attribute variability and increase choice difficulty (Dhar, 1997; Shugan, 1980). By enhancing usability, the addition of design scripts to options will produce assortments that are denser on the usability dimension. In addition, because an increase in the number of the assortment options also increases the density of the assortment (Fasolo, Ludwig, Hertwig, & Huber, 2009), consumers will experience more difficulty choosing from large high-usability-design assortments, which are perceived as less varied, than from small high-usability-design assortments, which are perceived as more varied.

This reasoning leads to the hypothesis that consumers will be more likely to experience choice overload when confronted with high-usability-design assortments than when confronted with low-usability-design assortments. This effect will be mediated by a reduced perceived variety between high-usability-design assortments compared with low-usability-design assortments.

The Evidence So Far

In a series of experiments we manipulated the design scripts of programmable thermostats (Visentin, Franssens, & Botti, 2014). We chose this product because it requires human–product interaction during the programming of an optimal heating/cooling schedule for one's house or apartment.

We initially selected a large sample of programmable thermostats and isolated the three most common design scripts that were already present, to different extents, in some or all of the thermostats: size and shape of the control buttons, color of the temperature buttons, and position of explanatory text-icon.

We then manipulated perceived usability by varying the presence or absence of these three design scripts (see Figure 20.1). In the high-usability-design condition,

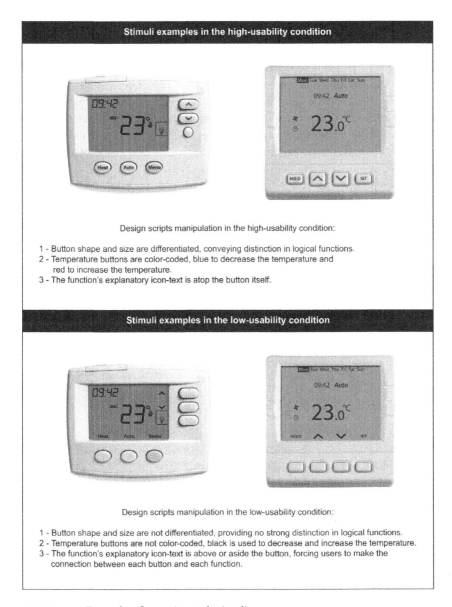

FIGURE 20.1 Example of experimental stimuli.

Source: Matteo Visentin.

the size and shape of the control buttons are differentiated according to their logical functions; for example, the confirmation button is different from the menu buttons and the navigational buttons. In the low-usability-design condition, the size and shape of the control buttons is not differentiated; for example, the confirmation button is the same as the menu and the navigational buttons (see Figure 20.2). In addition, in the high-usability-design condition, the temperature buttons are color-coded such that blue is employed for lowering the temperature (arrow pointing down) and red for raising the temperature (arrow pointing up). In the low-usability-design condition, in contrast, both buttons are the same color—not associable with hot or cold temperatures—although the arrow icons are the same as in the high-usability designs (see Figure 20.3). Finally, in the high-usability-design condition the function of some buttons is explained by a text-icon atop the button itself. In the low-usability-design condition, however, this text-icon element is placed on the side of the button or on the screen near the button (see Figure 20.4).

We conducted a pre-test to ensure that the presence of design scripts increased perceived usability. Each thermostat was presented in two versions on the same page, such that one version of the thermostat had the three design scripts active (high-usability design) and the other version of the thermostat had the same three scripts muted (low-usability design). Both thermostats were identical except

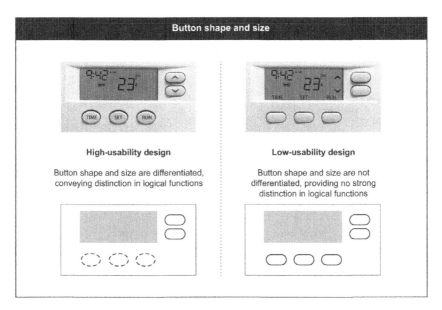

FIGURE 20.2 Design Script 1 highlights the size and shape of the control buttons.

Source: Matteo Visentin.

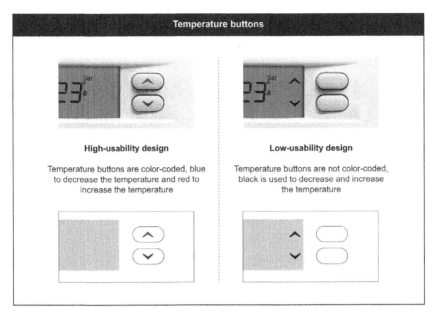

FIGURE 20.3 Design Script 2 highlights the color of the temperature buttons.

Source: Matteo Visentin.

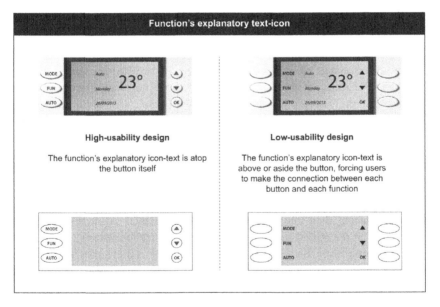

FIGURE 20.4 Design Script 3 highlights the position of explanatory text-icon.

Source: Matteo Visentin.

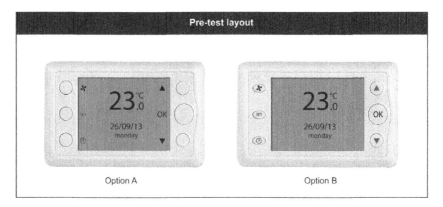

FIGURE 20.5 Stimuli layout used in the pre-test (Option B is the high-usability version).

Source: Matteo Visentin.

for the design-scripts manipulation (see Figure 20.5). The results of this pre-test indicated that although the high-usability option was considered to be as complex as the low-usability option, participants judged it easier to use, faster to program, and, most important, better able to convey clearer expectations about how the product works.

In a between-subjects experiment, we manipulated assortment size and usability to test the hypothesis that despite the fact that design scripts should facilitate the processing of information about product usability, choice overload is mitigated in the absence of design scripts. Participants were instructed to select their preferred thermostat considering that they would have to program it in their daily life. We assumed that these instructions would motivate participants to pay attention to the usability-design aspects of the options within the assortment. Participants were shown either 24 (large assortment) or 6 (small assortment) programmable thermostats with high-usability or a low-usability design. As noted above, thermostats in the high-usability-design and low-usability-design conditions differed only in the presence or absence of three design scripts: size and shape of the control buttons, color of the temperature buttons, and position of explanatory text-icon.

After making their choice, participants reported their satisfaction with and confidence in the option they selected, their preference for delaying their choice had they been given the chance, and the amount of variety they perceived in the assortment. Each of these dependent variables were measured with a 7-point Likert scale.

Results showed a series of interactions between assortment size and usability. When the assortment was composed of high-usability designs, participants were less confident of their choice, less satisfied with their choice, and more likely to delay their choice in the large-assortment than in the small-assortment condition. However, when the assortment was composed of low-usability designs, there was no difference between the large- and small-assortment conditions. In addition, in the high-usability-design condition, larger assortments were perceived as offering less variety than smaller assortments. Within the low-usability-design condition, conversely, larger and smaller assortments were perceived to offer the same product variety. Mediation analysis showed that in the high-usability-design condition, the negative effect of assortment size on satisfaction could not be explained by perceived variety, whereas in the low-usability-design condition, the positive effect of assortment size on satisfaction was mediated by perceived variety. This mediation suggests that implementing the same level of usability enhancement for all thermostats resulted in a more difficult discrimination process because the products looked more similar and less varied.

A follow-up eye-tracking test was conducted, maintaining the design of the previous experiment with a minor variation; the large assortments were composed of 20 instead of 24 options (due to the eye-tracking device's monitor resolution).

For the analysis of the eye-tracking data the entire screen was divided into smaller areas of interest, each corresponding to the footprint of a thermostat. In the large (small) assortment there were 20 (6) areas of interest, and fixation metrics were calculated at the area of interest level (i.e., per thermostat within the assortment).

As expected, results showed that participants in the two small-assortment conditions recorded more fixations per thermostat than those in the two large-assortment conditions. However, although for small assortments there was no difference in average fixation between the low-usability-design and the high-usability-design conditions, for large assortments average fixations per thermostat were higher for high-usability designs than for low-usability designs.

A measure of attention share for a thermostat was computed by dividing a participant's fixation duration for that thermostat by the participant's fixation duration for the whole set. This measure allowed us to rank each thermostat in terms of its ability to draw attention. We found that in both assortment sizes the high-usability-design condition showed equal levels of attention for a few top options whereas the low-usability-design condition showed the presence of a clearly dominating option. This suggests that it was easier for participants to identify the best option in the low-usability condition than in the high-usability condition.

These results suggest a potential explanation that corroborates the mediation by perceived variety observed in the first study: when the assortment is characterized by high-usability-design options, relative to low-usability-design options, consumers find it more difficult to identify their most preferred option and end up being less satisfied with the outcome of their choice, even though they are choosing from a pool of "better" options (Visentin et al., 2014).

Implications for Designers

In the present work we identified an untested design dimension—perceived usability—and showed that higher levels of perceived usability result in stronger feelings of choice overload. Above all, our findings suggest the importance of introducing an additional step within the design phase of a product. Since most designers are familiar with testing for product debugging and other qualitative purposes, we recommend, when possible, an additional test that simulates purchase decisions. The goal of this test would be to estimate the purchase likelihood and post-purchase evaluation of a new product both when evaluated in isolation and when displayed within an assortment representative of its category. This test would add the most value during concept selection—the process by which many concepts are evaluated and one is selected for the final stage of development—in that it will bring purchase-decision considerations into the design process before the product is finalized and will motivate designers to test design ideas through a new lens that is relevant for business.

Instead of testing primarily for product usability, as is the current practice, designers could also test the unintended effects of design characteristics on a purchase-decision scenario. In addition, the inclusion of this additional test may further connect the business side of product development with its design counterpart. One fundamental mismatch between these two interdependent parts is their apparent motivation. Designers are driven to produce good design, whereas business is driven by market success. Although designers should care about creating well-designed products, they should also create successful products, not simply because this benefits the business overall but because the design resources allocated to producing and commercializing products are less likely to be wasted if the product is successful in terms of sales.

Furthermore, a second test could aim at identifying the best visual display for a large assortment of products. This test bears implications for retailers. We previously outlined how large assortments can result in choice overload. An assortment-display test may reveal the best strategy to increase purchase likelihood and post-choice satisfaction at the product-category level. Designers could also explore methods for showcasing a large assortment of products using strategies to simplify information processing (e.g., visually suggesting how the assortment is structured, designing products labels that are effective at reducing choice overload). Established findings such as the mere categorization effect (Mogilner et al., 2008) could also be exploited for this purpose.

Implications for a Theory of Design

In this chapter, we introduced the concept of perceived usability via design scripts. This research raises an issue of interest for a theory of design. Purchase and use are two distinct phases of consumption, and our results suggest that some design elements, intended to deliver benefits while using the product, may have unintended consequences during the purchase decision. Although the design of a product is mostly carried out with end-user satisfaction in mind, we argue that individuals might evaluate the same product differently according to what they are trying to achieve—choosing which product to purchase among several alternatives versus evaluating one product on an important characteristic, such as usability. A theory of design implies that design should embrace and embody different goals reflecting different stages of consumption (e.g., consideration, purchase, and use).

Conclusions

We found that participants faced with high-usability designs were less satisfied with and less confident about their choice when they chose from a large assortment than when they chose from a small assortment. However, participants faced with low-usability designs were as satisfied when they chose from a large assortment as when they chose from a small assortment. Although high-usability designs offer superior value at the moment of use, they seem to be detrimental at the moment of purchase, because they do not prevent participants from experiencing choice overload (Visentin et al., 2014).

Although our studies tested the effect of design scripts on one product category only (programmable thermostats), our research documents a phenomenon that is both theoretically relevant and practically informative for the work of designers and businesses alike. We hope that our approach—directly manipulating a design element of the stimuli in a realistic manner—will set a precedent for research that can test purchase decisions in a way that is a step closer to reality while still retaining the rigor of experimental methodology. Extant scientific work on choice overload has not yet considered the role played by product design, maybe because of the difficulty of precisely isolating and modifying a single element of design in order to create stimuli that are comparable and free from confounding elements. We think that the high-usability- versus low-usability-design manipulation employed in our studies provides a solution to this problem.

References

Bergum, B. O., & Bergum, J. E. (1981, October). Population stereotypes: An attempt to measure and define. In *Proceedings of the Human Factors and Ergonomics Society Annual Meeting, 25*(1), 662–665.

Brenner, L., Rottenstreich, Y., & Sood, S. (1999). Comparison, grouping, and preference. *Psychological Science, 10*(3), 225–229.

Carmon, Z., Wertenbroch, K., & Zeelenberg, M. (2003). Option attachment: When deliberating makes choosing feel like losing. *Journal of Consumer Research, 30*(1), 15–29.

Chernev, A. (2003). When more is less and less is more: The role of ideal point availability and assortment in consumer choice. *Journal of Consumer Research, 30*(2), 170–183.

Chernev, A. (2005). Context effects without a context: Attribute balance as a reason for choice. *Journal of Consumer Research, 32*(2), 213–223.

Dhar, R. (1997). Consumer preference for a no-choice option. *Journal of Consumer Research, 24*(2), 215–231.

Diehl, K., Kornish, L. J., & Lynch, J. G. (2003). Smart agents: When lower search costs for quality information increase price sensitivity. *Journal of Consumer Research, 30*(1), 56–71.

Diehl, K., & Poynor, C. (2010). Great expectations?! Assortment size, expectations and satisfaction. *Journal of Marketing Research, 47*(2), 312–322.

Fasolo, B., Ludwig, M., Hertwig, R., & Huber, M. (2009). Size, entropy, and density: What is the difference that makes the difference between small and large real-world assortments? *Psychology and Marketing, 26*(3), 254–279.

Gourville, J. T., & Soman, D. (2005). Overchoice and assortment type: When and why variety backfires. *Marketing Science, 24*(3), 382–395.

Iyengar, S. S., & Lepper, M. R. (2000). When choice is demotivating: Can one desire too much of a good thing? *Journal of Personality and Social Psychology, 79*(6), 995–1006.

Iyengar, S. S., Wells, R. E., & Schwartz, B. (2006). Doing better but feeling worse: Looking for the "best" job undermines satisfaction. *Psychological Science, 17*(2), 143–150.

Kahn, B. E., & Wansink, B. (2004). The influence of assortment structure on perceived variety and consumption quantities. *Journal of Consumer Research, 30*(4), 519–533.

Karwoski, W. (2012). The discipline of human factors and ergonomics. In G. Salvendy (Ed.), *Handbook of human factors and ergonomics* (pp. 3–37). Hoboken, NJ: Wiley.

Lancaster, K. (1990). The economics of product variety: A survey. *Marketing Science, 9*(3), 189–206.

Malhotra, N. K. (1982). Information load and consumer decision making. *Journal of Consumer Research, 8*(4), 419–430.

Markus, H. R., & Schwartz, B. (2010). Does choice mean freedom and well-being? *Journal of Consumer Research, 37*(2), 344–355.

Mogilner, C., Rudnick, T., & Iyengar, S. S. (2008). The mere categorization effect: How the presence of category increases choosers' perceptions of assortment variety and outcome satisfaction. *Journal of Consumer Research, 35*(2), 202–215.

Sagi, A., & Friedland, N. (2007). The cost of richness: The effect of the size and diversity of decision sets on post-decision regret. *Journal of Personality and Social Psychology, 93*(4), 515–524.

Schwartz, B., Ward, A., Monterosso, J., Lyubomirsky, S., White, K., & Lehman, D. R. (2002). Maximizing versus satisficing: Happiness is a matter of choice. *Journal of Personality and Social Psychology, 83*(5), 1178–1197.

Shugan, S. M. (1980). The cost of thinking. *Journal of Consumer Research, 7*(2), 99–111.

Simon, H. A. (1955). A behavioral model of rational choice. *Quarterly Journal of Economics, 69*(1), 99–118.

Tversky, A., & Shafir, E. (1992). Choice under conflict: The dynamics of deferred decision. *Psychological Science, 3*(6), 358–361.

Ulrich, K. T., & Eppinger, S. D. (2012). *Product design and development*. Maidenhead: McGraw-Hill.

Visentin, M., Franssens, S., & Botti, S. (2014). *Ergonomic design and choice overload*. Unpublished manuscript, London Business School.

Wiebe, J., & Vu, K.-P. (2009). Application of population stereotypes to computerized tasks. In M. J. Smith & G. Salvendy (Eds.), *Human interface and the management of information. Lecture Notes in Computer Science Series: Vol. 5617. Designing information environments* (pp. 718–725). Berlin: Springer.

21

PRODUCT AESTHETICS AND THE SELF

Kelly B. Herd

INDIANA UNIVERSITY

C. Page Moreau

UNIVERSITY OF WISCONSIN

The success of design-focused companies like Apple, Target, and Sony suggests that both marketers and consumers realize that products—much like art—are often distinguished and defined based on their aesthetic value (e.g., Postrel, 2003). Former Target Vice President Ron Johnson explains, "Customers really respond to products that . . . connect with their souls" (Gibney & Luscombe, 2000). Even when these products are functionally equivalent to their less aesthetically pleasing counterparts, they can command a huge price premium simply because they look and feel better (Postrel, 2003). While aesthetics has been increasingly recognized as an important factor influencing consumers' behavior, the majority of recent research on the topic has focused either on the factors that make a product aesthetically pleasing or on the influence of product aesthetics on consumers' initial product reactions and choice (Bloch, 1995; Coates, 2002; Cooper & Kleinschmidt, 1987; Creusen & Schoormans, 2005; Townsend & Sood, 2012; Ulrich, 2011; Veryzer, 1995). In addition to this literature, we further consider how the use of products with differing levels of aesthetic appeal may influence consumers' self-perceptions. In the following sections, we provide an overview of product aesthetics, consider how aesthetics offers self-signaling value for consumers, and highlight implications both for practitioners and academics.

The Value of Product Design

While there are individual differences in aesthetic preferences (Bloch, Brunel, & Arnold, 2003), psychologists have found patterns across cultures and ages to suggest our response to beauty and evaluation of what makes something "aesthetically pleasing" is largely hard-wired (e.g., Postrel, 2003; Veryzer & Hutchinson, 1998). Extant research has considered how factors such as symmetry, prototypicality, and proportions all influence consumers' evaluations of an object's attractiveness (e.g., Coates, 2002; Raghubir & Greenleaf, 2006; Veryzer & Hutchinson, 1998).

Traditionally, the study of aesthetics has focused predominantly on objects whose primary value comes from an inherent beauty (i.e., artwork, music, and poetry) (e.g., Lasaga, 1947). Over the past two decades, however, firms have paid increasing attention to product design and aesthetics as sources of competitive advantage. "Competition has pushed quality so high and prices so low that many manufacturers can no longer distinguish themselves with price and performance" (Postrel, 2003, p. 2). Beyond the obvious industry leaders in technological products such as Apple, firms as diverse as Kohler (plumbing), Wolverine World Wide (footwear), and Black & Decker (power tools) are among the top 10 firms in the number of design patents awarded over the past 15 years (Nichols, 2013).

Products with "good" design offer firms a competitive advantage by creating value and benefits for the consumer that can be divided into three categories: utilitarian, hedonic, and semiotic (e.g., Bloch, 2011; Candi, 2006; Norman, 2005).

Utilitarian Value

Utilitarian value is found in a product's functional usefulness and the product's "ability to facilitate the accomplishment of a task" (Bloch, 2011, p. 378; Boztepe, 2007). A product with high utilitarian value is reliable and convenient to use. Firms such as OXO, which was founded in 1990 on the philosophy of Universal Design, have gained market success by producing products that "make everyday living easier" for "as many people as possible" (see http://www.oxo.com/aboutOXO.aspx).

Hedonic Value

Hedonic value relates to consumers' more visceral responses to product experiences. Specifically, hedonic value is comprised of both the aesthetic appeal of the product (i.e., the affective response to a product's ability to please one or more of our senses) and the experiential appeal of the product (i.e., the pleasure derived from its use) (Bloch, 2011; Desmet & Hekkert, 2007; Chitturi, 2009). Hedonic value is often evident in consumers' affective responses to the product, both in a purchase/choice setting and during product use. Car manufacturers, for example, design to enhance both the visual appeal of their products to drive purchase as well as the sensory experiences it offers to increase satisfaction (e.g., the "engine note" and the feel and smell of the leather seats) (Bloch, 2011; see also Leonard & Rayport, 1997). These affective responses are quick, involuntary, and evoked when experiencing an object via the sensory system (Bloch, 1995; Coates, 2002; Ulrich, 2011).

Semiotic Value

A third source of value is found in the semiotic benefits reflected in a product's messages, symbols, culture, and meaning (e.g., Norman, 2005; Pine & Gilmore, 1998; Stuart & Tax, 2004). Essentially, a product's design communicates important information about the product user and serves as a mechanism for his or her self-expression (Belk, 1988; Bloch, 2011; Mono, 1997). Car designs, for example, make statements about the driver and his or her values to others on the road. However, products are often used to define the self (Belk, 1988), and the information contained in the product's design may be most impactful to the person who owns and uses it. The most meaningful products are often those that "truly reflect the true story of who you are . . . and they help form the story you are telling yourself (and no one else) because that is the only audience that matters" (Walker, 2009, *Objectified*). Importantly, prior research on consumers' responses to product design has overlooked this third, but important, source of value, and instead, has focused solely on the utilitarian and hedonic sources (Chitturi, 2009; Chitturi, Raghunathan, & Mahajan, 2007).

All three sources of value—utilitarian, hedonic, and semiotic—suggest that design and aesthetics are not purely about the object or product, but instead reflect a complex "person–product relationship" (Veryzer, 1995). A design's value is not considered in isolation, but is instead based on an "aesthetic response," the response that arises from an interaction between an object's appearance and the perceiver of the object (Veryzer, 1995). Aesthetic value depends on the individual experiencing it and how that information is used (Postrel, 2003), though marketers can leverage appropriate positioning to influence consumers' perceptions of products' aesthetic value (Noseworthy & Trudel, 2011).

Aesthetics and Self-Signaling

Just as consumers infer information about others by observing the products they use, consumers also observe their own product usage and integrate this information into subsequent self-evaluations (e.g., Berger & Heath, 2007; Bodner & Prelec, 2002; Prelec & Bodner, 2003; Csikszentmihalyi & Rochberg-Halton, 1981). As Csikszentmihalyi and Rochberg-Halton (1981) note, "self-knowledge is inferential and not direct; when we say 'Who am I?', we attend to certain bits of information" including the objects around us (p. 3; Belk, 1988; Sirgy, 1982).

Researchers have long recognized that consumers examine their own behavior and use that information to make inferences about their personal qualities and characteristics (e.g., Bem, 1972; Dunning, 2007; James, 1884). In fact, early work in psychology by James (the James-Lange theory, 1884) suggests that people infer their own emotional states from observing their behavior (i.e., they feel afraid if they see themselves running). Building upon these theories of self-perception, recent work on self-signaling has demonstrated that consumers also use information about their own behavior to make themselves feel better (e.g., Bodner & Prelec, 2002; Dunning, 2007; Prelec & Bodner, 2003). Like related work on self-enhancement and other self-motives, research on self-signaling suggests that consumers like to see themselves in a positive light and will interpret information in a way that is consistent with this goal (Leary, 2007). While theories of both self-perception and self-signaling have been well established, many questions regarding the underlying process and moderating effects remain unexplored.

Self-Signaling in Economics

A limited amount of research on self-signaling can be found in the economics literature (e.g., Akerlof & Kranton, 2000; Bodner & Prelec, 2002; Prelec & Bodner, 2003). For example, Prelec and Bodner (2003) develop an economic model of strategic self-signaling that encompasses two utility components: outcome utility (i.e., the context-independent utility of an option) and diagnostic utility (i.e., the utility or disutility of learning about the type of person one is as signaled by one's choice). The latter component captures the value gained from self-signaling.

Self-signaling has been used to explain interesting behavior that does not follow traditional economics. For example, Shafir and Tversky (1992) use self-signaling to explain people's behavior in the Newcomb problem. In this problem, people are shown two closed boxes and are told that Box A contains a small, but significant, amount of money while Box B contains either nothing or $1 million. Participants are also told that an all-knowing deity has already made a decision about what Box B contains. If the deity thinks that the person is a nice person, the deity has put $1 million in Box B. If the deity has deemed the person greedy, the deity has left Box B empty. With this information, participants are then asked to choose between (1) Box B alone or (2) a combination of both Boxes A and B. Rational economics suggests that the second choice is dominant. Yet, most people tend to pick the first choice: Box B only. To an economist, this choice is irrational because the deity has already made his choice; nothing about the participant's decision will change the contents of Box B. Because the choice of Box B alone signals that the participant is not a greedy individual, the consumer attains utility from making this seemingly irrational choice.

Self-Signaling in Psychology

In psychology, Quattrone and Tversky (1984) conducted a study in which they asked participants to submerge their arms in a container of cold water until they could no longer bear the pain. Participants were then told that recent medical studies had discovered a connection between the effects of exercise on one's ability to keep one's arm submerged and a certain type of heart condition. Half of the participants were told that the heart condition was associated with *increases* in tolerance to cold water, while the other half were told it was associated with *decreases* in tolerance. Participants then rode a stationary bike for one minute and repeated the cold-water test. The majority of participants showed a change in submersion time in the direction correlated with "good news." While their behavior could not cause them to have a healthy heart, it could provide them with a signal that they were among the healthy.

Self-signaling has also been used to explain why people engage in a variety of "real world" behaviors. People recycle to see themselves as responsible people (Brekke, Snorre, & Nyborgb, 2003) and pursue challenging, even dangerous, activities like mountaineering to see themselves as brave and fit (Loewenstein, 1999).

Self-Signaling in Consumer Behavior

While there is likely an important connection between self-signaling and consumer behavior, limited research exists in this domain (Bennett & Chakravarti, 2008; Dunning, 2007). Dhar and colleagues (Dhar & Wertenbroch, 2012; Khan & Dhar, 2006) use self-signaling to explain consumers' self-control in their decisions regarding "virtues" and "vices." Consistent with the model laid out by Prelec and Bodner (Bodner & Prelec, 2002; Prelec & Bodner, 2003), Dhar and Wertenbroch (2012) examine how people use their choices between "virtues" and "vices" to generate self-attributions which either enhance or reduce the overall utility derived from these choices. In related work, Khan and Dhar (2006) find that once people have shown some type of altruistic behavior they feel licensed to engage in more self-indulgent behavior (i.e., the licensing effect). The authors propose that the effect works because the initial behavior dampens the negative self-attributions associated with certain indulgent decisions (Khan & Dhar, 2006). Similarly, Gao, Wheeler, and Shiv (2009) look at how product choice can restore self-views that have been temporarily brought into question. These authors find that when participants who believe they are exciting are temporarily made to question this self-view, they are more likely to purchase products with exciting brand personalities to bolster this momentarily shaken self-view.

Limited work has considered the relationship between self-signaling and product aesthetics. Townsend and Sood (2012) demonstrate that the choice of an aesthetically pleasing product can influence one's propensity to escalate commitment toward a failing course of action and openness to counter-attitudinal arguments. Further, their research demonstrates that when consumers engage in a self-affirming task prior to product choice, they are less likely to pick a highly aesthetic product. From these three studies, the authors conclude that good design is self-affirming.

Together, the work on self-signaling demonstrates how consumers may signal information to themselves in a consumption context; however, all of this research focuses exclusively on product choice, failing to consider how product use might offer similar self-signaling value. In our research, we demonstrate that simply using attractive products signals positive information to consumers about themselves, and that this effect is enhanced when uncertainty is high.

Self-Signaling and Uncertainty

Several economists have determined that signaling is most important when high levels of uncertainty exist (Akerlof, 1970). In general, people tend to be chronically uncertain about where they stand on a variety of dimensions, especially with respect to broad or abstract attributes (Prelec & Bodner, 2003). For example, when asked about one's "taste," there is little diagnostic information as to whether one has "good" or "bad" taste. Therefore, individuals look to their decisions, product choices, and current possessions to assess their own values, morality, taste, and ability to form a self-evaluation. Most researchers addressing self-signaling agree that uncertainty is a major contributor to the effect (Dunning, 2007; Loewenstein, 1999; Prelec & Bodner, 2003; Shafir & Tversky, 1992). In an analysis of Quattrone and Tversky's (1984) experiment, Shafir and Tversky (1992) explain it is their uncertainty of their prognosis that drives their willingness to do so (Shafir & Tversky, 1992). Loewenstein (1999) concurs: "People are, in fact, unsure of their own dispositions. To resolve this uncertainty in a manner favorable to themselves, people attempt to signal to themselves that they have desirable attributes by taking actions that they believe are consistent with those attributes" (p. 323). Similarly, Gao et al. (2009) show that when a self-view is temporarily cast in doubt, consumers choose products that bolster their original self-view. These findings suggest that consumers with a higher level of uncertainty have a greater need to self-signal, and thus, stand to benefit more directly from positive self-signaling than those with a lower level of uncertainty.

Building off of this literature, we conducted a series of experiments that demonstrate that using more (versus less) attractive products positively influences self-evaluations on domain-relevant dimensions; however, when participants are prompted with high certainty, this effect is attenuated (Herd & Moreau, 2015). For example, in the context of a writing task, participants who are prompted with uncertainty and who use attractive writing materials (i.e., pen and paper or a Microsoft Word template) evaluate their own writing abilities more favorably and report higher expected performance than those who use less attractive materials. The product aesthetics have no impact on non-domain relevant dimensions such as how nice or funny they are, suggesting the results are not driven by a halo effect (Nisbett & Wilson, 1977).

Conversely, we find participants who are prompted with certainty are unaffected by the aesthetics of the writing materials when reporting their self-perceived writing abilities. These effects are consistent across both online and offline contexts. Importantly, the experiments control for utilitarian and hedonic values in order to isolate semiotic value. In doing so, this research supports a self-signaling mechanism in which the product communicates important information about the user and serves as a mechanism for his or her self-expression (Belk, 1988; Bloch, 2011). By simply using attractive products, consumers gain confidence and evaluate themselves more favorably within a given domain. The process by which this occurs, however, is not well understood.

Self-Signaling and Awareness

The limited research on self-signaling suggests that it is an implicit process (e.g., Bennett & Chakravarti, 2008), yet we are unaware of research that has explicitly tested the underlying mechanism. As Prelec and Bodner (2003) explain, "while we do know that people engage in self-signaling, there is little experimental evidence on the level of subjective awareness of the process" (p. 293).

Anecdotal evidence from Quattrone and Tversky (1984) provides support for a nonconscious explanation. When the researchers followed up with participants following the cold water study, most denied that they were trying to bias the results of the bogus medical test suggesting that the self-signaling mechanism occurs at a nonconscious level.

In our research, we examine the process by which self-signaling occurs by manipulating participants' awareness of the products' aesthetics (Herd & Moreau, 2015). When participants become aware of the potential influence of the aesthetics on their subsequent judgments, they are likely to correct, or even over-correct, for the possible bias (e.g., Strack, Schwarz, Bless, Kübler, & Wänke, 1993). If the process is an implicit one, self-evaluations on domain-relevant dimensions should be lower (higher) when consumers become aware of a product's attractive (unattractive) aesthetics as compared to when they are not made aware. With awareness, consumers are likely to adjust for the positive or negative bias that the product may have on subsequent judgments.

The results of our experiment demonstrate that attractive (vs. less attractive) products positively influences evaluations of one's self-created outcomes, but only when attention is not drawn to a product's aesthetics. Using a scenario in which participants imagine cooking, the experiment provides evidence that aesthetic self-signaling occurs via an implicit process. For those consumers whose attention was not called initially to the products' aesthetics, the use of attractive products led to higher levels of both self-assessed cooking ability and expectations of the food's taste. When participants were made aware of the product's aesthetics, however, they appeared to adjust for that potential biasing effect.

Thus, our research demonstrates that the use of aesthetically pleasing products can influence consumers' self-evaluations, even when controlling for utilitarian and hedonic sources of value (Herd & Moreau, 2015). By simply using attractive products, consumers gain confidence and evaluate themselves more favorably within a given domain. Importantly, this semiotic value is attained only when participants are sufficiently uncertain about the judgment and are unaware of the potential biasing effect of aesthetics. In a final study, we introduce another potential moderator to better understand the semiotic value creation process: the presence of an audience.

The Role of an Audience

Unless completely engrossed in a task, people are often self-conscious when others are watching them perform. This type of public self-consciousness produces effects (e.g., emotions) that "are much more strongly tied to what people think other people think of them than to what people think of themselves" (Leary, 2007, p. 330). Self-conscious emotions (e.g., pride, guilt, embarrassment, shame) are more deliberative than hedonic emotions and result from cognitive appraisals (Hung & Mukhopadhyay, 2012; Leary, 2007).

Hence, the presence of an audience may lessen the aesthetic self-signaling effect because when observers are present, consumers are likely to consider how these outsiders might evaluate them. If motivated to make a positive impression, consumers are likely to reflect on both their behavior and their appearance to a greater extent than if no such motivation existed. Thus, the presence of an audience is likely to attenuate the self-signaling effect for two reasons. First, self-evaluations are likely to be more cognitive in nature as the consumer appraises him/herself by taking another's perspective. Second, in doing so, consumers are likely to pay attention to their own appearance as well as the appearance of the products and surroundings in which they are situated.

In the context of an actual cooking task, our experiment finds that using attractive cooking utensils (i.e., mixing bowls, measuring cups, measuring spoons, and other relevant tools) increases outcome expectations (Herd & Moreau, 2015). Specifically, participants expect that the cookies they made with more attractive tools will actually taste better. This effect only holds when the cooking task is completed in private. When an audience is present, the effect is attenuated and the self-signaling effect is diminished. The results suggest that this moderation occurred because the participants who cooked in front of an audience were more self-conscious and this awareness caused the participant to correct for perceived biasing effects of the aesthetic cookware.

Implications for Designers

As product competition evolves, few companies are now competing on the bases of functionality and reliability, and most are hesitant to compete on price, leaving product design and aesthetics as an important differentiator on which companies in a variety of industries are now competing (Christensen, 1997). Visual aesthetics are becoming increasingly important for a wide selection of products: "Vegetable peelers, wireless phones, car-washing buckets, and lawn tractors are all being designed with attention to the aesthetic value of their appearance" (Bloch et al., 2003, p. 551). While it is agreed that good design provides both value to consumers and a competitive advantage to firms, the sources of the underlying value remain largely unexplored (e.g., Schmitt & Simonson, 1997). Our research suggests that attractive products are not valued solely for their functional benefits or for the affective responses they generate, but also for their ability to help consumers create and develop a personal identity. When a product holds desirable qualities, consumers want to take on those characteristics (Coates, 2002). Simply using an attractive product allows us to do just that. This self-signaling process may help explain why, even for products that others may never see, "people will pay an extra five bucks for a little kitchen tool that looks and feels good" (Postrel, 2003, p. 14). A better understanding of semiotic value may provide insights into product development, positioning, and promotions. Importantly, the findings from the research presented may also extend to packaging design. Future research could further examine this relationship.

Implications for Theories of Design

Beyond functional benefits and the affective surge that comes when interacting with an attractive product, aesthetics offer a third important source of value: semiotic value (Bloch, 1995; Bloch, 2011; Norman, 2005). Semiotic value captures the interaction between a product and consumer and resulting changes in a consumer's self-identity (Norman, 2005, p. 38). Coates (2002) explains, "We don't just passively view products. We actively seek information from the watches on our wrists, our computers . . . in fact, *all* products talk to us" (p. 1). These products matter to people's sense of self, and are most influential under certain circumstances. Hence, product usage alone can influence evaluations of the self as well, even when consumers have made no intentional choice to acquire the product (e.g., Dhar & Wertenbroch, 2012; Gao et al., 2009; Khan & Dhar, 2006; Townsend & Sood, 2012). While prior research has shown that product ownership provides identity value that develops over time (Kleine, Kleine, & Allen, 1995), our research demonstrates that these effects can be observed over relatively short usage occasions.

References

Akerlof, G. A. (1970). The market for "lemons": Quality uncertainty and the market mechanism. *Quarterly Journal of Economics, 84*(3), 488–500.

Akerlof, G. A., & Kranton, R. E. (2000). Economics and identity. *Quarterly Journal of Economics, 115*(3), 715–753.

Belk, R. W. (1988). Possessions and the extended self. *Journal of Consumer Research, 15*(2), 139.

Bem, D. J. (1972). Self-perception theory. In L. Berkowitz (Ed.), *Advances in experimental social psychology* (Vol. 6, pp. 1–62). New York, NY: Academic Press.

Bennett, A., & Chakravarti, A. (2008). Self and social signaling explanations for consumption of CSR-associated products. *Advances in Consumer Research—North American Conference Proceedings, 35*, 1010–1011.

Berger, J., & Heath, C. (2007). Where consumers diverge from others: Identity signaling and product domains. *Journal of Consumer Research, 34*(2), 121–134.

Bloch, P. H. (1995). Seeking the ideal form: Product design and consumer response. *Journal of Marketing, 59*(3), 16–29.

Bloch, P. H. (2011). Product design and marketing: Reflections after fifteen years. *Journal of Product Innovation Management, 28*(3), 378–380.

Bloch, P. H., Brunel, F. F., & Arnold, T. J. (2003). Individual differences in the centrality of visual product aesthetics: Concept and measurement. *Journal of Consumer Research, 29*(4), 551–565.

Bodner, R., & Prelec, D. (2002). Self-signaling and diagnostic utility in everyday decision making. In I. Brocas & J. Carillo (Eds.), *Collected essays in psychology and economics*. Oxford: Oxford University Press.

Boztepe, S. (2007). User value: Competing theories and models. *International Journal of Design, 1*(2), 55–63.

Brekke, K. A., Snorre K., & Nyborgb, K. (2003). An economic model of moral motivation. *Journal of Public Economics, 87*, 1967–1983.

Candi, M. (2006). Design as an element of innovation: Evaluating design emphasis in technology-based firms. *International Journal of Innovation Management, 10*(4), 351–374.

Chitturi, R. (2009). Emotions by design: A consumer perspective. *International Journal of Design, 3*(2), 7–17.

Chitturi, R., Raghunathan, R., & Mahajan, V. (2007). Form versus function: How the intensities of specific emotions evoked in functional versus hedonic trade-offs mediate product preferences. *Journal of Marketing Research, 44*(4), 702–714.

Christensen, C. (1997). Patterns in the evolution of product competition. *European Management Journal, 15*(2), 117–127.

Coates, D. (2002). *Watches tell more than time: Product design, information, and the quest for elegance*. New York, NY: McGraw-Hill.

Cooper, R. G., & Kleinschmidt, E. J. (1987). New products: What separates winners from losers? *Journal of Product Innovation Management, 4*(3), 169–184.

Creusen, M.E.H., & Schoormans, J.P.L. (2005). The different roles of product appearance in consumer choice. *Journal of Product Innovation Management, 22*(1), 63–81.

Csikszentmihalyi, M., & Rochberg-Halton, E. (1981). *The meaning of things: Domestic symbols and the self*. New York, NY: Cambridge University Press.

Desmet, P., & Hekkert, P. (2007). Framework of product experience. *International Journal of Design, 1*(1), 57–66.

Dhar, R., & Wertenbroch, K. (2012). Self-signaling and the costs and benefits of temptation in consumer choice. *Journal of Marketing Research, 15*(5), 15–25.

Dunning, D. (2007). Self-image motives and consumer behavior: How sacrosanct self-beliefs sway preferences in the marketplace. *Journal of Consumer Psychology, 17*(4), 237–249.

Gao, L. S., Wheeler, C., & Shiv, B. (2009). The "shaken self": Product choices as a means of restoring self-view confidence. *Journal of Consumer Research, 36*(1), 29–38.

Gibney, F., & Luscombe, B. (2000). The redesigning of America. Retrieved from http://content.time.com/time/world/article/0,8599,2050262,00.html

Herd, K. B., & Moreau, C. P. (2015). Impress yourself: Self-signaling and product design. Working paper.

Hung, I. W., & Mukhopadhyay, A. (2012). Lenses of the heart: How actors' and observers' perspectives influence emotional experiences. *Journal of Consumer Research, 38*(6), 1103–1115.

James, W. (1884). What is an emotion? *Mind, 9*, 188–205.

Khan, U., & Dhar, R. (2006). Licensing effect in consumer choice. *Journal of Marketing Research, 43*(2), 259–266.

Kleine, S. S., Kleine, R. E., III, & Allen, C. T. (1995). How is a possession "me" or "not me"? Characterizing types and an antecedent of material possession attachment. *Journal of Consumer Research, 22*(3), 327–343.

Lasaga, J. I. (1947). Outline of a descriptive aesthetics from a structuralist point of view. *Psychological Review, 54*(1), 9–23.

Leary, M. R. (2007). Motivational and emotional aspects of the self. *Annual Review of Psychology, 58*, 317–344.

Leonard, D., & Rayport, J. F. (1997, November–December). Spark innovation through empathic design. *Harvard Business Review*, 102–113.

Loewenstein, G. (1999). Because it is there: The challenge of mountaineering . . . for utility theory. *Kyklos, 52*(3), 315.

Mono, R. (1997). *Design for product understanding*. Stockholm: Liber.

Nichols, B. (2013). Valuing the art of industrial design: A profile of the sector and its importance to manufacturing, technology, and innovation. *NEA: National Endowment for the Arts Research Report, 56*.

Nisbett, R. E., & Wilson, T. D. (1977). The halo effect: Evidence for unconscious alteration of judgments. *Journal of Personality and Social Psychology, 35*(4), 250–256.

Norman, D. (2005). *Emotional design: Why we love (or hate) everyday things*. New York, NY: Basic Books.

Noseworthy, T., & Trudel, R., (2011). The effects of functional and experiential positioning on consumer evaluations of incongruent product form. *Journal of Marketing Research, 48*(12), 1008–1019.

Pine, J. B., & Gilmore, J. H. (1998, July–August). Welcome to the experience economy. *Harvard Business Review*, 97–105.

Postrel, V. (2003). *The substance of style: How the rise of aesthetic value is remaking commerce, culture, and consciousness*. New York, NY: HarperCollins.

Prelec, D., & Bodner, R. (2003). Self-signaling and self-control. In G. Loewenstein, D. Read, & R. F. Baumeister (Eds.), *Time and decision* (pp. 277–298). New York, NY: Russell Sage Foundation.

Quattrone, G. A., & Tversky, A. (1984). Causal versus diagnostic contingencies: On self-deception and on the voter's illusion. *Journal of Personality and Social Psychology, 46*(2), 237–248.

Raghubir, P., & Greenleaf, E. A. (2006). Ratios in proportion: What should the shape of the package be? *Journal of Marketing, 70*, 95–107.

Schmitt, B., & Simonson, A. (1997). *Marketing aesthetics*. New York, NY: Free Press.

Shafir, E., & Tversky, A. (1992). Thinking through uncertainty: Nonconsequential reasoning and choice. *Cognitive Psychology, 24*(4), 449–474.

Sirgy, M. J. (1982). Self-concept in consumer behavior: A critical review. *Journal of Consumer Research, 9*(3), 287–300.

Strack, F., Schwarz, N., Bless, H., Kübler, A., & Wänke, M. (1993). Awareness of the influence as a determinant of assimilation versus contrast. *European Journal of Social Psychology, 23*(1), 53–62.

Stuart, I. F., & Tax, S. (2004). Toward an integrative approach to designing service experiences: Lessons learned from the theatre. *Journal of Operations Management,* 22(6), 609–627.

Townsend, C., & Sood, S. (2012). Self-affirmation through the choice of highly aesthetic products. *Journal of Consumer Research, 39*(2), 415–428.

Ulrich, K. T. (2011). Users, experts, and institutions in design. In K. T. Ulrich (Ed.), *Design: Creation of Artifacts in Society* (pp. 71–88). Philadelphia: University of Pennsylvania.

Veryzer, R. W., Jr. (1995). The place of product design and aesthetics in consumer research. In F. R. Kardes, & M. Sujan (Eds.), *Advances in consumer research* (pp. 641–645). Provo, UT: Association for Consumer Research.

Veryzer, R. W., & Hutchinson, J. W. (1998) The influence of unity and prototypicality on aesthetic responses to new product designs. *Journal of Consumer Research, 24,* 374–394.

Walker, R. (Producer), & Hustwit, G. (Director). (2009). *Objectified* [Motion picture]. (Available from Swiss Dot & Plexi Production.)

PART IV
Design Methods

22

EYE-TRACKING AIDS IN UNDERSTANDING CONSUMER PRODUCT EVALUATIONS

Ping Du

IOWA STATE UNIVERSITY

Erin MacDonald

STANFORD UNIVERSITY

Eye-tracking technology enables researchers to capture viewing processes of people and provides corresponding quantitative data, like where or what people look at (fixations), when they look at something and for how long (fixation time), scan paths between fixations, and pupil dilation during fixations. As the eye focuses on what the mind is cognitively processing according to the "eye-mind" hypothesis (Just & Carpenter, 1976), eye-tracking data are meaningful and can facilitate a wide range of research or investigations, especially in combination with other data sources. Eye-tracking can help inveistgate thoughts that are unconscious or difficult to articulate. The eye-tracking data can provide unique insights and are good additions to traditional self-report data, or even necessities in certain studies (Schiessl, Duda, Tholke, & Fischer, 2003). Eye-tracking is actively used in areas like psychology, marketing, industrial engineering, and human–computer interaction. Duchowski (2007) provides a review of eye-tracking's uses in these areas. Wedel and Pieters (2008) reviewed eye-tracking's uses in marketing research. We apply eye-tracking to facilitate understanding of consumer product evaluations from the lens of design research. This chapter reviews eye-tracking measurement approaches; introduces eye-tracking equipment; reviews different types of eye-tracking data; reviews studies that have employed eye-tracking to investigate consumer evaluations of visual designs; discusses strengths and limitations of eye-tracking in terms of its applications for understanding consumer product evaluations; and discusses implications of eye-tracking for designers and for design theory separately.

Eye-Tracking Methods

Eye-tracking measurement approaches can be categorized into two types based on the objects that are measured; the first type "measures the position of the eye relative to the head" and the other "measures the orientation of the eye in space," which is also known as the "point of regard" (Duchowski, 2007).

Electro-oculography (EOG), a method of the first type, was widely used in the 1960s (Duchowski, 2007). It identifies eye movements by recording corneoretinal potential differences, which are detected from skin electrodes that are attached around the eyes (Young & Sheena, 1975). EOG has the benefit of not requiring the eye to be visualized, but it can have errors that are resulted from eyelid interferences, alertness, muscle artifacts, and so forth (Young & Sheena, 1975). Contact lens method is another approach that measures the eye position relative to the head; a "mechanical or optical reference object" is attached to contact lens, which needs to be worn on the eyes in order to obtain measurements (Duchowski, 2007). This method is considered to be uncomfortable, and could potentially deform cornea or hurt accommodation muscles (Young & Sheena, 1975).

Other measurements based on the "point of regard" largely relax the restrictions on the head and have gradually come to dominate research. Pupil center/corneal reflection method is one of those, and is implemented in many commercial eye trackers available today. This method takes advantage of corneal reflections of incoming light. Infra-red is a commonly used light source. There are four types of corneal reflections that are determined by where the light reflections are formed (Crane, 1994). The one that forms at the front of the cornea is usually used in the pupil center/corneal reflection method (Duchowski, 2007). This reflection is relatively stable as long as the location of the light source is stationary, but the pupil center changes along with eye movements; because of this, the corneal reflection and the pupil center have changing positional difference that can be captured by a particular camera and be used to measure the eye movements (Duchowski, 2007). The pupil center/corneal reflection method can be realized in two ways, which differ in how the pupil is detected. The difference results from the position of the light source. If the light source is located near the optical axis of the camera, the pupil will be lit up and it is bright pupil eye-tracking; if the light source is located away from the camera's optical axis, the pupil will be relatively dark and it is dark pupil eye-tracking (Tobii, 2010). The effectiveness of these two types of eye-tracking can be affected by age and ethnicity of the person being tracked, as well as the environmental light (Tobii, 2010). Some eye-trackers use both types of tracking.

Eye Trackers

There are different types of eye trackers that can accommodate different experimental environment and needs. Common commercial eye trackers include: (1) monitor-based eye tracker, (2) snap-on eye tracker, (3) stand-alone eye tracker, and (4) eye-tracking glasses.

The monitor-based eye tracker integrates the tracking system into a computer monitor and is applicable for studies that focus on stimuli that can be displayed on the monitor, like still images, videos, websites, etc. It requires subjects to sit in front of it during eye-tracking processes. It looks and works like a normal computer screen to the subjects. The snap-on eye tracker does not have a monitor itself. It is much smaller and more portable than the monitor-based eye tracker. It can be attached to laptops, TVs, and external screens, and it tracks eye movements for the stimuli shown on those screens; it can also be used for studies on mobile devices and physical flat surfaces, but in these cases it needs to work in cooperation with an external scene camera that captures the objects being studied during the eye-tracking process (Tobii, n.d.). The stand-alone eye tracker has similar usages as the snap-on eye tracker, but the setup is different because it is not attachable. Eye-tracking glasses usually include a head unit, which is a pair of glasses with an integrated eye tracker, and a recording unit that records and saves eye-tracking data, images seen, and audio comments (SMI, n.d.; Tobii, n.d.). An advantage of eye-tracking glasses is that they allow subjects to move around, enabling studies in the real-world, like studies of shopping experiences, driving, and sports.

When choosing an eye tracker for a study, in addition to considering the type of the eye tracker, the technical aspects of the eye tracker are important. Eye trackers from different producers vary in their technical specifications. Some major specifications include the sampling rate, tracking accuracy, allowed operating distance, adaptation to head movements, use of monocular or binocular tracking, and adoption of bright/dark pupil tracking or both. Higher sampling rate captures saccades and miniature eye movements better, and is especially desired in research on reading(Andersson, Nyström, & Holmqvist, 2010). The implementation of bright/dark pupil tracking or both has effects on the eye tracker's adaptation to the sampled population as well as the experimental environment (Tobii, 2010).

The eye tracker is often used cooperatively with commercial eye-tracking software. The eye-tracking software manages the large amount of raw eye-tracking data that is collected by the eye tracker to determine eye fixations, pupil dilations, and other aggregated data for researchers. The software prepares and organizes data into easily interpretable formats for exportation, which makes post-analyses more straightforward. Some software also helps to visualize experimental results, results as introduced in the next section. Some software (like Attention Tool, Tobii Studio, etc.) offers a platform for setting up experiments and managing subjects. Some software (like Attention Tool) can also help integrate other biometric measuring techniques (like Electroencephalography [EEG], facial expression detection, etc.) with the eye-tracking process. An eye tracker can also be used without the commercial software, and in combination with a software development kit, for example Tobii's SDK.

Overview of Eye-Tracking Data

There are four major types of eye movements (Duchowski, 2007; Tobii, 2010): (1) fixations, which are "eye movements that stabilize the retina over a stationary object of interest" (Duchowski, 2007)"; (2) saccades, which are "rapid eye movements between fixations" (Tobii, 2010); (3) smooth pursuits, which are eye movements for moving objects so as to keep their images on the retina stationary; and (4) miniature eye movements like drift, tremor, and microsaccades, which help prevent images of the objects on the retina from fading. Most eye-tracking research focuses on fixations, because they are the most informative of cognitive states (Just & Carpenter, 1976). This section discusses the eye-tracking data that are associated with fixations, termed "gaze data."

Basic types of gaze data are *fixation time*—duration of fixation(s); *fixation count*—number of fixations; *gaze path*—trajectory of fixations; and *fixation location*. Fixation time and count are usually used in conjunction with areas of interest (AOIs), which are "areas of a given stimulus related to the research hypothesis" (Du & MacDonald, 2014) or research interests. Figure 22.1 shows an example

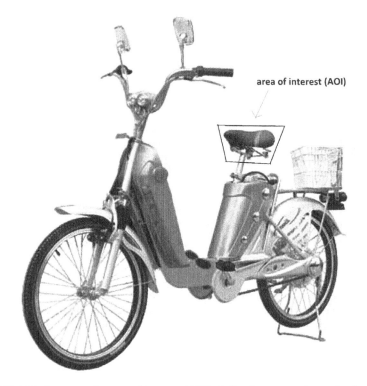

FIGURE 22.1 An example area of interest (AOI) defined on a product stimulus.

Source: Erin MacDonald and Ping Du.

AOI defined on a product stimulus. After identifying the fixations that are within an AOI according to the fixation locations, researchers can calculate the total fixation time and number of fixation counts for an AOI. Fixation time for an AOI can be seconds, while that for an individual fixation is usually milliseconds. *Percentage-fixation time* and *first-located time* are also useful gaze measurements. The percentage-fixation time for an AOI refers to the AOI's percent share of the total fixation time for the stimulus. The first-located time for an AOI refers to the timestamp of the first fixation located in the AOI during exposure of the associated stimulus. Other types of gaze data also exist, introductions of which are available in (Jacob & Karn, 2003; Poole & Ball, 2005).

Gaze data are often visualized for demonstration purposes. Three common visualizations are gaze replays, gaze plots, and heat maps (Nielsen & Pernice, 2010). Gaze replays are per subject. They map a subject's fixations on top of the corresponding stimulus and display them as if watching a video, with proper timings. They dynamically show the whole process of how the stimulus is viewed by the subject. Gaze plots are static presentations of fixations for their corresponding stimuli. Figure 22.2 shows an example gaze plot. Each dot represents a fixation and the longer the fixation duration, the larger the dot. The dots are numbered according to the sequence of the fixations. Different subjects' fixations can also be color coded and displayed on the same stimulus, so as to help identify if different subjects have varied points of interest. Heat maps, as shown in Figure 22.3, are another type of static presentation of the gaze data. They aggregate one or more subjects' fixations at each spot in certain ways (different eye-tracking software has different aggregation strategies), color code the intensity, and map the results on top of the stimulus. They quickly inform the "hot spots" in the stimulus, and show both the distribution and the intensity of the gaze attention. It is important to note that gaze attention does not necessary mean that the subject likes what they are looking at, for example, an ugly feature, a useless feature, or an unattractive color can also draw gaze to

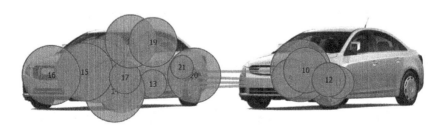

FIGURE 22.2 An example gaze plot. Each dot represents a fixation. The longer the fixation duration, the larger the dot. The dots are numbered according to the sequence of the fixations.

Source: Erin MacDonald and Ping Du.

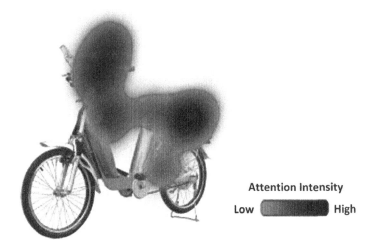

FIGURE 22.3 A heat map shows a static presentation of the gaze data.

Source: Erin MacDonald and Ping Du.

a specific area. Gaze can suggest what features a subject is thinking about, but not why they are thinking about it. That is one reason why it is important to use gaze data in conjunction with other sources of data.

Review of Related Eye-Tracking Studies

Use of Eye Tracking in Understanding Consumer Evaluation Processes

Eye-tracking has been used to help with understanding consumer evaluations of visual designs. Du and MacDonald (2014) collected gaze data while subjects were evaluating different product visual designs for preference decisions. Case products included cars and electric bicycles. They found significant correlations between gaze attention to product features and the importance of those features in consumers' product preference decisions, as rated by subjects later in the experiment. The correlation remained as significant while varying the type of the gaze data that was measured, the type of the product, sequential vs. side-by-side presentation of stimuli, and the number of subjects. It was shown that gaze data can statistically predict self-reported feature importance in product preference decisions. This suggests that gaze data could be used to supplement or replace attribute-ranking and choice-based product surveys, with further investigation. Gaze data were also found to predict when size-change in product features is noticeable to consumers. This can be useful in design, for example, when a company wants to decrease the size of a feature to save money on materials, but does not want the consumer to notice the change. Likewise, it can be used to enhance product differentiation within a portfolio. In another study, Du and MacDonald (in press) investigated how consumers evaluated products that had both shared and unique feature designs (e.g., two cars share the same headlight design while having different designs for their grilles). Cars and electric bicycles were both tested. Pairs of product images were provided to subjects for preference evaluations. They found that people tended to focus more on the differences than on the similarities during the evaluations. When the stimuli in a pair were presented to the subjects side-by-side, fixation time for the unique features were 592 milliseconds longer than that for the shared ones; when the stimuli were provided sequentially, the fixation time for the unique features were 99 milliseconds longer. This reveals a particular evaluation strategy that consumers use when making preference decisions.

Reid, MacDonald, and Du (2013) used eye-tracking in their investigations of product design representations' influences on consumer evaluations. It was found that, in some cases, consumers viewed the same product for a longer time when it was shown as a realistic rendering than when it was shown as a computer sketch. Different evaluation strategies by consumers were also observed. There were two distinct trends that split approximately 50/50 by question and/or subject population: either people gazed longer at the option they were going to choose, or the option they were not going to choose. The work did not indicate that people simply stare longer at the option they will pick. This is an important finding, because it contradicts a common but incorrect heuristic that people look longer at the option they will ultimately choose. Gofman, Moskowitz, Fyrbjork, Moskowitz, and Mets (2009) explored consumer evaluations of wine packages from several aspects using eye-tracking. They observed that most consumers started the evaluations from the center of the package and tended to ignore the tagline area, suggesting this area's uselessness for carrying important information. They found that first gaze locations had effects on purchase decisions and time spent evaluating the packages. They also differentiated features that kept the consumers wandering around the packages from the ones that focused the gaze on one area.

With the use of eye-tracking, Russo and Leclerc (1994) identified three major decision stages for consumers making choices between nondurable products, with different sizes and brands, displayed on shelves. There was an orientation stage at the beginning, during which the consumers had an overview of all the alternatives so as to facilitate the next stage. Sometimes, specific product screenings also took place during the orientation stage. The second stage was an evaluation stage, which had the most fixation time and count; during this stage the consumers thoroughly examined several alternatives. The third stage was about verification. The consumers double checked some alternatives before making the choice decisions. There could be an additional stage after the choices were made, in which the consumers revisited some alternatives. This revisitation was also observed by Clement (2007). Rosbergen, Pieters, and Wedel (1997) supplied subjects' fixation time for an ad's different elements (headline, body text, picture of a model, and picture of the product) to a latent class regression model, and categorized three segments of subjects. People in different segments differed in the fixation time spent on the ad as well as in the allocations of attention among different elements of the ad. They argued the importance of considering individuals' heterogeneity in the study of ad design.

Some studies have considered the effects of outside factors on consumers' evaluations of visual designs. Pieters and Warlop (1999) considered both time pressure and task motivation while using eye-tracking to examine visual attention for branding on shampoo bottles. As they expected, high time pressure decreased average fixation time spent on the brand while high task motivation increased the average fixation time. Time pressure and task motivation were found to have different effects on different areas of the shampoo bottle label: brand names, ingredient information, and pictures. The results indicated that the consumers strategically, rather than randomly, chose information to skip in the two conditions. They also found that brand choices were positively related to fixation time. Chandon, Hutchinson, Bradlow, and Young (2009) examined visual attention on products shown within the context of supermarket shelves and grouped by brand. They found that "in-store" factors, like number of products displayed for a brand and locations of the products on the shelves, were more influential to the visual attention on the products than "out-of-store" factors such as consumers' prior brand usages and shopping goals. Pieters, Rosbergen, and Wedel (1999) studied the effects of repetition on visual attention for print advertisements. They found that attention duration decreased substantially over the repetition of an ad; only about 50 percent was left for the third exposure to the ad. They also found the attention duration to be affected by consumers' natural differences in motivation. The consumers with higher motivation tended to pay more attention compared to those with lower motivation. A Markov model was used to examine scanpaths for the ads. They identified that repeated exposures to the ads did not alter the scanpaths.

As summarized in Table 22.1, the above studies use different approaches to analyze eye-tracking data, in terms of the number of stimuli per visual evaluation, and method. The analysis complexity varies with the focus of the study. For example, studying decision stages requires a combined use of advanced analysis methods, while studying the stimuli themselves is straightforward and can be accomplished by commonly used statistical analyses like t-test and ANOVA test.

Use of Eye Tracking in Understanding Visual Design

Eye-tracking has also been used to identify effects of different designs, the results of which are useful and beneficial for understanding, validating, or improving the designs. She (2013) used eye-tracking while investigating the usefulness of carefully designed sustainable-triggering features for toasters. She found that

TABLE 22.1 Summary of Eye-tracking Data Analysis for Literature Review

Literature	Number of stimuli per evaluation	Analysis focus	Analysis method
Du and MacDonald (in press)	1, 2	Design feature	Correlation analysis, Linear regression, One-way ANOVA, Logistic regression
Du and MacDonald (in press)	1, 2	Design feature	Pairwise *t*-test
Reid et al. (2013)	2	Whole stimulus	Welch two sample *t*-test, Descriptive statistics
Gofman et al. (2009)	1	Design feature	Descriptive statistics, Heat map
Russo and Leclerc (1994)	16	Decision stage	Descriptive statistics, Fisher's exact test, ANOVA, Bonferroni test, T-test, Regression analysis
Rosbergen et al. (1997)	1	Design feature, consumer segmentation	Latent class regression, Standard regression, Lognormal regression, Gamma regression, Hierarchical and nonhierarchical clustering algorithm
Pieters and Warlop (1999)	6	Design feature, whole stimulus, outside factors	ANOVA, Post-hoc test, Conditional logistic regression
Chandon et al. (2009)	96	Group of stimuli, outside factors	Descriptive statistics, Correlation analysis, Conditional logistic regression, Path analysis
Pieters et al. (1999)	1	Design feature, whole stimulus, outside factors	Gamma model, Markov model, Consistent Akaike information criterion test, Likelihood ratio test

during product evaluations, the presence of such triggering features on the toasters increased subjects' gaze attention on text describing on the toasters' sustainability, in terms of energy usage and shipping method. Räihä et al. (2006) used eye-tracking to monitor the product evaluation process, and used the information collected to answer product-design related questions, such as "what product features are brand cues?". Their findings included that the navigation panels on their tested cell phones played important roles in brand recognition; and that there were dominant features (e.g., the handles of bypass pruners) for subjects that were heavily fixated-on no matter what product aspect (e.g., ergonomics, aesthetics, durability) was being evaluated.

Eye-tracking helped Laughery, Young, Vaubel, and Brelsford (1993) identify features that improved noticeability of alcohol warnings on containers. Four features were considered: pictorial, signal icon, color, and border. The use of eye-tracking allowed the researchers to discriminate between the time needed to fixate the warning (first-location) and the overall time used to make a judgment. They found that the combined use of pictorial, signal icon, and color features resulted in an average first-location time of 465 milliseconds. This was significantly less than the 1096 milliseconds without the inclusion of these features. Piqueras-Fiszman, Alcaide-Marzal, and Spence (2012) investigated effects of four design features on fixation times for AOIs on jam jars. The four features included: the shape of the jam jar (either rounded or square), the use of a rippled or smooth surface texture of the glass jar, the presence of the word "natural" on the label, and the use of photo or text for ingredients' details on the label. Conjoint analysis identified that a rippled surface and square shape led attention to the border of the jar. Janiszewski (1998) studied effects of objects' overall layout on the attention allocated to each individual object. He found that "competition for attention," which was determined by both the sizes and locations of the surroundings of an object, negatively affected the attention for the object: more competition resulted in less fixation time. This observation supported Janiszewski's hypothesis of an exploratory-search behavior. Lohse (1997) investigated visual attention for ads in yellow pages, finding that the presence of color in the ads significantly affected the likelihood, order, and total time of fixation. Color ads performed better than non-color ads and larger size had longer fixation times.

Strengths and Limitations

Using eye-tracking to study consumer product evaluations has a number of strengths. Unlike some other biometric tracking systems that add attachments to the human body, eye-tracking can non-intrusively monitor human behavior. It can be used to design clever experiments that avoid asking certain questions explicitly in an experiment. It is also helpful for reducing bias resulting from social expectations, desirability of leaving good impressions, or political correctness (Schiessl et al., 2003). This is especially helpful for studies on certain sensitive topics. For example, She's study (2013), mentioned in the previous section, did not ask subjects for sustainability evaluations directly in order to avoid social desirability bias. Eye-tracking works well with survey questions. Having these two sources of data can help identify how a decision is made, and what aspects are influential to a response. Eye-tracking can also work together with other biometric tracking techniques like electroencephalography (EEG) and facial expression detection. Eye-tracking can be used with verbal protocols as well, particularly via replay of gaze paths, which can help the subject retrieve their thoughts during an experiment (Glaholt & Reingold, 2011).

Inevitably, eye-tracking has its limitations. The most important limitation of eye-tracking is the same as any form of bio-data: it should not be used in isolation. Fundamental experimental hypothesis should always be included and testable with more direct forms of data, such as survey answers. Eye-tracking should mainly be used to supplement or explain findings that are related to sound hypotheses, not as an "exploration." Because gaze data is noisy, though not as noisy as some other sources of bio-data, it should not be used in data-mining.

Currently, most eye trackers (except the eye-tracking glasses) have limited assistance for studies on physical objects. Eye-tracking works most robustly in situations where AOIs are within two-dimensional planes, such as surfaces of mobile devices, a monitor, a painting, etc.; but they could produce parallax errors when being used to track gaze in a third dimension (Tobii, 2012). Analyzing gaze path data remains challenging. Markov methods exist for analyzing the paths and predicting fixation locations (Hacisalihzade, Stark, & Allen, 1992; Pieters et al., 1999; Stark & Ellis, 1981). Researchers have also treated gaze paths as strings and used string-editing methods to measure the similarities or differences between different gaze paths (Hacisalihzade et al., 1992). But all of these approaches leave much to be desired in terms of testing and understanding how someone evaluates a product.

Another limitation is that analyzing gaze date for video or moving stimuli is complex. Contents in a video stimulus change in every frame, which makes the video a collection of thousands or even millions of still stimuli. Associating subjects' fixations in each frame with the specific content they are looking is data-intensive. Though some eye-tracking software enables generating moving AOIs to help map fixations to the contents shown in the video, the processes of generating those AOIs during the post-analysis are still labor- and time-consuming. Another limitation of eye-tracking is due to its "preference" for large AOIs. The most commonly used hardware and software offer more accurate data for large AOIs than for small ones. Researchers must carefully consider and experiment with the sizes of AOIs when developing research hypotheses and experiment designs. Achieving high accuracy for small AOIs, like a letter in a word, requires more sophisticated and likely more expensive equipment.

Future Directions

Just as web-clicks and internet purchases are currently being analyzed en masse for consumer insights, eye-tracking will provide "big data" for product researchers in the near future. It will play an increasing role in state-of-the-art design, as we are at the dawn of this new rich set of data for gaze analysis. To understand the magnitude of the data, consider the number of products people look at every day, whether on their phones, TVs, computers, tablets, or potentially via such technology as Google Glass. These data will facilitate both designers and the development of design theories, as discussed below.

Implications for Designers

Eye-tracking can provide designers with unique and rich input information to inform their decisions. For example, eye-tracking's ability to predict product feature importance and noticeability of feature size-change (as shown in Du & MacDonald, 2014) can help designers prioritize design efforts across a product's features. Gaze data can test designers' goals, such as to guide attention to a particular part of the product. Thus designers can test the effectiveness of different design alternatives in achieving such goals, as demonstrated in (Janiszewski, 1998; Piqueras-Fiszman et al., 2012; Räihä et al., 2006).

Eye-tracking can produce instant feedback from consumers that can be directly integrated into the design process. Designers can also create new products that have embedded eye-tracking, such as a personal recommendation system based on how consumers review a set of product images on a tablet. This opens the door for mass-customization without the need for consumers to articulate how they prefer a product to look. But developers of such technology should keep in mind that eye-tracking data from isolated evaluation, sequential evaluation, or comparative evaluation (e.g., side-by-side evaluation) of choice alternatives may provide different feedback. A suggestion to address this is to use the evaluation type that best matches the goal of the design process, such as simulating use circumstances or purchase circumstances. If the design process does aim to improve on-site selling, like for a personal recommendation system, a comparative evaluation that provides a reasonable amount of alternatives (an amount that does not overwhelm the consumer) at the same time is recommended. This is because direct comparison allows the consumers to determine good-and-bad or like-and-dislike clearly and efficiently, and it does not require the consumers to rely on memories as needed in a sequential evaluation situation. This makes the data collected easier to process and apply to improve the design.

Eye-tracking can also serve as a meta-tool for designers while they are designing or evaluating design alternatives using design software, as a type of training or assistance system. If designers are focusing too much on one area of a product design, the software can recommend other areas or features to think about. In this way, eye-tracking can provide real-time assistance or supportive information to the designers.

Implications for a Theory of Design

Eye-tracking's ability to monitor consumers' information acquisition processes makes it useful in the verification of design goals and the theories that have been developed to achieve these goals. For example, it can help explore the reasons why different designs have varied effects on consumer evaluations, such as why a symmetric design outperforms an asymmetric one in creating a product form that looks "calm." In this way, it can help explain and/or revitalize well-used design theories. Eye-tracking data could be indicators of consumers' decision processes (Hui, Fader, & Bradlow, 2009). This can help detect how consumers' preferences are constructed for product designs. From Russo and Leclerc's work (1994), it can be seen that eye-tracking is useful for investigating consumers' uses of existing decision-making strategies while viewing visual designs with certain decision goals (e.g., compensatory vs. consider-then-choose strategies). Further, it is also possible to identify yet-undiscovered decision strategies with the use of eye-tracking. Understanding how consumers make decisions regarding product designs can lead to improvements in design approaches.

References

Andersson, R., Nyström, M., & Holmqvist, K. (2010). Sampling frequency and eye-tracking measures: How speed affects durations, latencies, and more. *Journal of Eye Movement Research, 3*(3), 1–12.

Chandon, P., Hutchinson, J. W., Bradlow, E. T., & Young, S. H. (2009). Does in-store marketing work? Effects of the number and position of shelf facings on brand attention and evaluation at the point of purchase. *Journal of Marketing, 73*(6), 1–17.

Clement, J. (2007). Visual influence on in-store buying decisions: An eye-track experiment on the visual influence of packaging design. *Journal of Marketing Management, 23*(9–10), 917–928.

Crane, H. D. (1994). The Purkinje image eye tracker, image stabilization, and related forms of stimulus manipulation. In D. H. Kelly (Ed.), *Visual science and engineering: Models and applications* (p. 77). New York, NY: Marcel Dekker.

Du, P., & MacDonald, E. (2014). Eye-tracking data predict importance of product features and saliency of size change. *Journal of Mechanical Design, 136*(8). doi:10.1115/1.4027387

Du, P., & MacDonald, E. (2015). Products' shared visual features do not cancel in consumer decisions. *Journal of Mechanical Design, 137*(7). doi:10.1115/1.4030162

Duchowski, A. T. (2007). *Eye tracking methodology: Theory and practice*. London: Springer.

Glaholt, M. G., & Reingold, E. M. (2011). Eye movement monitoring as a process tracing methodology in decision making research. *Journal of Neuroscience, Psychology, and Economics, 4*(2), 125–146. doi:10.1037/a0020692

Gofman, A., Moskowitz, H. R., Fyrbjork, J., Moskowitz, D., & Mets, T. (2009). Extending rule developing experimentation to perception of food packages with eye tracking. *Open Food Science Journal, 3*, 66–78.

Hacisalihzade, S. S., Stark, L. W., & Allen, J. S. (1992). Visual perception and sequences of eye movement fixations: A stochastic modeling approach. *IEEE Transactions on Systems, Man, and Cybernetics, 22*(3), 474–481.

Hui, S. K., Fader, P. S., & Bradlow, E. T. (2009). Path data in marketing: An integrative framework and prospectus for model building. *Marketing Science, 28*(2), 320–335. doi:10.1287/mksc.1080.0400

Jacob, R. J.K., & Karn, K. S. (2003). Eye tracking in human-computer interaction and usability research: Ready to deliver the promises. *The mind's eye: Cognitive and applied aspects of eye movement research*, 573–605. doi:10.1016/b978–044451020–4/50031–1

Janiszewski, C. (1998). The influence of display characteristics on visual exploratory search behavior. *Journal of Consumer Research, 25*(3), 290–301. doi:10.1086/209540

Just, M. A., & Carpenter, P. A. (1976). Eye fixations and cognitive processes. *Cognitive Psychology, 8*(4), 441–480.

Laughery, K. R., Young, S. L., Vaubel, K. P., & Brelsford, J. W. (1993). The noticeability of warnings on alcoholic beverage containers. *Journal of Public Policy & Marketing, 12*(1), 38–56.

Lohse, G. L. (1997). Consumer eye movement patterns on yellow pages advertising. *Journal of Advertising, 26*(1), 61–73.

Nielsen, J., & Pernice, K. (2010). *Eyetracking web usability.* Berkeley, CA: Nielsen Norman Group.

Pieters, R., Rosbergen, E., & Wedel, M. (1999). Visual attention to repeated print advertising: A test of scanpath theory. *Journal of Marketing Research, 36*(4), 424–438. doi:10.2307/3151998

Pieters, R., & Warlop, L. (1999). Visual attention during brand choice: The impact of time pressure and task motivation. *International Journal of Research in Marketing, 16*(1), 1–16. doi:10.1016/s0167–8116(98)00022–6

Piqueras-Fiszman, B., Alcaide-Marzal, J., & Spence, C. (2012, July 11–13). An application of eye-tracking technologies to study consumers' attention to packaging sensory attributes. XVI Congreso Internacional de Ingeniería de Proyectos, Valencia, Italy.

Poole, A., & Ball, L. J. (2005). Eye tracking in human-computer interaction and usability research: Current status and future prospects. In C. Ghaoui (Ed.), *Encyclopedia of human computer interaction* (pp. 211–219). Hershey, PA: Idea Group Reference.

Räihä, K.-J., Koivunen, K., Rantala, H., Sharmin, S., Keinonen, T., Kukkonen, S., & Lahtinen, S. (2006). *Perception of design* (D.o.C. Sciences, Trans.). Tampere, Finland: University of Tampere.

Reid, T., MacDonald, E., & Du, P. (2013). Impact of product design representation on customer judgment. *Journal of Mechanical Design, 135*(9), 091008.

Rosbergen, E., Pieters, R., & Wedel, M. (1997). Visual attention to advertising: A segment-level analysis. *Journal of Consumer Research, 24*(3), 305–314. doi:10.1086/209512

Russo, J. E., & Leclerc, F. (1994). An eye-fixation analysis of choice processes for consumer nondurables. *Journal of Consumer Research, 21*(2), 274–290. doi:10.1086/209397

Schiessl, M., Duda, S., Tholke, A., & Fischer, R. (2003). Eye tracking and its application in usability and media research. *MMI-interactiv Journal, 6*(6), 1–10.

She, J. (2013). *Designing features that influence decisions about sustainable products* (Doctoral dissertation). Iowa State University, Ames.

SMI. (n.d.). SensoMotoric Instruments. Retrieved from http://www.eyetracking-glasses.com/

Stark, L., & Ellis, S. R. (1981). Scanpaths revisited: Cognitive models direct active looking. In D. F. Fisher (Ed.), *Eye movements: Cognition and visual perception* (pp. 193–226). Hillsdale, NJ: Lawrence Erlbaum.

Tobii. (2010). Tobii Eye Tracking: An introduction to eye tracking and Tobii Eye Trackers. http://www.tobii.com/Global/Analysis/Training/WhitePapers/Tobii_EyeTracking_Introduction_WhitePaper.pdf?epslanguage=en

Tobii. (2012). User Manual: Tobii Studio. http://www.tobii.com/Global/Analysis/Downloads/User_Manuals_and_Guides/Tobii_UserManual_TobiiStudio3.2_301112_ENG_WEB.pdf

Tobii. (n.d.). Retrieved from http://www.tobii.com/

Wedel, M., & Pieters, R. (2008). A review of eye-tracking research in marketing. In N. Malhotra (Ed.), *Review of marketing research* (pp. 123–147). New York, NY: M. E. Sharpe.

Young, L. R., & Sheena, D. (1975). Survey of eye movement recording methods. *Behavior Research Methods & Instrumentation, 7*(5), 33.

23

ENHANCING DESIGN INTUITION

Jeffrey Hartley

GENERAL MOTORS

In the late 1800s, a wagon maker was making a carriage for himself. He had all that was needed for a successful product. On one hand, he knew everything about making carriages: selecting materials, designing and integrating the various parts, making key tradeoffs, and tuning and refining the final integrated product. On the other hand, since he was the customer, he had a deep understanding of the customer's tastes, preferences, functional needs, and financial considerations. Not surprisingly, he developed a carriage that fit him perfectly and came in on time and under cost. The customer and manufacturer in him were both delighted.

The wagon maker's neighbor, seeing this wonderful carriage, then requested a wagon, and since the two men had been lifelong friends, the wagon maker agreed. But a source of uncertainty crept into the process. Now the company mind and customer mind were not housed in the same head. But through his intuitive understanding of his neighbor and by simply asking him direct questions when needed, the wagon maker produced a wagon that satisfied his friend.

The wagon maker's fame and business grew and his market steadily expanded, crossing county, state, and eventually international boundaries. The slight uncertainty he felt as he made his neighbor's wagon grew enormously as his customers became increasingly more distant geographically, demographically, and culturally. He had a very poor intuitive understanding of how his customers thought, what benefits they sought in their wagons, or how they would make any of the hundreds of decisions he had to make on their behalf.

But a second source of uncertainty also grew with his expansion, for the wagon maker had to hire hundreds of engineers, designers, blacksmiths, and carpenters. Now what might be called "the company mind" had disintegrated into many minds, and communication and understanding between these diverging minds became increasingly complicated. What were once smooth, intuitive, and dynamic tradeoffs among specialized skills in *one mind* now became tradeoffs that required careful planning and shepherding between groups of people. The final "design" of the product was affected by all of these company minds—not just designers—and their ability to work together affected the product integrity and ultimately its success.

Each of the company minds in large manufacturing companies (e.g., engineering, design, marketing, manufacturing, finance, etc.) spends each day working to a large extent independently, a problem so common that it has a name in the business literature—the silo problem (Aaker, 2009; Gulati, 2007). Each function fashions its meaning of who the customer is and what the product will be while nestled comfortably in its own thought world. And the requests for customer information from these different functions illuminate their different frames of mind.

Engineers tend to focus on functional needs and how things work. Their thought worlds are populated by parameters and mathematical precision. Aesthetics are typically not part of engineering education or thought. Designers tend to focus on how things look and they want to know about the tastes of customers and trends in product design. Their thought worlds are populated by images of artistically expressed product solutions. Mathematics are typically not part of designer education or thought. Manufacturing thinks about the assembly of the product, and they want to know how they can most efficiently build it and maintain high quality. Marketing wants to know how they can move customers down the purchase funnel from awareness of our product to consideration to purchase. Finance wants to know how they can reduce costs and, to a lesser extent, increase revenue.

Of course, each group is aware of the differences between functional thought worlds and each tries to comprehend the needs of the others, but it takes great effort to overcome the mental distance between world views and the possible cross purposes. In the wagon maker, such ideas would be preposterous—his "engineer" side wouldn't be distant from his "designer" side. His one mind would seek an optimal solution among these various interests. But in the modern, large-scale manufacturer, where geographic and psychological distance between groups is the norm and goals are oftentimes inconsistent, functional interference and suboptimal solutions are common.

Successful design of complex products, such as automobiles, requires that we address both of the wagon maker's problems. And the market research approach we use will succeed only to the extent that it reduces both problems. If market research is conducted as separate inputs to each company "mind," product meanings and customer depictions may diverge and foster opposition or confusion.

But suppose we insisted that market research activities be used as an arena in which the company minds would be encouraged to converge. And suppose that convergence were centered on a deeper understanding of the customer. The result would be a focused, customer-inspired singularity of thought—similar to the wagon maker's ideal situation.

Inspirational Research

Inspirational Research seeks to do just this. Based on a quarter century of experience in automotive design research, it has two philosophical goals. The Intuition Goal is to help the cross functional team develop an intuitive understanding of how their customers think and make product decisions. The Consensus Goal is to help this cross functional team develop a common intuition and then agree on what they must do to delight these customers.

The Intuition Goal

One might ask why the goal is to develop an intuitive understanding of how the customer thinks. Why isn't it sufficient simply to profile customers or hear "the voice of" the customer? There are many reasons why gaining intuition is not only preferable to profiling customers, it is essential.

To profile customers is to quantify and typify them in some static way: their average age, income, and education level; their geographic distribution; and any of thousands of other facts companies have about their customers. This information, even if it is about their product choices, doesn't help the team develop the ability to think like customers and make choices on their behalf, a skill crucial to developing customer-centric products. We are interested in understanding the *process* of customer thought, not the product of their thought.

We want our team to be able to go beyond the descriptive data and understand our customer in a *deep* manner. We want to understand their *dynamic* lives (as opposed to a static set of data). We want to know the customers *as individuals* (not as a collection of population averages). We seek to understand the customer using the product *in context* (not decoupled from that experience and placed in a contrived research setting). In short, we want to know the personal side of our customers, an intuitive understanding better obtained through observation and direct conversations with customers than through descriptive data.

Furthermore, several decades of psychological research have demonstrated that intuition takes precedence over more deliberative thought (Gladwell, 2005; Kahneman, 2013; Noblet, 1993). While we may think people make decisions impassively, much like a computer, methodically weighing all the evidence, what more likely happens is they first form an opinion and then find support for it. This makes it critical to nurture an accurate intuitive understanding or hunch about how the customer thinks as early as possible.

Once a hunch is formed, it is used as a filter through which subsequent information must pass. Data congruent with the hunch passes through the filter easily. Data inconsistent with the hunch meets with resistance and is often deflected. This "confirmation bias" is pervasive and often invisible to the mind it is affecting (Nickerson, 1998). For the present purposes, it also can obscure an accurate understanding of customers and how they think, if the initial hunch about them is wrong.

Thus, if market research is just delivering information to the minds of designers, engineers, and the like, and their minds already have different pre-existing hunches, the prism of each function will interpret the data differently. So we must target the hunches—the intuition—of all the functions and align them early, using the customer as our beacon, before "data" is to be interpreted.

There are other benefits of gaining an intuitive understanding of customers. Researchers can never anticipate all the decisions the product development team will be facing and so any "data" will be limited. But having an intuitive understanding of how customers think and make decisions can equip the team to represent the customer in even unanticipated decisions.

Information about aesthetic preferences is notoriously difficult to put into words (Cooper & Evans, 2006; Von Hippel, 1994), and so merely reporting the votes of target customers doesn't reveal much about what they will prefer in the future or why. Furthermore, the most successful products are those to which the customer is emotionally drawn, perhaps without even knowing why. Emotions are difficult to express or understand through sterile "data," but if a team has an intuitive understanding of their customers, they have a better chance of connecting with them emotionally. In fact, the brain circuitry involved in intuition overlaps greatly with the areas involved in emotion (Pigliucci, 2012).

The Consensus Goal

Design of complex products is very much a social and political activity. The final design will be affected by decisions of not just the designer, but also the engineer, the marketer, the manufacturer, and a cascade of other disciplines. So the second goal is to have the different functions all develop a common understanding of how their customers think and then forge this into harmonious actions they will take to delight those customers.

In a data driven world, the research team presents the data, and then the different functions deliberate and debate what it means. The data is the reference point for the joint decision. But in an intuitive world populated mainly by qualitative discussions and observation, reaching consensus requires a different approach. In essence the various team members must develop the same intuition about customers. Inspirational Research is thus structured to nurture this common understanding of customer thought, motivation, and behavior.

Executing an Inspirational Study

Intuition is the abstract knowledge that accompanies experience (Hartley, 2009) and as such it requires active involvement of the person whose intuition is being nurtured. If one wants to develop an intuitive understanding of how to dance, one has to dance. The logic underlying inspirational research is that to understand how customers make decisions, one has to experience them making decisions. In the following section, the details of how this is done are described. We'll take the realm of automotive design as our example.

Selecting Customers

As any well-educated market researcher will tell you, you should recruit a sample representative of your market. That is true for quantitative studies, but an Inspirational Research study is meant to inspire our team members who will be talking directly with customers. So the customers we meet have to be people whose opinion our team will respect. They will be affecting products which will be coming out well into the future so they must resemble lead users and social influencers. Based on our own basic research and on the work of several others (Rogers, 1995; Von Hippel, 1986; Zandl & Leonard, 1992), we use a filtering process to recruit. First we identify customers who own the relevant vehicles, who are then screened to get the younger, more educated, and more affluent end of this market. We also look for people who have demonstrated success in life through their profession. This initial set of people then goes through an articulation screener. For example, they may be asked to express their aesthetic ideals through metaphors or describe possessions they love because of their design. Those who can express these more figurative and introspective thoughts are allowed into the study. The resulting pool of people is usually a very interesting and influential collection of individuals who can hold their own in a discussion of aesthetic preferences.

We even go one further step. Of the 50 or so people we bring into the study, we handpick a half dozen of the most impressive customers to bring back for further, deeper discussions. These are the customers who, if we developed a product specifically for them, would lead many others to follow. They are selected, not because they agree with our preconceptions (in fact they often challenge some cherished beliefs among the team members), but rather because they have earned the respect of all team members. These "confidants" are sometimes empanelled to follow the product through development. For example, we often bring them back to see if the actions we took are in accord with their earlier-expressed desires.

Setting Up the Team

On any project there are key decision makers and these are prime candidates for the team. At a minimum, these should include the highest ranking designer, engineer, and marketer, but having key members of the other disciplines is highly encouraged. This team should be involved in planning the study, identifying the key questions, attending the study, and reaching consensus on its conclusions.

Most studies run for 4–5 days and it is critical that all team members attend from beginning to end.

Surfacing and Crystallizing the Research Questions

The nucleus of an Inspirational study is its research questions, which must be stated in the form of questions. It doesn't help to set vague goals (e.g., "know our customer better"). Ideally there will be a handful of important questions, although each one may have several secondary questions. Examples of typical questions (using vehicles as the example):

- *Passions.* What is at the core of their lives? Who and what do they value or love? What gives them joy? What worries them? These could be their family, a spouse, pets, friends, their job, school, religion, hobbies, health—just about anything.
- *Activities.* What do they do for work, leisure, family obligations, etc.? Obviously these topic areas should not be unrelated—things they love or hate are probably things they choose to do or are forced to do often. What activities make up the person's daily life?
- *Usage.* How do customers use their vehicle? What activities does it support?
- *Products.* How do the core elements of the person's life play out in their product decisions? Products can be expensive (e.g., homes, boats, furniture, vehicles) or inexpensive. They can be self-expressive or more functional (e.g., clothing, watches, shoes, glasses, appliances, tools). Note that observation of these things can be as valuable as direct questioning. Do they like to make a public statement or are they more humble?
- *Vehicles.* What is their vehicle history? What was their first vehicle, their most memorable vehicle, their last vehicle, any notable memories they have of vehicles? What vehicles do they currently have? For each one, what role does it play in the household and does it "belong" to one member of the household?
- *The Vehicle Purchase Process.* How did they end up with each vehicle? What guided their decisions? What objectives did they use to evaluate their selections? What role did brand play? What will they use to guide their next purchase?
- *Special Issues.* Often, at the time of the study, the team has identified where they expect to win and where they have to be at least acceptable to make it into the purchase funnel. For example, automotive teams often want to win in exterior styling. This begs the general question of: "What do we need to do to win in exterior styling?" That leads to other questions: "What role does the vehicle's exterior styling play in their purchase? How do they describe their ideal exterior styling? What vehicles have the type of styling they like? What proportion does a car need to be appealing to them? What are social 'moments of truth' that they envision when thinking about their exterior styling?"

Customer Benefits

Underlying all research questions is a foundation built on customer benefits (Aaker, 1996). The benefits they seek in their product can fall into one or more of four categories. A functional benefit is, as the name suggests, a functional performance of the product. The emotional benefit of a product is the emotion that it engenders in the customer during purchase or use. The social benefit involves the value the product brings its owner in a social world (e.g., prestige, dominance, a successful image, upward mobility, an appearance of being environmentally conscious, etc.). And an aesthetic benefit is that which the owner enjoys just for the beauty of it. Note that these benefits are not mutually exclusive but are more of a heuristic to make sure we have considered the full range of benefits that may determine the success or failure of the product.

Developing the Activities and Stimuli

Once the research questions have been clarified, the team must develop stimuli and activities which would engender a rich discussion with customers. For most of the lifestyle questions, a video or photographic journal usually suffices. Customers are sent the journal a few weeks prior to attending the study with topics aimed at documenting their family, their home, their typical activities especially with their vehicle, things they love and things they would change about their vehicle. We often ask customers to use visual metaphors for their ideal vehicle and for various brands, as metaphors offer an excellent window into deep thoughts (Zaltman & Zaltman, 2008).

So, for example, in a sporty segment, the ideal vehicle expressed as a person was often Angelina Jolie because of her sensuous, stealthy persona. The ideal as an animal was often a black panther for the same reasons. It did not take the team long to see the isomorphic relationships between Angelina Jolie, a black panther, and the design of the car's exterior.

For other research questions, the stimuli and activities can vary greatly. If the team is trying to understand how customers trade off a vehicle's interior spaciousness and exterior sleekness, for example, the design team might develop a large board showing a range of vehicle solutions from spacious, high roof designs to sleek, low roof designs. Then customers are asked which designs they prefer and why.

The stimuli can be quite abstract and still generate rich dialogue. In fact discussions at a nonliteral level may be best equipped to support design communication. For one truck brand, the design team developed "mood boards" that showed different environments (e.g., rain forest, desert, arctic, etc.) and asked customers which ambiance they would most like to feel in their truck's interior. Customers were quite enthusiastic in this exercise and the team got clear direction of which paths made positive emotional connections.

Common stimuli and activities are production vehicles, in which our customers are asked to identify examples of high and low quality or to go through a simulated shopping examination of the cars. We also bring the thinking in the studio out to the customer for discussion. This may include large boards with several dozen sketches, or sets of scale models, from which we ask customers to select their favorites.

In every activity we probe more deeply to understand the rationale underlying the response, always looking for the customer benefits. It is important to note that people are good at explaining functional benefits but less so for the other benefits and this is why we often resort to metaphors, which allow customers to express themselves safely. There is some evidence that people will more readily offer up functional benefits as an explanation for their choices, even if the true reason for their choice, which may be invisible to them, was another type of benefit (Nisbett & Wilson, 1977; Wilson, 2009), so diligent probing is required.

To unearth social benefits, we often ask for "moments of truth," which are situations that customers imagine when they purchase or assess a product. One teacher told us when she bought her car, she imagined the reaction she would get when arriving at school where all the parents, students, and other teachers would see her. She wanted to be taken seriously, so her car's exterior styling had to express "I have earned my professional success." It could not express "I am young and on the make" or "I am old and conservative." Clearly, vehicles have a huge social benefit theme, but we have also found that even supposedly functional products (e.g., kitchen utensils; tools) are judged by their emotional, social, and aesthetic benefits.

For a small handful of customers (i.e., the confidants) we may go to their homes and conduct a thorough profile of their everyday life and vehicle choices (Homma & Ueltzhöffer, 1990). This is analogous to the common practice of developing a "persona" to represent desired customers (Grudin & Pruitt, 2002), except these are real customers whom our decision makers know at a personal, emotional level.

Debriefing and Consensus Building

The team spends an equal amount of time debriefing about the emerging answers to the research questions as they do with customers. This is one reason why it is so important to state the research objectives as questions, so the team can state their conclusions in the form of answers. It is not uncommon for the first few debriefs to be confusing and disjointed, or to have different team members drawing different conclusions. This should not be surprising, given what we know about confirmation bias. But after a few days of customer sessions and debriefs, the answers start to coalesce and be agreed upon by the team.

Results

The final debrief captures the key conclusions as agreed to by the cross functional team. Each team member is expected to believe in the results or not agree to the conclusion. It is rare when we leave an Inspirational Research event without unanimous agreement. While the report is important, the real value of the event is distributed across the minds of the cross functional team members. Spending five days with customers and team mates, fashioning common answers to vital program questions, is a tempering process that creates strong belief and commitment in the team members. The team usually leaves these events unified in their mission and willing to make the sometimes painful tradeoffs to achieve what they think will delight their customers.

Concerns and Remedies

An obvious first concern is that the team can only meet with small samples of customers and the conclusions drawn may not be representative of the larger market.

We first seek to minimize this problem by coupling the deep understanding we get in face-to-face meetings with data drawn from larger samples. This occurs in the initial briefing, and it can also show itself in the report and supporting video we produce. On the edited video of our project, we can overlay large sample results to bring the individual's responses into perspective.

The concern about small samples begs the question of what "small" is for learning of this sort (i.e., direct experience with members of the category). The human mind is quite capable of abstracting out central tendencies from experience. For example, after seeing several paintings by Renoir, one is pretty good at recognizing others by him. How many examples of his paintings would one have to see to learn his style?

There is evidence in academic psychology that by encountering as few as 9–12 examples of a category, you can recognize later members very accurately (Cook & Smith, 2006; Dinardo & Toppino, 1984; Hartley & Homa, 1981). This finding is quite similar to results found by market researchers (Griffin & Hauser, 1993; Zaltman & Higie, 1995). Therefore, we make sure that every team member interacts with at least 12 customers.

A second concern is selling the results to the rest of the product development team. It is one thing to be personally inspired in this activity. It is quite another to sell that inspiration to your colleagues who remained at their desks while you were away. We address this problem in three ways.

First, we return with digitized and searchable video records that can be used to bring our conclusions to life. For example, if one conclusion was that customers wanted easy access to the rear seat, and someone back at the office disputed this conclusion, we could access just the video excerpts that bear on this issue. That often can help resolve disputes.

Second, because the team was made up of high ranking representatives from each function, the results are brought back by respected "disciples" who are distributed among the staffs. This personal envoy can also make the results come to life and assure the team that their viewpoint was represented in the discussions.

And finally, the "proof is in the pudding." Many of the results are in the form of decisions linked to customer benefits. These are therefore subject to further testing with larger samples. So we confirm or disconfirm the hunches in later large sample studies.

Implications for Designers

Designers and in fact all the functional team members will enter any product's development with existing intuitions about both their specialty and customers. Designers, for example, will have an intuitive grasp of what constitutes good design (e.g., unity, harmony, balance, etc.). They will likely have hunches about where designs are going in the future, and they will have some inkling of who their customer is.

Inspirational Research seeks to complement this native intuition with a visceral understanding of the customer. Left to their own devices, designers would design to their own tastes and needs, but by helping them to think like customers, their design intuition can be exploited to fit the customer's needs and tastes. In this scenario, the customer does not dictate the design, but a deep understanding of, and empathy for, the customer adds to the other influences on designer problem solving.

The knowledge gained through this personal dialogue between the team and the customer is compelling, contextual, and memorable—just the sort of experience our team needs to understand their customer intuitively. This leads to "higher motivation to respond, higher potential for change, deeper understanding, and more opportunity to generate innovations" (McQuarrie, 1993). Because these activities are cross-functional, they decrease disputes and misunderstandings, and they increase consensus and integration between functions—the very goals we set for ourselves.

Implications for a Theory of Design

A universal principle in the arts is that people enjoy things in which the elements are integrated into a cohesive whole, with no superfluous parts. This principle holds for painting, music, literature, architecture, and even for less obvious arts such as comedy, detective work, and science. It certainly applies to product design. In fact, it is so pervasive that it appears to be a quality of human perception and aesthetic appreciation in general, as substantiated by the Gestalt principles of perceptual organization (Goldstein, 2010; Solso, 1994). So it is perhaps not surprising that it also applies to the *process* of product development.

Inspirational Research is similar to other design approaches, such as that of IDEO (Kelley, 2001) in its focus on integrating the team and focusing them around the customer. Whereas IDEO's approach is aimed more at early innovation, Inspirational Research is aimed at resolving inter-functional differences in very large organizations later in the product development process. When the different functions behave in an orchestrated fashion, with a unity of purpose, inspired by the soul of the customer, the product achieves an uncompromised integrity. Inspirational Research is one tool that encourages this harmony of thought and action in the team, ostensibly leading to a focused, successful product, since it integrates customer thought into the team's decision making. The heart-to-heart understanding that Inspirational Research nurtures sets each team member's internal tuning fork into sympathetic resonance with both customer and colleague.

> *It is the harmony of the diverse parts, their symmetry, their happy balance; in a word it is all that introduces order, all that gives unity, which permits us to see clearly and to comprehend at once both the ensemble and the details.*
>
> *Henri Poincaré*

References

Aaker, D. A. (1996). *Building strong brands.* New York, NY: Free Press.

Aaker, D. A. (2009). *Spanning silos.* Boston, MA: Harvard Business Press.

Cook, R., & Smith, J. (2006). Stages of abstraction and exemplar memorization in pigeon category learning. *Psychological Science, 17*(12), 1059–1067.

Cooper, R., & Evans, M. (2006). Breaking from tradition: Market research, consumer needs, and design futures. *Design Management Review, 17*(1), 68–74.

Dinardo, M., & Toppino, T. (1984). Formation of ill-defined concepts as a function of category size and category exposure. *Bulletin of the Psychonomic Society, 22*(4), 317–320.

Gladwell, M. (2005). *Blink: The power of thinking without thinking.* New York, NY: Little, Brown.

Goldstein, E. (2010). *Sensation and perception.* Belmont, CA: Wadsworth Cengage Learning.

Griffin, A., & Hauser, J. (1993). The voice of the customer. *Marketing Science, 12*(3), 1–27.

Grudin, J., & Pruitt, J. (2002). Personas. Participatory design and product development: An infrastructure for engagement. In T. Binder, J. Gregory, & I. Wagner (Eds.), *PDC02 Proceedings of the Participatory Design Conference,* Malmö, Sweden.

Gulati, R. (2007). Silo busting: Transcending barriers to build high growth organizations. *Harvard Business Review, 85*(5), 98–108.

Hartley, J. (2009). Improving intuition in product development decisions. In S. Raghavan & J. Cafeo (Eds.), *Product research: The art and science behind successful product launches* (pp. 3–15). London: Springer Press.

Hartley, J., & Homa, D. (1981). Abstraction of stylistic concepts. *Journal of Experimental Psychology: Human Learning and Memory, 7*(1), 33–46.

Homma, N., & Ueltzhöffer, J. (1990). The internationalisation of everyday life research: Markets and milieus. *Marketing and Research Today,* 197–207. Amsterdam: ESOMAR.

Kahneman, D. (2013). *Thinking, fast and slow.* New York, NY: Farrar, Straus & Giroux.

Kelley, T. (2001). *The art of innovation: Lessons in creativity from IDEO, America's leading design firm.* New York, NY: Doubleday.

McQuarrie, E. (1993). *Customer visits: Building a better market focus.* London: Sage.

Nickerson, R. (1998). Confirmation bias: A ubiquitous phenomenon in many guises. *Review of General Psychology, 2*(2), 175–220.

Nisbett, R., & Wilson, T. (1977). Telling more than we can know: Verbal reports on mental processes. *Psychological Review, 84*(3), 231–259.

Noblet, J. (1993). *Industrial design: Reflections of a century.* Paris: Flammarian.

Pigliucci. M. (2012). *Answers for Aristotle: How science and philosophy can lead us to a more meaningful life.* New York, NY: Basic Books.

Rogers, E. (1995). *Diffusion of innovation.* New York, NY: Free Press.

Solso, R. (1994). *Cognition and the visual arts.* Cambridge, MA: MIT Press.

Von Hippel, E. (1986). Lead users: A source of novel product concepts. *Management Science, 32*(7), 791–805.

Von Hippel, E. (1994). "Sticky information" and the locus of problem solving: Implications for problem solving. *Management Science, 40*(4), 429–439.

Wilson, T. D. (2009). Know thyself [Special issue: Next big questions in psychology]. *Perspectives on Psychological Science, 4*, 384–389.

Zaltman, G., & Higie, R. (1995). Seeing the voice of the customer: Metaphor-based advertising research. *Journal of Advertising Research, 35*(4), 35–51.

Zaltman, G., & Zaltman, L. (2008). *Marketing metaphoria: What deep metaphors reveal about the minds of consumers.* Boston, MA: Harvard Business Press.

Zandl, I., & Leonard, R. (1992). *Targeting the trendsetting consumer: How to market your product or service to influential buyers.* Burr Ridge, IL: Irwin.

24

DESIGN HEURISTICS

A Tool for Innovation in Product Design

*Colleen Seifert, Richard Gonzalez,
and Shanna R. Daly*

UNIVERSITY OF MICHIGAN, ANN ARBOR

Seda Yilmaz

IOWA STATE UNIVERSITY

Examples of bad product design are common (Norman, 1993). It is interesting, though, that poor design is not immediately salient to most designers and consumers. Products with less than adequate functionality remain on the market, and are sometimes successful despite their flaws in design. Product designers have a tremendous influence on how easily, and how well, individuals' goals are met each day. Norman (1993) has characterized good design as "user-centered," where the human interacting with a designed artifact finds it useful and easy to use, and readily adopts it in favor of existing alternatives (cf. Krishnan & Ulrich, 2001). But while good product design seems to have consensual, even testable, standards for evaluation (Obradovich & Woods, 1996), little is known about the cognitive processes leading to innovation in design, nor the group processes that identify successful design groups (Wilpert, 2005; Heerkens, 2006).

Most research efforts to understand design focus on the evaluation of identified designs through focus groups, prototypes, user testing, and design critique sessions. These studies operate in a context where a candidate design is complete (Otto & Wood, 2001). However, to create an innovative design, the process begins when the designer first considers possible ideas, or concepts, for a new or redesigned product. How do designers generate novel concepts for a product and consider a varied set of potential designs in order to select an innovative design? We suggest that the process of idea generation can be enhanced to help designers uncover a variety of perspectives on the design problem (Kruger & Cross, 2006). By building variations into the design process, the potential designs considered will be more likely to reflect new and useful concepts to address consumer needs. However, to impact the design process, we need to develop a method for intervention during the process of generating novel designs. How can we develop a process to stimulate innovation? The early stages of design often take place under conditions when the designer may not have clear view of consumer goals, functions the product might serve, and forms that may better suit the problem. Further, many studies show that designers may become "fixated" on a particular design or direction, and as a result, have increased difficulty in generating alternatives (Jansson & Smith, 1991; Purcell & Gero, 1996). Fixation may limit the diversity, and therefore the quality of ideas in the resulting set of ideas generated.

Our goal in this research is to apply the models and methods from the fields of cognitive and decision science towards understanding the designer's process in creating innovative designs. Can we help designers create more, and more varied designs to consider, resulting in final designs that are more innovative?

Cognitive Heuristics

Traditional problem solving theory begins with generating a search space of all possible features of the problem considered in all possible combinations, and then this space is searched for a solution (Newell & Simon, 1972). If done systematically, this approach guarantees that the designer will find a successful solution, though the search may take a long time. However, this basic characterization of an (artificially) intelligent search diverges from the observations of human reasoners at every level of expertise (Newell & Simon, 1972; Simon, 1981). Most human problem solvers engage instead in a "heuristic" search (Klein, 1993; Kleinmuntz, 1985). Simon (1990) argued that heuristics are "methods for arriving at satisfactory solutions with modest amounts of computation," suggesting heuristics are useful in reducing the effort associated with a task (p. 11). Heuristics have been identified as cognitive "rules of thumb" that reduce the effort required by a task (Shah & Oppenheimer, 2008) in specific ways, such as examining fewer cues or alternatives. The use of heuristics in problem solving and decision-making has been established through an extensive body of research in cognitive science (Gigerenzer & Todd, 1999; Klein, 1998; Newell & Simon, 1972). These studies have identified the characteristic pattern of reasoning where people "jump" into the problem space using heuristics, and may or may not be successful in solving the problem (Kotovsky & Simon, 1990).

As used to describe thinking, heuristics often play the role of reducing the amount of information considered (Tversky & Kahneman, 1973, 1974). Studies in consumer behavior and marketing also demonstrated the narrowing of choices facilitated by heuristic use (Chang, 2004; Darke, Freedman, & Chaiken, 1995), and been found to be important in designing product warning labels (Zuckerman & Chaiken, 1998) and in determining consumers' frequent purchases (Hauser, 2011). However, in some cases, heuristics are not limits to information considered, but instead, perform as guidelines for focusing on key features in complex problems. For example, in fire fighting, the context of the physical setting and a variety of factors in the blaze bring to mind heuristics for approaching the blaze (Klein, 1998). Research suggests that heuristics can lead to optimal solutions when they focus attention on key variables (e.g., Dijksterhuis, Bos, Nordgren, & van Barren, 2006; Gigerenzer & Todd, 1999). Cognitive heuristics in some complex domains serve as well-known paths frequently travelled, and known to lead to useful solutions. Heuristic use by experts is one feature that distinguishes them from novices (e.g., Klein, 1998), and evidence of their use appears in many creative endeavors, such as mathematicians working on research problems (Sriraman, 2004), successful negotiations (Huber & Neale, 1986), managerial decision making (Schwenk, 1988), project scheduling (Bock & Patterson, 1990), creating instructional games for learning (Malone, 1980) and software design (Guindon & Curis, 1988).

The problem space for the process of design has been termed the "design space" (Goel & Pirolli, 1989). One approach to organize the tools for searching the design space makes use of the extensive body of designs already created by expert designers. *TRIZ* captures specific design elements from an analysis of successful patent applications (Altshuller, 1984, 1997). Case-based reasoning (CBR; Schank, 1982; Kolodner, 1993) provides designers with previous designs that may help with new situations (Maher & Gomez de Silva Garza, 1997; see also Ball, Olmerod, & Morley, 2004). These tools make use of the same process seen informally in experts; namely, the use of previously used patterns in creating new ones (see Cross & Cross, 1998, for a case study in engineering design). Similarly, analogical thinking (e.g., Ball, Olmerod, & Morley, 2004; Visser, 1996) is sometimes used by experts to apply existing designs to generate similar solutions to new problems. Analogical reasoning focuses on specific past designs, and the designer applies these past designs to new problems (Dahl & Moreau, 2002; Markman, Wood, Linsey, Murphy, & Laux, 2009).

However, rather than considering a specific past design, it may be possible that expert knowledge is encoded at a higher, more abstract level than the specific case (cf. Bailey, 2006; Eberle, 1995; Gordon, 1961). Based on an experience, a strategy or guideline may be abstracted from the specific case, and recalled at later times to lead to a new solution. This seems more likely to happen in settings where task demands require shortcuts. Ash and Smith-Daniels (1999) argue that because product development is a time-based competition, designers would benefit from heuristic methods that lead to fast project completion. Studies of heuristics in the field of marketing have uncovered common principles that guide decisions, referred to as "market orientation" by Kohli and Jaworski (1990). Narver and Slater (1990) have suggested a series of heuristics that, when followed, will result in a firm being "market-oriented." By analyzing protocols from practicing marketers (Merlo, Lukas, & Whitwell, 2008), a consensus emerged that a firm must adopt and implement an orientation towards its customers and competitors, and respond to the intelligence received from these market factors in a coordinated manner (see Narver & Slater, 1990). While these heuristics for marketing may appear too general to be useful (Merlo, Lukas, & Whitwell, 2008), more specific heuristics such as a "competitor-oriented strategy" were also identified.

Building on this research in cognitive and decision science, we set out to identify the cognitive heuristics used by expert designers to generate innovative product designs. We focused on use of heuristics (or general guidelines already known) used by designers to create novel product designs. Our approach was to learn from expert designers by following their steps through the generation of designs and identifying specific strategies they use in creating variations in design. An experienced designer has likely considered a variety of products, and has examined objects from multiple sources and perspectives. Their experiences with design have taught them the cognitive "shortcuts" (Merlo et al., 2008) that are likely to be useful to consider when designing new product ideas. This is a *generative* use of heuristics, where multiple ideas are formulated for later consideration, rather than a "fast and frugal" jump to a single option (Gigerenzer & Todd, 1999). By studying the designs of experts, we hoped to uncover the cognitive heuristics they use to generate innovative ideas for products.

Evidence for Design Heuristics

In most design problems, the space of all possible designs is never defined. Rather, the goal is to create *new* features not previously applied to the given design problem, and not already identified as relevant. For example, creating a problem space for a design of a wedding cake could be accomplished by varying the

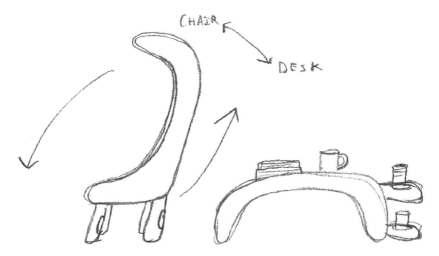

FIGURE 24.1 A design involving reorienting the form (a chair) for a new function (a coffee table). The idea of adding reorientation by the user to serve two purposes results in a novel form.

Source: Seda Yilmaz.

known attributes (tiers, color, height, toppings, flavors, etc.) to create an unusual combination. However, creating a novel design may require adding an element that was never before considered; for example, varying the shape of the tiers. Changing the design from round to square tiers may be an innovative option, but it cannot be discovered through simple combinations of existing alternatives. Innovation in design may require the *creation* of new features.

How would a designer use a heuristic to generate a new feature for a design? One heuristic involves transforming an object's orientation across an axis, either top to bottom or left to right, so that it can support a second, alternative use (see Figure 24.1). Once a dual purpose form has been identified, it necessarily differs from any canonical form. An object or its elements can be reoriented by the user in a new way, producing a novel design. The "Allow User to Reorient" heuristic is one specific strategy to create novel forms, and it is possible to apply it in many design problems to produce new concepts to consider. In this way, "Allow User to Reorient" appears to be a *design heuristic*: It's a rule of thumb that can be applied to introduce intentional variation into a design. It does not always lead to a viable alternative, but choosing to apply this heuristic generates a "guess" at a design that differs from existing ones. The design heuristic serves as a "short-cut" to a novel design that can then be considered for its value.

The heuristics employed by expert designers appear to have a quality of "suggestion," of introducing variation with intention and then considering the resulting concept. We posit that expertise in creative design arises from the accumulation of heuristics built through experience. An expert, then, may bring to bear their own personal toolbox of acquired "design heuristics," starting points for introducing novelty into designs. Heuristics offer a means of generating possible designs by guiding designers to apply specific, interesting variations to their designs. To explore how design heuristics may appear in the work of product designers, we conducted several studies of design involving a wide variety of products.

Longitudinal Study of an Expert Designer

A first source of evidence for use of heuristics emerged by studying a single expert industrial designer (Yilmaz & Seifert, 2011). Designers sometimes use "scrolls," a rolled paper record, to lay out their thinking during product design, working further down the scroll in each work session. As a result, the position of concepts, sketches, and labels on the scroll reflects the general sequencing of work, and suggests the types of designs and transformations that have considered during an extended design process. The scrolls provide a record of the designer's thought process and how ideas evolved in much the same way that a lab notebook provides a record of a scientist's work. For this study, a highly experienced designer with over 30 years of active work in the field was actively engaged on a single project over a two-year time period. The goal was to design a universal access bathroom that could fit within existing home spaces. For our study, the designer provided all of his scrolls for the project, and was interviewed retrospectively by prompting his thoughts as each design was reviewed. The scrolls included over 200 different concepts recorded sequentially on the scrolls. For example, at one point on the record, the designer drew three fixtures (shower, sink, and toilet) that all used the same form (a large rectangular block with a semicircle hanging below). As the designer stated, "So, that same shape represents the toilet to sit on, the sink to stand at, and a shower to stand under, and it just reminds me that there are three levels of function just like it said." The presence of this "repeated forms" concept on the scroll is evidence of a different type of design heuristic: "For multiple objects, consider a design that *repeats the same form.*"

The scrolls made it possible to follow the designer's thinking through each conceptual approach to a solution. Some concepts in succession appeared to be unrelated, such as a concept for the layout of fixtures in the space followed by a design for the control of water through a spigot. However, other sequences showed a relationship between concepts, such as a bowl drawn to capture waste water at the sink, followed by the same bowl form used for the toilet and shower. When a relationship was detected, we attempted to capture it in abstract form. Each potential heuristic described a specific change within a concept that added variation to produce a new concept. The occurrence of each heuristic was noted for every concept. The scoring of the heuristics was confirmed by a second coder who examined a quarter of the concepts with 91% agreement between coders. Each heuristic was described so as to be (1) readily observable as a new element within a given concept, and (2) applicable to other different design concepts.

The presumed goal of the designer is to generate as many varied concepts as possible in order to maximize the variety and novelty of candidate concepts for selection and refinement. The complete analysis of 218 different concepts sketched on the scrolls resulted in identification of over fifty different design heuristics. Because the heuristics can be applied repeatedly to a similar concept, and because multiple heuristics can be simultaneously applied to create a new concept, over 1,200 separate instances were noted. Each concept was identified as involving between 2 and 15 different design heuristics. The designs in this expert's work were rich with abstract connections across concepts, and allowed the observation of design heuristics in highly detailed, labeled concept drawings. Each design heuristic requires specific features within the problem in order to be applicable, and produces a changed concept altered in a specific fashion. As a result, the choice of which heuristic to use highly depends upon the immediate problem context. As implied by the use of "heuristic," there is no determinate heuristic that will lead to a definitive solution.

Interestingly, while the expert concurred with the analysis of the work, he did not identify specific heuristics in his work. He appeared to use the heuristics without conscious consideration, and implicitly invoked them as he worked. This observation fits Kavakli and Gero's (2002) protocol analysis findings, suggesting that experienced designers use strategic knowledge, but do not identify or communicate their existing strategic knowledge.

Comparative Study of Innovative Products

A second source of evidence for design heuristics is a study examining a wide variety of award-winning consumer products (Yilmaz, Daly, Christian, Seifert, & Gonzalez, 2012). Examining the specifications and sketches for winners in design competitions, and comparing their designs to existing competitive products, allowed us to identify places where heuristics may be useful (see Purcell & Gero, 1998, on ways to infer process from drawings). We found designs identified through existing, independent award competitions (the International Design Excellence Awards (2009),[1] Red-Dot Product Design Awards (2009),[2] iF Product Design Awards (2008),[3] Good Design Awards (2008–2009),[4] and the National Design Awards (2009)[5]) and published in compendiums of innovative products (Haller & Cullen, 2006; Hudson, 2008; IDSA, 2003; Lidwell & Mansacsa, 2009; Proctor, 2009). The information available about each product included the product descriptions, design criteria, constraints, scenarios, and sometimes critiques provided by professional designers. A detailed investigation was performed on approximately 400 products. We performed a content analysis of the major elements and key features of the products' functionality, form, user-interaction, and physical state. The descriptions of each heuristic were extracted by comparing these innovative designs to existing consumer product designs.

Across 400 diverse products, we identified 40 different heuristics appearing in at least four different products. In some of the products, multiple heuristics were observed, so that over 650 separate instances of design heuristic application were noted. For example, one award-winning product allowed a high-chair for feeding a baby to swivel on an axis to provide a lower "toddler chair" that fits at a standard table height. Comparing this product to existing highchairs, this product adds an entirely new function to the product to increase its value. The dual functions are accomplished by "flipping" the chair on a pivot point. In addition to "flipping," another heuristic identified in this product is, "provide multiple functions within a product," along with "adjust functions based on demographics of users."

Another heuristic identified was, "Use packaging as a functional component within the product." The packaging for the product performs a different function: Create a shell or cover for a component or the entire product that is uncovered when used. When opened, the package provides supporting structure, and functions as a necessary component rather than a separate, unneeded wrapping to be discarded (see Figure 24.2).

A third heuristic example from the award-winning products is, "Flattening design elements when they are not in use using elements nested inside each

USE PACKAGING AS FUNCTIONAL COMPONENT 73

WHEELED CUBE
Heinz Julen
This chair can be folded into a wooden box with wheels when not in use, protecting interior cushions.

FLIPBOX PENCIL CASE
Faber Castell
This set of colored pencils comes inside a package that also serves as a stand during use.

FIGURE 24.2 On the left, a set of colored pencils is located inside a package that also serves as a stand during use. On the right, the chair is packed in a way that it can be enclosed inside a box when not in use.

Source: Design Heuristics, www.designheuristics.com.

FLATTEN 35

FOLDING
Brainstream Design
This chair uses a parallelogram geometry that can be folded flat when not in use.

COLLAPSIBLE CONTAINERS
Rubbermaid
This container collapses like an accordian for storage when the product is not in use. It can be expanded to intermediate sizes based on user needs.

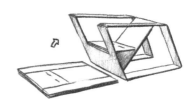

FIGURE 24.3 On the left, the bowl has several layers that are nested inside each other for storage when the product is not in use. On the right, the chair collapses flat when not in use.

Source: Design Heuristics, www.designheuristics.com.

other." This involves placing an object inside another object (entirely or partially), where the internal geometry of the containing object is similar to the external geometry of the contained object (see Figure 24.3). This heuristic allows the quick collapse of structure to flatten for easy storage.

There was substantial, but not complete, overlap in the design heuristics observed in the longitudinal study and the innovative products study. In sum, 74 separate heuristics were identified across the two studies. Thirteen of these were new heuristics appearing only in the innovative products dataset. These heuristics tended to address design issues that occur in the later stages of the process. For example, one heuristic observed in the consumer products was, "Cover joints for safety and visual consistency." This heuristic could potentially be applied to longitudinal design problem, but it would likely be considered only once a final concept had been selected, and further design refinements were taking place. This suggests that some heuristics may be suited to specific stages of the design process, may not be applicable to a given design task, and may depend upon the designer's personal preferences.

Protocol Studies With Experts in Engineering and Industrial Design

A third source of evidence emerged through a protocol project (Gero & McNeill, 1998) investigating professional and student engineering ($n = 36$) designers as they worked on a novel problem (Daly, Yilmaz, Christian, Seifert, & Gonzalez, 2012; Yilmaz, Daly et al., 2013). The problem involved designing a product that used sunlight to heat and cook food, and was portable and inexpensive. The participants were asked to draw as many concepts as possible and to elaborate on their designs with labels and descriptions. They worked for 25 minutes and generated an average of five different concepts. The designs varied in heat source identified (magnifying glass, reflectors), form (open box with extended sides, covered canister), and even function (water immersion, smoker).

The designers talked aloud as they worked, and their concept sketches and elaborations were captured. There was abundant evidence of design heuristics in the concepts created, and the more expert designers tended to display more evidence of heuristic use. Fifty-three heuristics used spontaneously by participants in this study were also identified in the previous research (Daly et al., 2010; Yilmaz & Seifert, 2010, 2011). By comparing how the concepts related to each other, it was possible to identify nine novel heuristics not observed in the previous studies.

77 Design Heuristics

Combining the results of these three studies (the expert's longitudinal design sketches, 400 award-winning products, and think-aloud protocol studies), a set of 77 Design Heuristics were extracted (see Table 24.1).

Each Design Heuristic is described on a notecard including a text and graphic description, and two examples of products where the heuristic is evident (see Figure 24.4A and 24.4B). The cards facilitate use of individual heuristics and comparison of product designs across cards (Daly, Yilmaz et al., 2012).

TABLE 24.1 The 77 Design Heuristics Observed Across Three Empirical Studies

1) Add levels	40) Incorporate user input
2) Add motion	41) Layer
3) Add natural features	42) Make components attachable or detachable
4) Add to existing product	43) Make multifunctional
5) Adjust function through movement	44) Make product recyclable
6) Adjust functions for specific users	45) Merge surfaces
7) Align components around center	46) Mimic natural mechanisms
8) Allow user to assemble	47) Mirror or array
9) Allow user to customize	48) Nest
10) Allow user to reconfigure	49) Offer optional components
11) Allow user to reorient	50) Provide sensory feedback
12) Animate	51) Reconfigure
13) Apply existing mechanism in new way	52) Redesign joints
14) Attach independent functional components	53) Reduce material
15) Attach product to user	54) Repeat
16) Bend	55) Repurpose packaging
17) Build user community	56) Roll
18) Change direction of access	57) Rotate
19) Change flexibility	58) Scale up or down
20) Change geometry	59) Separate functions
21) Change product lifetime	60) Simplify
22) Change surface properties	61) Slide
23) Compartmentalize	62) Stack
24) Contextualize	63) Substitute way for achieving function
25) Convert 2-D material to 3-D object	64) Synthesize functions
26) Convert for 2nd function	65) Telescope
27) Cover or wrap	66) Twist
28) Create service	67) Unify
29) Create system	68) Use common base to hold components
30) Divide continuous surface	69) Use continuous material
31) Elevate or lower	70) Use different energy source
32) Expand or collapse	71) Use human power
33) Expose interior	72) Use multiple components for one function
34) Extend surface	73) Use packaging as functional component
35) Flatten	74) Use recycled or recyclable materials
36) Fold	75) Utilize inner space
37) Hollow out	76) Utilize opposite surface
38) Impose hierarchy on functions	77) Visually distinguish functions
39) Incorporate environment	

Source: Adapted from Daly, Yilmaz et al. (2012).

UTILIZE OPPOSITE SURFACE

76

Create a distinction between exterior and interior, front and back, or bottom and top. Make use of both surfaces for complimentary or different functions. This can increase efficiency in the use of surfaces and materials, or facilitate a new way to achieve a function.

A

UTILIZE OPPOSITE SURFACE

76

FARALLON CHAIR
fuseproject
The back side of this chair has a pocket for storage.

980 TATOU
Annika Luber
The laces wrap around the bottom of this shoe and connect with the sole.

B

FIGURE 24.4 The information on the heuristic, "Utilize Opposite Surface," includes a graphic depiction, text description, and two product examples where the heuristic is evident. Each heuristic is demonstrated in a design for a chair to show that each can be applied to the same product problem.

Source: Design Heuristics, www.designheuristics.com.

These Design Heuristics represent an empirically derived body of cognitive strategies used by experts to add novelty to their designs. Collected from the work of many designers, these cognitive strategies provide specific directions for considering how to intentionally introduce variations among the concepts generated, and allow further exploration of the space of possible design solutions. As a result, the selection of a final concept can be made from among a richer, more diverse set of candidate concepts.

Implications for Designers

Now that these heuristics have been identified, they can be used by designers to prompt consideration of variations in design. Starting with a problem, the Design Heuristics can be applied to help the designer generate more, varied concepts to consider. Rather than relying heuristics built from experience (Moss, Kotovsky, & Cagan, 2006), designers can "jump start" the process of generating concepts by choosing to apply Design Heuristics. As a result, their process will be aided by the expertise captured by the Design Heuristics, and the result will be a larger set of concepts enriched by the variations introduced. Design Heuristics can provide explicit instruction on how to intentionally vary concepts during the design process.

For example, consider the problem of designing a liquid hand soap dispenser. How might Design Heuristics be applied to explore new concepts? In Figure 24.5, the design process begins with a concept, and then three different Design Heuristics are applied to suggest changes to create new concepts to consider.

The 77 Design Heuristics captured through empirical studies provides a new method for designers to add to their potential designs. A study to test this approach included design teams from a commercial product company (Yilmaz,

Initial Concept.	Make the individual parts attachable-detachable.	Attach the product to an existing item as an additional component.	Remove the moving parts.
Top part is nested inside the main structure, which holds the soap. Soap is dispensed by a push-motion from the top. The central open space is used for hand placement.	The two parts are separated easily with a snap-on motion. The location for connecting the parts is also used as the opening to fill it with soap.	The product can be attached to the faucet through a sliding motion. This way the soap dispenser does not occupy additional surface space on the countertop. Soap comes out from the channels on the sides, and the product can be filled with soap from the top part, which also serves as the part users push to receive soap.	Soap is dispensed through the top of the tubing component by rotating the entire product around its center. The cavity on the bottom of the product is used for filling it with soap.

FIGURE 24.5 An illustration of how design heuristics can be applied to a novel problem to generate three new concepts (shown in successive panels).

Source: Seda Yilmaz.

Christian et al., 2013). These professional designers had worked on a specific product line for many years, and were looking for new ideas. Working in a small group of seven, the engineers looked through a subset of 30 of the Design Heuristics in two, two-hour sessions, and discussed how they could be applied to their product concepts. Video recordings were analyzed to reveal how the heuristics were used to stimulate new designs for their product line. We found that Design Heuristics led to new ideas and further elaboration on ideas, resulting in novel designs even in this highly familiar problem domain (as reported by the participants). This case study shows using Design Heuristics can assist even expert design engineers to increase the variety of concepts generated, resulting in a larger set of ideas to consider.

Implications for a Theory of Design

The success in identifying Design Heuristics from empirical studies of professional designers points the way toward an evidence-based approach to design. While an innovative design can be viewed as something "magical," research in cognitive and decision science has been shown to provide a means to study the design process. By systematic analysis of designers and their work process and products, we can learn more about successful design. Interesting, innovative designers appear unable to tell us what they do to make the "magic" happen; instead, identifying the cognitive heuristics that occur instantly and seamlessly during their work must be performed by an observer. As with other heuristics, the individual is not able to reflect upon their use of specific strategies or information because of the speed of mental processing and the implicit nature of much of our cognition (Ericsson & Simon, 1980; Nisbett & Wilson, 1977). The approach presented here provides a means to systematically observe and analyze the cognitive processes in design.

Further research has shown that what we have learned—the 77 Design Heuristics—can help even novice designers create more varied designs, resulting in more developed and more creative concepts (Daly, et al., 2013; Daly, Christian, et al., 2012). Through identifying the heuristics used by professional designers, and facilitating the use of those heuristics in novice designers, we have demonstrated the feasibility of enhancing creativity and innovation in design. This understanding of successful design will improve instructional methods in engineering and industrial design, providing an opportunity to create new instructional methods. Further, the heuristic approach and pedagogical techniques studied in this project may transfer to other professional domains (e.g., art, choreography, software, marketing campaigns) and educational settings (such as K–12, business training, design workshops) to provide new approaches for teaching creativity and innovation (cf. Kokotovich & Purcell, 2000). In addition, identifying team processes that encourage innovation by helping groups to consider a wider variety of candidate designs may provide practical guidelines to make design teams more cost-effective (Hargadon & Sutton, 1997; Podsakoff, Ahearne, & MacKenzie, 1997; Sutton & Hargadon, 1996; Yilmaz, Christian, et al., 2013). Most importantly, specific methods for creating innovative designs may have a broad impact on products and consumers.

Acknowledgements

This research project was funded through the NSF Engineering Design and Innovation (EDI) Grant 0927474. Thanks to James L. Christian, who was an integral part of the Design Heuristics project. The authors would like to thank Panos Papalambros and Jan-Henrik Andersen for their support on the development of this research program.

Notes

1 http://www.idsa.org
2 http://www.red-dot.de
3 http://www.ifdesign.de
4 http://www.g-mark.org/english/
5 http://www.nationaldesignawards.org

References

Altshuller, G. (1984). *Creativity as an exact science: The theory of the solution of inventive problems.* New York, NY: Gordon and Breach.

Altshuller, G. (1997). *40 principles: TRIZ keys to technical innovation.* Worcester, MA: Technical Innovation Center.

Ash, R., & Smith-Daniels, D. E. (1999). The effects of learning on decision rule performance in Multi-Project Scheduling. *Decision Sciences, 30*(1), 47–82.

Bailey, R. (2006). *Work in progress: Using engineering design experts to validate a design process knowledge assessment tool.* ASEE/IEEE Frontiers in Education Conference, San Diego, CA.

Ball, L., Ormerod, T., & Morley, N. (2004). Spontaneous analogizing in engineering design: A comparative analysis of experts and novice. *Design Studies, 25*, 495–508.

Bock, D., & Patterson, J. H. (1990). A comparison of due date setting, resource assignment, and job preemption heuristics for the Multiproject Scheduling Problem. *Decision Sciences, 21*(3), 387–402.

Chang, C. (2004). Country of origin as a heuristic cue: The effects of message ambiguity and product involvement. *Media Psychology, 6*, 169–192.

Cross, N., & Cross, A. C. (1998). Expertise in engineering design. *Research in Engineering Design, 10*, 141–149.

Dahl, D. W., & Moreau, P. (2002). The influence and value of analogical thinking during new product ideation. *Journal of Marketing Research, 39*(1), 47–60.

Daly, S. R., Christian, J., Yilmaz, S., Seifert, C. M., & Gonzalez, R. (2012). Assessing Design Heuristics in idea generation within an introductory engineering design course. *International Journal of Engineering Education (IJEE), 28*(2), 463–473.

Daly, S., Yilmaz, S., Christian, J., Seifert, C. M., & Gonzalez, R. (2012). Design heuristics in engineering concept generation. *Journal of Engineering Education, 101*(4), 601–629.

Daly, S. R., Yilmaz, S., Seifert, C. M., & Gonzalez, R. (2010). Cognitive heuristic use in engineering design ideation. *Proceedings of American Society for Engineering Education* (AC 2010-1032), Washington, DC: American Society for Engineering Education.

Darke, P. R., Freedman, J. L., & Chaiken, S. (1995). Percentage discounts, initial price, and bargain hunting: A heuristic-systematic approach to price search behavior. *Journal of Applied Psychology, 80,* 580–586.

Dijksterhuis, A., Bos, M. W., Nordgren, L. F., & Van Baaren, R. B. (2006). On making the right choice: The deliberation-without-attention effect. *Science, 311*(5763), 1005–1007.

Eberle, B. (1995). *Scamper.* Waco, TX: Prufrock.

Ericsson, K. A., & Simon, H. A. (1980). Verbal reports as data. *Psychological Review, 87,* 215–251.

Gero, J. S., & McNeill, T. (1998). An approach to the analysis of design protocols. *Design Studies, 19*(1), 21–61.

Gigerenzer, G., & Todd, P. (1999). *Simple heuristics that make us smart.* New York, NY: Oxford University Press.

Goel, V., & Pirolli, P. (1989). Motivating the notion of generic design within information processing theory: The design problem space. *AI Magazine, 10,* 19–36.

Gordon, W. J. J. (1961). *Synectics.* New York, NY: Harper & Row.

Guindon, R., & Curis, B. (1988). Control of cognitive processes during software design: What tools are needed? In J. J. O'Hare (Ed.), *Proceedings of the SIGCHI Conference on Human Factors in Computing Systems* (CHI '88) (pp. 263–268). New York, NY: ACM.

Haller, L., & Cullen, C. D. (2006). *Design secrets: Products 2: 50 real-life product design projects uncovered* (Vol. 2). London: Rockport.

Hargadon, A., & Sutton, R. I. (1997). Technology brokering and innovation in a product development firm. *Administrative Science Quarterly, 42*(4), 716–749.

Hauser, J. (2011). A marketing science perspective on recognition-based heuristics (and the fast-and-frugal paradigm). *Judgment and Decision Making, 6*(5), 396–408.

Heerkens, H. (2006). Assessing the importance of factors determining decision making by actors involved in innovation processes. *Creativity and Innovation Management, 15,* 385–399.

Huber, V. L., & Neale, M. A. (1986). Effects of cognitive heuristics and goals on negotiator performance and subsequent goal setting. *Organizational Behavior and Human Decision Processes, 38*(3), 342–365.

Hudson, J. (2008). *Process: 50 product designs from concept to manufacture.* London: Laurence King.

Industrial Designers Society of America. (2003). *Design secrets: Products.* London: Rockport.

Jansson, D. G., & Smith, S. M. (1991). Design fixation. *Design Studies, 12*(1), 3–11.

Kavakli, M., & Gero, J. S. (2002). The structure of concurrent cognitive actions: a case study on novice and expert designers. *Design Studies, 23*(1), 25–40.

Klein, G. A. (1993). A recognition-primed decision (RPD) model of rapid decision making. In G. A. Klein, J. Orasanu, R. Calderwood, & C. E. Zsambok (Eds.), *Decision making in action: Models and methods* (pp. 138–147). Westport, CT: Ablex.

Klein, G. (1998). *Sources of power.* Cambridge, MA: MIT Press.

Kleinmuntz, D. N. (1985). Cognitive heuristics and feedback in a dynamic decision environment. *Management Science, 31*(6), 680–702.

Kohli, A. K., & Jaworski, B. J. (1990) Market orientation: The construct, research propositions, and management implications. *Journal of Marketing, 54,* 1–18.

Kokotovich, V., & Purcell, T. (2000). Mental synthesis and creativity in design: An experimental examination. *Design Studies, 21,* 437–449.

Kolodner, J. L. (1993). *Case-based reasoning.* San Francisco, CA: Morgan Kaufmann.

Kotovsky, K., & Simon, H. (1990). What makes some problems really hard: Explorations in the problem space of difficulty. *Cognitive Psychology, 22,* 143–183.

Krishnan, V., & Ulrich, K. (2001). Product development decisions: A review of the literature. *Management Science, 47,* 1–21.

Kruger, C., & Cross, N. (2006). Solution driven versus problem driven design: Strategies and outcomes, *Design Studies, 27,* 527–548.

Lidwell, W., & Manacsa, G. (2009). *Deconstructing product design: Exploring the form, Function, usability, sustainability, and commercial success of 100 amazing products.* London: Rockport.

Maher, M. L., & Gomez de Silva Garza, A. (1997). Case-based reasoning in design. *IEEE Expert: Intelligent Systems and Their Applications, 12*(2), 34–41.

Malone, T. W. (1980). What makes things fun to learn? Heuristics for designing instructional computer games. *Proceedings of the 3rd Association for Computing Machinery SIGSMALL Symposium* (pp. 162–169), New York, NY.

Markman, A. B., Wood, K. L., Linsey, J. S., Murphy, J. T., & Laux, J. (2009). Supporting innovation by promoting analogical reasoning. *Tools for Innovation, 1*(9), 85–104.

Merlo, O., Lukas, B. A., & Whitwell, G. J. (2008). Heuristics revisited: Implications for marketing research and practice. *Marketing Theory, 8,* 189–204.

Moss, J., Kotovsky, K., & Cagan, J. (2006). The role of functionality in the mental representations of engineering students: Some differences in the early stages of expertise. *Cognitive Science, 30*(1), 65–93.

Narver, J. C., & Slater, S. F. (1990). The effect of market orientation on business profitability. *Journal of Marketing, 54*(October): 20–35.

Newell, A., & Simon, H. (1972). *Human problem solving.* New York, NY: Prentice Hall.

Nisbett, R. E., & Wilson, T. D. (1977). Telling more than we can know: Verbal reports on mental processes. *Psychological Review, 84*(3), 231–259.

Norman, D. A. (1993). *Things that make us smart: Defending human attributes in the age of the machine.* New York, NY: Basic Books.

Obradovich, J. H., & Woods, D. D. (1996). Users as designers: How people cope with poor HCI design in computer-based medical devices [Special Section]. *Human Factors: The Journal of the Human Factors and Ergonomics Society, 38*(4), 574–592.

Otto, K., & Wood, K. (2001). *Product design: Techniques in reverse engineering and new product development.* New York, NY: Prentice Hall.

Podsakoff, P. M., Ahearne, M., & MacKenzie, S. B. (1997). Organizational citizenship behavior and the quantity and quality of work group performance. *Journal of Applied Psychology, 82,* 262–271.

Proctor, R. (2009). *1000 new eco designs and where to find them.* London: Laurence King.

Purcell, T., & Gero, J. S. (1996). Design and other types of fixation. *Design Studies, 17*(4), 363–383.

Purcell, T., & Gero, J. S. (1998). Drawings and the design process: A review of protocol studies in design and other disciplines and related research in cognitive psychology. *Design Studies, 19*(4), 389–430.

Schank, R. C. (1982). *Dynamic memory: A theory of learning in computers and people.* Cambridge: Cambridge University Press.

Schwenk, C. R. (1988). *The essence of strategic decision making.* Lexington, MA: Lexington Books.

Shah, A. K., & Oppenheimer, D. M. (2008). Heuristics made easy: An effort-reduction framework. *Psychological Bulletin, 134*(2), 207–222.

Simon, H. A. (1981). *The sciences of the artificial* (2nd ed.). Cambridge, MA: MIT Press.

Simon, H. A. (1990). Invariants of human behavior. *Annual Review of Psychology, 41,* 1–19.

Sriraman, B. (2004). The characteristics of mathematical creativity. *Mathematics Educator, 14,* 19–34.

Sutton, R. I., & Hargadon, A. (1996). Brainstorming groups in context: Effectiveness in a product design firm. *Administrative Science Quarterly, 41*(4), 685–718.

Tversky, A., & Kahneman, D. (1973). Availability: A heuristic for judging frequency and probability. *Cognitive Psychology,* 5, 202–232.

Tversky, A., & Kahneman, D. (1974, September 27). Judgment under uncertainty: Heuristics and biases. *Science, 185,* 1124–1131.

Visser, W. (1996). Two functions of analogical reasoning in design: A cognitive psychology approach. *Design Studies, 17,* 417–434.

Wilpert, B. (2005). Psychology and design processes. *European Psychologist, 10*(3), 229–236.

Yilmaz, S., Christian, J. L., Daly, S. R., Seifert, C. M., & Gonzalez, R. (2013). Can experienced designers learn from new tools? A case study of idea generation in a professional engineering team. *International Journal of Design Creativity and Innovation, 1*(2), 82–96.

Yilmaz, S., Daly, S. R., Christian, J. L., Seifert, C. M., & Gonzalez, R. (2012, May 21–24). How do design heuristics affect outcomes? In M. M. Andreasen, H. Birkhofer, S. J. Culley, U. Lindemann, & D. Marjanovic (Eds.), *Proceedings of 12th International Design Conference (DESIGN)* (pp. 1195–1204), Dubrovnik, Croatia.

Yilmaz, S., Daly, S. R., Seifert, C. M., & Gonzalez, R. (2013, September 5–6). Comparison of design approaches between engineers and industrial designers. *The 15th International Conference on Engineering and Product Design Education,* Dublin, Ireland.

Yilmaz, S., & Seifert, C. M. (2010). Cognitive heuristics in design ideation. *Proceedings of 11th International Design Conference, DESIGN 2010* (pp. 1007–1016), Dubrovnik, Croatia.

Yilmaz, S., & Seifert, C. M. (2011). Creativity through design heuristics: A case study of expert product design. *Design Studies, 32,* 384–415.

Zuckerman, A., & Chaiken, S. (1998). A heuristic-systematic processing analysis of the effectiveness of product warning labels. *Psychology & Marketing, 15*(7), 621–642.

INDEX

Printed and bound in the United States of America by Edwards Brothers Malloy
on sustainably sourced paper.